THE AGONY OF ARRIVAL
Gandhi: The South Africa Years

THE AGONY OF ARRIVAL

Gandhi: The South Africa Years

Nagindas Sanghavi

Foreword by
Lord Bhikhu Parekh

Rupa & Co

Copyright © Nagindas Sanghavi 2006

Published 2006 by
Rupa & Co
7/16, Ansari Road, Daryaganj,
New Delhi 110 002

Sales Centres:

Allahabad Bangalore Chandigarh Chennai
Hyderabad Jaipur Kathmandu
Kolkata Mumbai Pune

Cover and inside photographs courtesy
Mr. Tushar Gandhi

Typeset in 13 pt. AmericanGaramond by
Nikita Overseas Pvt. Ltd.
1410 Chiranjiv Tower
43 Nehru Place
New Delhi 110 019

Printed in India by
Saurabh Printers Pvt. Ltd.
A-16 Sector-IV
Noida 201 301

Contents

Acknowledgements

A book necessarily depends upon the cooperation of many minds and labour of many hands and I am very heavily indebted to several scholars and academicians mentioned in the bibliography. Without their insights, this book could never have been written. Besides them, I have been helped and encouraged by numerous friends and well wishers many of whom are too close to be mentioned in print.

My friend Natwar Gandhi insisted that an analytical study of Gandhi's early years needs to be attempted using the sources in Gujarati language that are still largely untapped. Dr. Usha Thakker, director of research at Manibhavan, Mumbai was of immense help in ways more than one. She readily undertook to read the draft twice over and made very valuable suggestions. The entire staff of Manibhavan library was of great help in tracing and procuring the source material and Ramesh Oza loaned many valuable books from his personal library. Yogesh Kamdar critically reviewed the final copy and his comments were helpful. Rick Gunderson undertook the editing the text and sanitised it of several grammatical errors.

Lord Bhikhu Parekh was gracious enough to go through a few chapters of the draft in the initial stage and accepted my request to write a Foreword. He went through the final copy once again and got the copy discussed by Prof. Pantam of M.S. University at Vadodara.

Shri Tushar Gandhi of Mahatma Gandhi Foundation India readily agreed to share his treasure of photographs and help me choose the best ones that adorn this volume.

The list indicates but does not exhaust the list of persons who have been helpful one way or the other. I take this opportunity to thank them all.

Nagindas Sanghavi

Foreword

Although Gandhi has been a subject of nearly twenty full length biographies, over twice as many radio and television documentaries and an internationally acclaimed film, he remains an enigmatic figure. Some of his actions and utterances continue to delude even the most sympathetic explorations and parts of his innermost world of thought and some of his driving passions remain somewhat opaque. Apart from the obvious fact that every human being retains an element of inscrutability and even mystery, which is all the more so with someone of Gandhi's complexity and stature, three factors are particularly relevant in his case.

First, very little systemic work has been done on the Gujarat of Gandhi's time, its social and political structure, currents of thoughts, cultural ambience and religious traditions including the Vaishnavite movement and the Pranami sect that were the integral part of his familial environment. As a result we know little of the major influences on him during his formative years.

Second, while much valuable work has been done on Gandhi's three years in London, his twenty years in South Africa remain a relatively uncharted terrain. South Africa played a decisive role in shaping him. As he said it, it was in this God-forsaken country that he found his God.

And it was in appreciation of his work there that Tagore called him a Mahatma, a title that over time became an integral part of Gandhi's name and to which his own attitude remained ambivalent. South Africa gave him the emotional and the physical distance he needed to get a better understanding of India and its sorry state. He had more humiliations and indignities heaped on him in the first few years than any human being can bear, including being thrown out of a carriage, kicked into the gutter for daring to walk past the President's house, stripped and made to stand naked in public before being locked up in a cell with common criminals who carried on indecent activities in his presence and made homosexual overtures to him and narrowly escaping lynching by a racist white mob by disguising himself as a police officer. All this led him to reflect deeply on the nature, causes and mechanism of the racist and other forms of oppression as well as how to liberate the parties involved from a system that dehumanized and held them prisoners. Gandhi also had the unique opportunity to enjoy close intellectual and social contacts with his Christian and Jewish friends and to develop uniquely open and ecumenical approach to religion that makes him the patron saint of multiculturalism.

South Africa was also important for Gandhi's political development. It was a small enough place and sufficiently free from political rivals to allow him to dominate it, to grow after each mistake and build up his self confidence. Yet it was significant enough to draw attention to his activities in India, Britain and elsewhere and to give him an international stature. Taking full advantage of opportunities available to him, Gandhi evolved new forms of political praxis especially the Satyagraha, acquired organizational and journalistic skills, knew how to identify and put pressure on those who mattered and learned the vital lesson that those who behave like worms should not blame others for trampling upon them. All this and much more stood Gandhi in good stead on his return to India and holds vital clues to his later life and work.

The third factor why Gandhi remains an enigma has to do with the state of his voluminous writings. Just under half of them were written in Gujarati which only a few of his commentators can read. And the English translations on which they rely are seriously flawed. What is more, even his Gujarati writings are not free of difficulties.

They were written in a hurry, long after the events he described without the opportunity to check his fading recollections and naturally marred by some degree of unconscious distortion. Not surprisingly they left false trails and misled those who placed uncritical faith in them.

Nagindas Sanghavi's *Agony of Arrival* is happily free from these and related limitations. He is a distinguished historian and knows nineteenth century Gujarat better than most. He is an eminent writer in Gujarati language and has mined the primary sources in it. He has also wisely focused his attention on Gandhi's early years, education in England and above all, his time in South Africa. Few can match the care with which Sanghavi details Gandhi's social, political and other activities and traces the complex dialectics of his personal and political development. He provides much new formation on Gandhi's South Africa years and often many valuable interpretative insights. His meticulously researched and fluently written book fills an important gap and places Gandhi scholars in his permanent debt. Like any good book, the disagreements it provokes from time to time only adds to its value.

University of Westminster   Bhikhu Parekh
House of Lords

Preface

Sixty years after Gandhi was shot dead, he continues to be alive. He had promised, "I shall be alive in the grave and what is more speaking from it". [Gill 232] "He still inspires, aggravates and annoys". [Brown 2] He is the most frequently mentioned political figure in India and he is still at the center of several acerbic controversies very similar to the ones he provoked during his life. He declared his life to be 'an open book' and invited everyone to peep into his innermost feelings and experiences. There is hardly any aspect of his personal life and of his public activities that has not been minutely recorded and exhaustively commented upon. There is, therefore, no dearth of material [of both primary and secondary nature] for analyzing Gandhi from any point of view one wishes to adopt. There is also a continuous flood of commentaries and biographies of Gandhi.

Gandhi in fact, needs no biographer because he himself was his best biographer. In a prolific output of written and spoken word, he quite candidly discussed his experiences and opinions and thereby made the task of his biographers much easier than it would otherwise have been.

What the Japanese poet Basho said about Fujiyama would apply with much greater validity to Gandhi: so much has been written about the subject that to write anything more would be like adding a sixth finger to the hand. Such an addition is not of much use and may well become a deformity. A word of explanation is, therefore, due for adding this volume to the already copious literature on Gandhi.

In almost all the biographies, Gandhi is presented more or less as a miracle, a freak emerging from nowhere and evolving quite independently from the societal and situational context. Every biography of his has to, and does contain, historical references because Gandhi is too closely involved with contemporary happenings and personalities to be isolated from the story of his times. In all such historical projections, we are told about the impact of Gandhi on his surroundings but very little about how Gandhi himself was molded and shaped by the landscape in which he lived and worked.

Such simplistic, Gandhi-centric narrations fail to answer several nagging questions about Gandhi himself and about his achievements and failures. A few biographies that attempted to relate Gandhi to the landscape have focused only on his family background and even there they have indulged in several unwarranted romanticisms.

Gandhi, as much as anybody else, must have been conditioned by a much wider socio-eco-political situations he faced in his life; but such relationships are hardly ever taken into consideration while examining and explaining Gandhi. If societal context were a decisive sculptor of human psyche, then the omission of such a perspective would be a major lacuna in the literature on Gandhi. This volume seeks to establish such linkages between Gandhi and his environment at every step so as to examine how each acted on, and reacted to, the other.

One ought to be extremely cautious and hesitant to form an opinion about Gandhi or even to choose one from the several opinions expressed about him because Gandhi is many men in one. A mystic who was a hard-headed realist; a pacifist who was all his life a trouble maker; a revolutionary who was a very staunch conservative: a strict disciplinarian who challenged the established order in every field of life;

a shrewd politician who would implicitly trust all his opponents; a statesman who refused to look beyond one step ahead; a generous man of very stingy habits who would save his pennies and throw away his pounds; a great lover of children who often imposed very cruel punishments on them; a kind hearted captain who was a harsh task-master; a confirmed democrat with very pronounced authoritarian traits; a gentle spirit seeking to accommodate an amazing gamut of opinions and personalities and a high-handed patriarch insisting on total submission; a staunch Hindu respecting all faiths as his own; an orthodox devotee who opposed all rituals of all religions; an intense seeker after spiritual bliss devoting most of his time and energy to mundane power politics. An expert dietician, an educationist of note, an evangelist reformer of social evils, an enthusiastic naturopath, a superb organiser, a great publicity expert, a lover of humanity and an apostle of peace and nonviolence recruiting soldiers for the British army—a convincing case can be built for either side of all such mutually exclusive alternatives while depicting Gandhi.

It is hardly ever possible to present Gandhi in his entirety. Nehru expressed his doubts [Pre.Tendulkar] about a proper biography of Gandhi being ever written because like Terence, Gandhi too can claim "Homo sum, humani nil a mi alienum". [I am human and nothing human is alien to me.] Gandhi took the entire spectrum of life in his stride and, therefore, cannot be fitted into any single frame however spacious its dimensions. Gandhi fills up every frame and is yet left out by a span.

There is yet another reason why Gandhi is a biographer's despair. Apart from multiplicity of facets, Gandhi is full of bewildering contradiction. He kept on evolving and changing until the very last moment of his earthly existence. A shy, ignorant, timid Gandhi of 1888, or an active, gregarious and vocal Gandhi of the nineties, the failure of a barrister in India or the ablest and the most highly paid advocate in Johannesburg, a status conscious and comfort loving Gandhi or an ardent ascetic—which Gandhi can one focus on? His was essentially an empirical and contextual approach and he cared but little about self-consistency of opinions or behavior. "In my search for Truth I have never cared for consistency."... "I must admit my many inconsistencies...I might well endorse Emerson's saying that 'a foolish consistency is the hobgoblin of little minds'.[CWMG III 381] There is, I fancy a method in my inconsistencies". [CWMG Vol.48 P 314]

His biography becomes all the more complicated because his priorities underwent a metamorphosis half way through his life when spiritual yearnings became the single passion of his life. By their very nature, such changes cannot be subjected to historical or chronological analysis.

Since Gandhi cannot be viewed in his totality, each one of us will have to choose a part of him - a somewhat narrow and limited part of Gandhi and to project that part as realistically and critically as our competence permits. This volume seeks to mainly focus on his political leadership. Gandhi always underrated his political activities and achievements. "My experiments in the political field are now known not only in India but to some extent to the civilized world. For me they are not of much value".[Auto Preface] "I was born for constructive program. It is a part of my soul. Politics is a kind of botheration for me". [CWMG 77: 374] He attributed all his political abilities to his experiments in the spiritual field "from which I have derived such powers as I possess for working in the political field". [Auto Preface]

It can therefore be argued that to concentrate on the political aspect of Gandhi is to emphasize what he himself considered a triviality and that such an approach is not only to misunderstand him but also to misconstrue him. But Gandhi was not unaware of his political abilities though he spoke of them on rarest of occasions. "I find from experience that I possess in an especial degree the gift of analysis and of discriminating right from wrong". [CWMG XII 358] Moreover, this volume is not a self-portrait by Gandhi and his opinions about himself and about his abilities would be only one of several factors in understanding and evaluating him.

This book is primarily addressed to those vast numbers who are interested in discussing the structure and the parameters of one of the most amazing and one of the most successful political careers in modern history. Gandhi's deep commitment to spiritualism cannot be overlooked, but our focus and our angle of viewing Gandhi are quite different from his. "Every activity of his for him is spiritual; but for us [it is] mostly political". [Brown] His religious inclinations were so strong that his professional and political experiences about the seamy side of human nature, his intense worldly wisdom, the frustrations of public life and his own sharp rationality could never smother his commitment to spiritualism.

So much has been written about Gandhi as a moral force that very little attention has been paid to the fact that it is not his moral principles but his vast and varied political experiences, his great capacity and sharp genius in handling public affairs that made him a force to be reckoned with. It is often overlooked that it was as a political leader fighting for his community in South Africa and for his nation in India that Gandhi emerged on the world stage.

The world knows him as a political leader of India and all his announcements were heard and counted as those made by an Indian patriot. Throughout his entire adult life Gandhi was first and foremost a political leader immersed up to his neck in political struggles and controversies. He was a politician par excellence. Though his political approach may be difficult to define, there is no denying that political leadership is the single most important and the most remarkable aspect of his multi-faceted personality. Gandhi himself was not unaware of this fact. "Men say that I am a saint losing myself in politics, but I am a politician trying my hardest to become a saint". [Polak]

Gandhi as an eminent politician predates Gandhi, the Mahatma, by at least a full decade. Long before he was launched on his spiritual quest in right earnest, he had demonstrated his political abilities in South Africa. His effectiveness as a political leader was never a by-product of any moral principles or spiritual discipline.

In every society, political processes and personalities are a force Majeure and this is all the more true of twentieth century India. Gandhi reflects and epitomises the aspirations and the frustrations of the society in which he lived and strived: he shaped the opinions and the events that would reverberate long after his departure. His impact on the political structures and the contemporary social ethos are of crucial importance to understand the world we live in.

Gandhi returned from South Africa in a depressed state of mind. He did die with a sense of failure, not of fulfillment. "The events of Independence and partition brought a near complete marginalization of Gandhi and Gandhism". [Omveldt "Dalits and democratic revolution" p 226] But all this does nothing to detract from his glory even by a hair's breadth. Societies survive persons like Gandhi a bit changed and probably a little ennobled.

Gandhi was always too awesome to be bypassed. Inspired by his idealism, his sacrifices and his wisdom, thousands marched to jails and privations; thousands more adored them and idolised Gandhi. "Gandhi has been criticized by many but he was seldom scorned and could never be ignored". [Swan 178]

Gandhi figures alike in the list of those who are politically prominent and of those who are spiritually advanced and both these aspects are inextricably blended in a singularly complex personality called Gandhi.

He holds his place in both lists and holds them both simultaneously and neither is an emanation from the other. It is extremely doubtful whether Gandhi himself ever succeeded in disentangling this very complicated relationship between his political sharpness and his spiritual aspirations.

We are focusing mainly on one aspect, albeit the most important aspect of his life. While Gandhi insisted on approaching the world from within guided by 'the still small inner voice', we would be trying to portray and understand Gandhi largely, if not entirely, in external context depicting major transformations in his personality.

Gandhi's life, compartmentalised by geography and calendar, is a four-act drama in which the first three small acts are followed by the longest and most important portion of his life. His early life in Kathiawar, his sojourn in London and his Africa years can be treated as separate, independent and almost disjointed parts of his life story and each of these three offers distinctly different societal landscapes. These three, almost detachable chapters of his life experiences are also his formative years and the last three decades of his life are only a continuum thereof.

In a long and frustrating struggle for rights for the Indian community in Africa, Gandhi's beliefs and his tactics attained maturity. In a sense, there is nothing essentially new in his opinions after Hind Swaraj and his struggle in India is merely an extension and an enlargement of what he did in South Africa. The amazing flexibility of Gandhian techniques and weaponry were demonstrated by Gandhi using the same weapons in diametrically opposite situations of South Africa and India.

In South Africa, Gandhi operated in a society where the dominant elite was intensely hostile and the colonial governments only a shade less so to his activities. Gandhi was supported and often rescued by the governments of England and India and almost the entire British press befriended him. In India the elite was entirely sympathetic, if not actively supportive of Gandhi's fight to the finish with the governments in India and in England. During his Indian years, the British rulers and press turned intensely hostile. Such situational divergences may help explain Gandhi's ambivalence about Indo-British conflict and cooperation.

Introduction

Athena, the Greek goddess of war and wisdom was fully formed and armed when she jumped out of the head of Zeus: so also was Gandhi fully matured and adequately armed when he returned [1915] from South Africa to dominate like a Colossus the political scenario in India till he was felled by the assassin's bullets in 1948. Gandhi held and used tremendous political power. "This man today holds in his hands the destinies of his people...more truly than any other man who ever lived... From almost utter obscurity, this man has mounted to fame, which is as universal as it promises to be immortal. ..." [Sir J H Holmes quoted Jai Narayan]

Gandhi's impact on Indian affairs has been so strong that every good and evil in modern Indian society has been traced back to him because he gave to the last phase of the struggle for independence in India "the color of his outlook and the stamp of his personality". During his lifetime he was recognised all over the world as the highest embodiment of the genius and spirit of India. When he died, "people all over the world mourned, because some goodness, some power for love and peace and justice had been taken away from this earth". [Alan Peton Fatima Mir ed.]

The centenary of his birth was celebrated by all the nations as "a tribute to an unconquerable spirit in a frail body, as an immense power of Will, a hatred for cruelty and injustice, a passionate and unceasing resistance to them and as a powerful assertion of Good". [ibid] "He is perhaps the only man in the world to day who has once again demonstrated, on an immense scale the creative power of saintliness and faith in the reality of the moral values". [Radha 160]

Gokhale went into raptures over him. "Gandhi has in him the marvelous spiritual power to turn ordinary men around him into heroes and martyrs" and "A purer, a nobler, a more exalted spirit has never moved on this earth... In him the Indian humanity at the present time has reached a high water mark" .[Cong. Pre.Add. 1908] Einstein echoed these sentiments in a tribute he paid in July 1944 and which has now become the most frequently quoted epitaph for the Mahatma. "Generations to come may be, will scarcely believe that such a one as this in flesh and blood ever walked on this earth".

Others were not so generous. Gandhi has been denounced as a bungler who queered the pitch of Indian politics by injecting religion in it and for delaying the arrival of independence by introducing several fads and distractions to the Indian public life. "He was accused, variously, of being an irresponsible trouble maker by his colonial masters, a destroyer of social harmony by Indian traditionalists, a backward looking crank by modernizers and progressives, an authoritarian leader by those within the movement who resented his leadership, a Hindu chauvinist by many Muslims and a defender of high caste elitism by lower caste activists". [Hardiman p 4]

Churchill called him "a fraud and a scoundrel" [Wallport 62] and "Truth" dubbed him 'a humbug'. Gandhi has often been denounced as a cheat, an imposter, an astute politician in the garb of a saint and one who used the mask of religion to further his political ends. "Gandhi who poses as a saint and a holy man is the cunning agent [of princes, landlords and capitalists]... he is one of the greatest enemies of the workers and peasants in India. [quoted Muriel Lister-35] "Gandhi has been denounced in this country [England] even by responsible persons as an ordinary agitator, his acts have been misrepresented as mere vulgar defiance of law, ...suggestions [have been made] that his motives are of self interest and pecuniary profits". [Lord Ampthill pre Doke]

By 1907 Gandhi had become a subject of intense and acrimonious debates and the controversies have never stopped thereafter. But "it is doubtful if there has been any man in history other than Mr. Gandhi who during his life time has won over so many millions of men to his side by his efforts and example". [Lord Sankhey Radha ed.]

Such a vast and seemingly unbridgeable gap between divergent opinions about Gandhi would define how formidable a task would face a biographer who seeks to add nothing and would hesitate to subtract any thing from the life which is so rich, so variegated and so confusing.

To write about Gandhi is to feel like a dwarf admeasuring a Virat. But one cannot and should not avoid the duty to admeasure and evaluate him. Personalities like Gandhi would be repeatedly dragged to the bar of history, as each generation would seek to evaluate them by their own standards. "We are lesser guys to judge a prophet but sitting as we are in the chair of History, we have to go by our own little understanding; but we must then fearlessly pronounce what we feel and what we adjudge". [Nanda P]

Gandhi is too valuable to be lost to history. He is already being enmeshed into so many legends that in the minds of several Indians he stands among the celestial hierarchy because Indians are "excessively inclined to deification". [Vincent Sheen] Even during his lifetime Gandhi had taken on something of a character of a mythological figure endowed with miraculous powers and gifts. "There is much to be said for stripping away the legends that have started accumulating around him and to see him as plain and as simple as he was". [Payne 13]

We must strive to prevent Gandhi's image being distorted into divinity by listing his stupendous failures together with his marvelous achievements. No one else will be more eager and more willing to be thus evaluated than Gandhi himself.

In fact Gandhi would insist that his failures and shortcomings be counted first and more strictly as he himself has done in his autobiography. "I assure all my admirers and friends that they will please me better, if they will forget the Mahatma and remember Gandhiji ... or think of me simply as Gandhi". [CWMG XXVIII-142] Gandhi was singularly free from ego and he was always first to unabashedly denounce his mistakes and misdemeanors.

Gandhi's successes and his failures could be traced largely to the same source—his intense and incessant quest in midst of messy politics for religious and spiritual values which was the primary and the most powerful motivating force of his entire adult life. "What I have been striving or pining to achieve for the last thirty years is self realization, to see God face to face, to achieve Moksha. I live and move and have my being in pursuit of this goal". [Auto. Pre.]

Most of Gandhi's failures arise out of his habit of attempting the impossible both in South Africa and India. "He did promise more than he could perform: but if men had never promised to themselves more than it was possible for them to perform, the world would be much poorer because the achieved reform is the child of the unachieved ideals". [Radha ed. 160]

Gandhi cared neither for money, nor power nor again for glory but only for the happiness of his conscience and that was the secret of his success in midst of all his failures. Intensity was another remarkable ingredient of his personality. Whatever he did or believed at the moment, he did with the greatest sincerity: there were no half measures in his life. As Nehru [Preface Tendulkar] puts it "there was a fire in this man of peace and humility".

These traits also made his personality so magnetic that he could transform the lives of all his near and dear ones. "It was extremely dangerous to have any contact with Gandhi because any such contact will definitely alter the course of one's life". [Payne] The combination of spiritual faith and intensity of purpose made Gandhi a formidable force and Prof. Gilbert Murray [Hibbert's Journal 1914] issued a warning to all the powers that be. "Persons in power should be very careful how they deal with a man who cares nothing for sensuous pleasures, nothing for riches, nothing for comforts or praise or promotion but is simply determined to do what he believes to be right. He is a dangerous and an uncompromising enemy; because his body which you can always conquer, gives you so little purchase upon his soul".

Religion was Gandhi's forte. "Gandhi is religious by nature and his doctrine is essentially religious... Gandhi is a Tolstoy in a more gentle, more appeased and if I dare say I would say in to a more Christian sense". [Romain Rolland P. 36] But Gandhi was not religious in the usual sense of the word.

Gandhi's quest for spiritual salvation took him to many destinations but his quest was essentially non-theistic and shorn of all rituals. He never hankered after holy places or personalities, never performed any puja, and never did his Sadhana in any prescribed manner. He did have a deep and abiding faith in the existence of an omniscient, omnipotent and benevolent energy whom he prayed daily for solace and guidance. He revered the scriptures of all the religions but only as far so they confirmed and supported his ethical values. For Gandhi, religion is entirely a matter of behaviour and a basic code underlying all religious denominations. The Christians and Islamic concepts and principles abound in Gandhi's code of ethics though his belief system is almost entirely Hindu. "His views are too closely allied to Christianity to his being entirely a Hindu and he is too deeply saturated with Hinduism to be classed a Christian". [Doke 106]

Too much has been made about the impact of Jainism on Gandhi's belief system and the influence of Raichandbhai on his thinking.

During Gandhi's short stay in Mumbai in 1891 he had met Rajchandra at a time when he "could not be said to have any serious interest in religious discussion". [Auto. Pt.II Ch I] The contact, so established between the two, might have been continued by correspondence because they never met again. Rajchandra died in 1897. No letters except a very trivial one, have survived. It is possible that Gandhi might have destroyed these letters as he had done with his correspondence with Maitland. Gandhi later on regretted his action as regards Maitland but not with regard to Rajchandra. When he heard about the death of Rajchandra he felt sorrow and commented that "Rightly or wrongly I was attracted to him and I loved him deeply too". [CWMG III 231]

In his lectures on Hinduism, delivered at Johannesburg [March 1905] Gandhi mentioned Jainism in passing as 'the most logical of faiths' [CWMG IV 370] but omitted even that reference in the summary he published in the *Indian Opinion* of 15-4-1905.

Gandhi was somewhat influenced by Buddhist tenets; but he totally rejected the basic ingredients of Jainism and Buddhism, namely Upasham [passivity] and Sanyas [retirement from worldly activities]. Buddha and Mahavir were agnostics if not atheists, while Gandhi had intense faith in Hindu gods and theology. Even his nonviolence - Ahimsa differs rather sharply from Ahimsa as preached by both these religions.

Gandhi preferred violence to cowardice and participated in war efforts in 1899, 1906 and in 1915. He always praised the military training and discipline and compared the war camps with monasteries. [Calcutta lectures 1902] He actively supported war against raiders in Kashmir in 1947.

In spite of his intense yearnings for spiritual bliss, Gandhi was never a recluse: he was an activist seeking solutions to the problems of humanity through action. He always was there where there was action and where the battle raged thickest. "No one has a greater horror for passivity than this tireless fighter who is one of the most heroic incarnation of the Man who resists". [Romain Rolland]

Gandhi was never an armchair philosopher and had a sneaking contempt for mere academics and preachers who, from their ivory towers, watched and yet avoided the struggles for underdogs. Although by nature a man of conciliation and compromise, Gandhi all through his life fought against authorities.

Gandhi was a superb writer and a very persuasive speaker but much more than both these, he was essentially a doer. Gandhi was never a theorist and whatever he said or wrote was always contextual to the situation at hand. His thoughts were "set out to a large extent, in newspaper editorials, letters to individuals, speeches to audiences, in dashed out memos and the like". [Hardiman 7]

It is quite easy to find mutually contradictory statements in his speeches and writings because he always projected a context. He was a man of the world brushing against the most astute and canny political leaders and was always ready for compromises without sacrificing his basic principles. He sought the Hindu goal of moksha through the Christian mode of service to humanity thus deliberately traducing the dividing line between the secular and the spiritual. Gandhi was a fascinating mixture of the mundane and the spiritual. "For me the road to salvation lies through the incessant toil in the service of my country and humanity". [C F Andrews 353-4]

Gandhi sought spiritual fulfillment where it was least expected to exist—in the messy political and public activities. "If I seem to take part in politics, it is because politics today encircles us like the coils of a snake and from which no one can go out no matter how much he tries. I want to wrestle with that snake. I want to introduce religion into politics". [R. Rolland] "I enter politics in so far as it develops the religious faculty in me".

Such a bifocal approach has baffled several observers and the apparent dichotomy between the spiritual and the secular is responsible for the mutually contradictory opinions about Gandhi as a person. "Gandhi is an unusual type of humanity whose peculiarities, however inconvenient are not devoid of attraction... His ethical and intellectual attitude based upon a curious mixture of mysticism and astuteness baffles the ordinary processes of thought". [Smuts in Walport.]

Gandhi has been described as a medieval mind seeking solutions of modern problems in a discarded jargon and reacting to the stress generated by modernity by rejecting modernity itself and by going back to a simpler and less complicated era of human history. Gandhi himself was not unaware of such anachronisms and advised that 'all my writings should be cremated with my body. What I have done will endure but not what I have said or written'. [intro. Last phase]

Gandhi's image as a saint has become so deeply ingrained in public mind that even an attempt to examine Gandhi in terms of non-spiritual qualities and abilities would be treated as a blasphemy. Gandhi himself always underrated his abilities because he himself was strongly convinced that all his political achievements were the by-product of his spiritual growth and he endlessly talked about the efficacy of the spiritual force as expressed through satyagraha. But such statements are not supported by objective and verifiable facts and hence ought to be treated only as his beliefs.

The strength of Gandhi's leadership does not seem to be an outcome of any ethical or spiritual discipline. On the contrary, Gandhi's emphasis on primacy of values has, at times, weakened his impact and his authority in public life as witnessed so often during the satyagraha in Africa [1909-13] and the suspension of satyagraha [1922] and also during the later half of his career in India. In his earlier years, Gandhi never allowed his quest for spiritual values to interfere with maneuvering which was so necessary for ensuring the safety and the security of the Indian community in South Africa. As a mystic Gandhi did rely on his intuition or his Inner Voice, but he was sufficiently pragmatic to act only on those of inner voices that were confirmed by the logic of his sharp and observant intellect.

Gandhi was no simple mystic. He was intensely religious minded but he also had a lawyer's trained mind. There was a simple directness in him, which was very winning but this was accompanied by a subtlety that could be very disconcerting. He was a formidable opponent while arguing his case as all those who negotiated with him were forced to acknowledge. In spite of all his humility and his readiness to acknowledge the weakness of his case, he could be very stubborn once he was convinced about any matter. "At times, he could be very intolerant and not at all open to dialogue". [Hardiman 10]

His great organising capacity, his vast and varied political experience, his sharp intellect, his practical common sense, his worldly wisdom, his quick and correct assessment of men and matters, his persistence in face of very heavy odds, his quiet courage in face of mortal dangers and his indomitable will, his industry and tireless zeal, his erudition, the originality of his concepts and his tactics, his grace and charm so captivating for his admirers and even for his enemies, his quick and correct analysis of problems and situations, his tremendous persuasive powers, his vast reading, his masterful command over English language, his capacity to sum up all the complexities of a problem in a nutshell, his readiness to hit the nail on the head at the right moment, his unique techniques of publicity and propaganda, his insistence on delimiting the area of conflict and his fairness of never taking a disadvantage of opponents' difficulties, his steadfast moderation in midst of conflict, his empathy and instant rapport with the masses everywhere, his shining transparency, total selflessness and humility to understand and acknowledge his blunders—these and many such other qualities ingrained in his personality were far more potent and important factors in his successful handling of public affairs than anything spiritual.

The life long, and very intense, quest for spiritual values made Gandhi a Mahatma but that quest did not make him an outstanding political leader either in Africa or in India. His colleagues in Africa and in India were impressed more by his political abilities than by his spiritual achievements. He was often disowned by his colleagues, in spite of the great respect he always inspired for his principled stand.

Gandhi is not the usual run of the mill politician. If politics implies an incessant urge to secure and retain political power and office, then Gandhi is the most apolitical of persons. He had no inclination to power and never displayed any desire or interest in capturing power or position. He did hold a few positions but only under great compulsion that he could not avoid. Very often he voluntarily stepped aside and allowed others to take over leadership. But occasionally he did participate in politicking. The use he made of coolies in the satyagraha of 1913 and the role he played in the Subhash Bose episode are very highly controversial.

On account of his stupendous abilities and great sacrifices, Gandhi did acquire a tremendous influence over his companions and compatriots. But he never sought to convert such influence into power. He always refused to use even his influence over anybody except those who willingly surrendered themselves to his guidance.

"Gandhi never asks men for more than they can give. But then he asks for all that they can give". [R Rolland 44] He never demanded from his friends and followers anything that he did not demand first and more rigorously from himself. He was often deceived by his followers. "You ask too much of people. You ask more than they are able to give. Then in self defense, they try to deceive you". [Millie 119] Gandhi took hold of ordinary men and women who are mixtures of heroism and cowardice and made heroes out of them all. As Nehru put it "he taught us to stand up and fight".

Few things about Gandhi are more impressive than his complete freedom from fear and hatred. He transmitted the first to his followers but they could not absorb his love for opponents. He was a traditional Hindu aspiring to spiritual experiences for self and others around him. Convinced very firmly that such a growth needs a proper social and political environment, he strenuously fought against every form of injustice in every corner of personal and public life.

It is rather uncomfortable for Indians to acknowledge that Gandhi, the most resplendent epitome of all that is best and most adorable in Indian traditions, was mostly structured and shaped beyond the geographical and cultural boundaries of India: he is as much a product of the West as he is of his native land.

Gandhi's childhood illustrates the Biblical parable of the seeds being thrown on the rocks and the birds hovering above them to eat them away. It was a fortuitous accident in the life of Gandhi that he was whisked away in the nick of time and planted in the culturally fertile soil of England where he immediately flowered with the amazing speed of a bamboo shoot. This happened once again when he was rescued from the boredom of a brief-less barrister's life. During the last decade of the nineteenth century, the racist and the arrogant society of South Africa was far superior to the land of Gandhi's birth. It was in England, but more especially in South Africa that Gandhi went hammer and tongs to work upon himself and forged a Mahatma out of a rich and prestigious lawyer leader.

Like all Indians of his day, Gandhi was essentially bicultural. He was a stunning amalgamation of the East and the West. Gandhi is a product of two civilisations or if one so likes, of Hindu and Christian cultures. The impact of Christianity and Christian value system on his mindset and on his activities and his approach to life has been seldom emphasised and all sorts of weird explanations are offered to explain his approaches and his attitudes instead of tracing them to their correct roots.

Gandhi's greatest contribution is his synthesis of the best of Indian and western values. In England and South Africa, some of his best friends and supporters were Europeans. Gandhi absorbed only the best that the west had to offer and never allowed his Indian-ness to get drained out of his psyche. Gandhi is nothing if not an Indian and that too a pious, believing Hindu. Hence his life style and his opinions are the products of the traditional approach of a typical Indian mind. The Gandhian approach always found a resonance with tradition oriented Indians but was often repudiated by the half-baked Indian elite.

We sent a dumb, raw, matriculate to England and it sent back to us a self-confident barrister, a journalist and a vocal crusader for whatever cause he believed to be true. India sent barrister M K Gandhi to South Africa and received in return a Mahatma.

It is true that having attained maturity, Gandhi seemed to repudiate everything western: he denounced western civilisation and all its legal, political and economic structures and institutions. But Gandhi did not repudiate the European culture; he denounced the industrialism that had acquired a stranglehold over Europe and India alike and which inculcated a mechanical and an amoral approach to life. That modernity had been denounced by several western thinkers and writers like Ruskin, Tolstoy, Kropotkin and Carpenter with far greater vehemence than Gandhi. Gandhi quoted them all in his *Hind Swaraj*.

Gandhi's approach to politics can be much better appreciated by tracing the concept of politics back to the Greek society where it originated. For the Greeks and also for Gandhi, politics was an extension and implementation of ethics—applying ethics to the management of the affairs of their city state-polis that for the Greeks was both the state and the society. For Socrates and for Plato and to some extent even for Aristotle, politics is an activity to uphold and to utilise the ethical values in the mundane life of the polis.

This concept is an antithesis to the Machiavellian concept of politics as a mode for acquiring power. Politics for Greeks was a duty, a burden, not a possession or an acquisition. That is why Pericles denounced all those citizens who do not participate in politics as so much burden to the polis for shirking their duty to participate in public affairs. Politics still remains the art of management and it does involve compromises and maneuvers; but such politics insists on what is ethically sound and possible and it is circumscribed by the ethical objectives. Bereft of such ethical values, politics is an anti-polis activity.

Gandhi in this sense is a Greek in his political approach and the Greeks would have understood him more easily and would have empathised with him more than modern society ever did. That is why Gandhi as a political leader was a tremendous success and a disastrous failure. Gandhi's insistence on the primacy of moral values and his equally assertive participation in messy game of politics is very difficult for modern mind to reconcile.

These are some of the contradictions in Gandhi's political career that have for long baffled his biographers and attracted researchers from all over the world to laborious inquiries into the ingredients of such a surprising political leadership.

Chapter 1

THE LAND OF GANDHI

Gandhi has become a symbol, even a Totem and hence all biographies of Gandhi are mostly hagiographies and a few of them are demonologies and his human face gets clouded in all such projections. But his admirers and his critics have one thing in common. They all depend largely on Gandhi's own narration, to depict his life, especially the early years of his life. Much of what is written about his childhood and adolescence is either directly copied or largely derived from his autobiography.

In a very candid autobiography, Gandhi told all that he thought was worth telling about himself, about his family, about his early escapades, his failures and his experiments with food and Truth. Gandhi is analysed and explained and psychoanalysed on the basis of data provided by Gandhi himself. Gandhi certainly was a very keen observer of men and events and he is quite an honest recorder of facts and experiences even if they were unpleasant or inconvenient. But this autobiography, although a very important historical document, is not a reliable source of history.

Gandhi's Autobiography is unique amongst this class of literature, because it is not a narration of a life as it was lived or even as it was remembered; it is not even a collection of stray reminiscences. It is "a highly idiosyncratic choice of events and experiences stressed or lightly touched". [Brown 8] The value of this autobiography as a source material is very severely vitiated by the occasion for which and the way in which it was written and by the perspective adopted by Gandhi.

It was written as a weekly column for his journal *Navjivan* [1925-29] and it was written without the help of any record or documents to stimulate Gandhi's memory about the events and personalities that were fast fading out of his life. Therefore the autobiography is "full of misremembering of the earlier events and experiences". [Stephen Hay]

Moreover, Gandhi did not tell us everything. He either forgot or deliberately omitted several pieces of information that he considered unimportant or irrelevant. "I do not set down in this story all that I remember. Who can say how much I must give and how much omit in the interest of Truth"? [Auto Part IV chap.XI] Gandhi, for example does not mention the religion of his mother, his friendship with Ranjitsinh of Jamnagar, his frequent visits to theatre and the lectures he delivered in London. He also does not mention his very close association with The Theosophical Society in Transvaal and his lectures to the Society or the misunderstanding that these lectures created amongst the Muslims.

Some such silences and memory lapses are quite trivial—e.g., the date of his arrival in London [1888]. The titles of the books he read are often incorrect and even the summary of these books is not very accurate. Ruskin's *Unto This Last* is an epoch- making book in the life of Gandhi; but the summary of this book [Auto Part IV Chap.XVIII] is a mixture of Ruskin, Carpenter and the Trappists.

Such errors might have crept in either because Gandhi had forgotten the details or because he was in a hurry to meet the deadline and had no time to either remember or revise. The autobiography never had the benefit of a proper editorial scrutiny. A few of such memory lapses will be noticed and corrected in course of our narration. The autobiography is also full of reconstructed conversations that are expository rather than factual. Such memory lapses and reconstructions do not distort the overall picture and can therefore be treated as permissible lapses.

What is *not* permissible is the approach. Gandhi's narration gets enormously distorted on account of the purpose for which it was written and the perspective adopted by Gandhi. The purpose was didactic and the perspective was teleological. "It is not my purpose to attempt a real biography. ....My purpose is to acquaint the reader with my *faults* and *errors*. [emphasis added]. In judging myself I shall be as harsh as Truth as I want others to be". [Auto pre]

It is a Mahatma Gandhi who is reviewing, annotating and judging the life story of a young, brilliant and highly sensitive person called Mohandas Gandhi and it is absolutely necessary for the readers to keep in mind that Mahatma was always very severe and even cruel in pronouncing judgements about himself and others close to him. "A streak of censoriousness was one of the marks left on Mahatma by the puritanical role of a young preceptor and a guide to his community [in Africa] freed from all traditional restraints". [Chandran 287]

The teleological approach adopted by Gandhi makes him review his early life on the basis of what he aspired to become. The narration does not reflect his mind and the opinions as they were at that time and his motives get coated with his later day views. He depicts the story not as it happened, but on the basis of concepts that became important to him in later life. The motivation and the rationale for his actions at that time are coloured by the hindsight provided by his experiences and might not have been there when the actual events were taking place. The autobiography is full of such afterthoughts.

The Autobiography does not describe the child or the person that Mohandas was, but as he would have been expected to be, by Gandhi of the twenties. Because of such a teleological approach, Gandhi's motives and opinions as presented in the autobiography are not contemporaneous: they needs to be supplemented by contemporary documents. Only then, can we hope to project a more correct and accurate picture of Gandhi as a person and to better understand his motive for what he did or did not do.

In the autobiography, his approach is totally negative and he is altogether too harsh and unjust to himself. Throughout his narration Gandhi degrades himself: he understates his leadership and his achievements to such an extent that, were we to depend exclusively upon the Autobiography as a single source of information about Gandhi, we would never get to know about his marvellous achievements and the dizzy heights that he occupied in the public life in Africa and in India. Under-valuation of self is as much a misstatement of facts as is hyperbolic boasting. Gandhi's penchant for self-abnegation makes his self-portrait an unacceptable caricature.

Gandhi ought to be studied in a larger societal perspective. Such a perspective is far more important for Gandhi than for many others. The child Gandhi is a Janus-faced figure standing on the threshold of a rapidly disappearing past and an equally rapid emergence of a perplexing and somewhat frightening modernity.

The society in which Gandhi passed his childhood was so crude, so barbaric and so poor that it can be safely asserted that Gandhi was born in the medieval age. Gandhi during his teens witnessed the onslaught of modernity that burst upon his homeland with a bang and with the fury of a whirlwind. Within a decade or two everything was changed with a velocity unheard of previously. When Gandhi left for England, Saurashtra had leap-frogged by a century within a decade.

As a teenager, Gandhi underwent three major culture shocks in rapid succession—a mild one in his vision and aspirations due to his education in an English school in Rajkot, a bewildering but a highly pleasant shock when he went for further studies in England and finally a shattering jolt in South Africa where he went to earn his living.

Gandhi was born and brought up in the vile atmosphere of Saurashtra, then known as Kathiawar. The region was a backwater lagoon where conditions of life were not conducive to the growth of a sensitive and brilliant child. Compared to the other areas of Gujarat under the direct rule of the British, Kathiawar was socially, economically and educationally a wild desert where human growth was stunted and frequently wilted.

During the major portion of the nineteenth century, Kathiawar was a concrete manifestation of what Hobbes has described as a State of Nature, where the hand of everyone was against the throat of every one else and where life was "nasty, poor, brutish and short" and where, as Gandhi himself said, a brother would cut the throat of brother for half a penny. [Payne] The Census report of 1881 speaks of ninety-three percent of people dying before they reached the age of fifty. Most of such dead were women, thereby pushing the sex ratio down to the uncomfortable level of 923.08 females against every thousand males. 86.37%. males and 99.66% females were illiterate. Kathiawar in the fifties and sixties of the nineteenth century, had no railways, no electricity, no drainage, no roads, no banks, no administration, no peace, no proper schooling and no intellectual activities.

"The social and the political system of Kathiawar is best described as a system of sanguinary disputes and of murder, robbery, abduction, arson and outlawry". [Gazetters 329] "Up to 1875, crime had practically, save in very grave cases gone unpunished". The crime was so rampant, because over most of Kathiawar, there was no jail, no police, no law and no court to punish the criminals. "Bear in mind that up to the present, no state in Kathiawar has any judicial system, any written law or any recognized civil or criminal law". [Col. Keatinge, Sept. 1863 quoted by Harilal Biography of Shamaldas Permanand preface V] The first court of criminal justice was established by the British Agency at Rajkot in 1860. Captain LeGrand Jacob commented, "Of civil and criminal law, the people of Kathiawar have no idea, nor do they seem sensible of the want". "Up to the beginning of the nineteenth century [1820], a murder was not a crime in Kathiawar. Only a wanton killing without any rhyme or reason and involving some important family was punished if the authorities wanted to". [*Saurashtra No Itihas* p 735 Desai Shumbhuprasad]

The reasons for such a ruinous landscape can be traced largely to the political conditions obtaining in Kathiawar. Fractured into 193 petty, quarrelling princedoms, and broken up into 418 jurisdictions— some of them as small as a single tiny village or even a part of such a village, Kathiawar was a cesspool of capricious, ineffective tyrannies; a theatre of the absurd. The White Paper on the Indian States published by the Government of India in 1947, mentions a sovereign state in Kathiawar—Veja No Ness which ruled over two and a half acres and had the royal income of thirty Rupees or $ 0.60 per annum. The Maharaja of Bikaner is quoted by Thompson and Garret [*Rise and Fulfillment of British Rule in India* p 229] as mentioning a ruler who had sovereign power over nothing else but a well.

With a very, very few honourable exceptions, almost all these rulers were ignorant, effeminate, cruel idiots and quite a many amongst them were downright criminals. K.M. Panikkar calls these princedoms "the theatre of the most degraded debauchery and the most horrible mismanagement" [Native States and the government of India.] and quotes *London Times* mentioning "their imbecility, their vices and their crimes." "Kathiawar," says Panikkar "was a veritable museum of sovereignties".

British rulers treated them as comic flunkies with their absurd costumes, jewels, silk pajamas and their dummy swords. Gandhi himself has called them Khansamas—the menial servants of the viceroy. [Auto. Part III Chapt. XVI] He has quoted with approval the sneering contempt expressed by Amanulla Khan, the Amir of Afghanistan [CWMG VII P 7] about their effeminate dress and ornaments.

"Kathiawar was, for many years one of the most lawless countries in the world. ... The chiefs sought every pretext of harassing the underlandholders [Bhayats and the Garasias] and the underlandholders when they found redress denied to them, sought shelter in outlawry". [The Gazetteers of Bombay Presidency Vol VIII Kathiawar 1888] "Between 1850 and 1880, thousands of such outlaws roamed all over Kathiawar striking villages and working all sorts of mischief". [Ibid] At any given time there were about two hundred such lawless brigands plundering and killing people.

Almost every prince gave shelter and support to the outlaws who were ravaging the areas of his rivals and harassing the subjects of his opponents. Since his opponents would do the same, entire Kathiawar was in constant turmoil. "The events.... were full of horrors. The internecine wars, the blood feuds, the plunder and the devastation of one or the other state were the order of the day. Everybody cut everybody else's throat and whoever was strong in the field successfully encroached on his weaker neighbors. ...... (Prior to 1806) every species of plunder and desolation—the ripe crops were swept off the fields, the villages were wantonly fired and destroyed, nothing was allowed to remain except the bare walls of the houses...every hamlet in the territory reduced to a heap of smoldering ruins". [Harilal Savailal Preface]

British Suzerainty was imposed on Kathiawar in 1822 and "the sole supreme power has been vested in the Political Agent subordinate to the Governor of Bombay". [Karaka-Kathiawar Directory (1884) p 15].

It was in 1844 that the Political Agent ordered the princes not to give shelter to the criminals from the areas of other rulers. The directive was honoured more in breach than in observance and the practice continued for more than a century till the princedoms were swept away by the currents of history in 1948.

The capricious and the unruly princes of Kathiawar were held somewhat in check by the fear of the British overlord and the Political Agent's office at Rajkot exercised undefined and unlimited powers to regulate the affairs of the states in all matters great or small. The most unruly princes trembled while facing even the lower grade officers in the Agency and meekly swallowed the orders and the directives of the Agency usually couched in rude, insulting and even threatening language. All the princes were warned by the Agency "there was a point beyond which mismanagement could not be allowed to proceed".

In order to bring some order out of the prevailing confusion and to define more clearly the powers and the functions of the princes, the states in Kathiawar were grouped into seven classes [1863] by Col. Keating and each class was assigned fixed protocol as well as the powers of administration and jurisdiction in a graded manner. None of the states had any political powers and all were to work under the strict supervision and guidance of the Agency office at Rajkot. In 1863, only four states –Bhavnagar, Junagadh, Dhangadhra and Navanagar—were classified as the first class states having full judicial powers in civil and criminal cases. [G.P. Makwana Administrative and political activities of the Rajkot Agency. Samshodhan Jan-Mar 2003]

The second grade was given to eight other states with their powers restricted to try the less important cases. Such powers were severely curtailed as the scale went down to the seventh grade and most of the States were no better than mere estates. Porbunder and Rajkot where Gandhi spent his childhood belonged to the third category and could exercise very limited powers. In case of misrule or any major transgression, the Agency would dethrone the ruler of any state for an indefinite period and manage the state though an administrator chosen by the Political Agent. The British authorities and their Indian staff treated these rulers and their officials with undisguised contempt.

There is no wonder that a sensitive child like Gandhi growing up in midst of such a landscape would develop an intense and long lasting love and loyalty for the British Raj which was the only civilising force in the region. So deep rooted was that love and loyalty of Gandhi to British rule that it took repeated rebuffs by the racist regimes in Africa followed by the Jallianwala Bagh in India to turn Gandhi into a rebel against the British Raj. He was almost the last of the prominent Indians to lose faith in British rule. "Hardly have I known anybody to cherish such loyalty, as I did to the British Constitution" [Collected Works IV]. Indians "have very little idea of how regretfully Gandhi withdrew his loyalty to the Crown and how long a time he took to come to a conclusion that he must become a rebel". [Chandran 162-63]

In the midst of such violence and oppression, society had developed a crude technique called *tragu* for the redress of grievances. The exasperated victim of the crime or injustice would torture himself or herself in the presence of the offender. Such self-torture might result in failure or death and the victims were fully aware of such possibilities. For the redress of minor grievances like recovery of debts or of stolen or robbed property, the victims usually belonging to the castes of Brahmins or Bhats or Charanas would sit at the door of the culprit and will refuse to eat or drink till the offender was shamed or socially pressurised into redress. Such a suffering or death at one's doorstep was believed to be a curse and would draw heavenly punishments. The dead victim may return as a tormenting ghost.

A far more gruesome variety of *tragu* was resorted to, mostly by the Bhats and Charanas. The victims would stab themselves with sharp weapons and sprinkle the blood of selves or companions on the house of the offender till their grievances were redressed or they died of self-inflicted wounds. They would also resort to self-immolation. This would lay a severe curse and would result in the eternal damnation-both social and spiritual for the criminal and his descendents for several generations.

The British authorities condemned all such practices as blackmail and suicide and made them criminal offences, but the writ of British rulers could hardly prevail and the practice continued almost unabated till the second decade of the twentieth century.

The massacre at Kanera is the most gruesome example of such *tragu*. In December 1882 [Gandhi was 13], some 200 Mahiyyas sat for a *tragu* on the hillock of Kanera in a peaceful and passive protest against imposition of a tax by the Nawab of Junagadh. One male member from each family of the caste was participating in the protest; and a young girl of nine or ten had brought her baby brother because the family had no other male member.

The sit-in continued for a month. On the thirtieth day, a police party fell upon the crowd, killing eighty-one persons on the spot including the young girl. Their heads were severed from their bodies and were taken to Junagadh for identification. The incident created a furor all over Kathiwar and Political Agent severely reprimanded the Nawab and his Diwan. [Desai Shambhuprasad]

Prof. Rushbrook Williams drew the attention of the Gandhian scholars to *tragu* and he traced Gandhi's satyagraha to this practice that was made more effective by borrowings from Western sources like Non-conformist passive resisters, the suffragettes, and the Irish freedom fighters who often resorted to fasting and hunger strikes.

It is argued that Gandhi refined and expanded *tragu* as passive resistance or satyagraha by synthesising the Indian and the Western techniques of self-torture and altered its application and scale by using it not for personal but for public purposes against more civilised and more law-abiding governments of South Africa and India.

But such explanations overlook a fundamental difference between *tragu* and satyagraha. Satyagrahis violate the laws and cheerfully suffer the cruelties and the tortures imposed on them. Such punishments may result in deprivations, injuries and even death. But satyagrahis never indulge in any self-torture nor were they ever allowed to do so. Gandhi did undertake several fasts; but he always discouraged others from joining him in fasting.

As a voracious and thoughtful reader of contemporary debates in the press, Gandhi was quite familiar with the nineteenth century language of protest. "Passive Resistance is one of the most approved methods of securing redress and is the only course that good, law-abiding and peaceful citizens can adopt without doing violence to their Conscience". [CWMG VII 211] Post-1850 England provided him with numerous such incidents involving Irish nationalists and the passive resisters to war services. Quakers in U.S. offered non-violent resistance to unjust laws and Gandhi himself was an admiring witness to the struggles of the Suffragettes. Satyagraha is almost entirely rooted in European experiences and any similarity with *tragu* is only verbal and superficial.

Gandhi himself traced the origin of satyagraha to the English Radical non-conformists and to Henry David Thoreau.[CWMG VII] His intellectual debt to Thoreau has been handsomely acknowledged. He refers to Irish Sinn Fein and their passive resistance movement [1905] leading to a boycott of British goods, courts and parliament. Gandhi has mentioned Dick of Austria-Hungary who led a no tax movement and a refusal of all services to the government.

Pre-Gandhian leaders in India were out of touch with contemporary currents of thought. Gandhi studied and adopted these concepts and he brought this technique to India. He was no innovator, but a very great and thoughtful adopter of the latest techniques of the twentieth century and therefore he remains modern and very relevant to our times. He gave back to the western world in a crystallised form what he had borrowed from it as crude ore.

It is not at all difficult to imagine the plight of the common man in the anarchy prevalent in nineteenth century Kathiawar. The economic activities and the productive classes were crushed under heavy exactions either from the rulers or from the dacoits. The economy had ground down to subsistence level. Any display of prosperity was risky and rich people pretended to be poor, leading simple and even austere lives. There were no banks till 1884 and money lending was an immensely profitable though a highly risky business.

There were no travel or transportation facilities except for the most primitive- bullock cart or camel/horse riding. That is how young Gandhi travelled in 1888 from Rajkot to Porbunder taking five days to cover a distance of 120 miles. Travelling without an escort was extremely dangerous and up to 1863, there were no postal services. Letters and goods were reached to the major destinations by armed and organised Angadias There were no roads and bridges up to 1865. "It was between 1871 and 1886 that there was a rapid and all round growth of roads, railways, post offices and telegraphs in Kathiawar .... Where there was not a single mile of road in 1865, there are now [1886] more than 600 miles of roads for the most part bridged and metalled". [Karaka P 19]

The railway line from Bombay to Baroda was extended to Ahmedabad in 1865 and came to Vadhwan only in 1872. The ruler of Bhavnagar got the line extended to his capital city in 1880 and likewise the ruler of Gondal to his capital in 1888. There was no railway in Rajkot when Gandhi left for England. Gandhi saw and travelled on the railway for the first time in 1887, [he was eighteen] when he went to appear for his matriculation examination at Ahmedabad.

Kathiawar economy was almost entirely pastoral and revolved round agriculture and animal-husbandry supplemented by labour-intensive village industries. This region was a flourishing center of hand spinning and hand weaving cotton textile production. But that industry had started rapidly disappearing by the middle of the nineteenth century. "Local arts and manufacturing has been nearly annihilated by the combined power of English capital and steam powered machinery". [LeGrand Jacob quoted in the Gazetters p 199] The spinning wheels and the handlooms were silenced by the textile mills in Bombay reducing, thereby, a large number of villagers to unemployment and starvation. The hand ginning and pressing of cotton also disappeared because the mills preferred the cotton ginned and pressed by machines. Kathiawar was being "steadily integrated into the rest of India by the threads of cotton and the iron of rails as the cotton presses and the ginning factories, roads and railways developed in the peninsula". [Chandran 71]

Gandhi was a first generation witness to the decline and the rapid disappearance of the old economy and the resultant human misery. Much of the Gandhian economy may have been an unconscious harking back to these childhood memories. His insistence on hand spun and hand woven cloth might have been rooted in these shocking experiences.

There was a great paucity of modern educational institutions in Kathiawar. The London Missionary Society and the Irish Presbyterian Church had established schools at Gogha, Porbunder and Rajkot between 1817 and 1820. Since these schools were mainly the agencies for conversions to Christianity, none but the depressed classes would attend them.

The strident and foolish denunciations of Hindu Gods and rituals by the lesser missionaries were so heinous that Christianity was the only religion for which the young Gandhi developed an intense dislike. [Auto

Part I Ch. X] Reverend H R Scot, who was at that time [1883-87] at Rajkot, denied Gandhi's charges and claimed that it was he who was very often attacked and maltreated by the people of Rajkot. [Pyarelal] Gandhi, in reply to Scot, stuck to his own version. [1926] Rev. Scot might have been an exception, but the experience with the early Christian missionaries was rather ugly all over India.

The missionaries often acted as the religious representative of the conquering race and hence "Christianity was undistinguished from British Imperialism in the eyes of the Indian people" [Chandran 49] and Baptism a mere indulgence in wine, beef and western dress. Even the Parsis, the most anglicised section of the Indians in Bombay dubbed the missionaries as "Devils in human form".

Several attempts to convert Gandhi to Christianity by better and higher types of missionaries in England and South Africa did not succeed probably because Gandhi and his missionary friends failed to overcome this mental block created by his childhood experiences. Gandhi, of course, was later on profoundly influenced by Christian ethics and developed an intense love for Christ and Christians. He probably was the only practicing Christian of his times.

Apart from missionary schools, there were several native schools known as Dhudi schools, [so called because students wrote letters and figures in dirt-Dhud] imparting elementary education and teaching only alphabets and rudiments of arithmetic. There was no systematic, secular school structure in Kathiawar till the second quarter of the nineteenth century.

In 1853 the Political Agent, Capt. Lang raised an education fund and established a central school in Rajkot. The Kattyawar High School established in 1867 was then, the only high school in Kathiawar. The census report of 1881 mentions a total of 600 schools in Kathiawar out of which only 11 were the middle schools. There were only four high schools [Bhavnagar, Rajkot, Junagaadh and Navanagar] that prepared students for the matriculation examination of the University of Bombay. The students studying up to that level were very few. Only thirty-eight students appeared for matriculation examination in 1881. It was only in 1885, that the first college in Kathiawar—the Shamaldas College started functioning at Bhavnagar, but there were hardly any students. The College in 1888, had only seven teachers and sixty students, Gandhi being one of them. When Gandhi passed his matriculation examination he was the first to do so not only in his family but also in his community.

Young Gandhi never read a newspaper because there was none to be read. There were only a few, irregularly published weeklies in Kathiawar. Writing or working for a newspaper was considered a reprehensible activity, which an educated person would undertake only to keep his body and soul together after he had failed to secure a government job. [Dalpatram in the first issue of *Buddhiprakash*.] There was very little literary or intellectual activity in Kathiawar and hardly any books other than religious or didactic literature were published in the region. But Kathiawar did hear the distant echoes of what was happening at Surat and Bombay, which were centers of numerous literary, social and intellectual movements.

The oppressive situation, the deprivations and the insecurities of life and belongings could not rob these sturdy people of their resilience and their *joie de vivre*. They were protected by intense religious faith and rituals and were buoyed up by numerous minor poets and saints of the region. Swami Sahajanand had just concluded his crusade in Kathiawar against drugs and crimes and Swami Dayanand Saraswati was campaigning in western India against untouchability and child marriages.

Chapter 2

THE FAMILY AND THE CHILD

Gandhi, the sixth child of his father and fourth of his mother, was born in the Modh Vania caste in the sub group known as Gobhva. The Gandhis originally hailed from Kutiyana in the state of Junagadh but they migrated to Porbunder in 1777. Modhs are a community of petty traders and shopkeepers but the family of Gandhi had taken to state service.

What Gandhi wrote in his autobiography about his father and grandfather are mere family legends and they are somewhat at variance with available records. Gandhi mentions them as Diwans of Porbunder, Rajkot and Vankaner. He himself translated the word 'Diwan' as 'prime minister' in the interview he gave to *The Vegetarian* in 1891. This misnomer was copied by the translator of his autobiography and has subsequently been accepted uncritically by all his biographers. Pyarelal has further embellished the term by mentioning the Home minister and the cabinet. All this is a gross misrepresentation because in nineteenth century no such offices existed anywhere in India.

In Kathiawar, only the first class states had Diwans and there never was any Diwan either at Porbunder or Rajkot or Vankaner. The documents so diligently collected by Pyarelal, invariably mention the father and grandfather of Gandhi as Karbharies i.e. the estate managers in the third class states that had no political power and could exercise very limited administrative functions.

The main and the most important function of the karbharies was to collect the Princes' share from each farmer on the sharecropper basis (Bhagbatai). A fixed share of agricultural products belonged to the ruler and the crops had to be assessed, weighed if necessary and the share of the prince collected in kind by the state servants and then sold to the traders, usually by auction. All the revenue so collected was the personal income of the prince to be spent at his own sweet will and was usually wasted on luxuries and escapades of the most abominable type.

In the native states, all servants including the Karbharis were chosen and dismissed at the whim of the princes. Their tenures and even their salaries were not safe from princely caprice and they could survive only through abject subservience and manipulation. Gandhi's father lost his salary for the entire service period of nine months with the ruler of Vankaner and he had to go on a fast to get released from the service. [Pyarelal]

The ancestors of Gandhi have been idolised by some biographers. Pyarelal describes all of them as persons of "exalted character, of indomitable courage, extremely truthful, exceptionally versatile, possessing vigorous and original minds". All these adjectives are a sheer waste of words. Such personalities would not have survived even for a day in the company of the capricious kinglets of Kathiawar. Good persons in a bad society are usually thrown on the dung heap.

Gandhi had a different opinion about his ancestors "a notorious... band of robbers and oppressors" because they were in league with the princes pursuing their own selfish interest. "Judging by the common standards, it would seem that they had acted with a fair measure of

justice i.e. they treated people with smaller measures of oppression...
At present the family has fallen on evil days". [CWMG XII 380]

Porbunder, where Gandhi was born, was the capital of a tiny state and Gandhi's father and grandfather spent the best years of their lives as the karbharies of this state. The state [pop. 71,072] was situated in western Kathiawar, an extremely arid, treeless, austere and gaunt area and a backward and a crime-infested region. The turbulent Vaghers were a constant source of trouble and their last uprising was crushed in 1859: one of them, Mulu Manek or Devo took to brigandage in 1862. The hills in the vicinity of Porbunder were his den and the ruler of Porbunder [Vikmatji] was suspected of being in collusion with him.

Porbunder was a poor state. Most [90.13%] of its population was Hindus. The tiny and mostly illiterate Muslim community had well established and flourishing commercial establishments in Arabia and South Africa and many of them had settled in South Africa as traders and merchants.

Prabhudas, a nephew of Gandhi, has popularised a romantic episode in the life of Uttamchand, the grandfather of Gandhi who was the Karbhari of the Khimoji Rana of Porbunder. Khimoji died in 1831 and one of his queens, Rupaliba became a regent for her young son Vikmatji for a decade.[1831-41]

We are told that she wanted to unjustly punish a storekeeper [bhandari] who sought and secured protection of Karbhari. When Ota Gandhi insisted on the due process of law, he was threatened, the guns boomed against the walls of his residence and the Gandhi patriarch quietly prepared to meet death for the sake of justice and for keeping his word. His guardsman Gulam Mahomed Makrani was killed in the skirmish and his memorial stone [Palio] was placed in the nearby Vaishnav temple. [Pyarelal] The political agent at Rajkot was alerted and intervened to save Gandhi; but the infuriated queen confiscated his property and exiled him. Ota Gandhi retired to the ancestral village of Kutiyana.

The entire story is an unadulterated fairy tale. There is no documentary evidence either in the state or Agency records to support it and it is very highly unlikely in the prevailing conditions. The most authentic historian of Porbunder, Manibhai Vora, not only does not mention it, but he, and the traditional history of Porbunder as also the Kathiawar Directory describe Rupaliba as a very wise, a very balanced and a very just ruler in all her dealings and decisions. Memorial stones can never be placed in Vaishnav Havelis and Narottam Palan who has made an extensive study of such memorial stones [Palias] of Kathiawar has not been able to find any single memorial stone anywhere in Porbunder. [Interview 27 August 2001] In 1838, there were no courts and no laws in Kathiawar and poor Ota Gandhi would not have understood the notion of law and legal process. Contacting the Agency at Rajkot by the fastest communication would have taken at least a week.

The *Makardhawajavamshiya Mahip Dipmala* [The string of lights of the kings belonging to the dynasty of Makardhwaja] edited and published by Pathak has a rather shocking story to tell. The well-entrenched Karbhari—Ota Gandhi taking advantage of his closeness to Rana Khimoji, had poisoned his ears against his second wife Rupali to such an extent that she was driven back to her parents. She befriended a dreaded dacoit Natha Modhwadia who threatened Karbhari, attacked his residence, took potshots at his house and forced him to run away to Kutiyana.

The story recorded by Gandhi in his autobiography about Ota Gandhi saluting the Nawab of Junagadh with his left hand because his right hand was pledged to the Rana of Porbunder is also a myth. The officials of the states would have to salute hundreds of petty officers of the Agency several times a year. Such an insult—left hand salute—would invite condign punishment from the Nawab for a serious breach of protocol.

The year Gandhi was born was a year of stress and difficulties for the family. Gandhi's father Karamchand, after serving for seven years in a minor position, was made a Karbhari of Porbunder [1848] in which capacity he served for about two decades. When the ruler had gone on a pilgrimage, his son prince Madhavsinh, an incorrigible alcoholic, died in 1869: his boon companion Lakshman Khavas was held responsible for leading the prince astray. He was detained by Karamchand Gandhi and on his return, the outraged Rana ordered Khavas to be mutilated by cutting off his nose and ears. Khavas committed suicide.

For such an act of wanton cruelty, Rana was severely reprimanded by the Agency. Karamchand also shared the odium and was under a cloud. Soon after this, [1870] Karamchand Gandhi left or was made to leave Porbunder for ever. He lost his job and was unemployed for a few years.

After 1870, he had to frequently change jobs and the intervening periods of unemployment explain the subsequent poverty of Gandhi family. The Gandhis were never to return to Porbunder though some members of the family continued to stay there and the major social events in the family were celebrated at the ancestral home in Porbunder.

After some three years, Rana deputed his faithful servant Karamchand to be one of the six assessors to the recently [1873] established Rajashtanik Court at Rajkot. On 1 September 1873, Karamchand was so appointed. The court had been established by the governor of Bombay to settle the disputes between the princes and their Bhayats and Garasias. It was not a court of law but a tribunal for settlement on the basis of existing possession and whatever little documentary evidence was available. The court did not adopt a legal or a judicial approach but sought to settle the disputes by an informal mode of persuasion and arbitration.

Karamchand served as an assessor only for a year. On 16 November 1874, Karamchand became Karbhari of Rajkot—a very tiny state [pop. 36776]. Three years later, Karamchand took [March 1878] a year's lien to become the Karbhari of Vankaner [pop.28750]. He had to suffer such humiliation there, that he resigned after nine months [1 January 1879] and reclaimed his lien. But he had to wait for some time and he was reappointed to the old post only on 4 April 1879. All these ups and downs must have been a strain on the family and its finances.

While travelling to Porbunder to attend the marriage of his sons, Karamchand met with an accident, [1882], which left him bedridden till his death in 1885. Gandhi has described his father as "truthful, honest but short tempered". The story of his tussle with an Agency officer either for not keeping an appointment or to defend the honor of the Thakore of Rajkot might well be a myth. Thakore himself would not have dared to displease even a minor functionary in the Agency office, much less an English officer.

Rana of Porbunder himself was not out of trouble; he was forced to appoint the persons approved by the Agency to various posts. Vikmat dared not disobey the instructions, but he refused to co operate with them. He was deposed in 1886 and was forced to live in Rajkot till his death in 1900. The state of Porbunder was put under the Agency administration for fourteen years. Frederic Lely was the administrator for the first two years and was followed by seven other administrators appointed for varying terms.

Neither Lely at Porbunder nor Watson at Rajkot seem to have any very high opinion about Gandhi family as can be surmised from the way they treated young Gandhi's request for financial assistance. The continued association of Gandhi family with the deposed Rana might have made them suspect in the eye of the Agency. Tulsidas, a cousin of Gandhi, was thrown out of Porbunder service by Lely.

Karamchand had two daughters from his earlier wives and his third wife was too sick for him. At the age of forty-five, Karamchand took Putlibai, aged fifteen, to wife and had one daughter and three sons from her. Since the third wife was still alive, Karamchand had to marry a bit below the rank of his caste status. [Pyarelal 186] Mohandas the last child of his parents was born on 2 October 1869 at Porbunder in the "Prime Ministerial"[?] quarters—a dark, dingy, ground floor apartment where Karamchand lived with his wives and children. The apartment consisted of a tiny kitchen and a small verandah with additional two rooms with a total area of about 600 sq. ft.

Gandhi stayed in Porbunder till the age of seven. The stories about his childhood as told by his relatives are suspect because all of them were told after his emergence as a Mahatma. He grew up like any normal Indian child, protected and constrained by the joint family atmosphere; but being the youngest in the family, he might have received more attention and more love from his parents.

Though Porbunder had a Taluka School maintained by the Agency, Gandhi attended one of the three private Dhudi schools. The school was owned and instructed by Virji Kamdar who was lame and hence the school was known as the Lame teacher's school [Lulia Masterni Nishal]. Gandhi remembered all the adjectives used by the children for the teacher. "The fact that I recollect nothing more of these days would strongly suggest that my intellect must have been sluggish and my memory weak". [Auto Part I Ch.I] Gandhi was six when he attended this school for a year [November '74-November '75] He also had the benefit of private coaching and it was Anandji Tulsi Adhyaru who taught him the Ramraksha Stotra, which Gandhi used to recite when he wanted to show off. [Upadhyaya]

While Karamchand was the assessor, he must have been travelling to and fro between Porbunder and Rajkot. When he joined the Rajkot service as a Karbhari in 1874, the rest of the family waited for a year and then followed him to Rajkot. [1876] Gandhi was sent to a nearby Taluka school for primary classes [1876] and studied there for the next four years. His performance at the school examinations bears out Gandhi's statement in the autobiography. "Gandhi, on the whole was a very mediocre student". [Upadhyaya]. In 1880, all the three brothers joined the Kattyawar High School [later to be known as Alfred High School]. The two brothers of Gandhi were very poor students. In their company Gandhi often played truant, attending, for example only 74 days out of the total of 222 working days in 1882.

After his vagabond brother Karsondas failed in the examination and left the school, Gandhi began to shine out and his academic performance improved, Gandhi has overemphasised his own mediocrity and painted a picture of himself as a dull, lazy, bum, but the picture is not true. The high school record compiled by Upadhyaya shows him to be an industrious, fairly intelligent and at times even a brilliant student. "I was not considered a dunce in my high school". He had to skip the examination in the year that he got married [1882] but he was allowed to jump up to the next grade examination "a privilege which was usually allowed to industrious students" [Auto Part I Ch V]

In the school examination in 1886, Gandhi stood third in a class of forty, he was declared to be the best reader of English prose and secured a scholarship of rupees fifty per annum. Next year, he stood fourth in his class and was awarded the scholarship of Rs. 120 per annum [but] "I did not have a high opinion about myself and was always surprised when I got prizes and scholarships". [Auto Part I Chap. V] These scholarships were huge amounts and would be equivalent to Rs. 15,000 and 36,000 at current price level. Gandhi and Jayashanker Booch were the only two students who successively passed every examination and cleared the matriculation examination at first attempt. Gandhi could no longer be described as mediocre.

Gandhi respected his father but he loved his mother. "When Mr. Gandhi speaks of his parents, those who listen, realise they are on the holy ground" [Doke 20] Gandhi has written tenderly and lovingly about his mother and Doke mentions [p.22] that even in later life, "his voice softens when he speaks of her and the light of love is in his eyes".

Gandhi has mentioned her great qualities of patience and wisdom and her intense faith, which often led her to fast for many days especially in the rainy season. This is the Krachchh-Chandrayan Vrat when women will eat only after seeing either the sun or the moon as the vow may be. All this might sound strange and unusual to the Western society, but such traits and austerities were quite common among the Indian women of that generation.

Too much has been read in Gandhi's adoring references to his mother about her piety and austerity. These were the usual traits of Indian women in those days. Gandhi has traced the religious bend of his mind to her influence, but she does not seem to have played any such role in the lives of her other sons and so long as Gandhi was with her, even he did not display any religious inclination.

Gandhi, however, has not given us a very important and a very interesting piece of information about his mother either because he forgot to mention it or because he considered it irrelevant to his purpose of writing the autobiography. The parents of Putlibai and Kasturbai were the followers of a very small sect of Vaishnavism, popular among the caste to which Gandhi belonged. They were Pranami Vaishnavas.

This sect originated in this region and traces its origin to Devchand Kayasth. [1562-1656] His disciple—Meghraj Thakkar—[1618-1694] or Prananatha was a rich merchant who had stayed for six years [1646-52] in Arabia attending to his family business. He claims to have studied Islam, Christianity and even Judaism and to have incorporated their teachings in his sectarian writings. The scriptures of the Pranamis accept the Quran and the Puranas as revealed texts. Prananatha used both Hindi and Urdu to preach his doctrines.

The Pranami sect has been profoundly influenced by Kabir, Nanak and Dara Shukoh and presents a synthesis of Hindu and Islamic concepts and beliefs—a process which begun with Kabir and went on for four or five centuries. Pranamis worship Krishna, God of Vaishnavas but reject idol worship, untouchability and all distinctions between the castes: they support gender equality and insist on the essential equality and unity of all religions, denouncing all rituals as the bane of spirituality.

The similarity of this belief system and Gandhi's value system is too clear to need any specific or elaborate description. Gandhi has told us often that his religious beliefs were profoundly influenced by the beliefs and practices of his mother.

Immediately after marriage, Gandhi and his bride were taken by Putlibai to the Pranami temple, which is next door to Gandhi's ancestral residence. Gandhi noted that there was no idol and the walls were covered by quotes in Sanskrit as well as in Arabic script. The dress of the priests as also the rituals resembled a Muslim shrine. [Pyarelal]

Gandhi has mentioned his early doubts about untouchability and his inquiry about this nasty practice was addressed to his mother. He has not recorded his mother's response. As was, and still is, the usual practice, Putlibai and later on Kasturbai, might have adopted the Pushti Vaishnavism of their in laws and they might have even taken to idol worship and the practice of untouchability. But their childhood beliefs might have remained unchanged and might have got imprinted on the young mind of Gandhi. Moreover, such an impact was not limited only to domestic influence because several caste fellows of Gandhi were also Pranamis.

Gandhi made a hugely significant contribution to the abolition of untouchability and the present day empowerment of the deprived sections of the Indian society is largely due to his impact. But Gandhi is not a pioneer in the crusade against this horrible system nor is he the only one to denounce it. All the social reformers and almost all the educated persons of nineteenth century India criticised it and repudiated it. Gandhi, a scion of a high caste Hindu had not only to witness but also to personally experience in South Africa the scorn and the tortures that the untouchables suffer at the hands of Indian elite.

Gandhi has mentioned [Auto Part I Ch X] his early contacts with Jains, Muslims and Parsis who visited his sick father. In a multi-religious society that India is, such contacts and interactions between persons belonging to diverse religious faiths is quite common. Gandhi mentions regular recitations of *Ramayan*, and *Bhagawad Gita* by the sick bed of his father and he mentions his having read *Manusmruti*.

But he must have been a very inattentive listener. He confessed his ignorance about *Gita* in London and his ignorance of Hindu scriptures is shocking. The queries he raised in June 1894 [CWMG I] more especially about the Trinity of the Hindu pantheon would not be expected from any educated Hindu of his age and education.

The impact of Jainism on Gandhi has been over-exaggerated. Jains are a very small but a very rich and very influential section of the Bania community in Gujarat and it would be quite difficult to isolate or even to distinguish the Jain Banias from Hindu Banias. The intermarriages between them have helped in wiping out the distinctions. Jain monks accept food from the Hindu banias if there are no jain families in the locality. The Jain influence in the literary, artistic, social, economic and even political development of Gujarat is too important to be overlooked. The widespread prevalence of vegetarianism in Gujarat is one such example.

But Gandhi as a child does not seem to have any direct contact with Jainism as such and even later, when he discussed the spiritual issues with a jain master Raichandbhai, they hardly ever discussed Jainism as such. Gandhi, in fact, knew very little about Jainism and he never followed their lifestyle. Gandhi's mindset is singularly non-Jain in his activism and in his belief system.

Gandhi's childhood stories revolve mostly round the unsavoury incidents he himself has mapped out in his autobiography. He imitated his elders and started smoking at the age of eleven or twelve and started stealing copper coins from the family servants to purchase *bidis*. Gandhi has not explained the reasons for the act but he and his brother attempted suicide by eating seeds of dhatura, [Belladonna] and thereafter gave up smoking in sheer disgust.

Several other self-derogatory remarks made by Gandhi in his autobiography are contradicted by the text itself. He often insists on his own mediocrity as a student but his high school record is quite brilliant and his academic record in London is quite meritorious. How can a student who was a dullard emerge with such brilliance after only three years?

Many of his statements are self-contradictory. "I had a distaste for reading beyond my school books" and "there was of course no question of extra reading". Almost in the same breath we are told about his having read not only the play Pitrubhakt Shravan but also a very serious and heavy tome like *Manusmruti*. He is quite familiar with the *Ramayana*, *Mahabharata* and even with *Bhagwad Gita*. At the age of thirteen, he has read "from cover to cover" several pamphlets discussing serious subjects like conjugal love, thrift, child marriages and such other subjects. He has also read about the benefits of long distance walking in the open air. He fluently quotes several lines from poetry. He had read Narayan Hemchandra's books while at Rajkot. This author befriended him in London. If he had no habit of extra reading up to 1888, how could he turn into such a voracious reader in London in 1889? Such habits take a long time to grow.

As was the custom of the day, Gandhi was betrothed at eight and was married at the age of thirteen [1882] and started acting as a typical Indian husband. Kasturbai came to Rajkot for the first time after her marriage. Gandhi later on claimed "I have learnt the lesson of non violence from my wife when I tried to bend her to my will. Her determined resistance to my will on the one hand and her quiet sufferings my stupidity involved on the other, ultimately made me ashamed of myself and cured me of my stupidity that I was born to rule over her and in the end she became my teacher". [Gandhi to Hoyland, *The Indian Crisis*. Quoted by Nanda 21]

Like millions of Indian women then and even now, Kasturbai was a mere puppet and was always treated as one by her husband: she never had any option but to submit to his dictates. Gandhi hardly ever treated her as a person in her own right and Louis Fischer is quoted by Ved Mehta to show that they hardly ever conversed in later life. Gandhi's treatment of Kasturbai all through her life is an ignoble part of Gandhi's patriarchal misbehavior with the members of his family and is one of the most repulsive aspect of this apostle of love and non violence.

Gandhi's brother Karsandas had left a legacy for him in the form of a friendship, which was to plague Gandhi for more than a decade. Sheikh Mehtab was the bosom friend of Karsandas and was three years older than Gandhi. He was an outstanding sportsman in the school and the leader of a gang of school brats. He was looked upon with envy and admiration by the weaklings like Gandhi. Mehtab had also failed in the examination and left the school with Karsandas in 1883.

Gandhi has attributed two of his failings to the evil influence of Mehtab. Gandhi's visit to the brothel in company of Mehtab cannot be dated with accuracy but a newly married Gandhi might be feeling a bit nervous and might have been taken there as a confidence building exercise. This happens very often in India where young boys [Gandhi was only thirteen] feel awkward in company of conjugal partners on account of the seclusion in which boys and girls are made to grow up.

Gandhi has described at great length, how under the influence of that friend, he started surreptitiously eating meat. Non-vegetarian food would amount to a great sacrilege in a very orthodox Vaishnav family like his. Gandhi indulged in such occasional non-vegetarian feasts for about a year and even cultivated a taste for such food. He had to give up meat eating because of financial stringency and the strain involved in secrecy, but even after he had given it up, Gandhi did consider meat a much better diet. [Interview *Vegetarian*]

Had Gandhi put the matter in its proper perspective in his autobiography, such clandestine meat eating would appear neither so untoward, nor such a great misdeed, and one would understand why Gandhi never felt apologetic about it. In nineteenth century India, English educated scions of strictly vegetarian higher castes of Hindus all over India had started aping the English rulers. Meat eating was considered to be a patriotic duty to become physically strong "so that we might defeat the British and make India free." [AutoPart I Cp. VI] Among the 'reformed' [westernised] sections of the Indian society meat eating and drinking alcohol were considered at that time and are still considered to be symbols of a progressive, free and rational mindset. Gandhi was getting English education and he therefore would not consider anything wrong in cultivating a food habit that was taboo in his family. His Muslim friend is unnecessarily blamed by Gandhi and others.

Gandhi lied to his family, offering excuses for skipping meals at home after such clandestine dinners outside. "My parents never knew that two of their sons had become meat eaters". [Auto Part I ch.VII] He did find it very uncomfortable telling lies but "I would remind myself that meat eating was a duty and so become more cheerful". He even offers a convenient justification for such untruths. "I persuaded myself that mere hiding the deed from the parents was no departure from truth".

The meat eating must have started around 1883, because the famous incident of stealing Karsandas' golden bracelet took place in 1884. Gandhi's confession came after the theft had been noticed by the parents and the lies told by both the brothers might not have convinced the parents.

Too much has been made about his written apology to his father for the theft. But it is overlooked that he was not so straightforward and truthful on several other occasions. He never apologised for far more serious lapses like thieving petty cash from the servants or for visiting the brothel or for smoking or eating meat and all these were far more serious offences in a Vaishnava family.

The nursing of his sick father had prevented Gandhi from participating in the physical training and games but his schoolmate Ratilal Ghelabhai [Upadhyaya] said that he used to play cricket and was a good batsman. Gandhi was a good swimmer and a great lover of music. [Chandran] As a teenager, Gandhi used to play the tunes of the then popular drama songs on his concertina and on S S Clyde, he often played piano. [Diary] He was a great connoisseur of ragas and always insisted on good quality music at his prayer meetings. He deplored the absence of mass singing in Indian society. [*Young India* 8-9-1920]

In view of Gandhi's statements in his Autobiography it might be of some interest to note that Gandhi showed no interest in the medical studies when there was an opportunity for it. B. J. Medical School at Ahmedabad had made a public offer of a stipend of rupees nine per month for any student who joined the medical course and Gandhi was aware of it but did not react to it. [Upadhyaya] Gandhi's interest in medicine is a by-product of his vegetarianism and his experiments with food leading him to naturopathy. It was in 1905-06 that Gandhi seriously thought of going to England for medical education. [CWMG XII]

There is one incident of this period that has been quoted by all biographers from Gandhi's narration and has been subjected to elaborate analysis. Gandhi lashes himself to no end for going to his wife on the night that his father died. "If the carnal passion had not blinded me,"..."the shame of the carnal desire even at this crucial hour"..."It was a blot that I have never been able to efface or forget…my mind was in the grip of lust". [Auto Part I Ch. IX]

But his own narration of the incident shows that Gandhi is whipping himself unjustly and quite unnecessarily. His father was ailing for three years and the end came rather suddenly and was totally unexpected. "No one had dreamt that this was to be the fateful night. The danger of course was there".

Gandhi must have been going to his wife every night during this prolonged sickness and he went that night in the normal course because there was nothing untoward which warranted a change in the routine. To blame a young husband for lusting and an accidental collapse of a patient after a prolonged sickness are two unrelated events and Gandhi's self denunciation is an insult to his wife and a pure masochism for the husband. In the autobiography, Gandhi on several occasions has made mountains out of molehills on account of his later day opinions and this may be one such. Moreover, the remorse about sex is a typical Christian concept. Hindus have no guilt feelings about sex. Gandhi himself had no such inhibitions and felt no such guilt for the next twenty years.

Now that the fledgling was about to leave the nest for the wider world, we must sum up the impressions and the experiences he was to carry with him to the next phase that was about to begin. Gandhi was too young and immature to analyse and understand the socio-eco-political situations around him but he must have unconsciously absorbed the ethos in which he grew up.

The entire Gandhi cannot and should not be explained in terms of Kathiawar of his childhood: but this environment does provide the substratum on which his personality developed and it does help to illuminate some of the most deep-rooted thought currents of Gandhi. Gandhi, like all the sensitive minds in Kathiawar was intensely oriented to the religious values that provided the only anchor in an oppressive society. An eyewitness to the all pervading violence and injustices,

Gandhi recoiled with horror from violence in any form and at any level. He was quite familiar with the practice of self- suffering—*Tragu* as a technique to soften the hearts of the cruel tormentors when all other avenues and remedies failed. He developed an instinctive repugnance against machines, which deprived the poor of their livelihood and the rich of their dignity. A return to simple village life prevailing in Kathiawar of his childhood appeared to be an alluring alternative to the problems of industrialisation as was advocated by several of his mentors during his stay in London.

It is interesting and important to reflect upon Gandhi's ambivalent attitude towards law. Gandhi passed his childhood in Kathiawar where the law and the judicial processes had a minimal role to play in sustaining social equilibrium. In London, he was to live in a society which was very law abiding and very just and humane. In South Africa, the law benefited only the dominant section of the society—the Whites and was, for all others an instrument of deprivation and torture. Professionally, Gandhi was intensely devoted to law and to the legal processes as the implementation of the social ethics but he had to fight against the law as an engine of oppression in South Africa. By the time he returned to India, Gandhi had lost all faith in law and judiciary and advocated peaceful defiance—satyagraha as the only path to the solution of all the problems faced by the individuals as a social being.

Chapter 3

JOURNEY TO LONDON

It was only after Gandhi had scraped through his matriculation examination securing only 247.5 out of the total of 700 marks that his true personality began to emerge under the pressure of his intense yearning to go to England. The Autobiography deviates at this point sharply from the actual flow of events as noted by Gandhi in his Diary [1888] written in Gujju English, and in the interview that he gave to *The Vegetarian* in 1891 and in his Guide to London written probably in 1892-93.

The Diary begins in September 1888 and ends 23 November 1888 and it details the events leading to his journey and the journey itself. In the interview, he has discussed his motives for coming to England and the difficulties he had to face. The Guide to London was written in response to the persistent queries about the conditions and the cost of living in London. All the three sources confirm, supplement and at times contradict his Autobiography in many important and interesting details. These sources are more authentic and more reliable because they are contemporary records untouched by later day opinions.

All the three are matter of fact descriptions full of trivial details but they, together with the Autobiography provide a fascinating chart of Gandhi's growing personality. In the Autobiography Gandhi is a mere straw buffeted hither and thither according to the opinions of his elders. The Diary and the Guide reveal Gandhi to be a determined and even an obstinate architect of his decisions from a very young age. The flow of events and the part played by various personalities will be better understood if the Autobiography, the Diary, the Guide and the Interview are juxtaposed and interwoven.

Gandhi, the only matriculate in the family was sent, much against his will [Upadhyaya] to Shamaldas College at Bhavnagar for his graduation. "I found my self entirely at sea. Everything was difficult. I could not follow, let alone take interest in the professors' lectures.... I was raw". [Auto Part I Chap.XI] But at Bhavnagar, Gandhi was not a dullard: he was uncomfortable and sick. "I suffered from constant headaches and nose bleedings". [CWMG I 42]

He went to Bhavnagar in January 1888 and almost immediately seems to have set his heart on going to London. By the beginning of April, he discussed with Jayashanker Booch, a school-mate and a fellow student, the possibility of getting a scholarship from the state of Junagadh for going to London. [CWMG I-2/3] If Gandhi was so raw and failed to follow the lectures of Indian professors—five out of his seven professors were Indians—how could he ever dare think of facing the teachers in England?

Gandhi, like any other young person, was ambitious to make a career and to earn a lot of money. When he was asked as to why he decided to come to England in spite of great obstacles, his reply was "in one word- ambition" ... "It [graduation] would take three years and I could not expect even after graduation, any very great income".

[CWMG I-42] "I had a secret design in my mind to come here to satisfy my curiosity of knowing what London was like."… "I had in my mind an intention of visiting England and I was finding means to that end". [CWMG I-2]

Gandhi returned to Rajkot on 13th April for his summer vacation. By the end of the month, Gandhi and his brother paid a casual visit to Mavji Joshi—an elderly family friend—whose son Kewalram was practising law in the city. When told that Gandhi was finding his studies difficult and had no hope of passing the examination that year, Dave suggested that Mohan be sent to London to be called to bar. "While I was incessantly brooding over these things, [Dave] as it were fanned the flame that was burning within me". [CWMG I-42] In the autobiography, Gandhi mentions his preference for medical education and the probable goal of diwanship. But there seems to have been no talk about medicine and it would be ridiculous for a barrister who expected fabulous income to aspire to diwanship.

The expenditure for London education was estimated at only Rs. 5000 and Dave suggested seeking scholarship from the states of Junagadh, Rajkot and Porbunder. He advised cooking to reduce expenditure but insisted that Gandhi be sent even if the family had to sell its furniture and household goods. Laxmidas agreed to do so and the matter was discussed between the brothers. Their mother does not seem to have been consulted or even informed till four or five days later. Women in those days had hardly any say in such matters. The problem was mainly financial. "I thought to myself that if I go to England, not only shall I become a barrister but I shall be able to see England the land of philosophers and poets, the very center of civilization".[CWMG I- 42]

Gandhi saw Kewalram the next day and was warned about the temptations of women, wine and meat. Kewalram doubled the estimated expenditure and bluntly refused to give any assistance in raising the amount. Gandhi felt very dejected. "But I am not one who having formed any intention, leave it easily". [CWMG I 4] Gandhi now broached the subject of his travels to London with his mother and was advised to seek the permission from his uncle who was staying at Porbunder. None of his close relatives had any strong objection to his going to London though he would be the first person in his caste to do so. It was hoped that if approached, the state of Porbunder would give some help to the son of its former Karbhari.

Gandhi travelled from Rajkot to Porbunder with the twin purpose of seeking financial assistance from the state as well as from his relatives and to get permission from his uncle. He failed in both. His meeting with Frederic Lely—the state administrator was brief, curt and futile and he was dismissed with advice to first become a graduate. His uncle was hostile to his travels but Gandhi exacted a reluctant and conditional consent from him. Immediately thereafter and without consulting anyone else, Gandhi rushed to Bhavnagar straight from Porbunder, vacated the rented premises and sold off the furniture.

A very anxious and restless Gandhi had to wait for six weeks for the return of Col. Watson who was to be solicited for scholarship. His cousins had promised to finance the entire London trip, but went back on their promises and began to malign Gandhi. "But all of them knew that I should not leave of anything having began it". [CWMG I-7]

Col. Watson dismissed him with a mere note of introduction, which he said was worth a lac of rupees. "It really made me laugh". Gandhi was pressurized to go again to Col. Watson and the Thakor of Rajkot. "The fulsome flattery that I had to practice this time made me angry. Had it not been for my credulous and dearest brother, I would not have resorted to such gross flattery". [CWMG I-8] But this meeting also proved futile and the Thakor gave him only his photograph.

The obstacles he faced was a "tale of misery and woe and they were of four types- money, the consent of the elders, separation from the relatives and the caste restrictions". [CWMG I-43] When all attempts at securing scholarships failed, the jewellery of his wife was sold and brought in a substantial amount [Auto, part I Chap XI, Prabhudas 30 and Gandhi's letter to Harilal 1919] and "I requested my elder brother to devote all the money that was left, for my education in England". Laxmidas provided Rs. 10000. This loan led to a very bitter quarrel between the brothers later on. Though Gandhi paid back to the family Rs. 60,000, he was accused of ungratefulness.

Going to England was not such a novelty by the turn of the century. Dr. Pranjivandas Mehta and Dalpatram Shukla had gone there and they were going to be very close companions of Gandhi during his stay in London. "I was a pet of my mother. However by showing exaggerated advantages of coming to England, I got her to accede, with much reluctance to my request". [CWMG I-44]

But Gandhi's father-in-law raised several objections. The journey was risky and there was a possibility of his [Gandhi's] dying. During his prolonged absence, where would Kastur stay and who would take care of her? "It was no easy task to sit, night after night with my father in law and to hear and successfully answer his objections". [CWMG I-45]

Gandhi had become obsessed with the London trip. "Sleeping, waking, eating, drinking, walking, running, reading, I was dreaming and thinking of England". His school organised a farewell function at which Gandhi spoke a few words urging others to follow his example and initiate social reforms [Kathiawar Times]; he left Rajkot on 10th August. There was no railway in Rajkot and the journey to Bombay started from Gondal. In the Diary Gandhi mentions a long list of persons who came to see him off at Gondal.

But Gandhi still had to cross a great hurdle. "The collisions with my caste fellows in Bombay defy description". [CWMG I-45] According to the vivid account by Gandhi, he was marked out, mobbed, hooted, pestered by several groups trying to dissuade him from going and finally, there was a large meeting of the caste elders—the Mahajan. "We are definitely informed" said these elders to Gandhi "that you will have to eat flesh and drink wine in England. Moreover you will have to cross [ocean] waters." "I replied I am sorry I can not change my decision. What I have heard about England is quite different from what you say. One need not take wine and meat there. As for crossing the water, if our caste brethren can go to Aden, why can't I go to England? I am deeply convinced that malice is at the root of all these objections". [CWMG 46] Gandhi was expelled from his caste and even his close relatives were debarred from keeping contacts with him on the threat of a heavy fine.

This conversation and the caste meeting described in the interview are not mentioned in the Diary, which merely notes "My caste fellows tried their best to prevent me from proceeding further. Almost all of them were opposed to my going". [CWMG I 8] Gandhi's reply is too mature for a shy young lad that Gandhi was in 1888 and any such talk would be impossible in a caste meeting. Gandhi knew and felt that he was tough. "Had there been some other man in the same position as I was, I dare say, he would not have been able to see England". [CWMG I-47]

Gandhi's troubles were still not over. He was to sail on 21st August but his journey was delayed because of the possibility of sea-storms during the monsoon season: his brother left Bombay leaving the fare money with Khushaldas Makanji. Trambakrao Mazumdar, a lawyer from Junagadh was leaving in September and Gandhi decided to risk it. But Khushaldas refused to part with the money. Gandhi borrowed money from Ranchhoddas Patwari and sailed by S. S. Clyde on 4th September after three weeks in Bombay. Mazumdar and Abdul Majid were to be his companions on the steamer. A large number of people saw him off and gifted him small cash and a silver chain. [CWMG I-9]

The most important and the most interesting point here is that in these so elaborately detailed contemporary records, there is a total omission of the three vows insisted upon by his mother and administered by the monk Bechar Swami. The autobiography makes very frequent and very emphatic references to the vows, as if they were the protecting shield and a sheet-anchor of everything that Gandhi did or did not do in England. Surprisingly nowhere in the Diary, or in his writings in England or in the Guide to London, is there any mention of any Swami or any such vows so solemnly administered.

The interview mentions a promise given to his mother and in his speech to the London Vegetarian Society, [20-11 1891] Gandhi refers only to "the adherence to a vow administered to me by my mother" [CWMG 48-326] In the Guide, Gandhi classes himself with "Indians who are not *over-scrupulous in their religious vows* and not much attached to caste restrictions".

It cannot be over-emphasized that though Gandhi had stopped eating meat, he was convinced that meat was a superior and more nourishing food. It was not his mother or his vows, but Englishmen who converted him to vegetarianism. The first mention of the vows and the Jain monk was made to Doke in 1908.

In the autobiography, Gandhi declares his readiness to return to India, if he had no other alternative to non-vegetarian food left to him. But the interview tells something different. To the continuous advice given to him during his journey about the necessity for flesh eating, wine drinking and tobacco smoking to withstand the cold climate and to be saved from tuberculosis, "I replied that I would try my level best to avoid all these things: but if they were found to be absolutely necessary, I did not know what I would do". [CWMG I-48]

Gandhi found all such warnings to be false. "They said, I would require it after leaving Aden. When this turned out to be untrue, I was to require it after crossing the Red Sea. And on this proving false, in the Bay of Biscay you will have to choose between death or meat and wine. That crisis too passed away safely". [CWMG I-48]

The interview [1891] reveals an interesting trait in Gandhi's character. He expresses his contempt for "gratuitous advice poured into unwilling ears", "I may here mention that my aversion to meat was not so strong then, as it is now", "I was even betrayed in taking meat six or seven times at the period when I allowed my friends to think for me".

The constant dinning of advice in his ears might have brought out the streak of obstinacy in his personality. "On the steamer my ideas began to change. I thought, I should not take meat on any account. My mother before consenting to my going had exacted a promise from me not to take meat. So I was bound not to take it, if only for the sake of a promise". [CWMG I-48]

Gandhi chose to cling to his own life style and grew more and more confident that there is no real danger in keeping away from meat and wine. "After reading [H S Salt] I adopted vegetarianism from principle. Till then I considered flesh to be superior diet from the scientific point of view". [ibid] There is here a passing reference to a promise, but the solemn vows are nowhere mentioned.

The name Bechar Swami would be extremely unlikely for a Jain monk.* The term 'Swami' often denotes a Jain nun. Such an absence of any mention of vows is very puzzling and it cannot be very easily explained, unless we argue that by the first decade of twentieth century, Gandhi was obsessed with the spiritual life style, so full of vows and abstinences and that this was a throw back to the earlier times.

During his voyage to London, Gandhi mentions his having depended "principally on the provisions" [Auto Part I Chap. XIII] The Diary

---

* Chatrabhuj Bechar was the name of the firm managed by Raichandhai and the name might have stuck in his memory.

notes that after two days, the arrangements for vegetarian food were made by Mazumdar by engaging a cook boy for all the three passengers who did not use the mess, and only took provisions from the store.

Gandhi specifically mentions [Guide] that there is no difficulty for the vegetarians during the journey. 'The passengers are overfed from 6.00 a.m. to near midnight and there are plenty of things he can take. The steward, if informed, makes special arrangements for vegetarian dishes and facility for separate food and even for self cooking is permitted'. [CWMG I-80]

We have fairly dependable sources of information about Gandhi's stay in London. The autobiography outlines the major incidents and activities while the Guide to London fills up the details, if it is presumed that what Gandhi wrote in it, was what he himself had actually done, even though he does not specifically say so.

Besides these original sources, researchers like Hunt, Chandran and Stephen Hay have unearthed enough information about the amazing and even a stunning growth chart of Gandhi as he rapidly matured in London in a mere three years. It was in London that Gandhi emerged as a free spirit guided only by his own will. Gandhi in London was just an ordinary, English educated young man—just one of the two hundred and seven Indian students in London in 1890. But he deserves to be noted for his grit, his insistence on practicing what he had promised or what he believed and his enormous capacity for hard work.

Gandhi arrived on 27 October 1888 and disembarked and travelled to Victoria Station and thence to the luxurious Victoria Hotel to be overwhelmed by the very sight. "I was quite dazzled by the splendor of the Hotel". [CWMG I-16] He was greatly intrigued by the elevator, the brilliant lights and the luxury of the Hotel premises. "I thought I can pass a life time in this room". [CWMG I-83]

Young Gandhi catapulted from Rajkot to the wonderland of London, must have experienced a tremendous but a very pleasant culture shock.

Everything from the floodlights on the steamer to the elevator in the Victoria Hotel was for Gandhi a strange world created by Alladin's magic lamp—a world of comfort and luxury in spite of a few inconveniences like waterless closets and the use of toilet paper. Much of this was beyond his wildest imagination and Gandhi bursts out into a poetic description of the stars dancing on the smooth floor of the ocean.

After two days, he shifted to a cheap accommodation arranged by Mazumdar. But the very next day, he went to stay with Dalpatram Shukla at Richmond for a month to get trained in spoken English and to be familiar with the prevailing etiquette of English society. During the initial period of homesickness when he felt forlorn, he was enormously and constantly comforted by Pranjivandas Mehta and Dalpatram Shulka; both were his fellow students and befriended him in every which way.

By the end of November 1888, he went to stay with an Anglo-Indian family at 20, Baron Court Road, West Kensington. He stayed there for six months during which he searched and found vegetarian restaurants. During the first ten months of his stay, [October 1888 and July '89] he got adjusted to English life style and attempted to become an English gentleman and then launched his economy drive. His decision to appear for the London University Matriculation examination was taken by August 1889 and he worked very hard for the examination that was due in December of that year.

He had already moved out of Kensington and had started living on his own. He took his Roman Law examination [March 1890] and then went to Brighton for a month long holiday where he started cooking his breakfasts. [April 1890] He returned and took residence at Tavistock Street, reappeared for his matriculation examination [June 1890] and took his final examination in Law [December 1890]. The results were declared in January 1891 and he was free from academic work. The next six months were spent in active promotion of vegetarianism in London. He got to know Dr. Joshia Oldfield in July 1890 and attended the Ventnor Vegetarian conference in January 1891. He went to stay with Dr. Oldfield at Bayswater in March 1891. He left England in June 1891.

Gandhi got quickly adjusted to his new surroundings and so thoroughly enjoyed his stay in London that at the end of three years' stay, he talks of London in endearing terms. "It is not without deep regrets, that I left dear London... so much was I attached to London and who would not be? London with its teaching institutions, public galleries, museums, theatres, vast commerce, public parks and vegetarian restaurants is a fit place for a student, a traveler, a trader and a faddist as a vegetarian may be called by his opponents". [CWMG. I 51] Gandhi confided to his friend and biographer Rev. Joseph Doke [p 50] "Even now [1907], next to India, I would live in London than in any other place in the world".

London in 1888 was the largest city in the world, its population of 5.5 millions being more than twice that of Paris and three times of New York or Berlin, and it was the capital of the mightiest and the most vast empire on which the Sun never set. It was the financial hub of the world economy and was agog with intellectual fervour and intense debate in every field of life. Darwin, [*The Descent of Man*] Karl Marx, [*Das Capital*] Prince Kropotkin, [*The Conquest of Bread/ Mutual Aid*] the critical study of Bible and the works of Leo Tolstoy had set London on fire.

Socialist groups of various hues, the assertive trade unions and the emergence of the Labor Party had made political debates intensely volatile. The London Dock strike [15 August-16 September 1889] was the biggest labor demonstration in British history till then. London with its free debates on every conceivable subject- political, religious or social, was a world of ever expanding horizons; it was "a paradise of individuality, eccentricity, heresies, anomalies, hobbies and humor". [Hay 74]

While in London, Gandhi was as curious as a cat, rushing out in several directions and trying out several new modes of living. He visited Paris, went to several water resorts, made friends with many men and women, attended several meetings addressed by Dadabhai Naoroji, used several libraries and associations, was present at the funeral of Charles Bradlaugh [January 1891], went to congratulate Cardinal Manning for his successful handling of the Dock strike and was often present at the meetings of the Anjuman-e-Islamia. [Nanda] He met and heard some of the celebrities of the day.

But out of the imposing complexities of the metropolitan London, Gandhi experienced only a few and selected segments. During his entire stay in England, all his contacts were with the middle class and he never had any contact either with the very rich and the very powerful or with the very poor groups in London. Gandhi hardly ever reacted to most of the issues and the currents and much of the intellectual ferment left him untouched.

He was mostly out of the roaring debates and did not merge in any current except vegetarianism and religion that rather confirmed his earlier attitudes and opinions. In a way, Gandhi in midst of a changing world, clung fast to his ingrained belief system and even to his orthodoxy. He did not imbibe the rational or the mundane approach of the Webbs or Shaw or Darwin, much less that of Marx—and these were the torch-bearers of the New Age.

But Gandhi did pass more than thirty-three months in this atmosphere of intense debates and activities of a very free and a very highly cultured society of vibrant London. During his London stay, we find a steady increase in his competence and self-confidence. He could not but breathe in such a free and congenial atmosphere of London and it proved to be quite a great stimulant to this precocious teenager [he was only nineteen] who with his tremendous, but hitherto suppressed energies now blossomed forth in several directions, some of which would stay with him till the very end of his life. Therefore it is very important to analyse what Gandhi did in London and what London did to his personality.

Gandhi responded to the London atmosphere with energy and enthusiasm and apart from his professional and academic studies, developed a strong affinity for two somewhat eccentric groups –the Vegetarians and the Theosophists. We should trace the development of Gandhi's personality in these three major directions that are clearly visible—his academic and social activities, his vegetarianism, and his religious studies. Gandhi's major occupation was with his studies but his enthusiasm was for vegetarianism and religion. The law made him a professional but the later two shaped him into a character.

Gandhi was so intensely devoted to his studies of law as well as to his Matriculation examination of London University that he hardly had any time for anything else. Gandhi never lost sight of the basic objective of his coming to London and never allowed anything or anybody to come between him and his studies. Almost immediately after his arrival, he embarked upon his academic career and purposely and deliberately undertook more academic work than he was expected to handle. Out of the four Inns of the Temple, he chose the most expensive, the most prestigious and the most sought after institution of legal studies—the Inner Temple Inn where he got himself enrolled on 6 November 1888.

In order to become a barrister a student had to be twenty-one years of age, must pass two examinations—one in Roman Law and the other in Common Law. He had to keep twelve terms that were very short with plenty of free time in between. He had to attend at least six out of the twenty-four dinners held every term each costing three shillings and six pence. Vegetarian food was provided on request: eating at these dinners was not compulsory but payment of fees and the attendance for an hour and a half was a must.

The examinations were both written and oral. A student could take the examination in Roman Law after keeping four terms, while the one in Common Law was permitted only after nine terms. The textbooks were prescribed, tutors were available and lectures were organised at the Inner Temple.

Gandhi discovered very soon that there was not much of studies. "The examinations were easy and the examiners were lenient". [Auto Part I-chap.] Most of the students took it easy, wasted a lot of time and passed the examinations after cursory reading of readymade question answer books. Gandhi was different and refused to walk the easy way out. Unlike other students, Gandhi purchased all the textbooks at the cost of ten Pounds and struggled hard to study them thoroughly and diligently. Gandhi has listed the books, along with the price for each of them.

In London, Gandhi was always very sober and disciplined and he felt a bit lonely. He scrupulously kept the promises given to his mother. He mixed freely with women of all ages but avoided sexual intimacies. He had neither the time, nor the money, nor even the urge for frolics. He was a workaholic and labored hard to improve his record of academic achievement.

He sought after the university education that he had missed in India. Gandhi joined [August 1889] a coaching class preparing the students for the matriculation examination of London University, choosing Latin and French as the optional languages. He must have realised the importance of Latin for his legal studies. He failed at the first trial [January 90], but reappeared in June of the same year and got through. In a short time of six months, he had become fairly acquainted with two languages that were entirely unfamiliar to him before.

He became quite proficient in Latin and read the textbook of Justinian's Code of Roman law in Latin itself, with the help of a commentary in English. His study of Roman Law was not of much use in India, but it proved to be of great advantage in South Africa because Dutch Law is based largely on Roman precepts. This brush with Latin made his English crisp, simple, terse and lucid. Though Gandhi's masterful command over the English language developed to its full maturity in South Africa, there was a vast improvement in his linguistic competence in a mere three years. The linguistic distance travelled by Gandhi can be measured by comparing the Diary [the end of 1888] and the articles he wrote for the *Vegetarian* [in the beginning of 1891].

Gandhi appeared for the Roman Law examination in March 1890. Out of the forty students who cleared the examination, Gandhi stood sixth. In the Common Law examinations in December 1890, Gandhi stood 34th among the 77 who passed. He got the news of his success in the examination on 12 January 1891. But he had not yet completed the twelve terms: so he could not be called to bar and had to spend another six months in London. He had no academic work left for him. But he did not waste this time and spent this period in intense crusading for vegetarianism. "Gandhi was quite proud of his legal qualifications and used to recount his early triumphs that he had when he went to practice in South Africa" [Radha ed. 381] and he was so emotionally attached to his Alma Mater that "when I heard that Inner Temple was bombed [1941], I bled". [Tendulkar VI 125]

The Bar examinations were easy and opened the doors to a very lucrative profession in India; most of the Indian students in England therefore got so qualified. The legal studies equipped Gandhi with the virtues and the defects of a professional education with its "definite, but narrow body of knowledge". [Hunt] But by passing the matriculation examination of London University, "Gandhi attained an educational standard, which for its day, was very high", [Hunt 12] because, in those days, there were very few matriculates even in London.

Gandhi had, from the very beginning of his stay at Kensington, cultivated the habit of reading three newspapers, which were his university keeping him posted with public affairs and currents of opinion. "In India I had never read a newspaper, but here I succeeded in cultivating a liking for them by regular reading". [Auto Part I-Chap. XIV] *The Daily News* was a Liberal, while the *Daily Telegraph* represented the conservative point of view. Gandhi specially enjoyed reading the magazine Answers "at times smutty, but witty and always very readable". [Pyarelal 232] It was *Pall Mall Gazette,* however, which was intellectually, the most influential paper and always supported all radical causes. But somehow Gandhi entirely missed the radical issues and also the emerging forms of Socialism of either the Fabian or the Marxist variety.

Apart from attending meetings and using libraries, Gandhi was not much connected with Indian affairs. He had a letter of introduction to Dadabhai Naoroji but it was only in 1891 that he handed it over to him. He did attend a few meetings and public lectures of Dadabhai organised under the auspices of the London Indian Society. Gandhi never mentions and he was probably not aware of the British Committee of the Indian National Congress, which was organised in 1889 and which with its mouthpiece *India,* published from 1890, carried on very active propaganda for Indian cause.

Anjuman-e-Islam, established by Abdulla Al Mamun Suharawardy, was also known to Gandhi. The National Indian Association was an association of young Indian students who gathered to hear lectures, to organise tours and trips and outings, to entertain one another and to meet the visiting dignitaries. Its secretary, Miss Elizabeth Manning maintained an excellent reading room with magazines useful to Indian students and arranged tea meetings that were sometimes attended by Gandhi. Manning knew Gandhi personally and introduced him to Narayan Hemchandra who occupies an entire chapter in the Autobiography as a comic diversion in an otherwise very somber reading. Gandhi in personal contact was extremely light-hearted but there is no humour either in his writings or his speeches. Hemchandra was a very well-known literary figure in Gujarat and Gandhi had read some of his books at Rajkot.

The Northbrook Indian Society acted as the guardian of Indian students and maintained a clubhouse and a library, which Gandhi visited very often. During his stay in London, Gandhi indeed wandered over a wide range of activities and interests but carefully restricted himself and was his own master in choosing all his contacts.

Gandhi himself and many of his biographers have described his efforts to ape English society as an attempt to compensate for the embarrassment caused by his staunch devotion to vegetarianism. But there is no such link between his food habits and his extravagance. Gandhi was always something of a dandy and was very scrupulous about his appearance and dress even after he adopted the simple, short dhoti as his only dress.

On his voyage [1888] to London, he had a coat, which he could loan to Mazumdar as a proper dinner dress and he ridicules his travelling companion for dressing shabbily. [CWMG I- 16] Gandhi has mentioned his embarrassment when he landed at the London docks for finding himself as the only person wearing flannels.

Almost as soon as he landed, he started cultivating the dress, the habits and the manners of the society in which he had to live for some years and which he considered to be culturally superior to his own. He purchased the most fashionable clothes from the costliest and most fashionable stores, tried to learn dancing, which led him to music classes and the violin and he even tried his hand at cultivating elocution. He was not the only one to do all this and his companions never noticed anything amiss about Gandhi's sartorial escapades.

"Isolation from the familiar surroundings, and the urge to get on with the unfamiliarity of the social set up with which they had to adjust, compounded as it was with the lack of linguistic fluency, made all Indian students suffer a lot and drove most of them to waste a lot of money and time in aping the English. Young Indian students felt rejected and therefore aped it all the more vigorously. ...It was observed that all Indian students would suddenly dress up like peacocks and parade their feathers for a few weeks or months. Then the infatuation would pass up, as they saw that they gained neither status nor girl friends by their display (and were left) with their debts and their broken hopes". [Payne 70]

Gandhi had enough time and a good lot of money for all such diversions and he used to enjoy all the good things in life and insisted upon all the creature comforts till 1904. The expenses for study and stay in London had been estimated at Rs. 10000 and Gandhi had brought Pounds 666 with him and he expected about Rs. 5000 more from the state of Porbunder or Rajkot. [CWMG I-16/17] Also Gandhi would have to conform to the prevailing dress code. "Everyone in the City or the Temple wore black clothes, stiff white shirt with cuffs and a tall silk hat. Even the junior Solicitors' clerks were so attired. In the Temple especially, such a costume was de rigueur". [Hunt 37].

Gandhi was spending quite a lot of money and his was certainly not a dull life. He went to the Paris exhibition for a week starting 5 May 1890. In the Autobiography he says very little about the exhibition, but goes in ruptures over the Cathedrals. He condemns the Eiffel tower and reproduces Tolstoy's amazing comments about the tower being a 'monument, not of man's triumph but of man's folly that could have been perpetuated only under the subtle, narcotic effects of the tobacco fumes'. [Auto I Chap XXIII]

But in 1890, Gandhi had different ideas. He was so impressed by the steel tower a thousand feet in height, that he climbed it not once, but twice or thrice and spent a lavish amount to lunch at the restaurant on the first floor of the tower. Apart from Paris, he often visited the seaside resorts like Brighton and Ventnor. He very frequently went to theatres, which he considered 'a school in English manners and customs'. He was greatly fond of Shakespeare plays. "I adored the incomparable Ellen Terry...I worshipped her". [CWMG XVIII p.2]

But Gandhi never tried to befriend the girls. Gandhi in London was shy and comparatively poor; he was intensely busy with his studies and his deep-rooted orthodoxy would prevent him from illegitimate sex. In spite of all his protestations to the contrary, Gandhi's sexuality was never very aggressive. For many long years, he could stay away from his wife without any complications. All the three times that he was in a brothel or semi-brothel surroundings—Rajkot, Portsmouth and Zanzibar, he would not or could not perform.

Gandhi never had any problem in befriending women. Women adored him especially after he became famous and assertive. "Except very gentle and loving eyes, Gandhi was not a particularly good looking man. But his bravery and his transparency won him the love, and the adoring devotion of several Indian and European women". [Polak] "Mahatma Gandhi was not much to look at, but he has a wonderful winning way with the ladies, a charm which is very lovable". [Maulana Shaukat Ali—Gandhi as Others Saw Him]. Millie Pollack ['This was Bapu'] mentions an appealing touch of womanliness in him. But a simple and more plausible reason may be his transparent sincerity, his bravery and his honesty, which would debar him from taking disadvantage of anybody either male or female. Bravery and sacrifice won for Gandhi many friends of both sexes.

Gandhi's extravagance lasted just for three months and he blew away thirty pounds which was quite an alarming waste of money. He had the old world habit of keeping the daily accounts in the minutest details. Gandhi saw, to his horror, his cash reserves rapidly sinking before his very eyes. He was stopped in his tracks of becoming an English gentleman, not from any remorse or for any love for simplicity but primarily because of the paucity of funds. The way in which Gandhi wasted money after his return to India and also in Africa shows that the economy he practiced in London had nothing to do with any love for simplicity.

He had come to London with strictly limited funds; he had wasted a lot of it in the first eight months in London. He had lost all hope of getting any scholarship from India by first months of 1890. In his Guide to London, Gandhi has warned the newcomers about the impossibility of getting money in London on loan and remittances from India would take a long time to come.

Gandhi in fact, was much quicker than others to realise the futility of wasteful expenditure and was strong-willed in firmly getting away from extravagance. After wasting a few months and a lot of money, he went back to the simple and frugal life style befitting his means and his childhood habits.

He gave up the unnecessary waste but retained the fastidiousness in dress for many years to come. Gandhi, in London and thereafter in South Africa [up to 1910] was always properly and even fashionably dressed. In Durban and even in Johannesburg, Gandhi loved to live comfortably and even luxuriously.

Sachchidanand Sinha who saw him at Piccadilly Circle in February 1890, describes him in details. "He was wearing a high silk top hat, burnished bright, Glastonian collar stiff and starched, a rather flashy tie, displaying all the colors of the rainbow under which, there was a fine stripped silk shirt. He wore as his outer clothes, a morning coat, a double-breasted vest and dark striped trousers to match and not only the patent leather boots, but also spats over them. He carried leather gloves and a silver-mounted stick but wore no spectacles. He was, to use a contemporary slang, a nut, a blood, a masher—a student more interested in fashion and frivolities than in studies". [*Amrit Bazar Patrika* 26-1-50 Nanda 28].

The impression carried by Sinha is very wrong. Gandhi might be wearing fashionable clothes, but there was nothing frivolous about him and he always was a very serious student devoted to his books and to his work

Once Gandhi decided to cut down unnecessary expenses, he went hammer and tongs and rebounded from extravagance to meticulous economy. The Kensington boarding and lodging with the Anglo-Indian family was costing him a fortune—nearly twelve Pounds per month [CWMG I-117]. As he grew familiar with London and developed more self-confidence, he moved out on his own, frequently changed his quarters and cooked his own breakfast and dinner to save money.

He had already discovered the restaurants serving cheap but wholesome vegetarian dishes. He hunted for and secured cheaper, self contained one room apartments which would be nearer to his place of work, saved enormously on conveyance by walking everyday an average of eight or ten miles going and coming from his workplace. Gandhi advises others to do the same. Walking this distance, said Gandhi in his Guide, is no exertion in the climate of London and one gets stiff and cold in the bus and the tram. Gandhi even mentions the conductors running along the vehicles for short distances to warm themselves up. [CWMG I-84]

In June 1889, Gandhi started living independently for the first time at Store Street residence, which was much nearer to the Temple Inn and also to the London University. He visited Brighton for a month in June 1890 and attempted self-cooking for the first time. Returning from Brighton, he stayed at Tavistock Street, paying the rent of fifteen shillings a week for a one-room bed-sit. He spent one shilling a day for food. [Breakfast 3 d. dinner 3 d. and lunch in a hotel 6 d] By the middle of 1890, he started cooking his breakfast and dinner and avoided costly hotels and costly dishes, bringing his monthly expenditure to five pounds. This was not only economy, but also the beginning of dietetic experiments, which Gandhi continued almost till the end of his life. Gandhi economised on rent and simplified his food habits; He economised on everything [in the Guide, Gandhi gives detailed information about the washing expenses and how to economise on it], but he never stopped buying books or purchasing proper clothes.

All these experiments in self-reliance and economy are interesting and important, but it ought to be kept in mind that he was not the only person doing it. There were several others—Indians as well as Europeans—who did the same. Gandhi himself has quoted in his Guide several such examples of people who lived even more simple and frugal lives.

Gandhi knew several Indian students who lived in the poorer quarters and spent much less than Gandhi. "It was not for me to think of emulating him". [Auto Par I Chap. XVI] Gandhi kept within moderate limits and maintained a proper status. He always lived in decent areas and never in poorer quarters. All the three addresses of his in London—Store Street, Tavistock Street and St. Stephen's Gardens are "the areas of middle class, well to do housing". [Hunt]

There was hardly any colour prejudice or racial discrimination in London of those days. Queen Victoria's personal valet [and rumours say her lover] was an Indian Abdul Karim and Hay has quoted an Indian saying that "I am never slighted for my color or nation or creed. The more I have of difference, the more I am respected". [Hay 74] During his three years stay in London Gandhi never had any single experience of racial bias or discrimination or hatred as he freely entered and moved into the High London society. That is why the South African experiences proved to be all the more traumatic as they were totally unexpected blows which surprised and stunned Gandhi.

Chapter 4

GANDHI IN LONDON

Apart from his studies and his attempts to live independently, it was his bold and even obstinate vegetarianism, which turned out to be a talisman for Gandhi in ways more than one. In London, the first and the most important direction of Gandhi's growth was his conversion to vegetarianism in principle.

The efforts and arguements of friends could not shake Gandhi from his obstinate adherence to vegetarian diet and when Gandhi was at Kensington, the landlady did provide him with vegetarian food. But it was a monotonous, insipid and tasteless routine, consisting of eternal rounds of bread, butter and jam, the boiled vegetable was mostly potato and there was no milk. "The food they used to provide for dinner was third rate" [CWMG I-118] because the landlady did not know vegetarian cooking.

The food was a torture and Gandhi was almost always underfed, often even hungry because it was bad manners to ask for more. Gandhi had to eat outside, which added to his expenses. With the additional rounds of social outings and hotel dinners, Kensington was very costly.

Getting vegetarian food was not a problem: the problem was to get vegetarian food that was tasty and nourishing.

The landlady gave Gandhi a wonderful piece of information that there were quite a few vegetarian restaurants in London but she knew nothing about them. Gandhi was given the name of the Porridge Bowl and he immediately set out on a long and hard hunt, searching for that restaurant in an unfamiliar city. He roamed all over London often walking eight or ten miles a day searching for that restaurant. He failed to find it, but found instead the Central Restaurant at 16, St. Bride Street, off Farrington Street, which was far away from his residence, but was quite in the vicinity of the Inner Temple. [Hunt] He was beside himself with such a palpable joy that even at this distance in time, that joy is felt in the cold print of his autobiography.

The date of this very important discovery cannot be determined with any accuracy, but it should be somewhere in March or April of 1889. The menu card of this restaurant that Gandhi has reproduced in his Guide to London is dated 22-10-1888. But at this time, Gandhi was living in Richmond with Dalpatram Shukla. Gandhi has declared "For months, I did not come across any vegetarian restaurant". The restaurant might be using the menu card long after it was printed or more probably it was an old and discarded menu card, which Gandhi had preserved to illustrate the variety and the courses of the vegetarian lunches and dinners available in London.

Even while entering that restaurant, Gandhi proved himself to be different from ordinary mortals. He saw Henry Salt's *Plea for Vegetarianism* and first purchased the book and then had his first satisfactory meal since he came to London. Salt presented a scientific and a moral case for vegetarianism "after reading which I adopted vegetarianism from principle. Till then I considered flesh to be a superior diet from the scientific point of view". [CWMG I-49] Gandhi was greatly impressed by that book and he wrote to Salt many years later "your book was of immense help to me in steadying my faith in vegetarianism". [CWMG XXXXI-553]

When Gandhi found the Central Restaurant, he, in a sense, found himself. Vegetarianism was the lynchpin of his relationship with the English society. Gandhi found wholesome food and very friendly English companions. He found the addresses of many vegetarian restaurants from the *Vegetarian Messenger*. There were ten such restaurants in London and others were in Manchester, Brighton and even in Paris. Gandhi mentions a Vegetarian Hostel where he stayed for some time. Food henceforth was no problem for Gandhi and even when he visited other cities, he never had any difficulty in finding vegetarian food.

He read and digested all the available literature on vegetarianism. Such reading converted Gandhi into a staunch and a confirmed vegetarian and backed him up with scientific data. His lifelong devotion to the gospel of vegetarianism dates from London. He had gone there a convinced meat eater and was intellectually converted to vegetarianism.

Far more important was the transformation that came over Gandhi. It linked up Gandhi to two major interests that dominated his entire life thereafter. He got interested in dietetics and health and was ultimately led to naturopathy "Health was the principal consideration of these experiments to begin with: but later on the religion became the supreme motive". [Auto Part I Chap. XIV] The spiritual aspect of dietetics was revealed to him only in South Africa

Secondly, his newly found passion was to turn him into an activist and was to overcome to a large extent, his shyness and his isolation. Vegetarianism opened the doors for him to enter and reach some of the best and the most progressive elements in the English society and put Gandhi in touch with "some of London's most eccentric idealists during the final year of his stay in their city" [Hay].

Gandhi had very little time—hardly a year to interact with them. But Gandhi rapidly blossomed forth in company of this modernist, fashionable, exciting group that led him to the most up to date currents of thought. He came to hear about Tolstoy, Thoreau, Morris and Ruskin from them. On account of their company, Gandhi anglicised himself in a better and a truer sense of the term, not merely in terms of dress, language and etiquette, but in terms of thoughts and beliefs.

Gandhi was a voracious reader and read extensively about the most modern controversies. He thereby surged far ahead of the leaders in India who were still stuck with eighteenth century Burke and Pitt.

By 1890, Gandhi was fully "in the orbit of this dynamic community of high-minded souls whose anti-urban, anti-industrialization philosophy of self-control and purification in many ways prefigured his own". [Hunt 23] Gandhi, of course was still not involved in such philosophical depths of vegetarianism, but he was going to be dragged into the same by the logic of the circumstances.

For Gandhi, vegetarianism was rooted in the traditional lifestyle and it was very commonplace for him; but for the English and the Americans, it was something revolutionary. The vegetarianism in USA and England was not exclusively concerned with food and food habits. It was a movement that began and continued as a part of the Humanitarianism and Idealism. The London Vegetarian Society was led by many stalwarts for whom vegetarianism was an expression of spirituality, intimately webbed with the Christian gospel providing simplicity and purity as the foundations of spiritual life.

The Society had launched its weekly, The Vegetarian [7th of January 1888] that was to be "a paper for the promotion of Humanity, Purity, Temperance, Health, Wealth and Happiness". The LVS launched many missions, campaigns, and conferences and Gandhi was to get involved in some of them.

The vegetarians were not a faddist group but a group of intellectuals, artists, thinkers and writers. In a sense they consisted of some of the best elements of the English society. Henry Salt, Edward Carpenter, Bernard Shaw, Annie Besant—made a motley crowd consisting of Fabians, mystics, rationalists, and theosophists. Almost all the leading lights of vegetarianism were writers and activists. Most of them were ardent supporters of simple living.

Edward Carpenter [1844-1929] was the high priest of vegetarianism in England and a staunch supporter of simple living in tune with nature and back to nature ideology. He was profoundly influenced by the teachings and the text of *Gita*. His *Civilization —its Cause and Cure* powerfully reminds of Gandhi's Hind Swaraj. It is a strong condemnation of Industrial civilisation and a call for return to simple rural life. Carpenter had founded his Humanitarian League and Gandhi used to attend many of its group meetings where he might have met Carpenter himself for a brief and impersonal interaction.

Henry Salt, the mentor of Bernard Shaw, a Fabian and an agnostic had a passion for social reforms based not on social and political considerations but on ethical principle. He used to praise Ruskin as a teacher of pure life. He and his wife were deeply interested in the study of Sanskrit language.

Gandhi was not the only Indian in London who was a vegetarian. There were vegetarian restaurants in quite a few localities of London: Gandhi has mentioned a few Indians who were vegetarians and one of them was a Parsi [Pestonji Padshah]. None of them, in spite of their vegetarianism, underwent any such development or growth as Gandhi. It was the way Gandhi took to vegetarianism and his habit of going to the roots of whatever he was doing—that made vegetarianism so fruitful for him. .

The London Vegetarian Society office was quite near the Central Restaurant, where tea meetings and discussion groups were frequently organized. Gandhi made it a point to attend such meetings; but only as a shy and silent spectator. Stephen Vincent [Salt and his Circle P 118] records an appearance of Gandhi at one such meeting in 1889. He was in silk hat and black coat and he introduced himself. "My name is Gandhi and of course you do not know me". Salt noticed him as a possible new recruit for his group, but soon thereafter forgot all about him.

Gandhi got acquainted with the leading members of the LVS; but could develop no rapport with them—most of them were old and sick. They "had a habit of talking of nothing but food and of nothing but disease". [CWMG XXXXVIII-326] Gandhi's activism was limited to reading the literature on vegetarianism and eating at the various vegetarian restaurants. "There was hardly a vegetarian restaurant in London that I had not visited".

Gandhi was too busy with his examinations to be more active in the group till the end of 1890. But he started practicing what he had learnt. Gandhi gave up tea and coffee and replaced both with cocoa. Gandhi experimented with Salt's vital foods that involved uncooked foods, fruits, vegetables and nuts and it made Gandhi sick. His strict adherence to vegetarianism was severely tested, when an ailing Gandhi refused beef tea pressed upon him by the doctor. He visited the editorial office of *The Vegetarian* to seek expert advice about his experiment and met the editor Dr. Oldfield who noted him as 'a shy, diffident youth—slim and somewhat weakly.'

The London Vegetarian Society was the most powerful influence on Gandhi's outlook on life. Gandhi joined the LVS in May 1890 and in no time, the circle of his friends expanded beyond his expectations. In the letter he wrote to the *Vegetarian* in 1894, Gandhi has listed seven reasons for his joining the movement and one of these reasons appears rather farfetched. "Vegetarian movement will indirectly aid India politically also in as much as the English vegetarians will more readily sympathize with Indian aspirations". [CWMG. I -125]

Gandhi's enthusiastic support to the movement led to a lifelong friendship with Dr. Josiah Oldfield who found Gandhi to be 'a gentle, quiet, reserved man who was very self-controlled and ready for any sacrifice'. [Shukla] Dr. Oldfield, came to know Gandhi through Dr. Pranjivandas Mehta; the contact between Gandhi and Joshiah ripened into a friendship and Gandhi maintained relations till 1931. Oldfield had become the editor of the *Vegetarian* in July 1890 and invited Gandhi to attend the International Vegetarian Congress held at Ventnor [11-13/7/1890.]

Gandhi had become an active member of the London Vegetarian Society in the beginning of 1890, but it was between December 1890 and June 1891, when Gandhi was absolutely free from all academic work that he came into close contacts with the Society and became its devoted propagandist.

These six months [January-June 1891] were the happiest and busiest period of his stay in London. Gandhi threw himself wholeheartedly in promotion of the vegetarian movement and he went to stay with Dr. Oldfield at St. Stephens' Quarters, Bayswater. [March-April '91] "Josiah was the only Englishman with whom young Gandhi lived on the basis of friendship and equality and the relationship was to be an enduring one". [Hunt 27] Dr. Oldfield got Gandhi elected to the Executive Committee of the society on 19 September 1890 and he was there for the next eight months.

The duo became great friends. "We spent all our spare time going out in the evenings and lecturing at clubs and any other public meetings where we could obtain a hearing for our gospel of peace and health". [Joshia Shukla 188] "We lived in the same diggings, shared the same table, sat on the same committees, wrestled with the same social problems and were faced with the same temptations of youth". [Oldfield Hay 91]

At Bayswater, Gandhi organised the West London Food Reforms Society with himself as the secretary, Dr. Oldfield as president and Sir

Edwin Arnold as vice-president.* The society folded up almost immediately after Gandhi left for India, but 'it gave me some valuable lessons in organizing and running an organization'. [Auto Part I-Chap. XVII]

The contact with the vegetarian movement encouraged and trained Gandhi to express his views and opinions both in spoken and written word: Gandhi thereafter never stopped speaking and writing till the very end of his life. While in England, he spoke to several groups and conferences and began to contribute articles to *The Vegetarian*.

He started writing almost regularly and his six short articles on Indian customs and habits and three articles on Indian Festivals were published in the issues of *The Vegetarian* between February '91 and April '91. There is nothing much to be noted in these articles in terms of either contents or style: the subjects are trivial and Gandhi's knowledge is quite superficial. But there was a noticeable improvement in his language and presentation though he is still uncomfortable with both.

Gandhi read a paper on Foods of India at the Waverly Restaurant [2 May 1891] meeting and it was very highly acclaimed. He was selected as a delegate of LVS to the Federal Vegetarian Union conference at Portsmouth [5-6 May 1891] and read that paper with some additions and expansion. T.T. Mazumdar, who was his companion on the S.S. *Clyde*, also spoke to the delegates.

Gandhi, in this paper has mentioned that he had given up eggs after taking them for six weeks. There was an intense controversy going on at that time among the vegetarians about the use of eggs and milk on physiological and moral grounds. Gandhi's paper was very highly appreciated and widely discussed and Gandhi himself participated in the discussions, which followed. His recommendation of sesame [til] oil for

---

* Hunt hints that it was an old club that was revived and reactivated by Gandhi and Dr. Oldfield.

Gandhi at age seven

Mohandas with Sheikh Mehtab

Gandhi and Kasturbai (date uncertain)

Farewell function at Durban, 1914

With British army officers in London, 1914

Gandhi with Natal Indian leaders, 1912

Send off function at Durban, 1909

Gandhi and Kasturbai with family and children at Porbunder, 1914

Felicitation at Porbunder, 1915

Welcoming Gokhale, 1912

Gandhi with Kallenbauch, Polak and Sonia

Gandhi leads the March, 1913

Indian Ambulance Corp. Boer War, 1899

Stretcher bearer group, 1906

Sergent Major Gandhi

Medals for war services

Law student in London

Barrister Gandhi – Durban

Gandhi with London Vegetarian Society members

Gandhi, Kallenbauch and Sonia

Indian community at Durban

Gandhi with C. F.
Andrews and Pearson

Barrister Gandhi in turban

Gandhi, 1910

frying evoked great interest and Gandhi promised to procure some sample supply of oil. [Pyarelal]

His articles on the food habits of India grew out of this paper and they were published in *The Vegetarian* after he left London. It was at this conference, that the shortage of accommodation forced Gandhi and Mazumdar to stay with a woman of easy virtue. While playing cards with the lady in the evening, Gandhi [starved of sex for three years] felt tempted: but he was warned and saved by Mazumdar. He immediately left Portsmouth. 'God saved me' is the only comment Gandhi makes about the incident [Auto.]

Gandhi spoke at Ventnor [May 1891] on "Vegetarianism- is it reasonable?" By the end of May, Gandhi spoke at the Galborne Liberal and Radical Club meeting and in the first week of June, he spoke for fifteen minutes to the Band of Mercy at Upper Norwood and quoted Shakespeare to bring out the inherent contradiction between mercy and non-vegetarian food.

While in London, Gandhi addressed public meetings at least four times. He read his papers at the meetings of LVS and at two widely attended conferences where he also participated in the debates to elucidate and defend his papers. Gandhi must have spoken at several small meetings with Dr. Oldfield. His statement about his total inability of speaking in public is flatly contradicted by Dr. Oldfield but Gandhi was still shy and hesitant about public speaking.

Gandhi regularly attended all the meetings of the executive committee of LVS where most of the time he was a silent and tongue-tied spectator to such an extent that Dr. Oldfield often taunted him as being a drone. But Gandhi was, by no means, an inert member and fully participated [Auto Part I –Chap.XVIII] in a storm that was brewing in the Society.

In the executive committee meeting held on 20 February 1891, Gandhi had the guts to oppose the most influential patron of the

Society. Gandhi very strongly protested against the chairman Mr. Hill's attempt to denounce and drive out Dr. Richard Thomas Allinson, a very staunch advocate of vegetarianism and of artificial methods of birth control. Such methods were then considered immoral and the Christian ethics insisted on purity or self-control for preventing pregnancy. These were the views adopted by Gandhi in later years.

Hills, the chairman and the patron donor of LVS, was upset with Dr. Allinson. Gandhi was in full agreement with Hills, but he insisted on the freedom of dissent. When the resolution to remove Dr. Allinson from the executive committee was presented, Gandhi's written submission against it was read out. Gandhi mentions in the autobiography that the protest failed and the resolution was carried. Dr. Allinson had to resign and he [Gandhi] too resigned from the executive committee in sympathy.

Gandhi seems to have totally forgotten the incident. In fact, Gandhi was swimming with the current; most of the executive members were of the same opinion as his. The chairman was forced to withdraw his resolution against Dr. Allinson and Gandhi continued to be the member of the executive committee till the very end of his stay in London. [Pyarelal 235 et al] The last meeting of the executive that Gandhi attended was in May 1891. Gandhi resigned his post thereafter because he was leaving for India in June '91.

Gandhi has omitted or more probably, he was unaware of the unsavoury details about his vegetarian friends and associates who were, for Gandhi, mere passing shadows. Henry Salt, for example, was a known homosexual and his wife a self confessed lesbian. Gandhi was never that intimate with them. He was only on the periphery: he joined the society in May 1890, and left for India in June 1891. He stayed with the society hardly for a year and for half of that period he was very busy preparing for his final examinations.

Gandhi was immensely relieved and greatly happy with his success in sticking to vegetarian diet while in London: but he does not mention it as a fulfillment of his vows. "During my nearly three years stay in England, I have left many things undone and have done many things which perhaps I might have better left undone. Yet I carry one great consolation with me that I shall go back without having taken meat or wine and that I know from personal experience that there are so many vegetarians in England". [CWMG I-49]

Before leaving London, Gandhi spent lavishly to throw a grand and a very costly vegetarian party for about twenty of his friends and associates at the posh Hallborn Restaurant and made a short after dinner speech. Gandhi [Auto Part I Chap XVIII] says that he only succeeded in making himself ridiculous. Gandhi's memory about the Hallborn speech bears no relation to either the contents or the length of his speech. "He made a graceful, though a little nervous speech and it was a fairly long speech" [The Vegetarian 13-6-91] thanking LVS and particularly Dr. Oldfield. The other speakers praised Gandhi very highly for his patience and his persistence.

Unlike other Indians, Gandhi had penetrated into the best of the English society and was put in touch with the concepts and writings of Tolstoy, Thoreau and Ruskin. All these thinkers rejected Society as it existed and insisted on reexamining the prevailing concepts about food, [vegetarianism] sex [contraceptives vs. celibacy] and religion [Theosophy, agnosticism and even atheism e.g. Shaw and Bradlaugh]. The vegetarians discussed and were usually supportive of simple life, moral force and philosophical as well as Christian anarchism based on non-violence and civil disobedience. Gandhi was going to practice and preach all these concepts in South Africa.

The open sessions of the Humanitarian League were often attended by outstanding intellectuals and celebrity writers some of them being theosophists. Thus vegetarianism provided Gandhi with linkages with several streams of contemporary thought. He emerged as a Mahatma, not in London but in South Africa; but he had picked up several ingredients for that career in London by and through vegetarianism.

Contact with vegetarianism led Gandhi to religious quest. Most of the vegetarians were devout and ardent Christians. Gandhi's friend and the editor of *The Vegetarian*, Dr. Josiah Oldfield was an intensely devoted Christian and tried very hard to lead Gandhi to salvation through Christ. When Gandhi hedged in because of his ignorance about his own religion, Josiah persuaded Gandhi to at least read the Bible and Gandhi became a life long devotee of the Sermon on the Mount.

Gandhi, for quite some time, made it a practice to regularly attend Church services and he heard many famous preachers. His favorite preacher was Rev. Joseph Parker. "I went again and again". [Doke p 50-51] Gandhi's life long love for the hymns like "When I behold the Cross" and 'Lead Kindly light" date from this period and his charming phrase in his interview "I have left many thing undone' etc. is a phrase from protestant litany.

The missionaries in India had familiarised Gandhi with mostly a "beef and beer" Christianity; but Gandhi was fortunate to get associated with better and higher type of missionaries both in England and in South Africa. Gandhi's strong attachment to Christianity that had developed in England began to wane after his experiences in Africa where the Christian precepts and the practices of Boers who were staunch Christians, differed so sharply.

Gandhi discovered his own heritage—vegetarianism and Hindu religion in London. He was initiated into reading Hindu scriptures by the theosophists some of whom were active members of the vegetarian movement. Gandhi refers [Auto Part I Chap. XX] to two Theosophist brothers, who having read the Song Celestial of Sir Edwin Arnold, sought [the end of 1889], Gandhi's help in reading *Gita* in the original. But they were not brothers. Chandran Devnesan has identified them as Betram and Dr. Archibald Keightley who were a very rich uncle and nephew duo who had put their vast and luxurious residence at the disposal of Madam Blavatsky. Gandhi had to shamefully confess that he had not read the *Gita* either in original text or even in vernacular versions. Gandhi was shamed into reading it in the original.

Gandhi was welcomed, befriended and provided spiritual nourishment first of all by Theosophists. Gandhi met Mrs. Annie Besant and had great respect for her. It was Theosophy rather than Christianity that led Gandhi back to his roots and made him study more deeply the Hindu texts—more especially the *Gita* which became a guiding star of his later life. Gandhi was persuaded to read Blavatsky's *A Key to Theosophy* which renewed his faith in Hinduism and it had a great impact on him. "This book stimulated in me a desire to read the books on Hinduism and disabused me of the notion fostered by the missionaries that Hinduism was rife with superstitions" [Auto Part I Chap. XX]

Gandhi read the *Song Celestial*, which is "neither very accurate nor very faithful to the spirit of the original". [Payne 72] Gandhi was led to read Edwin Arnold's *Light of Asia*—the life of Buddha, which is far superior as a poem. Gandhi had great respect for Arnold and persuaded him to be the vice-president of the Bayswater society.

Under the impact of theosophy, Gandhi turned to the study of Islam and read Carlyle's *Mahommed as a Hero*. He greatly admired Prophet Mahommed for his austere simplicity, his strictly disciplined life and his intense faith in God.

Madam Helena Petrovna Blavatsky [1831-91] and Col. Olcott had in 1875 established in New York the Theosophical Society that was the first western cult of Hindu derivation. The British Theosophical Society was founded in 1878 but by 1883, the Society was in trouble. The investigations by the London Psychic Research Society resulted in a very damaging report exposing its occultism to be a sheer hoax and Gandhi was probably aware of this report.

It was in May 1889 that the Society received a shot in the arm when Mrs. Besant, a prominent activist in several fronts and fields joined the movement. Gandhi met Blavatsky ['a cheater'] when she visited London in December 1890 and took instant dislike for her because of her cigarette smoking. He became an associate member of the Society with its motto "There is no religion higher than Truth". He was there only for six months and did not renew his membership in spite of being pressed to do so. But Gandhi had very close relations with the Theosophical Society in Transvaal and often spoke at their meetings. Almost all his European friends in Transvaal were Theosophists.

Theosophy is a curious mixture of Asian lore and traditions as found in the prevalent beliefs of the orthodox [Sanatani] Hinduism and pseudo science. Its motifs are mostly from Hinduism and Buddhism. Theosophy became a shield to save Gandhi from the onslaught of Christian proselytism. Gandhi took from Theosophical society only what he wanted and he would have none of its occult teachings then or even later. "Though Society's rule respecting brotherhood appealed to me, I had no sympathy for its search for occult powers". [CWMG XI 64] "A credulous Besant was duped by Leadbeater...as to his humbug, I came to know later". [ibid]

But Gandhi never outgrew some of their beliefs e.g. the existence of spirits and the communications with the dead through mediums. "I have no evidence to disbelieve the possibility of such communications. But I do strongly disapprove the practice of holding or attempting to hold such communications...... The practice is harmful both to the mediums and to the spirits. As for the mediums, it is a matter of positive knowledge with me that all those within my experience have been deranged or [rendered] brainless and [were] rendered disabled for practical work.... I can recall no friend of mine who having such communications, has benefited in any way". [*Young India* 12-9-29]

Religion was one aspect in the growth of Gandhi that was *not* very prominent or much noticed in England: but religious interest roused in London stayed with Gandhi for ever and grew more and more compelling with the passage of time. His innate interest in mysticism led Gandhi first to theosophy and later on to esoteric Christianity, which had a great impact on his spiritual quest in South Africa.

The intense religious feelings that Gandhi had imbibed from his family were nourished and awakened and further fortified in London. He journeyed to Hinduism via Theosophy and Christianity. It was in London that he seems to have heard about Tolstoy and might have read some of his opinions and books. The teachings and the opinions of Tolstoy were the single most important force in shaping Gandhi in Africa.

We should refrain from exaggeration while interpreting the impact of London on Gandhi, because Gandhi never became that intimate with any of the groups in London. He might have met a few celebrities on rare occasions and that too from a distance. But London inculcated in Gandhi two of his passions, which were life long—dietetics and religion. The third, political activism was the gift of South Africa.

Though Gandhi later on disowned his heritage of the English culture, he always had a deep and sincere admiration for England, which grew out of his contacts with the finest elements of the English society during his long stay in London. "Gandhi had experienced many facets of Europe and had absorbed many doctrines propounded by the European thinkers within his own philosophy of life". [Hardiman 17] After such pleasant experiences and contacts in London, the bureaucratic brazenness of the whites in India or their barbaric racialism in South Africa came as a much greater shock to Gandhi than for other Indians who were accustomed to putting up with such arrogance and brutalities.

By the time Gandhi left London, he was a very highly intelligent professional and an extremely well read person with a long and truly formidable list of readings. While in London, he must have read Shakespeare, Thackeray, Tennyson all of whom he quotes frequently, but never Dickens. Besides all the prescribed textbooks for his legal studies and for the London University Matriculation examination, Gandhi read James Mill's *History of India* and W.W. Hunter's volume of the same name.

He read extensively the literature on vegetarianism, which included several volumes of Henry Salt, Edward Carpenter and Anna Kingsford and Dr. Allinson. He also read Howard William's *Catena of Authorities* and his *Practice of Flesh Eating*. He studied with great attention the books written by Dr. Allinson. After getting interested in Theosophy, he read Blavatsky's *Key to Theosophy* as also Mrs. Besant's *Why I Became a Theosophist*. He mentions in his autobiography *The Song Celestial* and *The Light of Asia* by Edwin Arnold as also the *Hero as a Prophet* by Carlyle. Gandhi also studied Latre's volume on physiognomy to understand the character of persons from their external appearances. This is quite a long and impressive list.

But Gandhi felt diffident about his competence as a professional because he was a perfectionist and was wont to compare himself with the best barristers like Pherozeshah Mehta. He sought and obtained the advice of Frederic Pincutt who put all his doubts at rest. Pincutt gave him very sound advice that for a successful professional career in India, Gandhi must "know India, know Indian laws and know Indian history".

Gandhi in London grew fairly fast and fairly tall, but the shell was not yet broken when Gandhi returned to the dreary existence in Kathiawar. Gandhi returned from England a better Indian and a more believing Hindu than he was when he had left India. He discovered the soul of India in England and was going to discover his own in South Africa.

"To judge from all the available evidence on these student years, not political but academic, and moral and religious matters were most on his mind, as the last two were going to be in his later years". [Hay 95] Gandhi did not show much interest in politics- either British or Indian but he was quite familiar with the political happenings around him on account of his careful reading of newspapers and his prodigious memory. He did attend several lectures of Dadabhai Naoroji and students at the Anjuman I Islam were always discussing politics and current affairs.

Like all educated Indians of his times, Gandhi was already culturally bifocal but in a sense, London made him more so. His English education in India and then in England had made him belong to the class of Indians Macaulay had hoped for and dreamt about—"a class of Indians who may be interpreters between us and the millions we rule over—Indians in blood and color, but English in taste, in opinions, in morals and in intellect". Gandhi was all this.

But London added cultural ingredients that Macaulay could not have imagined would ever be available in England. India's cultural and spiritual concepts had captured some of the best minds of Europe and America—Thoreau, Emerson, Carpenter, Salt, Blavatsky and Besant. Captured Greece took Rome captive. Similarly, but to a much lesser extent, India had attracted the westerners. In England and in America there emerged "a class of persons English and American in citizenship and skin color, but enchanted by the spiritual heritage and often by the dietary practices of the Hindus. Gandhi was drawn to and was welcomed by these men and women. Their friendships, lectures, articles, pamphlets and books made both England and India even more dear to him". [Stephen Hay]

It would be a great mistake if all the elements of Gandhi were to be traced back only to this period and only to this city. Gandhi probably had neither the time nor the inclination to come into contact with all the intellectual or ideological currents that dominated London then. He was hardly aware of either Liberalism or Socialism or Anarchism both in its philosophical and revolutionary varieties.

It is rather surprising that, while in London, he had very little or no contact with Indian students. Gandhi was always a keen observer of contemporary affairs; and yet, he hardly ever mentions the current politics of either England or India, though lot of activities were going on, on both fronts and the two were often closely dovetailed together, e.g. the Liberal party was campaigning to get Dadabhai elected to the House of Commons and succeeded in doing so in 1892.

For Gandhi, this stay was truly the most important shaping event of his career on account of his intellectual awakening and also because of the opening of his mind to some of his life long interests—dietetics, naturopathy and spiritual quest. No other Indian, not even Nehru who stayed in London much longer than Gandhi, did or could have done more to absorb the London atmosphere as much as Gandhi achieved during this short stay: such an amazing growth of Gandhi must be attributed to his innate worth as much if not more than to the atmosphere.

Chapter 5

BRIEFLESS BARRISTER

Gandhi was called to the bar on 10th June and sailed for India three days later, "with just a little leaven of hope mixed with my despair". [Auto Part I Chap. XXV] Gandhi had left Bombay and returned to Bombay during the monsoon months, which are usually a period of sea storms. He was returning with a personality much fuller, more enlightened, more mature, more free, more assertive, more vocal and a little bit more self-righteous. "It [Guide to London] may cost me even friendships and some will call me rash and tactless but I have resolved upon bearing the storm for the sake of Truth." [CWMG I 67] During the voyage to Bombay, he mixed very freely with the passengers, comforted them during a minor sea storm and was yearning to give a talk on vegetarianism, which could not be delivered for no fault of his.

Gandhi underwent a purification ceremony at Nasik and gave a community dinner after which he was readmitted in the caste. But the readmission was partial. He was accepted by the caste in Rajkot but the Porbunder group refused to do so. Poor Kastur was the helpless victim of this split. Her parents were in Porbunder and her in laws in Rajkot.. "They [Kastur's relatives] were prepared to secretly evade the prohibition [on contact with Gandhi] but it went against grain with me to do a thing in secret which I would not do in public". [Auto Part II Chap II]

Gandhi after his return from England, troubled Kastur and after a petty quarrel drove her away to her parents. After being forced to stay with her parents for three months, the poor woman had to crawl back to him in great humiliation: Similar and worse experiences were the lot of Kastur and they continued for quite a long time thereafter.

The foreign returned Gandhi was a westernized dandy who insisted on several costly changes in the family routine. Tea and coffee were replaced by Cocoa and porridge: fashionable and costly crockery together with forks and knives and spoons was introduced. Children had to wear boots and socks. Gandhi himself always dressed in western fashion. He wasted a lot of money.

After staying in Rajkot for three months, Gandhi shifted [October 1891] to Bombay to seek wider pastures. But he was a misfit in India. Though technically qualified, he knew nothing about the personal laws of the various communities or the procedure for conducting civil and criminal cases in Indian Courts. He struggled hard to overcome his limitations but could not do much.

Gandhi has elaborated on his failure as a lawyer but he was no failure. The professional competition in India was quite intense and every barrister in India had to survive a fairly long period of briefless existence, Gandhi being no exception. Barristers charged heavy fees and handled more complicated cases. Such important cases would naturally go to experienced and more reputed lawyers.

Gandhi learned the lesson from bitter experience and in his Guide, he has advised newcomers to save Rs. 2000 which will see them through the lean period of about two or three years. He was disillusioned about the prospects of quick and great earning. "Barristers are at a discount... that is an undisputed fact"..."they are too many of them, they are too inefficient and they are too expensive". [CWMG I-101] After he failed to conduct his first case, he could never secure another client, more so because he declined to pay the touts. The personality that Gandhi had developed in London did not have much of a scope in contemporary India.

He attempted to take a part time job in Bombay as a teacher with a salary of rupees seventy a month, but he did not have the necessary qualification of being a graduate and was rejected. He returned to Rajkot in April 1892 and for a year eked out a living by drafting the plaints and memorials of various sorts for other lawyers and clients. His plan to go abroad for legal practice was shot down by his brother and he was so hard up that he had to request Patwari for a big loan, [CWMG I 56] but it failed to materialise.

Business, however, slowly picked up and Gandhi started earning a fairly good income of Rs. 300 a month but he was still in despair and yearned for an outlet. The twenty months that Gandhi spent in India after his return from London are the darkest years of his life and a severely depressed and listless Gandhi fretted and fumed all to no purpose.

But he did not waste his time. He started writing his *Guide* to London in response to many persistent queries about the conditions of living in London from many people who were eager to emulate his example and stay there without spending a lot of money. Such a Guide was a long felt need because "Nobody gives useful information for going and studying in England" and "no one is bold to tell his countrymen how he managed to live in London" for the fear of controversies, reproaches and condemnations. [CWMG I-67]

The *Guide*, the first full-length book written by Gandhi, shows him a very intelligent and very sharp observer of things and situations and he has a remarkable memory. The *Guide* [CWMG I-66-120] is a very interesting revelation about Gandhi's personality as it was in the nineties and that picture is a very sharp contrast to Gandhi as we see him after 1908. He is greatly enamoured of England and the English in every way. He wants every person who can afford the expense, to go to England for trade or for education.

He emphasises again and again that "this is a book meant for those who want to live cheaply and yet respectfully" and that it "is not written for those who would make a show —very often false show of their riches". He insists that a fashionable living in London is a must; 'fashion is to be adored as it ought to be more or less'.

Based upon his own experiences, he is quite confident that cheap and comfortable living in London is quite possible and even enjoyable, provided it is a disciplined and purposeful living. "It is better to impose some sort of examination task upon one self" and he is frank enough to advise "Indian not over-scrupulous in his religious views and not much of a believer in caste restrictions should partly cook and partly eat outside".

The Autobiography provides a glimpse of what would have happened to him had he been confined to Kathiawar for long. He was dragged into the whirlpool of petty politicking and was pressurised by his brother to misuse his London contact with the Assitant Political Agent Mr. E.C.K. Ollivant.

Gandhi family had continued its relations with the degraded and the deposed ruler of Porbunder and his family. Gandhi himself had worked as companion tutor to prince Bhavsinh, the heir apparent to the throne of Porbunder, who had stolen some jewellery from the state heirlooms: [Pyarelal] Lakshmidas, the elder brother of Gandhi was either an accomplice or at least an accessory post facto.

Gandhi, much against his will and better judgement met Ollivant and pleaded for his brother who was involved with the errant prince. Gandhi was summarily thrown out of the office. Gandhi was clearly and totally at fault and his behaviour was most annoying. Ollivant who was handling the case, was merely obeying the instructions issued by the Governor of Bombay Sir Richard Temple to all administrators. "[The officers should] while being courteous, not allow interested persons to make separate or personal representations to him regarding the matters under investigation: he should not be too accessible to all sorts and conditions of natives".

Ollivant chose to be cautious and refused to hear a word more from Gandhi and got him pushed out. Gandhi could never see his own fault. He was rash enough to threaten penal action for assault and battery against the officer concerned who very rightly refused to relent. Instead of realising the grave mistake he has made, Gandhi blames the officer for misbehaviour even in his autobiography. [Part II Chap II] The threat recoiled against Gandhi because he had often to appear before the same officer to plead his cases. Sir Pherozeshah Mehta advised Gandhi to shut up and forget the behaviour of the officer concerned.

The dark clouds lifted a little, when Laxmidas found an opening for Gandhi. Sheth Abdul Karim Haji Adam Zaveri of Porbunder offered an assignment to Mohandas for a year in South Africa. Zaveri was a partner in one of the oldest and richest business firms of Indians in South Africa—Dada Abdulla and Co., with a vast network of commercial establishments in Natal and Transvaal.

A prolonged and a ruinous litigation involving a staggering amount of Pounds 40,000/- had been going on now for many years between the two business tycoons of the Indian community in Africa—Dada Abdulla and Haji Tayyab. A barely literate Dada Abdulla found it very difficult to explain his case to his European lawyers. The accounts had been maintained in Gujarati style and most of the important documents were in Gujarati language which the European lawyers were not able to read and which the court would not admit as evidence.

Gandhi was not employed as a lawyer because nobody would entrust a novice like Gandhi with such an important and complicated case.

Gandhi had to serve more or less as a legally trained clerk who would act as a liaison between the firm and its lawyers, explain to them the intricacies of Gujarati style of book keeping and translate documents from Gujarati into English as and when needed. The employers also expected him to do sundry odd jobs "to get some experience". [Auto Part II Chap V] Gandhi was going as a legal adviser cum translator cum clerk. His service contract was only for a year and the stipend he was offered for the entire year was commensurate with the insignificance of his duties. He was to be paid a lump sum of twenty-one Guineas. [£105] in addition to the maintenance, out of pocket expenses and the first class fare for all his travels.

This new assignment would involve financial loss to Gandhi because he was earning more than double the amount [£240] at Rajkot. But Gandhi jumped at the offer. After his frustrating experiences in Bombay and Rajkot, anything else was welcome. Africa was famous all over Gujarat and more especially in Porbunder as a land of promise and prosperity. "I wanted somehow to leave India" [Auto Part II Chap V] "I was fond of novel experiences.. .The atmosphere of intrigue in Saurashtra was choking me". [SSA] Africa offered an escape route and Gandhi went without regrets.

It was Gandhi's habit to always look for opportunities. "Wherever I go, I keep inquiring about the opportunity in the foreign countries for the members of our family and for others". [CWMG III 268] Gandhi found great opportunities for business in Africa and he persuaded some of his relatives and professional friends to come and work in Natal.

In spite of his failure as a lawyer, Gandhi seems to have developed, by now a very pleasant personality with surprising powers of persuasion. He succeeded in securing a berth in the overcrowded S.S. Safari after more experienced and better-connected travel agents of his employers had failed to get it for him. He travelled [16-4-1893] as a cabin companion of the Captain of the ship, played chess with him and befriended him to such an extent that at Zanzibar, where Gandhi broke his journey to change the ship, the captain took him for 'an outing' in the red light zone of the city. Gandhi was so singularly free from lust that for the third time {Rajkot, Portsmouth and Zanzibar} he failed to perform with women of easy virtue. "God saved me" was his only comment, but God usually does not help that much that often.

When Gandhi sailed for Africa, he was heading for an arena bristling with the problems and issues about which he knew nothing and which he was least prepared to face. He was going there for a temporary stay of a year and strictly in search for employment. "I had gone there on a purely mundane and selfish mission. I was just a boy returned from England wanting to make some money". [Radha. Ed. 120] He was to stay there more than twenty years and returned a world famous Fakir without any possessions whatsoever.

"Africa the land of exile provided the opportunities and the context for the development of a man of action, of vision and of hope". [Brown 30] "In this new raw society of South Africa, many races and nationalities of Europe and Asia struggled for a place. This turmoil was the training ground in which young Gandhi learnt his lessons" [Hunt 56] and he learned them the hard way through a series of triumphs, failures, frustrations, sufferings, accusations, betrayals and calumnies.

This lawyer who had failed so miserably in India, very soon emerged as the tallest among Indians in South Africa. "Operating in a sphere where he really had no rivals, Gandhi was able to rid himself of the uncertainties and the inferiority complex... A highly skilled lawyer greatly respected in Natal and Transvaal, he also proved to be a political leader of great maturity, flexibility and imagination ...[so much so that] one wonders what Gandhi would have been without South African experience". [Hutten 329]

There is no denying that "South Africa was indeed a great training school for Gandhi" [Smuts Radha Ed. P],and he emerged from it as "the only Indian in South Africa who demonstrated leadership ability and the real sense of direction in the political arena". [Swan 217]

In Africa Gandhi's rise to prominence was truly meteoric. In India, peer pressure and professional competition smothered him but here the field was free and open for him. He arrived in South Africa [May 1893] and jumped into the public life in April 1894. By December 1894, he was the tallest among Indians in Natal—leading delegations to the prime minister and to the governor of the colony and corresponding with the highest power centers in Natal, India and England. He was barely twenty-five when he was acknowledged as the sole spokesman for his community.

One more year and Gandhi dominated, in absentia, 1896 Immigration Bill debate of the Natal Assembly as the enemy most widely feared and most severely denounced. On a short visit to India, [1896] Gandhi spoke to crowded meetings, interacted with the front rank leaders of India and established personal contacts with some of the major media personages. After the dastardly attack on him by the white hooligans [January 1897] Gandhi was the best known personality in South Africa. Questions were asked about him in the British Parliament, he was interviewed and commented upon by all the leading newspapers in Africa, India and England. The *London Times* the most prestigious among them all spoke of Gandhi as one "whose efforts on behalf of his fellow subjects in South Africa, entitles him to respect".

No other political leader of comparable age and qualifications had has ever attained such eminence in such a short time. Gandhi had to pay a huge price for such prominence. His bona fides were suspected, he was very often accused of misusing the public funds, of making money out of the political activities and of being a professional agitator, if not something much worse.

He emerged as a towering personality and had neither rivals nor companions. When he left Africa, he left behind him a vacuum. He had no successors. In India, Gandhi trained and disciplined an army of future leaders; but in Africa he could not do so for reasons beyond his control. He himself was too young and was still training himself. Moreover in South Africa there was hardly any human material worth training.

Besides being a launching pad for his political career, South Africa was for Gandhi a Sadhana Kutir for his final emergence as a Mahatma. The process that began in England reached fruition in Africa. Gandhi embarked upon an intense search for the ultimate goal and purpose of life. As a professional expert in law and politics, Gandhi was immersed in thousand little duties and worries, but he simultaneously emerged as a determined pilgrim in search of spiritual light and eternal verities.

Gandhi in South Africa often seemed being tossed hither and thither. "In a life that consisted of many false starts and unfulfilled promises, he seemed to have no steady aim, no ideal vocation. As a lawyer or a politician, he would fight valiantly for a year or two against restrictive laws applied to Indians and then he would weary of the conflict". [Payne 127] But this would be only a very superficial view of Gandhi in Africa where Gandhi emerged as a totally matured personality.

It was in Africa that Gandhi transcended all the limitations of the pluralistic Indian society and became a true Indian to a much greater extent than most of his contemporaries. Leading the feuding groups of Indian community against mortal dangers, he repeatedly exhorted the community "We are not and ought not to be Tamils or Calcutta men, Mohmeddans or Hindus, Brahmins or banias but simply and solely British Indians and as such we must sink or swim together…If we have brought from India these divisions and differences as very valuable cargo…it would clog us at every step and hinder our progress". [CWMG III 497]

Between 1893 and 1914, Gandhi underwent a three-dimensional transformation. From a struggling draftsman of petitions and memorandums in Rajkot, [1993] he became the most successful advocate with a very lucrative practice: a diffident, shy and largely dumb Gandhi emerged as the most assertive and a highly vocal political leader whose voice rang over three continents in England, South Africa and India. A staunch and a devoted loyalist to the British crown and an ardent admirer of Western civilisation, Gandhi by 1914 was on the brink of rebellion against the British sovereign and had already repudiated every single vestige of Western culture in his *Hind Swaraj*.

But Gandhi does not belong to South Africa: he remained an Indian first and always. In spite of his very long stay and his total involvement, Gandhi never viewed himself as a permanent settler. Africa was always a halfway house for rich and upper class Indians—the elders and the more affluent of them retiring to India after about two decades or so and their being replaced by new comers.

Gandhi also was psychologically a temporary resident serving as a lawyer and a political leader for the community and the business establishments that were more or less permanent in South Africa. The yearning for India breaks through his writings and utterances more and more intensely as the years roll by. He left Africa for good in 1901, wound up his office, bid farewell to all his associates and was away in India for a year. Fate dragged him back. But in 1914, enough was enough and Gandhi resolutely turned his back on Africa even though the mission he had undertaken was still an unfinished agenda.

Chapter 6

INDIANS IN SOUTH AFRICA

Gandhi's brilliant achievements in India have overshadowed his somewhat underemphasised activities in South Africa. But these years [1893-1914]—some of them the most painful years of his life—are of crucial importance as the formative years for Gandhi. The political activism and spiritual fermentation contributed immensely to the final sculpting of Gandhi's personality. A mere lawyer emerged first as an outstanding politician and was then transformed into a Mahatma. His achievements and failures involve a few happenings that are still obscure and leave a number of nagging questions unanswered. Therefore this era needs to be evaluated more elaborately than has been done so far.

When Gandhi landed at Durban, he was stepping into a tri-lateral battlefield where each side was fighting against the other two. "The history of South Africa is a history of wars between the whites and the blacks and wars between the British and the Boers for the supremacy over the lands so acquired". [P.C.Joshi] The Indians arrived very late on the scene and had to struggle hard for survival in this atmosphere of animosities and hatreds.

South Africa, in 1893 consisted of four separate units—two colonies [Cape and Natal] and two autonomous Republics—Transvaal and Orange Free State. The Republics were fully autonomous in their internal administration but both were under the hegemony of British Imperial authority. The population of all the four tiny units consisted of a small minority of the whites drawn from several European countries, dominating over the vast mass of various native African tribes collectively known by a pejorative term—Kafirs. South Africa was a plural society "where different nationalities are in a melting pot and a South African nation has yet to rise in a dim and distant future". [CWMG VII 2]

The whites—mostly Boers, were a tough and crusty community of Afrikaaners who lorded over the blacks and the coloureds and regarded them with contempt as some sort of barbaric or even a subhuman species of the animal world who were to be tamed, controlled and used by the superior race of the whites. This deeply ingrained attitude of racist arrogance raised an impassable barrier against all the non-whites including Indians.

Gandhi's agitations and confrontations spread over two decades brought him into conflict with three different polities—the British Natal, the Boer Transvaal and the Union of South Africa and each had a distinctive socio-political ethos.

Of the four units, Transvaal was by far the richest and 'most sought after piece of geography in the world' [Leo Marquard] on account of its diamond mines and rich deposits of gold. By the end of the nineteenth century, the whole world was rushing to this El Dorado glittering with a third of world's gold and nearly half its diamonds.

These outsiders-Uitlanders-were perceived as a threat to the independence of Republics. Fearing that they may misuse the franchise to take over the political control of Transvaal, President Kruger deprived them of voting rights. The Europeans immediately formed a

Political Reform Association and launched a furious agitation bombarding British Colonial Office in London with memoranda and petitions signed by hundreds of whites.

Gandhi, then in Pretoria, must have been a keenly interested observer of this agitation that was so similar to the one that he would be leading a year later in Natal. "The drama of Gandhi's agitation was a re-enactment using the lessons learnt...in the protracted and grim struggle between the Boers and the Uitlanders". [Chandran 251]

The arrival of Indians laid the foundation for the Indian Question that Gandhi handled so superbly. The Indians had not come on their own. They had been invited, persuaded, tempted and even cajoled to come, work and settle in Natal, which suffered intensely from an acute shortage of labour for its coalmines and sugar plantations. The colony was prepared to pay very high wages for importing labor. India was an inexhaustible source of surplus labour. A contractual system for labour supply known as indentured system had been structured and supported by the governments in Britain and India. It was a well-paid, temporary bondage, perilously close to slavery.

Natal offered very tempting terms and from 1860, a steady stream of ever increasing number of indentured Indian coolies arrived in Natal. Between 1860 and 1911, Natal imported 1,52,184 coolies and most of them chose to settle in Natal. Within less than a decade, these coolies, most of them Tamil or Hindi speaking, converted Natal into a prosperous 'golden colony'. The legal services rendered by Gandhi to these poor Indians earned him their unflinching devotion and their support and sacrifices saved Gandhi and his satyagraha from a total fiasco in 1913.

The terms of labour contract were very fair but there was a wide gap between law and practice. The coolies were overworked, exploited, cheated out of their wages and were often treated with cruelty by their employers. But after the term of bondage was over, they were allowed to stay and settle in the colony as free labor.

Much has been written and spoken about the hardships and torture suffered by these poor, illiterate and totally helpless coolies. But the very fact that they chose to go there and stay on would imply that for most of them economic and social conditions in South Africa were much better than those available in India.

The bulk of indentured labour was "the products of socio-economic system which offered at best, mere subsistence but too often starvation". [Swan 20] The social degradation and exploitation, intense poverty, recurrent famines and seasonal unemployment drove them to starvation and hence to South Africa where they were assured of employment and food. People always prefer slavery to starvation. They "domiciled in Natal in a manner that a free Indian never does. His home is where he can keep his body and soul together". [CWMG III 540-41]

"The life in South Africa at its worst was much better than life in India". [Hutten 28] and Gandhi himself has certified "I do not think that their lot is worse than the lot of Indians similarly placed in other parts of the world". [CWMG II 77]

Coolies hardly ever renewed their indentures and chose to work as free labour either on the plantations or they took up odd jobs as domestic servants, railway porters, cooks, waiters, laundrymen, fishermen, etc. Many of them owned or leased small plots of land to grow vegetables and fruits. They were expert farmers or gardeners earning twenty times the income they could ever hope to get in India and lived much better quality life. Some of them started small shops and stores. Their ever increasing numbers and their prosperity created a stir within the white community. Coolies were welcome as labourers but they were not wanted either as permanent settlers or as rivals in agricultural or commercial pursuits.

The coolies were a submissive but a licentious, unscrupulous, dishonest, illiterate society with very dirty habits. A skewed sex ratio [only 30/40 women for every 100 males] drove them to live without too many social or moral taboos. Wives were often shared. "Those who know the conditions of life on the estates wonder that there is any purity of life is left among their inmates and that violent crimes are so rare as they are". [CWMG XI 319]

Coolies were often employed for scavenging and for cleaning sewers and drains. They lived in the most unsanitary conditions and were much prone to various diseases. [CWMG IV 161] Theirs was a miserable lot. They were hated and maltreated by the whites and despised by elite Indians. Both men and women were heavy drinkers. Gandhi attributed [1903] the high rate of suicide amongst the indentured coolies not to any maltreatment but to depression and isolation.

The coolies constituted ninety-five percent of the Indian community; but they were only a part and a small part of the Indian Question faced and handled by Gandhi. Far more exacerbating element was the Indian merchants and much of the anti-Indian fury was directed against them. The settlement of large number of coolies in South Africa had been followed by the influx of merchants—most of them from Porbunder and Surat in Gujarat and most of them Muslims. On account of their turbans and flowing robes, the ignorant colonials called them Arabs.

Indians proved to be better merchants than Europeans. They were more polite, more hard-working and could supply better goods at cheaper rates because of their less expensive life style. The coolies as well as the natives found it safer and more pleasant to deal with Indian merchants rather than with the whites. In Durban there were only 37 Indian stores in 1880; the number rose to 132 in 1891. By 1903, Indians in Natal had virtually monopolised all the retail trade in the colony.

Indians hawked the goods in the rural and remote areas of Natal and very rapidly spread all over the colony. By 1904, there were 1260

Indian stores and shops as against 658 owned by the whites. [Seminar papers. University of Natal 1984] The rich but largely uneducated Muslim merchants employed educated Parsis and Hindus as clerks and accountants.

The number of Indians in Natal rose very fast. In 1870, there was not a single Indian trader in the colony and there were only 5000 Coolies: by 1885 the number rose to 30159. By the turn of the century, there were 51000 Indians in the colony as against only 50000 whites: by 1912, there were 150000 Indians in South Africa and in Natal there were more Indians than whites. [1,20,000 in Natal, 10000/15000 in Transvaal and the rest in Cape Colony] The rapidly increasing numbers, skill and wealth of Indians made them an eyesore to the White community.

By 1880, Indians from Natal began to spill over into Boer republics—more especially into the rich Transvaal, which offered immense business opportunities. Between 1881 and 1885 numerous Indian merchants had their establishments in Pretoria and Johannesburg. Boers hated Indians on racial as well as political grounds. Boers were intensely racist and Indians insisted on being the loyal subjects of Britain, which was deeply hated by the Boers.

It was in these Republics that the anti-Indian laws were first enacted and enforced. The Orange Free State took the initiative in closing its doors tightly shut against the Indians. All Asiatics were prohibited from farming and trading and three Indian shops in the republic were given a year's notice and then were closed down with meager compensation.

In Transvaal the infamous law no 3 of 1885 listed Indians as the "semi barbaric Asiatics belonging to uncivilised races of Asia". But there was no restraint on the entry of the Indians. They had to get registered and pay twenty-five pounds: they would have no property rights, no franchise and could live and trade only in locations reserved for them.

Since Indians were British subjects, this law was a flagrant violation of the rights granted to ALL British subjects. The governments of Britain and India protested very strongly and the law was amended next year. There would be no registration and the fee was reduced to three pounds. Governments of Britain and India kept up prolonged correspondence to press for the better treatment of Indians in Transvaal and therefore the law No. 3 of 1885 could not be implemented till 1899.

Indians entered Transvaal in ever increasing numbers and the British Agent in Pretoria encouraged and protected Indians in defying the law. Indians stayed wherever they wanted and traded as they liked with or even without proper licenses. The British protection of Indians was not entirely altruistic. Britain was using the Indian issue as an excuse and an occasion for asserting her sovereign authority and as a means to discredit the Republic so as to finally destroy its independence.

The continuous and enormous influx of Indians—coolies, merchants free labour, and the white collar workers in Natal and to some extent in other colonies as well, led to intense social tensions and a raucous debate erupted among the dominant White community. Their racial arrogance and their contempt for the non-whites were further exacerbated by the economic factors.

Several white traders were driven out of business by the competing Indian merchants while the coolies were taking over kitchen gardening and the odd job market. The large number of Indian merchants and their prosperity loomed much larger in the overheated imagination of the whites and gave them the nightmare of whites being economically ruined and politically overwhelmed by a flood of Indian migrants who would eventually take over the colony by becoming a dominant community in this white men's land.

The anxiety stoked by fear and envy burst into volcanic fury in the last decade of nineteenth century and Gandhi was caught in this tornado. Race relations deteriorated very sharp and very fast

"Whatever was the root cause of the anti-Indian hostility, the manifestation was always racial discrimination". [Swan 44]

Indians were accused of every conceivable crime and misdemeanour. They were vermin, breeding like rabbits: they lacked in human decencies and were lecherous brutes preying on every woman white or black: they were the carriers of loathsome diseases on account of their very dirty, unsanitary habits and shabby life style. Indians were denounced for unfair business competition, for their sharp practices, for receiving stolen properties, for exploiting their servants, and for fraudulent bankruptcies. They were charged with short weight and adulteration, cheating their customers and society. These despicable creatures were very bad citizens and drained Natal of all their savings when they retired to India. As Gandhi noted with sarcastic amusement 'no word in English dictionary is sufficiently strong to damn the Indian with.'

The press continuously denounced Indians in the most extreme language and painted them in the worst possible colour. The illiterate coolies and semi-literate merchants were hardly aware of such sinister accusations and were much less capable of refuting them. Therefore the charges went unanswered for a long time and created a stereo image of Indians which Gandhi valiantly but unsuccessfully strove to change.

Such widespread and intense hatred often resulted in maltreatment and violence against the persons and the properties of the Indians. They were often attacked, their shops were at times plundered and even burnt while the police looked the other way.

After 1890, there was a spate of anti-Indian laws in all the colonies. The disabilities and indignities that had been devised for the Natives were now sought to be applied to Indians too. The term Coolie or Sami—a descriptive term for Indian labour degenerated into a pejorative term expressing contempt and hatred and was used for all Indians irrespective of status, wealth, life style, education or profession. There were coolie merchants, coolie teachers and Gandhi was a coolie barrister.

The humiliations and difficulties that Indians in South Africa had to face, have been vividly described by Gandhi in great detail in the pamphlet he wrote in 1896—the famous 'Green Book.' Indians were not allowed to travel in first or second class during railway journey and could use only lower deck or footboard in tramcars. They could not use footpaths and would be kicked off if they did.

They were subject to the vagrancy law and could be locked up by the police if they moved out of their residences between 9.00 pm and 6.00 am. Indians were not admitted in hotels and theatres and would have to use separate facilities like restrooms and lavatories. There were separate entrances for whites and blacks at the post offices and railway platforms. Every municipality treated Indians as more or less untouchables and sought to push them away into distant locations where sanitation, water supply and electricity were either totally unavailable or hugely inadequate.

But it was not possible for whites to expel Indians or prevent their entry by law because Natal and Transvaal were a part of the British Empire and Indians were the fellow subjects. Indians were felt to be thorn in flesh and every means and method legal or ultra legal was used to make their life so miserable that they stop coming or even withdraw from the colony.

At every turn, Indians faced insults, threats and even assaults and yet they did not even complain about such incidents. "In all cases of assault, our mode of action as a rule is not to take any notice of them…Sufferance is really and truly the badge of the Indians in South Africa especially in Natal". Gandhi hastens to add that "we follow this policy not from any philanthropic principle but from purely selfish motive...to bring offenders to justice is a tedious and expensive process...The offender would either be discharged with a caution or would be fined five shillings or a day. The very man...assumes a threatening attitude and puts the complainant in an awkward position". [CWMG II 6-7] Gandhi himself followed this path of wisdom in 1897 and refused to register the complaint against his tormentors even though he had the support from the highest quarters.

By the end of the century, humiliations, violence and wanton harassments had piled up so high that it was almost impossible for any self-respecting Indian to stay in Africa for long. In spite of such harassments and insecurities arising out of racial hatreds, more and more Indians kept on coming to South Africa. Gandhi himself stayed on for more than twenty years and he even persuaded his relatives to settle for business in the colony.

Gandhi was always hard put to explain why Indians suffer so much misery and maltreatment and stayed on. Gandhi's explanation was that the high earnings and profits that were available in South Africa attracted Indians. "Indians pocketed the insults as they pocketed the cash".

But this, by no means, is a sufficient explanation. Most of the Indians were lower caste coolies and they did not feel too much about such indignities and cruelties. In the hierarchical and status conscious society of India, they were used to the same or very similar indignities and cruelties in their own homeland. The merchants and the middle class Indians were irked by the treatment meted out to them in South Africa: but then Indians were treated with contempt and cruelty by the whites in India itself. The conditions in South Africa were indeed much worse but not that unbearable.

The superb and patient handling of this very complicated and almost intractable Indian Question in South Africa is an epic of Gandhi's sagacity, bravery and tenacity. The problem and the ways in which

Gandhi handled it can be best understood by viewing it from the Colonial, the Imperial and the Indian points of view because each side had a case of its own.

The colonies of South Africa, more especially after they were granted autonomy and self-government insisted upon free and full authority to determine the composition and shape of their society by admitting or rejecting outsiders on terms and conditions most suitable for themselves. For the colonies this was an internal matter in which the Empire had no reason and no authority to interfere. They were determined to maintain the white character of the country, which they had opened up with their blood and developed with their sweat.

They needed and eagerly sought a large import of Indian labour and were willing to pay a good price for labor work. Indians were wanted all the time, but only as laborers or as mere beasts of burden: Indians were not wanted as settlers, traders, farmers and artisans who would compete with the whites on a footing of equality. Gandhi puts it tersely. "Had Indians continued to work…as mere laborers, no agitation would have ever started against Indian immigration".

The tiny White community of around 12,50000 living in midst of vast mass of Natives in South Africa was worried about being submerged by the unlimited influx of the second alien element-Indians who claimed rights of migration and settlement as fellow subjects of British Empire.

British government and leaders of public opinion in England strongly upheld the Imperial theory that all subjects of the Empire irrespective of race, colour or origin must enjoy freedom and full opportunity to live and labour in any part of the British domain. The autonomous colonies were certainly free to manage their own internal affairs, but migrants from one part of the empire to the other part should not be hampered by racial discrimination or by any socio-political disabilities. To protect such migrants, the British authorities, while conferring autonomy on the colonies always retained final authority to disallow and veto any discriminatory law or administrative action against her subjects who usually had no voice and no power to protect themselves. Gandhi again and again insisted upon such protection and he was always heard with sympathy by British authorities.

After granting responsible government to the colonies, the colonial office declined to interfere in internal affairs and sought to control only Imperial affairs. London's theoretical power to disallow colonial laws was very rarely exercised for the fear of jeopardising the loyalty of White settlers by direct confrontation. The conflict between the Imperial theory and the colonial autonomy was never satisfactorily resolved. As far as South Africa was concerned, there was an additional handicap. The area was most suited for colonisation by the British people and therefore Britain needed South Africa more than the other way round.

The Imperial theory was an ideal that was found very inconvenient to be implemented in practice. The dominant white communities in all colonies were unwilling to treat brown and black subjects of the Empire on a footing of equality on account of racial arrogance. It was impossible for Britain to compel any self governing colony to accept that British Indians would be placed in the same position as European British subjects. "British Imperialism was tempered by as much humanitarianism as was compatible with its political and economic interests". [Chattopadhyaya Pre.]

The loyalty and the contentment of Whites were far more important than the sufferings of a small community like Indians in Africa. The British masses had a strong affinity with the White colonials and shared their racial prejudices. British bureaucrats too had a soft corner for the colonials who were determined to maintain White dominance over the rich and fertile areas of South Africa and to preserve the colonies as White-man's land. The Whites in India too were in general sympathy with the Whites in South Africa.

In fact, Britain herself was discriminating against Indian merchants in Zululand in matters of property and mining rights while that area was under direct administrative control of Britain. Gandhi had to carry on a long struggle to secure redress for them. "It was hardly possible for the British Government to throw the first stone against the Boers in matters of anti-Indian legislation". [Hutten 70]

British rulers and officials in England and in India were greatly worried about the adverse effects that anti-Indian measures in South Africa would inevitably produce on the prestige and peace of British rule in India and they always sought to mitigate such impact by championing Indian cause to the extent that they dared.

Buffeted between the racial affinity and the shared prejudices on one side and her Imperial interests and responsibilities on the other, Britain was forced to walk on both the sides of the fence and to speak from both the sides of mouth. They would always insist on face saving formulae that the restrictive laws should not be overtly racial in terms. It was always high-sounding phrases about principles, offering little actual help in practice. Britain had to compromise with racist discrimination by brilliant equivocation.

"Embarrassed and frustrated, the British government compromised. It insisted that the letter of any particular law be indiscriminating but cared little about the spirit or the contents". [Hutten 69] Such compulsions were reflected in the attempts of the Colonial office to preserve the appearances rather than the substance and it "was more interested in the technicalities of the legal constructions rather than in the spirit and the true purpose of the legislation". [Huten 107/8]

Indian viceroys did protest against anti-Indian legislation but their main efforts were directed towards the protection of the coolies. Lord

Curzon was the only one who showed interest in protecting the entire Indian community as such.

Dispatches from the colonial office soothed the Indian wounds and elated their spirits but they were bitterly disillusioned when the all of such verbiage turned out to be mere fireworks ending in nothing but flashes and smoke.

Indians and more especially Gandhi strongly and enthusiastically upheld the Imperial theory and claimed rights and securities as the most loyal and law-abiding subjects of British Empire even though they differed from the Europeans in race, manners, customs habits and religions. Gandhi, like most of the educated contemporary Indians, was dazzled by Queen's Proclamation of 1858 and repeatedly pronounced it to be a Magna Carta for India. He was totally convinced about the eventual implementation of all the commitments made therein. Gandhi often romanticised about British Imperialism. "There is no true Imperialism unless we have oneness, harmony and toleration among all classes of British subjects....How to weld the differences of British dominions into one beautiful, unbreakable whole is the problem which the greatest of British politicians are endeavoring to solve". [CWMG III 300-301]

A misty eyed idealist, Gandhi refused to see the facts in their face and always talked about the moral values, the justice and fairness of the British Empire. "We do not despair. We have an unfailing faith in British Justice". [CWMG III 402] Gandhi had deep rooted faith in British sense of justice and fair play and he was never tired of urging the uniqueness of British Empire as being the only one of its type as based on equity and justice.

Both these presumptions were factually invalid and Gandhi, a victim of his own rhetoric, was destined to realise that this Empire too was as red in teeth and claws as any other one. After several rejections and frustrations, Gandhi's hopes were going to be shattered on the hard rock of reality. In a way, South Africa started to drain Britain out of Gandhi.

Gandhi was an enthusiastic devotee of British society, British Culture and British government. His gushing loyalty to the Crown is imprinted on every page that he wrote. Every event involving the Royal family—jubilees, deaths, coronations and even casual visits evoked an intense emotional upsurge in Gandhi and he responded both verbally and in action. The vocal and influential sections of the Indian community in Africa too shared Gandhi's beliefs and responded to his initiative in presenting their grievances to the British sovereign. But they had no trust in Whites and were quicker to grasp that racial affinity was far more potent than Imperial responsibilities.

Indians in South Africa were "an ignorant and docile minority crushed under the heavy boots of racist whites. ...Theirs was a depressed sub-world [in which] the limbs of a trampled minority [were] powerless to generate forces on its own" [Ash] and needed a catalyst like Gandhi.

Indian community was its own worst enemy. "The multiplicities of Indian life...were transplanted across the waters of South Africa". [Hunt 50] making it impossible for them to stand and speak in one voice. Indians in South Africa consisted of three major groups that were divided into several sections and subsections cutting across one another on religious, linguistic and economic considerations.

The largest [ninety-five percent] group was the poor, illiterate coolies- indentured as well as free labor. These coolies were divided in two linguistic sections—one speaking Hindi and the other speaking Tamil or Telugu. Most of them were low caste Hindus and many were untouchables. All caste distinctions were very soon wiped out in this small and poor community as they were forced to mate and marry among themselves.

The second group consisted of colonial born and English educated second-generation coolies who lived and dressed in English style. They were working as teachers, clerks, policemen etc, in the municipal offices and government as well as in non-government establishments. Many of them had been converted to Christianity and were looked down upon with suspicion by the better placed Indians for their being under the thumb of the clergy controlled by government. [Auto. Part II Chap.XVI]

The third group was a very rich, active, influential and assertive group consisting of merchants [most of them Gujarati speaking Muslims called 'Arabs'] and their staff of Parsi and higher caste Hindus. These 'passenger' Indians were a small [hardly 5000] and floating group.

All such crisscrossing groups of Indians—coolies, merchants and white collar workers: Hindus, Muslims, Christians and Parsis: speaking different Indian languages like Hindi, Tamil, Telugu Gujarati—hardly had any contacts, much less any fellow feelings of solidarity.

Gandhi, an upper caste Hindu, strongly tinged with Christian culture and English manners, serving Muslim merchants and fighting in the courts on behalf of various linguistic groups of indentured as well as free labour provided in his person strong linkages between all the groups and sections of Indians.

By his personality and activities, Gandhi played the role of a catalytic agent and galvanised the Indian community into a political unit fighting for the redress of grievances arising out of a total denial of civil and political rights. The momentum of Gandhi's activism was sustained by active participation of all sections of Indian community. The rich Muslim merchants provided funds and lent their prestige to the movement. The Parsis, the higher caste Hindus and the second-generation Christian coolies were the educated classes and looked after the enormous quantity of paper work.

It is one of the greatest achievements of Gandhi in South Africa that in almost no time, he could forge unity and harmony, albeit only for a temporary period among all sections of Indians. Gandhi's claim that "Hindu Mohmeddan problem had been solved in South Africa". [Col.Wor.IX 507] is "to be understood not in the sense of being totally eliminated but in the sense of achieving temporary unity that had to be continuously renewed and maintained against the centrifugal forces". [Hunt 54] Gandhi failed to sustain such unity and after 1905, communal and class antagonisms intensified the divisions and the mutual hatreds among Indians.

The entire struggle between the two minorities—Whites and browns was fought out without any reference to the vast and silent majority [eighty-two percent] of the blacks who were held unworthy of being even noticed in this clash of the Titans. The Indians had only commercial interest in the Africans and had absolutely no cultural or social contacts with them. Indians felt themselves to be racially different and culturally superior to the Africans whom they treated with undisguised contempt almost to the same extent as the Whites had for Indians.

Up to 1903, Gandhi too shared this attitude and endlessly whined about "being classed with the natives- the Kafir races". [CWMG. II 7] "It will be better in so far as it is possible to have Indians working with us instead of Kaffirs". [CWMG V 196.] Gandhi never employed any black either in his office or in his Ashrams. He did not hate or deride them. He had no contempt for them, but he did not want to mix with them. "It was a wise policy on the part of British Indians... to keep themselves apart and distinct from all the colored communities in this country".[CWMG V 242]

Gandhi was both the focus and the spearhead of the earliest struggle against unabashed racism and led the earliest protests against the scourge that ultimately emerged as the horrible Apartheid and this makes him a pioneer and a model for the African struggle against racism in spite of his personal attitude towards the blacks.

Gandhi does not belong to South Africa. "In Africa, Gandhi would remain an Indian leader rather than a leader of South Africa".

[Chandran 329] He worked as the leader of only one community, not of the society as a whole. He never participated in any political activity dealing with wider issues facing South Africa, though he constantly commented upon them and analysed the happenings as they affected Indians. He took no interest and played no part even when the political structure of Africa was taking up a new and a permanent shape during 1906-10.

He fought, not for human rights but consistently and exclusively for the rights, interests and benefits of Indians and that too mostly for the merchants. During the first fifteen years of his stay in Africa, "Gandhi's constituency was always the rich Muslim merchants" [Swan] "He was more involved in defending the interests of Indian merchants than in that of Indian labor". [Chandran 311].

Gandhi was not unaware of the limited area of his leadership and his defense was that "As it was considered that the free traders were the chief target of attacks, the measures of defense were limited only to that class". [SSA 54] Gandhi always took humanitarian interest in the conditions and troubles of coolies and personally helped them in every possible way, but he devoted most of his time and energy to the problems of the merchant class and prior to 1910 worked mostly as a spokesman of middle class interests.

Even after staying in Africa for two decades, Gandhi never took a full view of the totality of the situation and concentrated all his tremendous energy and his brilliant intellect on the Indian question in isolation rather than on the problems of Indians as a part of the South African society. The fault was not entirely his. The dominant White community was so disdainful of all Asians that it was hardly possible for Gandhi to build up bridges or establish any meaningful dialogue with them.

Gandhi's relation with the Africans is another question. Gandhi was quite aware of the inhuman exploitation to which the Africans were subjected both by whites and Indian merchants. Gandhi was upset with the racial discriminations against the Indians, but he hardly ever protested against much worse treatment given to the blacks by the Europeans and Indians alike.

Gandhi intensely resented the pejorative term coolie used for the Indians but he himself always referred to the Native Africans as Kaffirs and was probably unaware of the resentment caused thereby. His contemptuous reference to the natives in his Green Book is an evidence of his ignorance and his isolation from the African society as such. A gregarious Gandhi did not have a single African friend or supporter.

Gandhi might have been forced to keep away from Africans due to the realisation that even the slightest mixing up of Indian cause with Africans would harm the Indian community. They would then be accused of rousing subterranean fury of African tribes who were intensely hated and also intensely feared by Whites on account of their vast numbers as also for their volatile and violent tempers. This in fact, was one of the accusations levelled against Indian Natal Congress.

Indians and even Gandhi deeply resented that the rules made for the blacks were being applied to Indians. Gandhi himself argued continuously and emphatically that Indians though coloured were different from and superior to the 'Kafirs.' Gandhi's monster petition of 1894 noticed "with shame and sorrow the zealous attempts to compare your petitioners with the natives of Africa...[it] would rank Indians lower that the rawest of the Natives".

"My impression is that he [Gandhi] resented that his people should be and were placed in the same category as the uncivilized and the primitive natives and that they should be consequently be subjected to the same restrictive laws". [Dr. Krautze C Shukla] Hunt [55] has quoted Younghusband's wry comment. "They [Indians] complain of being classed separately from the Europeans...[But] they are much offended at Kafirs being classed with them".

In his fight on behalf of the Indian community Gandhi was never without numerous and powerful allies. His legal and constitutional struggles against the racist measures in Natal and Transvaal were strongly supported by the Indian leaders as well as by the governments in India and Britain. Gandhi expressed "gratefulness for the efforts o fthe Indian government to ameliorate the conditions of Indians in South Africa". [CWMG III 460] The Indian cause was championed by several British MPs in both the houses of the Parliament, and more especially by Dadabhai Naoroji, Manchersha Bhavnagari, Lord Ampthill, Lord Curzon, Sir W.W. Hunter, Sir William Wedderburn the president of the British Committee of the Indian National Congress and numerous others.

Lord Curzon's blistering attacks, denounced the South African colonies in far more virulent terms than Gandhi ever used. "Britain enjoys the benefits of the Empire but shirks its responsibility of protecting Indian traders and settlers". [Guildhall speech.] "It was the duty of the Indian government to protect Indians and they will continue to discharge their duty". [Curzon. CWMG IV 401] 'The Indian Question was totally above party politics and about which there is no difference of opinion between the powerful Anglo-Indian elements and the Congress'. [CWMG IV 52]

The East India Association, a very influential society consisting mostly of retired British bureaucrats who had served in India, very strongly supported every demand made by the Indians in South Africa. Gandhi splendidly acknowledged "the deep debt" to the Association for its constant support to the Indian cause [CWMG III 298] and "a silver lining to the cloud that overhangs the Indian community in South Africa". [CWMG III 451] The entire Indian press and a very influential section of British press led by the *London Times* consistently extended their support to Gandhi.

Gandhi's objectives and his opponents in Africa and in India stand at diametrically opposite poles. In Africa Gandhi fought for the rich Indian merchants against the dominant section of local society. He actively sought and often secured the help of Imperial Authority in London. In India he championed the cause of the poorest of the poor and of the most downtrodden and fought against the British authorities.

In Africa Gandhi as a lawyer and an activist, did sympathise with the poor, ignorant and helpless indentured Indians and fought several cases on their behalf securing for them all the redress which law and equity could provide for them. But he took no interest in, and made no special efforts for, improving their conditions or ever suggested better terms for the contract, which bound them and brought them to Africa. Gandhi's statement that "the labor was ignorant of the burden [poll tax] and the agitation on their behalf was carried on by the Indian traders actuated by the motives of patriotism and philanthropy" [SSA 38] can hardly be accepted as statement of facts.

In India, Gandhi was supported by the dominant sections of the society in his fight against the governments of India and England who were his allies in Africa. In India, Gandhi fought against unjust laws: in Africa up to 1906, he mostly strove for the more humane implementation of laws. In Africa, he often fought the administration with the help of laws and courts; in India he fought against the laws and repudiated the courts.

During his Africa years, Gandhi laboured under a few personal handicaps. He was an Asian and as such a natural target of intense racial prejudices from whites: for Africans, he belonged to the community of merchants who cheated them, exploited them and treated them with disdain.

Gandhi's intense interest in religious studies led to very close association with missionaries like Spenser Walter and Baker and Michael Scots. He was also very close to the Welsyan church. Such associations would damn Gandhi in the eyes of Muslim merchants and orthodox Hindus. Gandhi had several devoted friends among the Whites. Several missionaries supported him in Natal and in Transvaal: many Jews he met either in Theosophical circles or in vegetarian restaurants in Transvaal befriended Gandhi and fought in his ranks.

Gandhi's intense and emphatically professed loyalty to the British Empire must have galled the Boers whose hatred for Britain was both intense and outspoken.

This young man, [he was only twenty-five,] undertook and successfully accomplished the great task of arousing and organising the Indian community in Africa. "He found them dispirited and sunk into apathy accepting their depression without protest. He recalled them to a sense of their manhood as a moral basis for demanding to be treated as men by the Whites of South Africa". [Hoernle Radha Ed. 116]

While fighting on their behalf, Gandhi forged himself into an outstanding forensic expert, a superb and skilled mass mobiliser, a master builder and an astute manager of the strongest political party in South Africa.

Apart from his legal profession and his political leadership, there is a third aspect of Gandhi. The spiritual quest that had begun in London gradually became the dominant and later on, the sole purpose of his life. But in Africa, Gandhi's spiritualism did not lessen his capacity for tenacious fights or hard bargains

Gandhi arrived in Natal at a wrong time. British control was ebbing and Imperial authority was about to be replaced by local autonomy. This change would facilitate the process of converting anti-Indian prejudices into legislation. The endgame was being played out; the horizons were darkening and gloomy and the situation was simmering for a final boil over.

It is in this wider and somewhat weird context that we should describe Gandhi's responses to the prevailing situation so as to measure up his leadership qualities and his political acumen displayed through out "his unequal struggles in South Africa which he rarely won and mostly lost". [Payne 116]

The contours of Gandhi's strategy as well as his tactics were largely shaped by the political landscape in which he had to operate and partly also by his maturing personality. In the stubborn resistance that Gandhi offered to the racial hatreds, his courage and his character proved to be as decisive as the legal remedies he sought or political maneuverings that he employed.

Chapter 7

THE FIRST ENCOUNTERS

Gandhi landed in Durban [23-51-93] and he was observant enough to feel something amiss the way in which his host was being treated by the Whites. [Auto Part II chap VII] He was in Durban hardly for a week or so, but even during this short period, he made several friends and made himself thoroughly familiar with the intricacies of the Gujarati style of bookkeeping that being the main reason of his being brought into this case.

Gandhi's casual visit to Durban court, his refusal to remove his turban and the *Natal Observer*'s note on the 'Unwelcome visitor' have been quite wrongly depicted by many biographers. Gandhi's cryptic comments in Chap. VII in Part II of his Autobiography ["I was asked to remove my turban; I refused and left the court"] have provided grist to their mills. But Gandhi's comment is at variance with his apologetic letter to *Natal Observer* that details the incident and clarifies that there was nothing racial about the incident and no discourtesy was intended on either side.

The turban was not a major issue at all. Gandhi entered the court without removing his turban and without curtseying to the bench and he sat at the horseshoe with other lawyers. He was asked by the judge not to sit at the horseshoe and to show proper respect to the court by removing his headdress. The magistrate's disapproval was not about the turban but about Gandhi's mistake in sitting with the advocates without formally presenting his credentials. Gandhi had been misinformed and misguided by the clerk of the court. He was politely asked to vacate his seat but instead of sitting with common people, he left the court.

"I had not the slightest idea that I was offending His Worship…I beg His Worship's pardon if he was offended by what he considered to be my rudeness which was the result of my ignorance and quite unintentional". [CWMG 57-58]

It is the European custom to remove the headdress as a mark of respect. The Indian custom is to keep the head covered to show respect and devotion and 'Arabs' used to keep the turbans on in the courts of Natal. Gandhi was in European dress but his turban was Indian. Gandhi explained in the letter mentioned above that in keeping his turban on and in not curtseying, he was following the practice as obtained in the High Court of Bombay and in the high society in London. This last reference made Gandhi's letter quite 'piercing' and was so noted. "The response of the young stranger was piercing in its quiet sarcasm". [Natal Mercury 27-5-93]

The press comments of his being 'an unwelcome visitor' has nothing to do with his turban or the court incident and Gandhi never had any trouble in removing his turban when he started practicing in South Africa though Gandhi makes it sound like a deliberate compromise. [Auto Part II chap. XVIII]

The press comment is concerned with professional rivalry. "There is quite a flutter of excitement among the legal fraternity, especially among those gentlemen who are apt to look for good clients among the Indian community…An Indian gentleman holding an English barrister's diploma is about to fix his tent and try his luck". [Natal Mercury 30-5-93 Fatima Mir Ed. 100]

Nobody knew that he had come for a short period and only for a single assignment. The same lawyers were going to oppose his enrolment as an advocate, not only because of racial feelings but also because of professional jealousy and fear of losing corporate clientele of rich Indian merchants. The anxiety of European lawyers proved to be just. As soon as Gandhi was enrolled, he almost monopolised the entire Indian business.

On being called up by the senior lawyers of his employers, Gandhi started for Pretoria. This business trip took only five days: but for Gandhi it involved a series of nightmarish experiences of racial arrogance, insults and even assault. He was travelling first class in railway that no 'coolie' was allowed to use. He and his baggage were pushed out and thrown on railway platform of Maritzberg. A frightened and a lonely Gandhi shivered through the cold, dark night debating his future course of action.

To many biographers, this was the beginning of his anti-racist campaign and of his quiet determination to stay and fight against the discriminations and the disabilities suffered by Indians rather than to desert his mission and rat upon his compatriots in Africa. It is argued that it was at Maritzberg that Gandhi broke out of his shell and emerged as a potential leader. Such projections are inspired and supported by Gandhi's vague description [Auto Part II Chap. VIII] about his musings on that fateful night. Many years later Gandhi claimed that "Maritzberg was the beginning of Active Ahimsa" [CWMG 10-12-1938] and he has described the incident as "the most creative experience in my life". [John Matt Gandhi and Christian missions P 193]

It is rather difficult to accept such statements and interpretations as valid. The choice before Gandhi on that fateful night could not have been either to struggle against racism or to submit to it. He was on a professional visit only for a year and had no reason to hope that he would be able to extend his stay. In fact, his stay was *not* extended. He had been in this strange land for only about a week and he knew nothing about the problems and issues faced by Indians in Africa. His incredulous surprise at racial disabilities is strewn on every paragraph of chapters VIII and IX of Part II of his autobiography.

What Gandhi has written in his SSA is far more plausible. The options before Gandhi were purely personal—whether to quit the contract and return to India or to face whatever was in store for him and complete the term of the contract.

The decision was not easy for him. He was a man of considerable self-respect. "I had a positive aversion to earn money or sojourning in a country where I was insulted". [SSA 56] But he had yearned so intensely and so long to go abroad for legal practice [CWMG I 55] that "to run back to India would be cowardly. I must accomplish what I had undertaken. I must reach Pretoria. ...The case was being fought there. I made up my mind to take some steps if that was possible side by side with my work". [SSA 57] There was nothing for him in India and the decision to hang on to his job was prompted by personal rather than public considerations. He would have returned to India a failure and as one who could not keep a job even for a year.

If he was determined to fight racism, he did pretty little in that direction for the next ten months. He merely wrote two letters to the newspapers in the closing week of September 1893. "I did nothing beyond occasionally talking with Indians in Pretoria on the subject." [SSA 58] Gandhi did approach the British Agent in Pretoria to complain about the conditions of Indians. The Agent expressed his sympathy but pleaded helplessness because Transvaal was beyond the orbit of the British control. Such inactivity is very unlike Gandhi as we saw him in London and as we shall see him soon in Durban.

His public life and his leadership were the accidental by-products of the Franchise Law Amendment Bill of 1894 about which nobody and certainly not Gandhi could have any premonition. Active Ahimsa was not on the horizon for more than a decade thereafter. All the activities and the agitations that Gandhi led up to 1905 were entirely legal and constitutional and nowhere do we find any trace of defiance of law-nonviolent or otherwise.

Gandhi's telegraphic complaint to railway authorities was rejected out of hand and the action taken against him was justified because non-Whites were not permitted to travel first class if objected to by the white passengers. His telegram to his employers brought immediate help and relief by the local associates of Dada Abdulla & Co. Next day, with a properly reserved ticket, Gandhi travelled first class untroubled to Charlestown by the next train.

There was no railway line between Charlestown and Johannesburg and the coach journey proved to be the most horrifying experience for Gandhi. His ticket had expired because of the delay at Maritzberg: the coach leader could have accommodated him for a proper seat, but he did not do so. Gandhi had the option to travel by the next coach but that would mean further delay. The only way he could travel the same day was to sit outside the coach next to the driver. Gandhi had no option and had to accept the uncomfortable and degrading seat.

At Pardekoph, the conductor ordered him to move over to a still more degrading seat. Gandhi refused to accept it: he was assaulted and boxed by that White bully. The other passengers intervened and Gandhi retained his seat much to the chagrin of the conductor.

At the night halt at Standerston, Gandhi was met and comforted by Dada Abdulla's men who informed Gandhi about such insults and beatings being the everyday lot of Indians in Transvaal. Gandhi's complaint to the Coach Company brought forth an immediate response and an apology. For the next day's journey, Gandhi was provided a proper seat within the coach and travelled to Johannesburg without any further trouble.

Gandhi was so inexperienced and so ignorant about prevailing conditions that he sought hotel accommodation that was politely refused. Gandhi's narration of the incident amused his Indian hosts to no end. Sheth Abdul Gani enlightened Gandhi about the situation faced by Indians.

Gandhi had to flaunt his European dress and his status as a barrister to get a first class ticket from Johannesburg to Pretoria being conditionally issued to him. The courtesy of a White fellow passenger saved Gandhi from a repetition of Maritzberg and Gandhi travelled in peace and comfort in the very heartland of intense racial hatred.

In Pretoria, Gandhi had grown wise enough to seek local advice and was taken to an American hotelier who not only gave him accommodation but also allowed him the use of dining room as other White customers had no objection to his presence.

Throughout this horrible journey, Gandhi was helped and comforted by the protecting arms of Dada Abdulla & Co.'s network of agents and associates. Gandhi found it extremely galling to tolerate racial discriminations and violence so meekly accepted by Indians. "my mind became more and more occupied with the question as to how this state of things might be improved". [Auto Part II Chap?].

Gandhi had been instructed by his clients to keep away from Indians and more especially from the defendant Taiyyab Sheth. Gandhi took up a costly accommodation with an English lady at thirty-five shillings a week. Baker, the senior advocate of Dada Abdulla informed Gandhi at the very outset that there would not be much work for him in the court. But Gandhi was determined not to treat his job as a sinecure: he diligently studied all the documents submitted to the court by both the sides, mastered all the details and prepared a full brief on which the advocates could work further.

Gandhi still had plenty of time and a workaholic like Gandhi would never waste even a little of it. It was during this sabbatical year that Gandhi completed his *Guide to London* which he seems to have started writing while he was in India. He undertook an intensive study of Christianity, Hinduism and Islam and read nearly eighty books and pamphlets about these religions and about Indian history and culture —some of them being scholarly works like *History of Sepoy Mutiny* by Malleson and Kaye. He opened his correspondence with Raichandbhai whom he respected as a highly knowledgeable person asking him questions on Hindu theology and philosophy. [CWMG I 127]

Baker, besides being a rich and renowned lawyer, was also an enthusiastic lay preacher of Evangelical Christianity and made strenuous efforts to convert Gandhi to Christian faith. Gandhi was befriended by persons like Mr. Coates, Ms. Harris, Ms. Gaff and others who hoped to save his soul. Gandhi regularly attended their prayer meetings and church services. Baker took Gandhi with him to Wellington Convention though both of them were put to a little inconvenience because Gandhi was a non-white. Gandhi's friend Dr. Oldfield told him about Esotoric Christian Union founded by Maitland in 1891 and Gandhi quickly and completely took to its philosophy.

Gandhi was immensely shocked by racism prevalent amongst the devout Christians and even among the priests and preachers. His understanding of Christianity was that it was a religion of universal love and service. He always appealed to the Christian spirit and especially to the clergy to counteract and repudiate the racial virus that was infecting European children who would often pester and hit the non-Whites just for the fun of it.

Gandhi spent every minute of his leisure time either for study or for socialising. His London habit of activism broke through all inhibitions. With the help of Taiyyab Sheth and others, he called a meeting of Indians in Pretoria [August '93] and delivered his first speech in Africa. He urged upon a handful of Hindus and Muslims who attended, [Briton 32] the importance of truthfulness, cleanliness, unity and public hygiene. Gandhi also suggested an association that could speak to the authorities on behalf of Indian community. [Mir Ed.]

He mixed so freely with Indians of all categories and classes and to such an extent that at the end of the year, "there was hardly any Indian in Pretoria who did not know me or whom I did not know personally". [AutoPart II Chap.XII] Urging all Indians to acquire a working knowledge of English, Gandhi offered free tuitions to any one willing to learn. He had three students—a barber, a clerk and a shop assistant—and he, a barrister, volunteered to go to their places and teach them at their convenient time. He came to be known as a very sweet, selfless and obliging person ever ready and eager to take great pains for the benefit of others.

The high court of Pretoria took up the Dada Abdulla matter in December 1893 and while the hearings were on, Gandhi made tremendous efforts to persuade both the parties to agree to arbitration. He succeeded and the arbitration proceedings began on 11 April 1894.

On 25th of April, the case took a bizarre turn when a former employee of Dada Abdulla—one Ujamshi Mulji Shah accused Dada of large scale smuggling of goods into Transvaal in 1889/1890. The police arrived in arbitration room for the seizure of the relevant documents: but Baker refused to surrender his personal papers.

A scuffle between Baker and police resulted in Baker being arrested, handcuffed and marched down the streets to the jail custody together with Abdulla. [Britton41: Mir 110] Both were released on bail and the Supreme Court of Transvaal denounced the highhanded behavior of the police. The documents were eventually returned and the arbitration proceedings were completed. [14-5-94]

Having finished his assignment, Gandhi left Pretoria as he had booked his passage to India by S S *Reichstad* sailing on 25th May 1894.

The high court ordered [19 May 1894] the defendants Sheth Taiyyab to pay 37,000/- Pounds together with the cost to Gandhi's clients. Taiyyab Sheth did not have that kind of money to make the payment within thirty days.

Gandhi, then at Durban persuaded Dada Abdulla with very great difficulty to accept the payment by installment. The only alternative would have been an ignominious bankruptcy for Taiyyab Sheth and a near total loss of money for Abdulla.

Apart from such professional and personal activities, Gandhi had already jumped into public controversies. While in Pretoria, Gandhi drew up [28-9-93] a welcome address to the incoming governor of Natal, drawing His Excellency's attention to "the special affairs of the Indian community in Natal, ... owing to the extending Indian influence there". [CWMG I P-62]

What Gandhi did by himself was more important. His protests against the racial prejudices are of very great interest and importance. Gandhi began to issue trenchant, sober and highly stinging replies to false and unwarranted accusations against Indians in the local press in very forceful rebuttals.

A Mr. Pillay, a graduate of Madras University had been pushed off the footpath in Pretoria. Pillay's letter of protest to the *Transvaal Advertiser* was reproduced by the *Natal Advertiser* with editorial comments using very abusive adjectives for Asiatics. Gandhi's letter to *Natal Advertiser* [19-9-93] was a strong and a sophisticated protest against such vilification of Asians, which Gandhi described as 'unethical' and 'barbarous'.

Gandhi used facts, logic and satire in almost equal proportions, quoted profusely from contemporary sources and ended with rhetorical questions "Is this fair play? Is this Christian like? Is this justice? Is this civilization"? [CWMG I 59-61]

His barbed arguments were presented in very polite language and his command over English language was impeccable. Gandhi returned to the attack on 29th September 1893 when *Natal Advertiser* published the details of a campaign unleashed by anti-Asiatic League for disfranchisement of the Indians.

The argument was that the Indians have no traditions of voting and no capacity for franchise. Such 'coolie' votes would swamp the voice of Europeans who were more enlightened and more capable. Gandhi described all such fears as baseless and irrational and contradicted the supposed inexperience or unfitness of Indians for franchise. [CWMG I 63-65]

With impressive erudition, and relentless logic, Gandhi demolished every single arguement used by those who denounced Indians and wanted to humiliate them. He quoted Queen's proclamation [1858], referred to the very high offices held by Indians under the British administration. He even referred to Emperor Akbar and his minister Todarmal, who devised the revenue system adopted by British rulers as the one best suited to Indian conditions.

The letters coming in rapid-fire succession consisted of furious declamations and beautiful phrases. The Whites were surprised by his courage and charmed by his presentation. Such spirited and eloquent refutation stunned the rabble rousers among the Whites because the semi literate and largely apolitical community of Indians had so far suffered all the calumnies heaped upon them in agonised silence and had never shown the capacity and the courage to join issues in a public debate.

With the emergence of Gandhi the picture was going to suddenly and radically change. Gandhi single-handedly proved to be more than a match for the whole lot of detractors of Indians in terms of eloquence, arguments, logic and moral precepts of Christianity.

Chapter 8

THE PLUNGE

Gandhi does not seem to have much impressed his employers and his professional colleagues. He was cashiered off at the end of the contracted period. But the events took an unexpected turn at a party arranged by Sheth Abdulla on his ten-acre farm [Britton 48] at Sydenham on 22 May 1894. The party was a send off function for barrister Gandhi who was soon leaving for India.

Gandhi's description of the event in his autobiography adds a touch of drama. He is said to have casually noticed a news item that a bill to disfranchise Indian community was due for second reading in Natal Assembly: he alerted the community of the impending danger. Gandhi telegraphically requested the Speaker of the House to postpone the reading so as to hear the plea of Indians. The Speaker postponed it *only* for two days.

This narration by Gandhi [Auto Part II Chap XVI] appears to be a case of jumbled memories and he himself is a bit unsure about the dates and the readings of the bill. The documents preserved in the Collected Works tell a more coherent story. The full-page press report noticed by Gandhi and Indian leaders was actually two days *after* the second reading of the bill was over; the third reading of the bill was to be held on

2nd July 1894. There was plenty of time for petitioners. The first petition to the Assembly was presented on 28 June 1894 i.e. more than a month after the farewell party.

It was the third and the last reading that Gandhi requested to be postponed. Since the third reading is more or less a formality and new issues cannot be raised or admitted, the bill was passed on the same day and sent to the Council.

It was much more important that Gandhi succeeded in rousing the anxiety of merchants over a political matter like loss of franchise which he described as 'the first nail in the coffin for the Indian community'. Gandhi's warning went home because the proposals to deprive Indians of municipal franchise and to impose poll tax were in the air and had secured wide spread support of the White community.

His description carried conviction because the Education bill of April '94 had excluded non-White children from the government secondary schools and a proposal to debar all the non-Whites from civil service was defeated only by the casting vote of the speaker. Gandhi related the political move to disfranchise Indians with the status and business interests of Indians that might be seriously jeopardized as had happened in Orange Free State and Transvaal. "This could be only the beginning of the end of whatever little rights they were enjoying". [SSA]

What came as a shock to the merchants could not have come even as a surprise to Gandhi. As a regular and avid reader of the Natal newspapers while he was in Pretoria, Gandhi was well aware about the raging controversy with regard to Asiatic franchise and he himself has strongly defended Indian community against the charge of being unfamiliar with and unfit for franchise.

It is rather surprising that he had not alerted his compatriots earlier about the impending disfranchisement. It is quite possible that he was unaware of the actual bill for disfranchisement. His total preoccupation with the arbitration proceedings, which with its bizarre turns and twists, coincided with the progress of the bill in question and left him no time to think about it. He also might have felt himself to be an outsider not concerned with the matter.

Now that Gandhi had sounded the tocsin, the leaders of Indian community were alarmed into frenetic activity. The battle was to be joined on the delicate and explosive issue of franchise, which could be a great power generator for the Indian community.

Indians in Natal so far had enjoyed the ten Pounds franchise on the same footing as Whites: but coolies were too poor to qualify for it and merchants too apolitical to realize its importance. Prior to 1892, Indian merchants never got themselves even registered, much less ever used franchise.

But it was now decided to pick up the gauntlet thrown down by the Assembly and launch an agitation to claim the retention of franchise for Indian merchants as British subjects and as good citizens who were superior to the Africans culturally and to the coolies economically.

The farewell party turned into a working group and Gandhi leapt into leadership in a single jump. He emerged as the moving spirit of the ad hoc committee that was formed under the chairmanship of Seth Haji Mahommed. [SSA] The committee was entrusted with the task of drawing up a petition to the Assembly. Gandhi adopted the same tactics as Uitlanders had done in Pretoria, but he brought to bear upon the task his tremendous energy and his great forensic skill making his presentations far more effective.

The petition [28-6-94] he drew up is his first resounding shot in the political arena. This was the first petition of its type, which was not for redress of any grievance but for claiming a political right. The petition politely but firmly refuted the presumption underlying the bill that Indians were not acquainted with representative institutions and hence were unfit for franchise.

Gandhi mentioned the age-old village panchayats as also the caste-panchayats. He referred to the Mysore State Assembly, the municipal franchise in major cities of India as also the Indian Councils Act of 1891. Gandhi was a voracious reader and had a photographic memory with a computer brain. His vast reading and scholarship enabled him to quote a large number of renowned authorities like Sir Henry Maine, Thomas Munro, George Birdwood, Max Muller and several others in support of his contentions. Gandhi was very up to date and could quote from the latest reports, newspaper comments, court verdicts and government documents as well as commission reports.

The basic thrust of his arguements was that the bill violated an established and existing right of franchise and such disfranchisement would retard "the process of unification that the flower of British and Indian nations are earnestly striving for". [CWMG I 132] The petition therefore requested either the abrogation of the bill or a commission to inquire into the ability and fitness of Indians for franchise.

Gandhi did not rest content with a mere application to the Assembly. On the very next day, he led a deputation to the prime minister and assured him that Indians "have no desire to thrust ourselves as members on the brother nation that was unwilling to receive us as such". [CWMG I P 132]

This was obviously untrue and should have been repudiated by his fellow delegates. Indians had persisted in staying on in spite of clearly demonstrated hostility of the hosts. Gandhi was hard put to explain the inordinate delay in protesting the Franchise Law Amendment Bill of 1894. He frankly confessed "Our imperfect knowledge of English language prevents us from keeping in touch with important matters". [ibid]

In a polite but very blunt presentation Gandhi refuted the statement made by prime minister in the Assembly and called that speech 'unjust'. He quoted Max Muller, Morris, Grene and others to claim that Anglo-Saxons and Indians belong to the same stock: he, however, praised the premier for expressing sentiments of justice, morality and Christianity. Gandhi pressed for a commission of Inquiry.

Gandhi time and again, was to return to this argument and he was never tired of emphasising the glorious achievements of ancient India. He firmly believed in the theory of Aryan race and claimed brotherhood with the Anglo-Saxons. Gandhi's valiant efforts to enlighten the Europeans about the cultural status of the Indians were largely irrelevant because racial prejudices and hatreds were not based upon ignorance and had nothing to do with culture.

Gandhi's emphasis on ancient Indian culture was mostly romantic and untrue. The glories of ancient India had been wiped out by centuries of sloth and degradation and racial affinity of Aryans was based on similarities of languages long since dead both in Europe and India.

The deputation met attorney general and also other members of the Assembly. After two more days, an indefatigable Gandhi circulated [1-7-94] a five-point questionnaire to all legislators of Natal but got no response from any one of them. On the same day a meeting of the leading Indians was held and Gandhi led a deputation to the Governor requesting him to withhold his assent.

After the bill was sent to the Council [2nd July] Gandhi immediately rushed a petition [4 July] to the Council with the same request and almost the same arguments. The petition was signed by 500 Indians. But this petition had to be sent second time because of a technical error of procedure in presentating petitions.

Gandhi took the opportunity to express the dissatisfaction and disappointment of Indian community; he pointed out the anomalous results of such disfranchisement, quoted Queen's proclamation of 1858, quoted Macauley's remarks, mentioned several British administrators who had praised Indians for their noble culture and sharp intelligence.

He refuted the fear of Whites being overwhelmed by Asiatic votes and reiterated the demand for a commission of inquiry.

The Council took up the bill for consideration and in a mere matter of four days passed it through all the three readings and forwarded it to the governor for his signature, [7-7-94] With the signature of the governor, the Franchise Law Amendment bill was converted into an act; but the fight was not over yet. The act was subject to the approval of the Crown and was duly forwarded to British Colonial secretary, Lord Ripon.

Since the act was referred to London, the battlefield shifted to England. Gandhi was not the one who would give up the fight so easily as this. Gandhi was by now fully prepared and equipped. He drew up a detailed and exhaustive petition to the colonial secretary. This lengthy document was copied many times over and was reached to all towns and villages in the remote corners of Natal to be read and signed by Indians residing there. Few would be able to read it and fewer still would understand its purport, but all signed it.

Thus by a single stroke of genius, Gandhi converted a simple petition into a public agitation and galvanised a headless, disjointed community into a coherent phalanx. The exhilarating experience of the first public agitation so enthused Gandhi and the entire community that merchants as well as professionals responded with an élan. In less than a fortnight, nearly ten thousand signatures were collected from all over the colony [Auto]

The petition itself was a remarkable exercise. Aware that all earlier petitions sent to the authorities would be with the colonial office, Gandhi argued the Indian case de novo avoiding the points and arguements urged earlier. Summarising the recent past, Gandhi quoted at length, the 1894 debates in the Natal Assembly to illustrate that disfranchisement was a retrograde and unjust act of political malice and an outcome of a phobia of being swamped by Indian votes.

Gandhi tried hard to deny the possibility of any such thing ever happening. Most [ninety-five percent] of Indians settled in the colony were ex-indentured labour: they and even their children were too poor to ever attain the high property qualification needed to secure the franchise.

Indian merchants with enough property to be qualified for franchise, formed a very small minority among the Indians and they usually returned to India after retirement and were replaced by their younger kith and kin. This floating population of merchants and professionals were totally apolitical by temperament and pursuits. But Gandhi was never able to refute the argument of Europeans that such demographic actualities might change any time.

As a conclusive proof of his contention, Gandhi pointed to the voters' list. Though Indian population was almost the same as Europeans, Indian voters numbered only 251 as against more than 9000 Europeans. The second-generation coolies were highly educated and lived in European style and did deserve franchise. The petition criticised the Act as a thin end of the wedge for Indians who may eventually lose municipal franchise, jobs in the government and finally all civil rights.

The Indian protest was against racial discrimination. Gandhi noted with "shame and sorrow the zealous attempts at comparing Indians with the natives of Africa". Since educated natives were entitled to vote, the act would rank Indians lower than the lowest of natives and that would be an insult to the entire Indian nation.

Gandhi quoted the Blue Book of 1883 to show that a much more milder attempt at disfranchisement had been then rejected by Colonial Office and the act would be "an unwarranted interference with the rights of one section of Her Majesty's subjects by another". The colonial secretary was requested to withhold the royal assent to the Act as it was obviously discriminatory and racial and mentioned Indians by name [eo nominee] and violated the rights of Indians as British subjects.

The act also violated several legal and constitutional commitments made by government of Natal and ratified by the Imperial authority. In the end Gandhi repeated his demand for a commission of inquiry into the experience and fitness of Indians for franchise.

A thousand copies of this petition were widely distributed in Natal, England and India to make Indian leaders aware of the problem. The petition was widely noted in the London Press. The *London Times* very strongly supported the petition and denounced Natal Act of 1894 as unjust, oppressive and retrograde. Sir William Wedderburn mentioned the petition in Parliament.

The basic issue which Gandhi raised in this petition and which he was going to raise directly or indirectly very often was whether Indians can claim the same status and the same rights as British subjects in colonies. The contention was accepted as legally valid but was almost always denied in practice. Though Indians were occasionally granted some temporary relief the issue was never finally or satisfactorily resolved.

The petition was forwarded through proper channels and Prime Minister Robinson appended his note to the colonial secretary giving his reasons as to why it should be rejected. The Natal government contended that given the low level of political awareness among Indians and of absolutely no possibility of their ever securing franchise, "It is reasonable to assume that most of the signatories did not know what they were signing". All signatories claim fitness to vote and the number of signatories would be "the conclusive evidence of the danger that menaces the electorate, should Asiatics continue to be admitted to franchise" [Natal Govt. to Colonial Sec. 27-2-94. Swan p 75]

The Franchise Law Amendment Bill of 1894 provided the first, the most successful and the most memorable arena in which Gandhi battled. The franchise controversy proved to be a double edged sword for Gandhi and Indian community. Gandhi's submissions apart, the possibility of Indian votes swamping European ones in near future was quite real. The lawyer in Gandhi had clouded the politician in him. The line of arguement chosen by Gandhi would only confirm what the Whites had all along been clamouring about.

The Indian franchise had emerged as a major issue during the election campaign [September '93]. The possibility of Asiatic vote becoming important had been inadvertently demonstrated by Harry Escombe, the lawyer who was most popular with Indian businessmen. When he was contesting the 1894 Assembly elections, he persuaded a few of his rich Indian clients to get enrolled as voters so as to secure their support and he did get elected. He realised the implications of his action and quickly became the vociferous supporter of the disfranchisement of Indians.

In Natal, there was an intense hostility to any political rights enjoyed by Indians for the fear of 'Coolie' votes submerging White votes. Natal faced a serious problem because there were a large number of wealthy Indian merchants who could and would tilt the political balance. Several administrative efforts to deprive Indians of franchise were objected to by colonial office in London and by planters who feared the stoppage of labour supply from India.

If Indians, as Gandhi argued, were capable of franchise and if they secured and used that franchise, the European community was doomed to be submerged by Indian votes in next few years. Indians were as numerous as Europeans in Natal and their number was rising at an alarmingly fast rate.

Indian merchants were numerous enough and prosperous enough to become voters. Till now they were inert. But their attitude might change if they came to realise the political implications of franchise for safeguarding their business interests. The migratory and apolitical community of Indians could be easily politicized. Gandhi himself had done it and it could happen again. If the right of franchise enjoyed by them so far was to continue, the 'coolie' merchants' vote would become an important, if not a decisive, factor in the politics of Natal.

Gandhi was now fully launched on his political career that was to take him to dizzy heights in Africa and thereafter in India. Gandhi emerged as the 'chief agitator' for the Indian community. The next twenty years were for Gandhi the years of immense growth, even of metamorphosis. His personal life and his public activities started developing on parallel lines—extreme preoccupation with public affairs and of deep introspection in the spiritual domain. Very soon the lines began to converge and finally merged into a single integrated whole as Gandhi blossomed forth at an astoundingly rapid rate.

For the first three years, [1894-97] Gandhi struggled hard through numerous petitions, memorandums and letters written to several personalities and power centers and to the press, [averaging one item a month], to prevent discriminatory anti-Indian laws. In the next decade [1897-1906] Gandhi's efforts were not to block legislation but to mitigate the hardships by humane implementation of laws that could not be kept out of statute books.

During the ten weeks of his extended stay, a more than willing Gandhi had been prevailed upon by the merchants to take one of the most momentous decisions in his life. The merchants, anxious about their future status and about their stake in the country, realised the value of having an activist like Gandhi in their midst. They had got his departure delayed by a month and now urged Gandhi to stay and guide the community till franchise issue was settled one way or the other.

The question of his maintenance was raised by his patron and Gandhi very firmly and very wisely refused to be paid for public work or out of public funds. This refusal saved Gandhi from many more scandals and calumnies in which his opponents later on sought to involve him. Gandhi contracted his legal services to twenty Indian firms who agreed [July 1894] to pay the retainer fees in advance. Rustomji

Jivanji Ghorkhodu and Dawdji Mahommed were the first to pay him twelve Pounds each.

Gandhi launched his public career on the assured basis of a flourishing practice in Law. Natal had no Indian lawyer and Indians had to depend on Europeans in all legal matters. English language was a barrier between these lawyers and their clients.

Gandhi filled up a long-standing vacuum and began to shine out very soon. He was the only Indian barrister in South Africa and this gave him a chance to prove his talents. He soon monopolised almost the entire Indian clientele. He insisted upon living in style and in a proper locality. "According to my notions of that time, I thought I should live in style usual for barristers and reflecting credit for the community: and that would mean great expenses" [SSA 60] of at least 300 Pounds per year.

Dada Abdulla rented a house at seventy-eight Pounds a year and furnished it. It was a comfortable, two storied, five bedrooms house— Beach Grove Villa—in a posh locality where Harry Escombe, solicitor-general of Natal, was his neighbour. Gandhi maintained an open house crowded with friends and books.

Instead of calling his family, Gandhi brought in his notorious friend Sheikh Mehtab from Rajkot, and put him in charge of his household. There is no way of knowing whether Gandhi called him to Natal or he was there and just came to stay with him as many Indians used to stay with their acquaintances. Most of Indians in Africa did not bring in their families so as to save money and to work for longer hours.

Mehtab abused Gandhi's trust and brought in prostitutes when Gandhi was away either in office or court. An angry, shocked and disillusioned Gandhi threw him out of the house in spite of Mehtab's "threat to expose" him. [Auto Part II chap.XXIII] Gandhi, a very gentle and credulous person, also had a surgical touch in him and he could be very cruel and hardhearted as and when required.

The bargain of legal service against public work was beneficial to both the sides. The Indian community maintained Gandhi in a very comfortable and even a luxurious life style by allotting more and more legal work to him: Gandhi, on his part, devoted all his tremendous energies and his great forensic skills to whole heartedly champion the cause of the community. He was free from all professional worries and was not hampered by the trammels of family life for next two years. He was so fully engrossed in his professional and public activities, that he hardly had any time left for self.

Seeking the professional wings, Gandhi applied to get himself enrolled as an advocate of the Supreme Court of Natal. [September '94] The lawyers, fearing professional competition from a better-qualified Indian barrister and worried about losing Indian clientele, used the Natal Law Society to oppose Gandhi's application.

"It is anomalous that while an attempt is made to disfranchise Indians on the ground that they do not possess the necessary intelligence to vote in elections, an Indian should, in the teeth of opposition of the profession should take his seat as an advocate of the Supreme Court". [Natal Mercury Fatima Mir ed. 146]

The submission of the Law Society was opposed by the Attorney-General Escombe who was the senior legal adviser of the Dada Abdulla & Co. The plea of the Law Society was rejected by the Supreme Court and the Society came in for some well deserved ridicule from the press. Some of the editorials even congratulated Gandhi. [SSA 61]

Gandhi had no money to set himself up. His admission fee and the cost of law books were paid by Dada Abdulla. In almost no time, Gandhi was recognised as one of the best lawyers available in Durban. His political activism brought him in contact with very rich merchants and there never was any dearth of work for Gandhi.

He certainly was the most highly qualified, the most erudite and the most painstaking one. He was an incisive draftsman, and a very persuasive, convincing advocate. He worked very hard to master every detail, never overlooked contrary evidence, never resorted to falsehoods and refused to tutor witnesses. He never indulged into some of the most common unfair practices of the lawyers' trade. He would never knowingly accept a false case, would never enter 'not guilty' plea and would always plead 'extenuating circumstances'. [Milli Polak] He would always attempt settlement rather than litigation and aimed not, at winning the case but in helping law to prevail. He never used legal process to recover his dues from his clients or other debtors. He was an unusual lawyer as he was to become an unusual politician.

He came to enjoy such a formidable reputation for fairness and honesty that railway authorities approached him for arbitrating a dispute between the railway company and 255 coolies and he was thanked by the manager for the amicable settlement of the dispute. His legal practice brought him a huge and ever increasing income that Gandhi spent lavishly on himself, his family, his friends and associates, occasionally throwing quite grand parties.

In spite of being a practicing lawyer and such an outstanding political leader, Gandhi was never an orator and never indulged in rhetoric and theatricals. His low, calm, clear voice and a total absence of any gestures would deeply impress and move any court and any audience.

His instant and brilliant success as a lawyer in South Africa is often posed as a problem. Gandhi's statement about his miserable failure in India in 1892 is accepted at its face value and his performance anxiety and peer pressure have been offered as explanations. But Gandhi was not such a failure as he makes out for himself.

There were so many barristers in India that every barrister, however brilliant and well connected he may be, had to pass through a long waiting period. Gandhi himself advised the new aspirants [Guide to

London] to save some money to pass over such a waiting period. Even in 1902, Gandhi was informed by solicitors that it would take about two years before they can find some work for him.

The cause celebre for Gandhi as a lawyer involved an interpretation of Muslim law of inheritance. Gandhi had drawn up a plan to distribute the intestate property of Hasam Dawji giving a due share thereof to his stepbrother. The Muslim priests insisted on excluding the brother and on spending that portion on religious charities. The high court rejected Gandhi's plan on the ground that Gandhi was a Hindu and therefore he would know nothing of the Muslim law.

A feisty Gandhi tore that verdict to pieces by his critical comments in press. Employing vitriolic sarcasm, he boldly and entirely demolished the ground of himself being a Hindu. [CWMG I 193] The Supreme Court upheld Gandhi's plan as the most reasonable interpretation of Muslim law and entire White press held it to be the most just and proper distribution.

Gandhi's contacts with and his interest in the problems of indentured Indians and his understanding of the same widened and deepened when by a chance, he got professionally involved in a case of an indentured coolie—Balasunderam. The coolie came to Gandhi [June 1895] seeking redress against his employer who had assaulted him and had broken his teeth.

Gandhi enlisted the sympathy of the magistrate and succeeded in securing considerable relief for his client whose indenture was transferred. Gandhi was hailed as the savior of the coolies and thereafter fought several cases on their behalf. The coolies had, up to now, nobody to turn to for fighting against the violence and the injustice perpetrated by their employers. Gandhi was the first and the best lawyer who often rescued them. He provided them free or almost free service and more and more coolies trusted their 'Gandhibhai'. He emerged virtually as a one-man legal aid society for these poor Indians.

Gandhi was soon acknowledged as the most active and even an aggressive leader of his community. The Franchise Law Amendment Bill of 1894 and the resultant controversies had brought out all his latent strength—his infectious activism, his impressive scholarship and his formidable forensic powers cultivated over many years of silence and studies. Gandhi almost overnight flowered into a captainship of great maturity, of innovative strategies and of a persistency that refused to take any defeat as final. The franchise controversy set all his abilities ablaze with dazzling brilliance and Gandhi emerged as a one-man army fighting on three different fronts.

He faced a hostile press, a prejudiced White community and a racist government. He fought, almost single handed against aggressive and active Whites on behalf of a docile, apathetic and disunited community. His quick and labourious footwork exacted a grudging admiration even from the quarters hostile to the Indian community. Natal newspapers wrote several editorials highlighting his great abilities and his energy.

Gandhi kept on an unending barrage of petitions and memorandums directed at administrative and legislative centers of power. He strove incessantly to mould public opinion by a continuous flow of letters, rejoinders and press notes to newspapers, all the while presenting Indian case as well as replying to all the unjust criticisms against the Indian community. He wrote nearly one thousand such letters.

He cultivated the support of eminent Indians like Dadabhai Naoroji and Manchershah Bhavnagree in England. Dadabhai had become an M.P. in 1892 and it was his advice and guidance that Gandhi continuously sought. He was quite aware of the enormity of the task and quite hesitant to get involved. He wrote to Dadabhai Naoroji: "I am yet inexperienced and young and therefore quite liable to commit mistakes. The responsibility undertaken is quite out of proportion to my ability". But "I am the only available person who can handle the question". And so he has "taken this matter up which is quite beyond my ability". He made it clear that he is not doing all this for any pecuniary gain but because "the first session of the Assembly [1896] was largely engaged with anti-Indian legislation". [CWMG I 139-40]

Gandhi was not merely a highly successful professional and a brilliant leader of his community, but also a deeply introspective moralist, an ideologue, a spirit hankering after Truth and Right. He had "a complex mentality which allowed him to think little of his personal comfort and to eschew the shackles of Ego and ambition and not to harbor any resentment and rancor against others". [Hutten 47]

Gandhi had already begun to develop a distinctive personal philosophy and was seeking sublimation of his material needs and cravings. During these three years [1894-97], Gandhi continued an intensive study of Christianity and Hinduism. His close and constant contacts with missionaries of various denominations, his visit to the Trappist monastery of German monks and nuns at the Marian Hill near Durban, [CWMG I 222] his devotion to Evangelical Union, his study of Tolstoy, his correspondence with Raichandbhai, his study of Hindu scriptures and books of philosophy, especially Narmd's Dharmavichar [*Reflections on Religion*]—all these fall within this period.

This was the beginning of his transformation into a believing and practicing Hindu and an ardent seeker after spiritual bliss. He was still far away from ahimsa [non-violence] and satyagraha, but the journey to a higher plane had begun. Gandhi's disillusionment with "the dazzling and the bright surface of modern civilization" and his craving for better life, his fervent faith in Esoteric Christianity and the impact of Theosophy were reflected in letters he wrote to Natal Mercury [CWMG I 169]. Gandhi found "present day materialism and all its splendor to be insufficient for the needs of his soul." ..." the unity and the common source of all the great religions of the world".

He quoted Rev. Pulsford with approval "These [Esoteric] teachings were received from within the astral veil. They are full of compact and concentrated wisdom of Holy Heavens and of God". [CWMG I 191] These letters go a long way to show that Gandhi's *Hind Swaraj* took a long time germinating and that *Hind Swaraj* is rooted more in the Christian mysticism than in Hindu vision of life.

But Gandhi's spiritual quest [1893-1905] did not in any way hinder his public and professional activities and did not diminish his capacity to fight or his ability to drive hard bargains. He was no mystic recluse.

Chapter 9

NATAL INDIAN CONGRESS

G andhi was sharp enough to understand that the fight for Indian cause would be a long-drawn struggle and would need a permanent, strong and well organised political association to sustain the necessary momentum.

All groups of migrants to South Africa-Uitlanders, Irish, Jews etc. had their own associations and permanent organisations. The Indian community too was not totally inert or docile before the arrival of Gandhi. The leaders of the community had been making a few sporadic and ineffective efforts to assert themselves and to register their grievances by presenting petitions to proper authorities. Gandhi was certainly the best, most efficient and most devoted leader, but there were several leaders and groups of Indian community before and after him and quite a few of them were his contemporaries.

The best known of these groups was the Durban Indian Committee formed in 1890. The Committee got a petition "On the Grievances of the British Indians in Natal, South African Republic and the Orange Free State" drawn up by the solicitors Fazalbhoy Vishram of Bombay and got it presented to the governor of Bombay [6-1-91]. The petition was forwarded to the viceroy and copies sent to the colonial secretary, Prime Minister Gladstone, Dadabhai Naoroji and one was sent to the government of Natal too.

The Committee claimed to speak on behalf of 2000 merchants and 100,000 coolies. The petition opposed the granting of autonomy to Natal as "it would do us harm" and the petition also demanded appointment of Indians as magistrates and license inspectors. [Mir Fatima ed.] The committee also got a pamphlet on Indian grievances printed in 1892 and a second pamphlet on the conditions of Indians in Orange Free state. [June 1893]

But the earlier leaders were handicapped by their ignorance of law and English language. Indians in Natal had very poor knowledge of English and even in 1904 hardly 5% of them [5211out of 100918] knew English. Gandhi enjoyed a mastery over the language and was an expert in law.

Gandhi felt an urgent need to organise and strengthen Indian community for political activism and persuaded others about the need for a party. The community felt "the absolute necessity of establishing a permanent institution that would cope with the legislative activity of retrograde nature of the first responsible government of the colony with regard to Indians and to protect Indian interests". [CWMG I 245] "The Congress was formed chiefly by the efforts of Mr. Abdulla Haji Adam". [CWMG I 258]

Such polite attempts to share credits with others camouflage the fact that the party was entirely a brainchild of Gandhi and was always considered by others to be his personal achievement.

It was on 1st July 1894 that a hundred leading members of the community resolved on establishing a permanent political association to protect Indian interests by constitutional methods and to claim franchise as a right of British subjects.

It was decided to utilise the existing but largely dysfunctional Durban Indian Committee. That committee served as a nucleus for the new organization and all the seventy-six members of the Congress who enrolled on the first day were the active members of that Committee. [Fatima Mir Ed P?] "The new political organization was in terms of ideology and leadership, a direct descendent of the Durban Indian Committee". [Swan 50] The name of the new organisation- Natal Indian Congress was deliberately so chosen. "I was a Congress devotee" "and wished to popularize the name in Natal". [SSA /Auto Part II Chap. XIX]

The Natal Indian Congress with its precise and terse constitution and an elaborate formal structure was inaugurated on 22 August 1894 amid the scenes of wild enthusiasm. Abdulla Haji Adam was its president. Gandhi became and remained its general secretary for all the seven years that he was to remain in Natal with a break of one year when he had gone to India in the middle of 1896.

Gandhi made conscious efforts to give a cosmopolitan and composite character to the Congress [CWMG I 338]; but from beginning to the end, the Congress was dominated by Muslim merchants. Seventeen out of its twenty-three vice-presidents were Muslims. The executive committee consisting of all office bearers and thirty-nine ordinary members had only a few Hindus and fewer Christians.

Gandhi intended to make the Congress useful to both Whites and Indians and "a medium of interpretation of feelings of Indians on questions affecting them". [CWMG. I 262] He invited Whites to even join this organisation working for Indian cause. The conciliatory character of Congress party was emphasised in its very first objective "to promote the concord and harmony among Indians and Europeans residing in the colony".

Other objectives were to spread information about Indian history and culture, to inquire into the conditions of Indians and of indentured Indians and to take proper steps to remove their hardships and sufferings, to help the poor and the helpless in every possible way and to work for improving "the moral, social and political conditions of Indians". [CWMG I 162-63]

In an interview to the *Natal Advertiser* [CWMG I 339-40], Gandhi emphasised the twofold approach of Congress party to ventilate the grievances of Indians by petitions and publicity and to work for educational progress of the community. The political activities of the Congress were to be only defensive in nature, to protect the rights of Indians against all discriminations and disabilities. While the Congress did much for the Indian community in political and social fields, it did almost nothing for the educational progress of the community.

Unlike the Congress party in India, the Natal Indian Congress functioned continuously throughout the year; it held monthly and even weekly meetings of its executive committee to scrutinise the accounts and issues. These meetings proved to be "so informative and energizing" that all the ordinary members insisted on attending and participating to the extent that the executive committee became redundant and defunct.

The leaders of Indian community were so enthused that some of them travelled on their own to enroll new members. Before the year was out, the Congress had on its roll 228 members belonging to different religious, linguistic, caste and professional groups. The minimum annual subscription was three Pounds but those who could afford were persuaded into paying as much as they could, ranging all the way from seven Pounds to twenty-five Pounds.

Such a heavy subscription kept Indian labour out of portals of the party and it certainly kept all riff raff away. Gandhi had a tough time collecting subscriptions—promises to pay were often not kept and nearly half the members never paid anything. The N. I. C. was always an elite group and it never became a mass organization. Eighty-five percent of members were merchants while the white-collar workers formed twelve percent of its membership. [Swan]

Gandhi at this time had a great admiration for everything English and he insisted that all members of Congress must be able to read, write and speak English though this was easier said than done.

The party soon degenerated into a costly club meant only for the rich elite amongst Indians. "Whatever the Congress may have been in theory, in practice it operated like a very small private club". [Swan 54]

At the end of the first year of its existence, the party had a balance of 616 Pounds [CWMG I 247] "a net financial result which puts to shame the pecuniary support usually accorded to political associations of Europeans in South Africa." [Natal Mercury.]

Natal Indian Congress shifted [22-6-95] to rented office premises and by 1896 worked from a bigger office with a spacious hall. Gandhi had more ambitious plans and called for a special fund of 4000 Pounds so that the party can expand its activities. Gandhi promised to try and bring over "a number of good Indian lawyers" to Natal. [CWMG I 259] The call for funds was deliberately and widely misinterpreted by the White press as a plan to induce larger number of lawyers from India by offering money to them.

In May 1896, Congress purchased its own property worth 1080 Pounds and rented out a part of it at 10/- Pounds per month to secure funds for its running expenses. The Congress hall was a venue for political, social and cultural activities of Indian community and this building was used as a shelter for Indian refugees during Boer war.

The Natal Indian Congress under the stewardship of Gandhi emerged within two years as the richest and most highly organised political party in South Africa. It soon had 11 branches in Natal, though most of them were mere shadows and its members were concentrated only in the city of Durban. Similar organisations sprang up in Cape Colony and Transvaal.

The Natal Congress became a focal point of public life for Indians handling political issues, organising social functions and religious festivals. The associated bodies of the Congress-Natal Indian Education Association, [1894] and the C.M. School gave scholarships for English education, arranged debating competitions etc. It organised and maintained a small library—the Diamond Jubilee Library [1897] with about 200 books almost all of them gifted by others. "It is painful to report that the library has not been as successful in its career as was its opening". said Gandhi. [CWMG III 126]

The Congress also helped in establishing [14-9-98] and nurturing a small hospital—St. Adian Hospital under Dr. Booth to which Rustomji gave a generous donation. It was this hospital that roused Gandhi's interest in servicing the sick. For about a year, Gandhi served there for two hours every day as a medical assistant dispensing medicines and also as a social service counsellor. He picked up considerable expertise in medicine and nursing. This was his first experience of rendering medical service to persons who were not members of his family.

Congress spent a lot of money on publicity. It printed and distributed 7000 copies of Gandhi's 'Indian franchise: an appeal to every Briton' and spent about 100/- Pounds for preparing and forwarding the memorandum to the colonial secretary in 1897.

Congress was a pulsating publicity organisation and between 1894 and 1899, nearly 20,000 copies of various pamphlets, memorandums and open letters written by Gandhi were circulated on various occasions. Congress also paid traveling expenses of Mansukhlal Nazar who was sent to present its views at Colonial Premiers' Conference at London. [December 1896] Congress leaders toyed with the idea of starting a newspaper. [Swan.] No other political party had been able to do as much work as Natal Congress did under Gandhi's guidance.

Congress and more especially Gandhi soon became a center of admiration and envy of European community. Congress was mentioned in the debates of Natal Assembly [1896] as "the strong organization at the head of which stands a capable, energetic and ambitious man— Mr. Gandhi".

The formation of Natal Indian Congress roused the most horrifying suspicions and fears among Whites—all the more so because launching and organisational details of Congress were never published. It was a virile and an affluent organisation capable of fighting back, but it deliberately kept away from undue and unnecessary press publicity. It carried on active press campaigns for Indian cause, not in the name of the party but in the name of its prominent leaders.

Congress limited its activity to oppose racial discrimination. "The object of the Congress is to resist degradation, not to gain political power". "Its leaders have no intention to endeavor to place a single Indian on the Voters' list" [CWMG I 326-7] Gandhi firmly refused to be a voter. "I do not aspire to parliamentary honors whatsoever...Those who know me personally know well, in what direction my ambitions lie." He promised that "Natal Indian Congress would not sponsor any single candidate". [CWMG II 246]

Gandhi repeated this argument in an interview he gave to *Natal Mercury*. [May 1896] Indians have never tried to capture political power in any other colony of British Empire. Gandhi actively discouraged Indians from enrolling themselves voters as during the time when the bill to disfranchise Indians was pending with the Colonial office. This proved to be a serious strategic mistake.

The existence of Natal Indian Congress was first publicly mentioned in the infamous perjury case—Regina Vs. Ramaswamsi Padayachi. [September-October 1895] It was a minor case of scuffle and assault. Padayachi—a member of the Congress executive was accused of having pressurised a witness to give false evidence. All the three persons involved in the case were Congress leaders and the scene of action was Congress office. But it was the case of individuals acting in their personal capacities and not on behalf of Congress as an organisation. The episode had nothing to do with Congress as such and Gandhi was not involved either as a congressman or as a lawyer.

However, the resident magistrate of Durban in his verdict referred to Congress being "of the nature of an association of conspiracy, pernicious and fraught with danger to the whole community in this colony of whatever race".

The press picked up the refrain. The *Natal Observer* described the Congress as 'a clandestine organization'. "It has been quite through an accident that the existence of Natal Indian Congress has been discovered".

Gandhi in his capacity as a general secretary appealed to the Supreme Court to expunge the remarks of the magistrate: his appeal was upheld because "there is not even a particle of evidence" and the remarks would be "a miscarriage of Justice". [27-11-95.]

Meanwhile, Gandhi had taken on the press. Natal Advertiser had commented that if Congress could be proved to have resorted to wrong and pernicious practices, a swift and decisive punishment would be justified. Gandhi immediately and wholeheartedly agreed. "If Congress has attempted, even in an indirect manner to temper with a witness, it will certainly deserve suppression". [CWMG I 260] Gandhi pointed out that "Congress was a perfectly lawful and open organization and there is nothing sinister or conspiratorial about it".

The existence of Congress was never kept a secret from the press. But there were no press announcements because "its organizers were not and are not sure of its permanent existence...and therefore thought it prudent to let time alone to bring it to the public notice". [CWMG I 257] "The Congress has not as yet made itself known to the public because it was thought advisable not to do so unless it was assured of permanent existence. It has worked very quietly". [CWMG I 250]

The White press denounced Congress as a gang of conspirators extorting money from the Indians to fight against the government and of exciting coolies against their employers. Gandhi himself was accused of exacting money from coolies and from merchants, of misusing Congress funds for personal purposes, and of draining Congress coffers by drawing a monthly salary of 300 Pounds for working as its secretary. Gandhi duly replied to such calumnies with convincing clarifications.

Such accusations and charges in the press reflected the fears and misgivings felt by the Whites at the emergence of a powerful and organised party as a shield for Indian community; but more sober and wiser evaluations were not entirely absent. "It [Congress] shows that the time has passed when the child of India will be content to remain …in a position of servile dependence upon those to whom he owes his presence in this part of the Empire. He claims to have arrived at the age of discretion when his political and social aspirations should be recognized. …We have to reckon with the Indian society as one of the upcoming forces in this country. …To affect to ignore its existence would be a folly. …Mr. Gandhi's followers are capable of being a power for the good or for the evil and the prudent politicians will not fail to take notice of them". [*Cape Times* Payne 489]

The Whites continued to display a hostile attitude towards the Congress and the prime minister's remarks in the Assembly represented that attitude. "There is in this country a powerful body—a very powerful body, in a way a very united body though a practically secret body—Natal Indian Congress. It is a body which possesses large funds; it is a body presided over by a very able, a very active man—Gandhi: a body, the avowed object of which is to exercise a strong political power in the affairs of this colony". [Natal Assembly debates 14-5-96] Other speakers also were equally scared of Gandhi and his Congress.

A lynx-eyed Gandhi did not allow such calumny to pass unchallenged and he very strongly protested against the charge of secrecy levelled by prime minister. He insisted in a letter to prime minister that Congress was a lawful association and there was nothing secret or sinister about it. Its monthly meetings were open to all its members and to a few invitees who included Europeans. Congress does not hanker after publicity. "It has preferred to keep its own counsel until the society has found its own legs".

Gandhi's strong protest forced prime minister to withdraw his charge of secrecy and he was generous enough to publicly apologise for his remarks. Such courtsey led to a life long friendship between the two stalwarts. Gandhi wrote a very friendly letter to Sir Robinson [29-4-02] from India. When Robinson died, Gandhi wrote a moving obituary for him in *Indian Opinion*.

The Congress was denounced also as a subversive body fomenting discontent among the natives. The possibility of such misunderstanding might have been one of the reasons why a wise and cautious Gandhi scrupulously avoided all contacts with blacks. The prejudices against blacks that Gandhi shared with other Indians might have been thus reinforced by strong political considerations.

But Natal Indian Congress was neither as strong, nor as united as it appeared to be to its friends and foes. Gandhi's premonition about its long-term existence proved to be true and the party started dying after a year or two. Within less than five years i.e. by 1899, Congress was a moribund, if not a dead body.

Apart from incompatible class interests, Congress was ravaged by all the pluralities of Indian society. Gandhi had enough and more trouble collecting subscriptions; the attendance at monthly meetings was poor and painfully unpunctual. There were quarrels about the issue of cheques and who would sign them showing thereby mutual suspicions and distrust. At one time these differences threatened the very existence of Congress.

Gandhi remained the general secretary for seven years but there was a rapid flux of other office bearers as prominent Indians left either for

India or for other colonies. Gandhi struggled hard and long to nourish and strengthen the organisation but it was a divided house and rapidly fell apart.

The intense factionalism raised [June 1897] its ugly head on a trivial issue of presenting an address to Adamji Miyakhan, the retiring secretary who was returning to India and Gandhi could secure only a meager majority in his favor. Adamji "left for India unthanked and unhonoured" [CWMG III 127] though Gandhi personally hosted a party for him.

Congress continued to exist somehow and participated in Diamond Jubilee celebrations as well as in promotion of non-political activities till Gandhi was about to leave for India after the Boer war.

There are only two reports by Gandhi to the Congress party—1895 and 1899 and both are very factual and quite critical about the functioning of the party. The second report is only a draft and it is a very depressive document. "The fiery enthusiasm seems to have died out".[CWMG III-116] There was neither attendance nor any collection of dues and "it is difficult to form even the quorum at the Congress meetings". [CWMG III 130]

By 1899 "the outlook for Congress was gloomy as far as the internal working of Congress is concerned" because "there is no enthusiasm left for party work". [CWMG III-131] only 37 out of its 300 members paid the dues and Congress had no funds to pay off a debt of 300/400 Pounds. Gandhi explained this decline by mentioning that "The Indian community was facing serious political troubles in midst of all pervading gloom and had suffered most intensely from the ravages of Boer war".

Gandhi himself was not spared by the party elite and in 1899 report he had to defend himself against the criticism that it was his agitation and his strategy that were responsible for recrudescence of anti Indian fury in Natal. "It has been said that if we had not started the movement to obtain redress, our position might not have been so bad as it now is". Gandhi pointed to the situation in Orange and Transvaal where there was no agitation and yet the position of Indians was much worse than in Natal. [CWMG III 124]

The occasion of presenting an address to the Duke of York [Aug 1901] brought a rift in the party. Gandhi presided over a protest meeting that strongly disapproved the choice of only Musalmans for presentation ceremony, even though there were a large number of non-Muslims. But this protest was disregarded by Muslims leaders.

Even such a moribund and bankrupt Congress defrayed the travelling and office expenses of Gandhi for the promotion of African cause during his short stay in India [1902]. [CWMG III 305] No funds were collected after 1903 and the party was but a shadow by 1908.

Gandhi continued to take active interest in the party affairs even though he was in Transvaal after 1903. By 1907 the colonial born, second generation Hindus were dissatisfied with domination of Muslim merchants in Congress and wanted to form a new body. [1-1-07] Gandhi advised restraint. "To those who feel aggrieved at not being able to figure prominently in the work of Congress we strongly advise to steer clear of any movement that would bring about discord ... the entire community will suffer". [CWMG VI 291] Gandhi suspected "There must be some White person behind all this... Whites are very anxious to create dissentions among Indians". [ibid 298] Gandhi strongly advised the leaders of the Congress to get associated with the problems of indentured labor. [CWMG VII 40] But his advice was not followed. Congress turned a deaf ear to Gandhi's repeated pleas for funds to support satyagraha movements in Transvaal. The end came in 1913.

At a mass meeting called by Gandhi at Durban [19-10-13] to seek Congress support to the impending Satyagraha, Gandhi was severely denounced. The *Daily Rand Mail* reported that the dominant section of mercantile community held Gandhi responsible for leading the community into trouble. His work during the last twenty years was "not only worthless but was highly injurious to the community leading to deterioration of race relations with the resultant loss of rights and opportunities for Indians". The importance given by Gandhi to Polak and Ritch was intensely resented.

The meeting had to be hastily terminated and a small group of Gandhi's supporters formed Natal Indian Association thus splitting the party that Gandhi had formed and nourished since 1894. Gandhi expressed the hope that "the most reasonable and peaceful Indians would join the new body". [CWMG XI 246]

Gandhi's appeal to Natal Indian Congress to keep away from Solomon Commission was rejected by Congress leaders and Gandhi poured scorn on them for giving false and foolish evidence before the commission. {CWMG XII 345} Gandhi in a letter to Gokhale derided 'only about 100 pseudo leaders of Congress who are not important at all and who are anti-movement people'. "Indians support me."

The Natal Indian Congress functioned as an active organisation only for two or three years, but it provided a model and an inspiration for the African leaders who adopted its organization and its line of action. South Africa Native National Congress [1912] or Nelson Mandela's South African National Congress [1923] has preserved the name of Congress in South Africa.

Chapter 10

THE APPRENTICE

Gandhi soon grew beyond Congress and beyond Natal emerging as a champion of Indian cause all over South Africa. From the very outset, Gandhi had sought to widen his horizons and the focus of his writings and activities cover and involve the entire Indian community. "The breadth of Gandhi's concern and the complexities of his self appointed task of winning the dignity and respect for his fellow countrymen", [Hutt 98] from the very outset of his career, ought to be constantly kept in view.

He kept up an unceasing stream of correspondence with the governing authorities in Natal, Transvaal, England and India as also with the press besides writing letters to Dadabhai Naroroji and other friends of India in England. He was engrossed in petitions, test cases, and protests whenever Indian interests were adversely affected. He carried on a dogged struggle against administrative misuse of power even though the situation was hopeless and was ever getting more so.

Apart from major issues like franchise and immigration, Gandhi carried on a ceaseless fight against discriminatory laws that inflicted indignities on his fellow Indians e.g. the misuse of vagrancy law as applied to Indians. He would enter strong protests whenever respectable and educated Indians were arrested and locked up by police under this law.

Gandhi very soon began to take interest in Transvaal because most of his clients had huge financial interests there. After a prolonged correspondence between Britain and Transvaal authorities, the infamous Act no.3 of 1885 [denying property rights to Indians and enforcing compulsory trade and residence only in locations for them] had been referred to for arbitration. In April 1895, a judge of Supreme Court of Orange F. S. gave his award of arbitration [Bloemfontein award] upholding the validity of law but leaving all controversial issues to be settled by courts in Transvaal.

Gandhi submitted a strong protest against the award. His memorandum requesting rejection of the award was submitted to the colonial secretary [5 May 1895] with 1000 signatures. Gandhi's great expertise in law enabled him to challenge the legal validity of the award as it had violated the terms of reference.

He claimed for Indians the rights of British citizens who were culturally superior to the Africans. He pointed out that Indians already had huge vested interest to the tune of 1,00,000/- Pounds and that the Pretoria and London conventions enjoined equal treatment to *all* British subjects.

Since locations were to be enforced only on sanitary grounds, Gandhi collected several certificates from Dutch and British citizens. Three doctors, thirty-five merchants and bankers, innumerable burghers and European residents of Transvaal certified about sanitary habits and health of Indians, their creditworthiness and honesty and abilities and about their compatibility with European society.

Gandhi pointed out that continuous oppression "cannot but degenerate [Indians] so much from their civilized habits. Indians may be forced to adopt the customs, habits and thoughts of African natives".

The memorandum to the colonial secretary was followed up by an appeal to the Viceroy of India for succour and protection. But all was in vain because Gandhi's protest note reached England on 24th June 1895 but the award had been accepted only two days before. Britain had to accept the award in its entirety.

The *London Times* was upset with the award. "Are Her Majesty's Indian subjects to be treated as a degraded and outcaste race by a friendly government". [May '95] Dadabhai Naoroji led a delegation to Chamberlain [29 August 1895] who regretted that while Natal and Cape were autonomous colonies, Transvaal and Orange F. S. were independent republics and Britain was bound by the award.

But this award could not be implemented by government of Transvaal till 1902 because British officers on spot actively and continuously helped Indians to defy the legal notices issued by Kruguer ministry.

When Transvaal exempted British citizens from military service but excluded Indians from that facility, Gandhi protested [26-11-95] against such an unnecessary affront to Indians and pointed out that Indians do not have even the human rights in Transvaal and were treated as "a little more than chattels". [CWMG I 265]

In Zululand, then a British colony, building sites in a new township were reserved [1895] only for the Europeans and non-Europeans were excluded from applying for land ownership. Indians insisted on entering the bid for government plots. Gandhi jumped into the fray. "We have been fighting the battle of these Indians in the Dutch Republics and now the British government seeks to impose such restrictions on them in a purely crown colony". Gandhi carried on the campaign against the ordinance till it was rescinded by Britain. [February-March 1896]

He strongly protested every time that insults and indignities were heaped upon the Indians and quoted press reports to prove that the real reason for anti-Indianism was trade rivalry and jealousy. He always insisted that the status of Indians was an Imperial question and hence within the purview of colonial office. Gandhi's language was always polite and parliamentary but his furious and forthright denunciation of White community often contained several barbed phrases.

While fighting with grit and doggedness for the rights and status of Indians, Gandhi was never blind to the defects and shortcomings of his own community. His habit of self-analysis and self-criticism revealed to him the drawbacks and blemishes of Indians.

Indians were being denounced by Europeans for their dirty habits, insanitary lifestyle, their lack of decorum and discipline, their unpunctuality, neglect of education and their false economy of living in hovels and often residing and trading from the same premises.

Gandhi accepted the validity of such criticisms and joined Europeans in making very severe critical remarks about such defects. "Indians have so many blemishes and they are themselves, no doubt to be blamed to some extent for the present unsatisfactory state of feelings between the two communities". [CWMG I 286]

He was aware of very low level of Indian life style and "fought hard to improve the stereotyped image of Indians in the mind of Whites". [Chandran 282] He very strongly and almost continuously insisted on urgent and thorough reforms in domestic sanitation, personal hygiene, punctuality, for separation of residential quarters from business premises, and for comfortable life style.

From his very first meeting and his first speech in Pretoria [1893] "he was not only the staunchest champion of Natal Indians but also their very severe critic". [Nanda 46] His efforts to nag and improve Indian life style were resented and often made him quite unpopular.

Gandhi's insistence on cleanliness and punctuality can be dated from South Africa on account of such intense and long crusade. He stuck to his sophisticated life style and was always a well dressed, clean, sober and exactly punctual person. He insisted upon social and hygienic reforms as an indispensable prerequisite for public and political activities.

Up to 1903, Gandhi was very keen and enthusiastic about educating all Indians in English and western type of schools. He laboured hard to promote education and continuously urged his companions and co-workers to get educated in English. The Indian children were not admitted in public schools in South Africa and church schools were neither very proper, nor very popular with Indians. Government grants to private Indian schools were very meager. Gandhi therefore promoted Natal Indian Education Society for the children of the merchants and free labour.

While devoting his tremendous energies to all such public and political activities including social reforms and building up of Congress organisation, Gandhi also concentrated on his profession and gradually built up a roaring legal practice taking all the while public activities in his stride. He successfully dovetailed the professional and public activities but it was the profession that claimed most of his energies and much of his time up to 1906.

It is a measure of his titanic energies that he was simultaneously an immensely successful professional, a vocal and assertive political leader defending Indians from humiliations and fighting against their internal deficiencies. All these time-consuming preoccupations were never allowed to retard or delay his personal enlightenment and spiritual progress.

The most important and the most crucial issue for Gandhi and Indian community in Natal was the fate of franchise controversy. The Indian petition to the colonial secretary was the most challenging and embarrassing shot that put British authorities squarely on the horns of a dilemma. "The whole subject is perhaps the most difficult we have had to deal with. The colonies wish to exclude the Indians from spreading themselves all over the Empire. If we agree, we are likely to forfeit the loyalty of Indians. If we do not agree, we forfeit the loyalty of the colonies". [Hutten 69]

Disfranchisement was an affront to India and would certainly cause dangerous repercussions in India. But there was also a fear of "a union against us of the whole of South Africa over a political question and all other Colonies and States would also join it, if franchise for Indians is insisted upon".

It took the colonial office about ten months to arrive at a decision. While the petition was pending with the Colonial Office, [July 1894 to April 1895] the White press, dismayed by the outburst of Indian activism carried on a virulent campaign against Indian community in general and against Gandhi in particular.

The delay in approving disfranchisement Act by the Colonial Office was condemned by the Whites in Natal and Britain was accused of culpable negligence and of contemptible weakness. The disallowance of the bill was equated with the government by coolies in Natal and European leaders threatened to pass the same law again and again till it was approved.

"The question at issue really is whether Natal is to be governed in future by persons of European descent or whether persons of Asiatic descent are allowed a decisive voice in the government of the colony. The public opinion in Natal conceives that there is only one reply to the question and that it can best be answered by this law". [Gov. to Colonial Sec.]

As the days dragged by, European leaders became more and more fidgety and unleashed a campaign against the possibility of Royal disapproval. There was a mutinous air in Natal. "The White men should never consent to meet the blacks at the ballot box". [*Times of Natal* 4-9-95 Swan]

Gandhi was quite aware of this sullen and even a vicious mood that was developing all around and tried to mitigate the rancor by addressing

[December 1894] a long letter to all legislators of Natal who were bent upon disfranchising Indians: he sought to present Indian side and tried to reason with the opponents by marshalling forth facts and figures about the Indian problem.

He assured the legislators that his aim was only "to bring about a better understanding between European section of the community and Indians in this colony". Conceding that the agitation in England would be futile unless the local opinion is cultivated, Gandhi presented his case on four major counts.

Indians were hated and despised by average European "who hates him, curses him, spits upon him and often pushes him off... The press can not find a sufficiently strong word in the best of English dictionary to damn him with". [CWMG I 185] Gandhi described the privations of Indian community in all its vivid and horrible details.

He expressed his resentment that Indians were called Coolies and argued that only Europeans in the colony can accord better treatment to them. It would not be possible to oust Indians because driving them would ultimately harm and ruin Natal and it was impossible to root them out. Indian labour was indispensable and they have made Natal a golden colony in comparison to Transvaal which is 'a desert of dust.' If Indians were to be allowed to stay, they ought to be given humane treatment.

"Is the treatment given to Indians just or human or Christian or in accordance with the British traditions"? Policy regarding Indians "was not in consonance with the principles of Christianity". Accepting that Indians had very unsanitary habits and they were very often untruthful, he appealed to the Europeans to "raise Indians with them rather than rise on their ruins".

More than half of this letter was devoted to a scholarly description of India's cultural and mundane achievements and to claim that Indians and Anglo-Saxons belonged to the same stock. Gandhi deeply regretted that "Indian is being dragged down to the position of a raw Kafir". [CWMG I 177]

Even though much of the material and even the quotes in the letter are same as in the petition to colonial secretary, Gandhi's erudition and presentation is both dignified and impressive

Gandhi's effort to reach out to Europeans who were sympathetic to Indian cause or those who could be persuaded to do justice to them was a miserable failure because there was no response to this elaborate exercise. On the contrary, Gandhi was denounced by the leaders of the White community as an agitator making money out of public work and inciting Indians against government.

Dislike and hatred for Gandhi were mixed with envy and admiration for his ability and his personality. In fact he was more admired than hated. Gandhi was a superb advocate of his cause. He had a thorough grasp of every detail and kept himself up to date so as to quote the latest press reports and government documents.

His great industry, his sharp wits and his erudition enabled him to rebut every false charge and he would never allow any single accusation to go un-refuted. He was a formidable fighter and would not allow any grass to grow under his feet. He was better educated and had a better command over English language than most of his opponents. He was a tireless and enthusiastic crusader more or less free from professional worries and family entanglements.

The White press was fair enough to publish Gandhi's rejoinders and refutations even when the press was needled and upset by Gandhi's frequent and strongly worded diatribes about Christian spirit. Gandhi knew more of the Bible and about Christian philosophy than Christian journalists. In any battle of wits, an unflappable Gandhi proved to be much stronger and better equipped than all his opponents. "There are Indians here, like Mr. Gandhi, for instance who have come to stay in the colony and who are more capable than any Englishman of exercising their vote in an intelligent and patriotic manner". [*Natal Mercury* 19-11-95]

By January 1895, there were press reports about a likelihood of the Act being disapproved. After a long and frustrating delay, the colonial secretary decided [April 1895] to withhold royal assent to the Franchise Law Amendment Act of 1894. It was not an easy decision. But ultimately India weighed more and turned the scale.

The dispatch argued that Indians *were* British subjects and "all subjects of Her Majesty have an equal right to settle and earn livelihood anywhere in the Empire" and that no privilege could be denied to them on the ground of racial discrimination.

"To deprive a person of his privileges blatantly and openly because of his color is repugnant to the spirit of freedom and fair dealing which the entire British Empire and not merely British Isles plumes itself upon. ... The measures of such nature ... draw no distinction between aliens and Her Majesty's subjects or between the most enlightened and the most ignorant of natives of India. Such Indians are voters in England and are even elected to parliament.

"To assent to this measure would be to put an affront to the people of India such as no British government could be a party to. ... The basic principle of the British Empire is that no subject can be deprived of any right on the ground of race or religion". [Hutten P ?]

The decision withholding Royal approval of 1894 Act vindicated the stand taken by Gandhi and was a resounding victory for Gandhi and Indian community. It sent his score skyrocketing amongst Indian community to a height that was never surpassed thereafter. This is the climax of his popularity in Natal. With a single stroke, Gandhi emerged as the tallest stalwart who single handedly could checkmate entire European community as also the Assembly and government of the colony.

But this tremendous success proved to be a mere temporary respite because it scared the Whites and in the long run proved to be a pyrrhic victory, which was the undoing of the Indian interests in Africa. The decision of British authorities evoked immense enthusiasm in India and sympathy in England; but in Natal it roused all the low-lying racial hatreds and worsened the situation.

Gandhi, on behalf of Indian community, had disclaimed any aspiration for political power; but franchise *is* the most potent lever to power. The petition was a positive proof that there was a large number of Indian migrants who might be or become qualified for franchise and who were assertive enough to demand the retention of their legal right to get into the political arena. The collection of so many signatures in such a short time might have caused a boomerang effect. Gandhi's intense agitation and his success in getting the act vetoed had brought Indian question into a sharp focus.

The successful thwarting of the franchise act had excited racial antagonism and all that Gandhi did or said failed to heal the wounds or even assuage the exasperation of the dominant community of Whites because their ego was hurt. There was a fear that all enfranchised Indians would vote as a block because minorities often do so. The Europeans had hardly ten thousand votes and if the demand for franchise by more than nine thousand Indian signatories were to be conceded, Indians there and then would emerge as the most significant sector of the ruling elite.

But they did not so emerge. Gandhi and the Indian community refrained from enrolling themselves when it was possible for them to do so. They held back their fire and left the field free for their tormentors who soon returned to another and more ingenuous assault with a redoubled determination not to fail this time.

The vote might have empowered the Indian community to safeguard their interests by the White leaders eager to utilise them as the vote bank. But Gandhi argued that the mass enrolment of qualified Indians as voters would further exasperate racial hatreds and would prove to be more dangerous for the helpless minority that Indians were. Most of the rich Indians were the birds of passage and would lose franchise on residency grounds.

Asking for franchise and then keeping away and out of voters' list was a serious mistake of strategy. Gandhi, in 1894, lacked the experience to realise that in a modern state, those excluded from franchise, are excluded from all the benefits. Gandhi did realise his mistake. "The experience in Natal shows that disfranchisement of a class in a community enjoying self government means its complete effacement". [CWMG V 198] After 1910, Gandhi repeatedly regretted that Indians had no voice in the choice of legislators.

As a gesture of conciliation and reasonableness, Gandhi wrote [December 1895] a public letter to all Britons in Natal appealing to their British sense of justice and fair play and appealing to them to do their duty as clergymen, journalists, educators, merchants, lawyers and public servants. This was an appeal addressed to the better side of the dominant community.

Since "the question of Indian franchise has convulsed the whole colony, indeed the whole of South Africa", [CWMG I 266] Gandhi selected six major points of criticism of Indian agitation and answered each one of them. Gandhi raised issues that he considered to be the core of misunderstanding between Europeans and Indians and urged his addressees to do justice.

Claiming that his object was "to serve India, my native country and to bring about better understanding between European section of the community and Indians in this colony" [CWMG I 270], Gandhi appealed to all Englishmen "to unite Europeans and Indians and not to divide them".

He asserted that Indians do enjoy limited franchise and occupy high positions in judiciary and administration in India. To the criticism that Indians in Africa did not represent the best of Indian society, he boldly rebutted that "If the Indian community in Natal is not, nor is the European community here drawn from the higher classes". [CWMG I 269]

"Everyone I have met with in the colony dwelt upon the untruthfulness of the Indians" [CWMG I 183] The Whites considered Indians dirty, stingy, corrupt and confirmed liars. Gandhi conceded that these accusations were largely true and urged in defense the uncongenial surroundings, the fear of Whites who trouble, insult and assault Indians at every step and the difficulties of language. Gandhi asserted that if Indians were dirty and sick, so would be Europeans living under similar conditions. Coolies lack the moral and religious instruction and lying becomes a habit and a disease with them. Indentured labour does lie, but other Indians do not do so. The Indians in fact, were highly trusted by European businessmen and banks as honest and reliable.

He insisted that persistent indifference and retrogressive legislation would degrade Indians still further. "Shunned, despised and cursed, he will only do and be what others in similar positions have done and been". [ibid 269]

Indians were a highly apolitical community. Gandhi sought to dispel the fear of Indian votes swamping European votes by an elaborately detailed and academic analysis presenting a socio-economic profile of Indian voters in the colony and emphasised that only 251 Indians possessed the franchise as against 9309 European voters.

Gandhi was not for adult franchise and declared "no Indian will take exception to a reasonable and real educational qualifications and a larger property qualification than at present". [CWMG I 279] But he insisted "Indians do and would protest against... color distinction-disqualification based on account of racial distinction". [ibid 279]

He assured his readers that "the object of every right minded Indian was to fall in line with the wishes of European colonists as far as possible". Indians are not asking for a new privilege. Indians have the franchise in Natal. "An attempt is now being made to disfranchise him" Gandhi's statements that 'Indians as a rule do not actively meddle with politics' or that 'they have never tried to usurp political power' or that 'their religion teaches them indifference to mundane pursuits' would sound hollow from a leader who was so strenuously trying to retain a potent political privilege for his community.

Gandhi made a weird statement that the demand for franchise was "…no political agitation in the real sense of the term. But an attempt is … being made by the Press to father as it were such an agitation upon Indians". His defense was that "had not an attempt be made to tread upon their commercial pursuits, had not an attempt been made and repeated to degrade them to the condition of the pariah of society, had not an attempt been made to keep them for ever 'hewers of wood and drawers of water' … there would have been no franchise agitation".

To the argument that the country had been opened up by blood and sweat of Europeans and that Indians have no right to share it, Gandhi retorted that Europeans of several other nations also have done nothing in the matter and yet they are admitted to all privileges. He denounced the attempts to divide Indians and to put one against the other and to rouse Hindus against Muslims as 'the most mischievous'.

Indians were being treated as if they were intruders, but Indian labour had been the cause of the Colony's prosperity and Gandhi quoted several authorities and official reports to show that the Colony did not have enough coolies and still needed more of Indians. Driving Indians out of the colony being impossible, the only alternative was better relations between Whites and Indians.

The treatment given to Indians in South Africa would determine India's relations with Britain. "India belongs to Britain and England does not wish to lose her hold on India". The Indians were quite ready and even eager to adjust to the wishes of Whites as far as possible.

Barrister Gandhi in Johannesburg

Gandhi in Mumbai, 1914

With Gokhale at Phoenix farm

Gandhi addressing a public meeting, 1912

Women satyagrahis led by Kallenbauch

Members of Tolstoy farm

Count Leo Tolstoy

Ruskin

Laxmidas

Arrested at Palmford

Office staff of Attorney M K Gandhi, Johannesburg

Released

The mighty pen

As loyal and law abiding subjects Indians must get equal rights and equal treatment and their protest was only against racial discrimination. Their number in Africa was never going to increase because "many come every week and an equal number leave for India. As a rule the incoming ones take the place of the outgoings". [CWMG I-277]

He ended by mentioning the ties between India and England and exhorted that "your duty as Britons and as leaders of public opinion can not be to divide the two communities [Indians and Europeans] but to weld them together and to oppose the policy which is repugnant to British constitution, British sense of justice and fair play and above all hateful to the spirit of Christianity". He closed his letter by declaring "it is not the political power that Indians want. It is the degradation, it is the many other consequences and measures that will flow from and will be based upon that they dread and resist".

Gandhi in this letter chose to minimise or even to overlook the issues of racial hatred and trade rivalry. He even went on to the extent that trade rivalry is beneficial to White consumers who get the benefit of free market and goods that are better and cheaper. Indians do need a lot of improvement and should be helped to become better members of African society.

Seven thousand copies of this appeal to every Briton [Dec.'95] were printed and were widely distributed to the friends of India in England. The London Times wrote a special article on it and extended full support to the plea made by Gandhi.

But this effort was an exercise in futility. Gandhi was refuting the arguments put forward by White leaders but these arguments were a mere façade hiding the real hard core of racial prejudices and commercial rivalry at the grassroot level.

The White community and the government of Natal were stunned by the refusal of the Colonial Office to approve 1894 bill disfranchising Indians. The Natal government responded to the challenge by bringing forward a series of well planned anti-Indian measures forcing Gandhi to carry on a strenuous but futile struggle against them during the next five years of his stay in Natal.

The first such measure was a new disfranchisement bill. The Act 25 of 1894 was repealed to avoid a formal veto. A new Franchise Bill was introduced [March 1896] after securing prior consent of the Colonial Office to accept any measure to disfranchise Indians without naming them.

The franchise was granted to persons of European descent: non-Europeans "who are the natives or descendents ...of the natives of countries which have not...possessed elective parliamentary institutions...could not vote in parliamentary elections". [Natal Act 8 of 1896] The voters already on the list were to continue and the governor was empowered to grant franchise to suitable aliens.

Indians would lose franchise not on the basis of colour or country of origin but because of the lack of democratic institutions in India. The act avoided racial terminology through this was a mere exercise in semantics. It would get immediately approved as there were no grounds to withhold the royal approval. The Act did affect the rights of resident Indians. The Government of India registered its protest but it had no power of interference in colonial affairs.

Gandhi in his memorandum to the Assembly [April '96] pointed out the discriminatory nature of the bill since European migrants from non-democratic countries were granted franchise. He insisted that Indians had age old panchayats that were democratic and 'virtually' representative in their nature. Moreover, after 1888 Indians in all the major urban centers were exercising municipal franchise and had a representative system. The representative institutions had been introduced in the British provinces by Indian Councils Act of 1891.

Gandhi's presentations were factually invalid. The panchayats were neither elective nor representative and the Indian Councils under the

Act of 1891 were most certainly *not* elective bodies; the municipalities were administrative and not political assemblies. Gandhi had to concede that "in the popular sense of the term, we have no such institutions but in law, the Indian Councils can be considered to be such". Chamberlain, the colonial secretary was more correct than Gandhi when he declared: "India does not have and never had any elective representative institutions". [12-10-1895]

Gandhi urged strongly against "the vagueness and ambiguity [in the act which] are very undesirable and are fair neither to European community nor Indians...[and] the state of suspense which is painful to the latter". [CWMG I 316] He insisted that the fear of Indian vote swamping the European one is purely imaginary and pointed out that during the pending of disfranchisement act, not a single Indian have had his name placed on the voters' roll.

In the memorandum submitted to the colonial secretary, Chamberlain, Gandhi was more forthright and condemnatory. He very strongly criticised the prior approval granted by the Colonial Office. He repeated his argument that not a single Indian name was added to the voters' roll when the previous act was pending with the colonial office. He argued that rights and privileges of Indians as British subjects and the equality of treatment promised in 1858 Proclamation were far more important than the franchise in Natal.

Gandhi suggested several alternatives to allay the fears of Whites about Indian voters e.g. higher property qualification or an education test or exclusion of Indians by name. He urged an inquiry about the number of Indian who qualified to be voters. He pointed out that in Mauritius, where Indians had settled in large numbers, where they were more prosperous and where they had a franchise, they had not grabbed political power. Gandhi quoted the *London Times* that the issue involved is "the status the British Indians shall occupy outside India and in the colonies and in allied states".[CWMG I 326-333]

Gandhi's letters and his memorandums to the authorities were very factual and fervent and the Europeans had never heard such trenchant criticism and furious denunciations from Indian leaders. His letters and the memorandum were very forceful presentation of Indian case from economic, historical and cultural points of view. His scholarship showed as he quoted W.W. Hunter, Max Muller, Schoepenhaur, Sir Henry Maine, Andrew Carnegie, Bishop Heber, Sir Thomas Munro, Sir George Birdwood, Sir Charles Trevelyan, Macaulay, Mill, Burke, Bright, Faucet, Bradlaugh and Gladstone in these submissions.

The presentations were very well received and the White press was charmed by Gandhi's style and equipoise. His writings were praised as moderate, balanced and yet forceful, candid and strongly worded defense of Indian position.

"Mr. Gandhi writes with calmness and moderation: he is as impartial as anyone can expect him to be and probably a little more than might have been expected, considering that he himself did not receive very just treatment at the hands of the Law Society when he first came to the colony. Not only Mr. Gandhi writes with a marked moderation but the arguments he uses are very skillfully put and the 'Open Letter' is throughout distinctly creditable to him in every way". [*Natal Mercury* 7-1-96]

"Mr. Gandhi writes forcefully, moderately and well. He himself suffered some slight measure of injustice since he came to the colony. But that fact does not seem to have colored his sentiments and it must be confessed that to the tone of his Open Letter, no objection can reasonably be taken. Mr. Gandhi discusses the questions he has raised with conspicuous moderation". [Star of Johannesburg.]

Gandhi's presentations contain quite a few statements that are factually untenable. Ancient India never had any representative institutions and religion never stopped Indians from material pursuits. Gandhi's highly drawn projections of India's cultural heritage were more romantic than factual. India as imagined by Gandhi had never existed and ancient India had disappeared long back: by the eighteenth and nineteenth centuries, India was a degraded, dirty and poor community.

The number of Indians in Natal was increasing by leaps and bounds and that was the root cause of all trouble. His argument that political activism on the part of the Indians was not possible because they were not educated in English had been disproved by what he himself had achieved.

Believing firmly that "much of the ill feeling [between the communities] is due to the want of proper knowledge about India and Indians," [CWMG.II 59] Gandhi strove hard to emphasise the cultural achievements of India from very ancient times. He even sought to traduce the racial line by claiming that as Aryans, Indians and Anglo-Saxons belong to the same racial group.

But Gandhi either deliberately overlooked or missed the crucial point of the controversies in which he was involved. The basic issue was not the quality of Indians or culture of India but the social and the political structure of Natal, the intense racial prejudices, the trade rivalry and the fear of Whites being elbowed out in the country that was theirs by the right of conquest. It was not a cultural conflict but a racial, economic and political tussle.

The presentations by Gandhi almost always fudged this core issue that the recently arrived outsiders like Indians could not be given a share in political power [franchise] without jeopardising the future of Whites in the colony. That may be the reason why his arguments charmed his opponents, but never convinced them.

Gandhi's harping upon the culture of India was as irrelevant as the arguments of Europeans about their cultural superiority. Such presentations by European leaders were facile excuses put forward to cover up real reasons and fear psychosis.

Polak has protested that Gandhi's Open Letters to the Britons and to the legislators were very highly didactic in tone, but then Gandhi always wrote that way. Gandhi's prolific writings—memorandums, petitions, letters and even articles of this period were more or less lawyers' presentations and make very boring reading. The colonial secretary, Chamberlain, also expressed such boredom with the monotony of the complaints and documents submitted by Gandhi and Natal Congress.

Gandhi's writings are full of endless repetitions of the same arguements, the same quotes about the culture and capacity of Indians, in almost the same words. "He carried these quotations around with him almost like research students with their cards". [Chandran 285]

When the new disfranchisement bill was being discussed in the Assembly, Gandhi figured prominently in the debates. He was not a member of the Assembly, nor was he on the voters' list, nor again was he ever interested becoming a member of that august body. But he was the target of the most virulent criticisms and denunciations from almost all members.

Gandhi was "an individual who has been referred to more than once …as a man of considerable talent, of not great scrupulosity and of very large ambition. It has already and it will still more, in future, suit this leader to fight over such grounds in endeavoring to obtain for the body of his people the influence over electoral power …His arts, his cleverness and his resources though arrayed against our desire compel our admiration". [Maydon Assembly debates 14-5-96]

"If they [Indians] put this man [Gandhi] in the Assembly, they would have a superior man than anyone in this Assembly. They would have a man educated in England… who has an intimate knowledge of Eastern affairs. He would soon become the Prime Minister". [ibid]

Even the prime minister spoke of Gandhi as "an able, clever and influential member of his community". The petition submitted to the speaker and to the members of Assembly was "an emanation from one man—Mr. Gandhi representing a very small body of men," said the prime minister.

Referring to the petition submitted to the colonial secretary, the prime minister cautioned the Assembly. "It shows how formidable might be the influence of such an organization [Congress] if Indians possessed a larger degree of political power than they possess at present". [ibid]

Prime Minister Robertson was quite candid. "Interests of those of British extraction must be preferred to the interests of those of Indian extraction so as to preserve this fair land for those who are in the colony and to maintain it ... as a British colony and not have the whole country submerged under the Asiatic wave of immigrations". [Hutten 65]

"It is the manifestly the desire and the intention ...[of the assembly] that the destiny of the colony of Natal continue to be shaped by the Anglo-Saxon race and that the possibility of any preponderant influx of Asian voters be averted".

The Assembly debates echoed acute resentment against 'the migrants who would reap the benefits and advantages of the county opened at great risk and made habitable with great travail by original settlers. Europeans who conquered wilderness should not be forced to accept the aliens. 'India had been conquered by the force of arms and therefore Indians have no rights against the English in colonies'.

Gandhi's protests against the new franchise act failed. The disfranchisement bill was quickly and unanimously converted into a law. The bitter pill was a bit sugar-coated by assurances given to Indians by the prime minister and advocate general that since Indians were to lose representation, every member of the Assembly was duty bound to act as a guardian and look after the security, rights and interests of that community.

In later years, Gandhi used to remind Europeans time and again about these promises but all to no purpose. In politics what counts is power and not promises and assurances. The Act immediately received the approval of the colonial office. The British authorities had already agreed to the right of the autonomous colony of Natal to regulate its franchise on any non-racial ground. They pleaded inability and unwillingness to interfere with internal affairs of an autonomous and self-governing colony that Natal had become in 1895. Indian community lost franchise [1896] and Gandhi was deeply disappointed.

The disfranchisement was the most important but by no means the only one anti-Indian measure. Natal was keen on preventing coolies from settling down in the colony. The Wragg Commission [1888] [the coolie commission], had suggested a ten year indenture with higher wages and compulsory return to India after the period of indenture was over. The proposals had been discussed with and approved by the government of India with important amendments, [January 1894] Natal introduced [21-6-95] the Indian Immigration Law Amendment bill and quickly converted it into a law which enjoined that Indian coolies coming after 1896 must either renew indentures or compulsorily return to India at the expiry of the term of contract.

If a coolie did neither, he would have to pay a poll tax of Pounds three pounds per head for an annual residential license with its implied permission to stay but denying them all rights and privileges of citizenship.

The press in England was aghast and the *Star* bitterly commented [21-10-95 CWMG I 287] on the bill "which proposes to reduce Indians to a state of slavery...the thing is a monstrous wrong, an insult to the

British subjects, a disgrace to its authors and a slight upon ourselves. Every Englishman is concerned to see that the commercial greed of South African traders is not permitted to wreck such bitter injustice upon men who alike by the Proclamation and by Statute are placed upon an equality with ourselves before the law".

Gandhi protested to the Assembly that for a coolie to return to India after five or ten years in Natal was 'a pure fatuity' as all his ties and relations would have been cut off. The indenture, though voluntary in law, was entirely one sided and the act would drive poor coolies into perpetual slavery.

He pointed out that it was universally admitted that Indian labour had immensely benefited Natal. Indians were useful, honest, and peaceful; but now they were unwanted as free labour. Gandhi argued that to drive the poor coolies out after their best years have been spent in Natal would be both unjust and cruel.

Gandhi sent a memorandum to the colonial secretary [Aug.1895] repeating the same arguments but adding a note of belligerency that "if the colony can not put up with Indians, the only course... is to stop all future immigration to Natal". [CWMG I 241] He was bitter that even 'a foreign country' like Transvaal does not impose any such annual tax on Indians.

In a memorandum to Lord Elgin, the viceroy of India, Gandhi regretted that the viceroy had sanctioned the principle of continuing indenture or compulsory return. He pointed out that the viceroy should have been guided more by the interests of Indians rather than by the wishes of Natal. Gandhi requested Indian government to totally stop labor supply to Natal as a measure of arm-twisting.

But this plea was a drastic step. Such a measure would have ruined Natal economy and was opposed even by *London Times*—usually very friendly to Indian cause. "We can not afford a war of races among our subjects. It would be as wrong for the government of India to suddenly arrest the development of Natal by shutting off the supply of immigrants as it would be for Natal to deny the rights of citizenship to British Indian subjects". [CWMG I 338]

Gandhi failed again and the bill became the law on 16 August 1896. But this act was largely dysfunctional as far as coolies were concerned. They did not much care for citizenship rights; any way as they had very little of them in India. They hardly ever paid three Pounds tax but they stayed on. The Indian government while giving their consent to the principle of compulsory return, had stipulated that no criminal proceedings for deportation or expulsion could be instituted against coolies who did not renew their indenture and did not return to India.

The Natal government had to be satisfied with such a shadowy tax that was hardly ever paid by free coolies. Natal began to tighten the screw on such coolies. By 1903, the coolie had to pay the tax also for his wife and grown up children [boys aged sixteen or more and girls aged thirteen or more].

Due to economic deterioration in the first decade of the twentieth century with its depression and unemployment, the poll tax became an almost unbearable burden. Gandhi protested that the tax was driving men to crime and women to prostitution. When the government insisted on collecting the tax by confiscation of goods, Gandhi suggested with biting sarcasm that, "The authorities should have gone a step further and suggest that the poorest man can raise money for the payment of tax by mortgaging his body for dissection purposes". [CWMG V 179]

After 1905, it was a crime for the employer to employ a free coolie. But the coolies who were mostly self-employed in petty odd jobs were not much affected by such pressures and prohibitions.

Chapter 11

INDIA AND BACK

With prospects of a long and professionally very profitable stay in Africa so full of public activities, Gandhi began to plan a trip to India in January of 1896 with a twin purpose-to bring his family back with him and to "endeavor and persuade a number of good Indian barristers to come to Natal."

He was authorised [26 May 1896] by twenty-six leaders of the Indian community in Natal "to represent the grievances Indians are laboring under in South Africa before the authorities and public men and public bodies in India". [CWMG II 1] Gandhi took a six months vacation and sailed for India. It was a sponsored trip and Gandhi was to be paid seventy-five Pounds for the travelling and other expenses for public work necessary for his mission. [CWMG I-338]

At a farewell party on 4 June 1896, Gandhi was presented with addresses that praised him very highly for his public services together with a gold medal and gifts that he accepted as tokens of their love. [CWMG III-120-121] By 1901, however, Gandhi's views underwent a sea change and he then resolutely refused all such gifts. He returned even those that he had accepted in 1896.

Gandhi sailed for Calcutta on 5th June 1896 because ships for Calcutta were more easily and more frequently available. While on board, Gandhi wrote his famous pamphlet 'Grievances of British Indians in South Africa- an Appeal to the Indian Public', and added notes to it in Rajkot to complete it. "I prepared the whole of it while on voyage home". [CWMG II 121]

The pamphlet was based upon his personal experiences and observations as also on newspaper clippings narrating actual incidents; Gandhi had collected and carefully preserved them for over three years. His petitions and public letters contained almost the entire data that he used for this pamphlet.

Gandhi arrived at Calcutta on 4 July and left for Rajkot. Utilising an unintended break of journey at Allahabad, [5-7-96] he visited Mr. Chesney, the editor of *The Pioneer* "who told me frankly that his sympathies were with the colonials" [SSA] But Chesney was prepared to give a hearing to whatever Gandhi wanted to say or write about South Africa.

Gandhi reached Rajkot on 9 July 1896. After completing the notes which summarized the major points and thrust of the pamphlet, he got 4000 copies printed [14-8-96] and sent them to newspapers and leaders of public opinion all over India, believing that "Publicity was our best and perhaps the only weapon". [CWMG.II 65]

Gandhi described in all its horrible details the plight of Indians in the four colonies to bring out the indignities and injustice that Indians had to suffer. But he had no desire to blacken the image of Whites. The Green Book and the Open Letter had the same purpose-to rouse the conscience of Indians and Whites and both contained the same information, the same facts and almost the same quotes. "Gandhi's factual and very trenchant criticism did incite public opinion in India against South African society and laws". [Chattopadyaya 147]

Gandhi quoted extensively from the African papers and the presentation was not very comfortable for Whites. The purpose of the pamphlet was to inform and rouse the public and leaders of India who might start an agitation in India as a lever of pressure on the colony because Natal could not do without Indian labour.

He highlighted the problems of coolies and discussed the case of Balasunderam. The alternatives suggested by Gandhi were either to secure a right for Indians to settle or to close down labour supply. The labour class would suffer great losses if such opportunities for employment were closed down. But Gandhi justified the step on grounds of dignity and freedom for Indian community in Africa.

The insults and maltreatment suffered by traders were on account of trade rivalry: White traders and chambers of commerce led anti-Indian tirade. Indian question was an Imperial question but colonies were bent on having their way and drive Indians out and away.

Gandhi declared that British love for justice and fair play was "the sheet anchor of our hope". The help from England was not a remedy against the insults and indignities suffered by Indians at the hands of people. But England, if pressurised by India, could and should block anti-Indian laws as the Imperial Authority had a right to quash any legislation of colonies. "When legal disabilities are removed, social persecution will gradually disappear". [Letter to *The Statesman*].

The public hatred can be removed only by local good will. The only remedy was to publicise the wrong and rouse the conscience of better type of Whites. "Our policy in South Africa is to conquer by love...at least that is our goal and we do not attempt to have the individuals punished and as a rule patiently suffer wrongs at their hands". [CWMG II-29] This was not ahimsa, but pure pragmatism because the complaints were counter-productive. "Complaints brought no relief and often worsened the situation".

Gandhi called for, and expected, strong support from the government and people of India in fighting for the cause of Indians in South Africa. "We are hemmed in on all sides by restrictions and high handed measures". "It is not political power that Indians want. It is the degradation, and its many other consequences and measures that follow and will be based on disfranchisement that they dread and resist".

This shocking pamphlet was widely noticed in India: *The Pioneer* wrote an editorial. "South Africa, for better class of Indians was a country to keep away from". [CWMG III 121] *The Times of India* called for an inquiry into the conditions of Indians as depicted by Gandhi. Such an inquiry would put Natal in an awkward position as far as labour supply was concerned.

The agent general of Natal in India, Walter Peace, noted the pamphlet and protested against charges levelled by Gandhi. He declared that 'justice was never denied to Indians and that railways as well as the State never treated Indians as beasts'.

Gandhi's lengthy and highly sarcastic rejoinder came in his speech in Madras repeating what he had already written in a letter to *The Times of India*. He dismissed the agent general's defense as "a plea of the guilty" and wryly commented on "Mr. Peace's queer notions of 'good treatment' when Indians were kicked, abused and pushed away by railway staff including Station Masters themselves".

Gandhi was very active during his short stay at Rajkot. The outbreak of bubonic plague in Bombay led to a precautionary alert in Rajlot. Gandhi fully and avidly participated in all preventive measures. As a member of the sanitation committee, he visited the quarters of untouchable scavengers and found the surroundings cleaner than those of upper caste areas in the city. Gandhi also served on the committee formed to celebrate golden jubilee of Queen's coronation.

He visited Bombay [19-8-96] and accompanied by Sheth Abdulla [CWMG III 121] met several political leaders—Ranade, Taiyabjee,

Pherozeshah Mehta to finalise the arrangements for a public meeting at the end of September. He returned to Rajkot with his ailing brother in law who died after a few weeks.

Gandhi had to rush to Bombay to address the arranged public meeting [26-9-96] even without completing the final ceremonies for his dead relative. He was too tired to read his speech loudly enough but he did read his address. [CWMG III 121]

The draft of this long and brilliant speech makes a very impressive reading. "I am a man of few words but the rights of 300 millions of Indians are involved in the colonies. ...Ours is a continuous fight against degradation which is sought to be inflicted upon us by Europeans who want to degrade us to the level of Kafirs whose occupation is hunting and whose one ambition in life is to collect a certain number of cattle to buy a wife and then to pass his life in indolence and nakedness". There is no secrecy about the contempt for Indians and a determination "not to let them form a part of the future South African nation that is being built". [CWMG II 53].

Gandhi's wisdom and vision could be grasped as he sought to give the problem an all India dimension. Gandhi insisted that Indians in South Africa have a right to seek protection from India because if South Africa is not checked, chances of Indians for settlement in other colonies will be ruined forever. He made a ringing appeal for Indian help as "elder and freer brothers to lift the yoke of oppression from our neck".

From Bombay, he went to Poona to meet national leaders like Tilak and Bhandarkar and met his future guru Gokhale for the first time. He went to Madras [14-10-96] where his fame as the protector of indentured coolies had preceded him and he was greeted with enthusiastic welcome from the public and a very warm response from the press. Gandhi spent a fortnight in the city.

At a public meeting organised [26-10-96] by the Madras Mahajana Sabha and forty other prominent citizens, Gandhi spoke at great length and this was the best and the most important speech he delivered in India. A part of it was included as an appendix to the second addition of his pamphlet.

His banter, his humorous asides and his sharp words make his speeches in India very effective shafts. "Great men may change their views as often and as quickly as they change their clothes ...and some say that such changes are a result of sincere conviction". [CWMG II 76] He was aware that it was only starvation that forced the Indian coolies to stand the sufferings in Natal. "A starving man would generally stand any amount of rough treatment to get a crumb of bread". [CWMG II 80]

He even issued a certificate to himself. "I am not given to exaggerate matters and it is very unpleasant to me to cite testimony in my own favor...[but] I feel it my duty ...to tell you what papers in South Africa thought about my Open letter..." and then Gandhi quoted very laudatory remarks about self. [CWMG II 81]

He appealed for help. "We are young and inexperienced. We have a right to appeal to you-our elder and freer brethren for protection. ...The blame would lie on your shoulders if the yoke is not removed from our necks." [CWMG II 91]

At Madras, there was such a great demand for the 'Green Book' that an additional 2000 copies had to be printed as a rush job. He then proceeded to Calcutta [31-10-96] and met Surendranath Bannerjee and others. But the response from the Bengali press and leaders in Calcutta was so cold that even a meeting that was planned could not be organised.

Gandhi spoke to the British India Association committee in the city. The editors of *The Statesman* and *The Englishman* were the only ones who showed interest in Gandhi's plea. He was interviewed by, and wrote letters in both the newspapers.

He clarified that Indian merchants were prosperous and that the franchise agitation was not for political power but for removal of vexatious disabilities. The proposed three Pounds tax on the free coolie was very high in view of his low earnings.

While at Calcutta, he received a cable summoning him back because Transvaal Assembly –Rand––resolved to force all the Indians to stay in locations. [12-11-96] He left for Bombay; but he was in no hurry to leave.

He went to Poona to address the public meeting arranged by Sarvajanik Sabha. [16-11-96] He went to Rajkot to pick up his family members and left for Durban [30-11-96] by S.S. *Courland*. Before leaving the shores, Gandhi telegraphed Viceroy Lord Elgin to pressurise Transvaal to stop enforcing locations for Indians.

Gandhi maintained afterwards [Auto] that he had to leave Calcutta post haste because of the telegram; but this statement does not accord with his declared intention to leave by *Courland* on 29 November 1896 or thereabout [CWMG II 69 and 94]. S.S. *Courland* left Bombay on 30-11-96 i.e. a day after Gandhi intended to leave anyway. There was no particular urgency for his return and Gandhi did nothing very significant after reaching Durban.

Gandhi's speeches in India sound repetitive to us on account of the same facts and statistics, together with the same phrases and same quotes. But each time he was speaking to different audiences who found him fresh and shocking.

During his stay in India, Gandhi tried hard to persuade his lawyer friends–F.S. Talyarkhan and Padshah brothers to come to Africa for legal practice and offered partnership on very generous terms to whosoever would come. [CWMG II 67] There were very good prospects for earning but he requested them to treat the profession more as a public duty than merely as means of amassing money. "No one in our position would go to South Africa with a view to pile money. You must go there with a spirit of service. The money will come". [CWMG II 68]

This was the attitude and the approach he himself had adopted right from the beginning of his career. But no Indian barrister was ready to risk his career by going to Africa for public service. Only one advocate—R.K.Khan accompanied Gandhi. He had also requested Gokhale for "a few active prominent workers in India for our cause". [CWMG II 66]

During his India visit, Gandhi spoke only about South Africa. He had accomplished a lot. He had travelled to all important centers of political activity in India, contacted most of front rank leaders, had spoken at several, well attended meetings and had established personal contacts with major newspapers to enlist their support to the cause of Indians in Africa. Gandhi had spent 118 pounds [Rs. 1766] for accomplishing his mission; but he declined to accept more than 75 Pounds as earlier stipulated. [CWMG II 104-115]

Gandhi arrived at Durban [18-12-96] to face the storm he had been warned about. His arrival added fuel to a fire that was blazing for more than four months. An intense anti-Indian agitation had been going on since August 1896 and two newly founded bodies were conducting virulent campaigns to drive Indians out of Natal.

Gandhi has traced this agitation to April '96 proposal by the Tongaat Sugar Company to import twelve Indian artisans. This proposal gave rise to an agitation by artisans and led to the formation of European Protection Association at Maritzberg, [18-9-96] to curb and stop Indian immigration to South Africa.

The Colonial Patriotic Union at Durban formed on 26-11-96 had submitted a petition to debar Indians, as there were too many blacks in the colony. The White agitators argued that Indian coolies retarded the growth of Native labour and dirty habits of Indians endangered the health of Whites. Australia and New Zealand had closed their doors to Asiatics and Natal should do the same.

The colonials had valid reasons to be apprehensive. Driven by poverty, plague and famines, a large number of Indians were arriving just at that very period in South Africa. Between 1895 and 1899, each of the four shipping lines owned by Indians, made four trips a year between India and South Africa bringing about 300/400 Indians every time [CWMG V 70-71] and this downpour was rising to its climax by the end of 1896. Most of them went to Transvaal but quite a few settled in Natal too. This was the reason why anti-Asiatic agitation assumed a virulent and organised form.

Gandhi's pamphlet, his speeches and his intense activity to rouse the sympathy of people and press in India had created a scare together with anger and hatred for Gandhi among Europeans. His Green Pamphlet came in for special castigation because of its garbled summary published widely in Natal press.

Reuters had cabled [14-9-96] from London a four-line summary of Gandhi's pamphlet without mentioning his authorship. "A pamphlet published in India declares that Indians in South Africa are robbed and assaulted and are treated like beasts and are unable to obtain redress. The Times of India advocates an inquiry into these allegations".

The Whites might have been rattled more by the demand for an inquiry that might affect labour supply than by the accusations and charges that they knew to be true. Gandhi was accused of using irresponsible anonymity to malign the White community of Natal. The press was agog with fury and the leaders of the White community stoked the fire by denouncing Gandhi as a liar who had tarnished the name of Natal and the image of Whites by publishing falsehoods.

But the very next day, tempers cooled down. When copies of the pamphlet were made available and were studied, the entire White press absolved Gandhi of all guilt and some even upheld his activities and his opinions as just and fair.

The *Natal Advertiser* and *Natal Mercury* wrote editorials with a great sense of justice and fair play. "Mr. Gandhi on his part and on behalf of his countrymen has done nothing that he is not entitled to. ...He is within his rights and so long as he acts honestly and in straightforward manner, he cannot be blamed or interfered with.

So far as we know, he has always done so and his latest pamphlet we cannot honestly say is an unfair statement of the case from his point of view. Reuter's cable is a gross exaggeration of Mr. Gandhi's statements". [*Natal Mercury* 18-9-96]

"A perusal of Mr. Gandhi's pamphlet recently published in Bombay leads to the conclusion that telegraphic description of its objects and contents was considerably exaggerated. ...His is rather an old familiar grievance that Indians are regarded and treated by Europeans as belonging to a separate class and as not one of themselves". [*Natal Advertiser* 18-9-96] [CWMG II 142]

Gandhi on his part had a very clear conscience. "What I had written in Natal was far more severe and detailed than what I wrote and spoke in India. My speeches in India were free from slightest exaggeration". [SSA 71]

The pamphlet storm in the newspapers had blown away three months before Gandhi arrived in Durban. But the demagogues had kept the pot boiling to incite the White community. The European Protection Association and Colonial Patriotic Union fomented virulent anti-Indian feelings.

A Durban meeting of the Europeans under Sparks [26-11-96] had demanded total stoppage of Indian immigration by using Australian system of language barrier. At a public meeting on 25th December 1896, Gandhi was criticised for 'indulging in animated condemnation' of Natal Whites.

Gandhi was furiously denounced at a meeting [4-1-97] for accusing the colony of unfair treatment of Indians who were abused and robbed and swindled in the colony. "Mr. Gandhi returned to India and dragged them [colonials] in the gutter and painted them as black and filthy as his own skin" [Doke] All moderate newspapers criticised the language and adjectives used against Indians in general and against Gandhi in particular but the riff-raff enjoyed such outbursts and abuses.

The mob fury that Gandhi and Indian passengers had to face on their arrival in Durban [18-12-96] had very little to do with his writings and speeches in India. Between August and December 1896, several ships had docked in Durban bringing a large number of Indians many of them were artisans; their arrival had been prominently reported with exaggeration while the departures of several Indians were never reported by the press. [CWMG II 130]

Gandhi was suspected of promoting such influx by organising an Immigration Agency to bring into Natal thousands of Indians every year. Intense public pressure was mounting, not only in Natal, but in all the colonies to stop the Indian influx.

"Facts were at a heavy discount, the whole Indian question was opened up and Indians were condemned wholesale.... The Indians are the most hated and misunderstood community in the Colony". [CWMG II 141/42]

There were wild rumours that Gandhi had attempted to recruit many lawyers for Africa and this had some basis in truth. A report was circulated that funds that Gandhi had collected and was still trying to collect, were actually meant for importing artisans and professionals. This was a lie.

Gandhi had encouraged his relatives to come to Africa for business and he did try to bring a lawyer or two and a few activists. Gandhi would have been happy if educated and better qualified Indians came to Africa and in his farewell address [June '96] he had hinted at such a possibility but there was no organised attempt and certainly no conspiracy of any kind. In fact Gandhi temperamentally was incapable of any conspiracy of any type.

Gandhi, reasonable as ever, conceded that 'the agitation against any organized attempt to swamp Natal with Indians would be justified'. [CWMG II 124] The Indian community in Durban was trying to start a printing press in 1895-96 and "I had instructions to bring the material and Indian types for the press... I might have brought the material, but I failed". [SSA 125 and CWMG II 125] The planned newspaper could not be started because Gandhi had no time and there was no other Indian who could undertake the job.

The White community was being roused "to resist an Indian invasion" by any and every means. The accidental arrival on the same day, 18 December, of two boats—*Courland* and *Nadiri* so full of Indians seemed to confirm their worst suspicions and boosted up an anti-Gandhi fury. The memories of franchise agitation were revived to create a scare that "Indians want to take over the colony and rule over us".

Wild rumours asserted that Gandhi had returned with several artisans—fifty blacksmiths, thirty compositors and a printing press. The facts were different. Out of some six hundred passengers, only 120 were coming to Natal and most of them were clerks and women. Only sixty Indians were newcomers in Natal. Other passengers were bound for Delgoa Bay or Mauritius or Transvaal. Gandhi knew none of them except his family members.

Since the boats were coming from a plague zone, they were sent into quarantine for five days. During the week, there were numerous large meetings in the city where inflammatory speeches were delivered against the landing of Indians and such landing was to be stopped by force if necessary. There was intense excitement all over Durban and a determination that all passengers had to be sent back and no more Indians should be allowed in the colony.

A Demonstration Committee was formed and it issued an ultimatum to the captains of the ships to take the Indians back. Abusive and threatening speeches against Gandhi [beat him up, spit upon him, tar and feather him] were the order of the day. A huge meeting [4-1-97] resolved that all the Asiatics on board *Courland* and *Nadiri* be sent back or their landing would be prevented by force.

It was quite clear that the Natal government and political leaders sympathised with the mob that threatened to go out of hand. There was a call to "blow up the ships" and wide spread anti-Indian riots were feared. European working class had joined the agitation for the first time and the demonstrations became more and more rowdy.

In midst of this severe tempest Gandhi remained firm and calm throughout the crisis. His example and exhortations as well as the support of the captains of the ship helped the passengers to stand firm. "Poor Indians were in for tough time if they attempted to land; even if they remained on board afraid to land...they would be deafened and scared by the hysterics, by the hootings, groanings and the jeerings of the assembly". [*Natal Advertiser* CWMG II 159] The passengers were threatened with violence if they landed and were offered reimbursement of fare money if they chose to return. But the passengers refused to yield even an inch.

The rowdies established a mob rule in Durban and dared the government to use force against them. A few Indian shops were damaged and burnt and the government did nothing to control the violence. The new port authorities were in collusion with the mob and the political leaders like Escombe assured the mob that "we are with you and no force would be used to prevent violence".[CWMG II ` 153]

The five days quarantine was periodically extended to twenty-three days; "The power of quarantine was abused for political purpose" [SSA 75] to frighten Indians into returning to India. The passengers were harassed by frequent and unnecessary cleanings and fumigation and their blankets and bed sheets were burnt more than once under the pretext of sanitary measures. [28-12-96] There was a serious shortage of food and water on the ships and passengers suffered from cold and rain.

But the captains of the ships were firm and patient and passengers cheered by Gandhi were in high spirits. Gandhi has mentioned [SSA and Auto] that in his Christmas speech on board *Courland*, he strongly criticised western civilisation as based upon violence and fraud and that the behaviour of the Natal mob was a fruit thereof.

Such a speech would be somewhat incongruent with his dress and manners. In 1897, Gandhi was a great admirer of western culture. He had forced his wife and children to adopt western dress and etiquette and to use fork and knives: he himself lived very comfortably in western style.

Indians in the city organised a 'quarantine relief committee' to supply the necessities to passengers who stoically faced severe pressures and crude threats. The mob leaders exerted tremendous pressure on Abdulla & Co. as the owner and agent of the ships to take passengers back to India and the firm was offered the defrayal of expenses involved.

But such pressure was firmly resisted and Abdulla & Co. expressed its readiness to be ruined for the cause. "They [the firm] would fight to the bitter end but would not be coerced into committing the crime of sending away these helpless and innocent persons". [SSA 74]

The captains of the ships kept up pressure on the port authorities for permission to land the passengers. The port authorities informed Harry Escombe, the acting prime minister that the board had no legal powers to extend the quarantine any further after 7 January 1897.

Harry Escombe was an interesting character. He was a lawyer politician and frequently shifted his positions. He had a very rich Indian clientele and staunchly expressed pro-Indian views prior to his election to the Assembly. He assumed an anti-Indian attitude during his entire political career; but after his retirement, he sympathised with Indian community.

He had played a very prominent role in the anti-Gandhi agitation ['It was he who instigated them' [SSA 73]; but now he was at the end of his tether and quietly prepared to enforce the law. He informed the delegation of agitators "the colonial government at present has no powers...to legally prevent the landing of any class of Her Majesty's subjects". [CWMG II 131]

He also told them that demonstrations would be useless and unhelpful because if the situation persisted, the ministry will have no alternative but to resign and hand over the administration to the governor. Escombe placated them with a promise to shortly enact laws to prevent Indian immigration and thus save Natal from being overwhelmed by Asiatics.

Escombe denied press reports about his collusion with demonstrators and declared: "Government is responsible for the protection of passengers and cargo from the violence of rioters". "But there are intense feelings throughout the colony against the landings of Indians and they [Indians] should be informed of the existence and strength of these feelings". [CWMG II 156]

The quarantine had lapsed and Dada Abdulla issued a legal notice to the government claiming that it was costing them 150 Pounds per day to keep ships at anchor. Dada Abdulla proposed landing the Indians quietly at night so that the government was not forced to fight with rioters. [CWMG II 155]

Laughton, a senior advocate of the firm notified the government [11-1-97] of a defiant decision to land all passengers at night. "If no full answer is received within 24 hours and if rioters are not suppressed and we are paid 150 Pounds per day, we would disembark at night relying on the protection which we respectfully submit government is bound to give us".

Henry Escombe was needled. "The government does not need any reminders about its duties". Gandhi was firm and calm. When asked by the captain about his reaction in case he was attacked by the mob, Gandhi had replied in his cool way "I hope God will give me the courage and sense to forgive them and to refrain from bringing them to law. I have no anger against them". [Auto]

Spark, the president of the Demonstration Committee threatened conflict and violence and European shops were to be closed for the day to enable their employees to proceed to the docks. In an interview to the *Natal Advertiser* {13-1-97}, Gandhi had clarified all issues and scotched rumours and misinformation about his activities in India. Gandhi was not at all intimidated by the agitation and was quite forthright "We will fight against all discriminations and disabilities and the discriminating laws".

Gandhi was accused that he was inciting the passengers on boats to sue Natal government for illegal detention; Gandhi emphatically rejected the accusation. "I do not return here with the intention of making money but of acting as an humble interpreter between the two communities". "My object throughout is not to saw dissentions between the two communities but to assist at creating harmony between the two".

He pointed out that anti-Indian demonstration is an act of disloyalty to the Crown and would rouse anger in India. India is the most important part of British Empire and most of English trade was with India. The policy of exclusion was obsolete and Natal demonstrators were disloyal to Imperial interests. The franchise was a right. If Indians are not fully civilised, colonists should help them to become so. Natal wants and needs Indian labour but not Indian citizens. It is a leonine partnership with Natal getting the best of both the worlds. Natal has no right to stop Indians from entering the colony because they are British subjects.

He denied having maligned Natal. "I have not gone beyond what I said here and my stating the case in India has not prejudiced it in any way". If Indian merchants were not to be allowed, then there would be no labour supply [CWMG II 118-126]

Gandhi's statement in this interview that "the free Indian population really remains stationary... The law of supply and demand regulates the inflow and outflow of the passengers... For every Indian coming to Natal, one returns to India" can hardly be supported by ground realities.

Gandhi always adopted a very reasonable attitude. He never favoured free migration of Indians to Africa. "If Indians get free access and full status in Africa, the European community might be pushed away", but he insisted that those who were admitted and allowed to stay must be treated fairly and be granted a right to travel and re-enter.

On the day of landing, [13 January] about 3000 rowdies had collected on the docks but the violent tempered crowd was persuaded by its leaders not to harm Gandhi. 'Injury to Gandhi would make him a hero and a martyr. The greatest punishment which could be inflicted on him is to allow him to live amongst us so that we can spit on him'. [CWMG II 161] The menacing crowd was dispersed by the police and the rioters vanished. But there was tension in the air and all shops in Durban were closed.

Now that the decision had been taken, S.S. *Courland* came in and Harry Escombe himself arrived personally to assure all passengers that "they are safe under the Natal Government laws as if they were in their own native villages". In order to avoid un-pleasantries, all passengers including Mrs. Gandhi and her children were disembarked [13-1-97] at a different jetty and reached their destinations without any further trouble.

Gandhi had accepted the government's advice to land late in the evening and under police protection, [CWMG II 161] because Gandhi was the chief target of hatred. Laughton, however, disliked the idea of

Gandhi "entering the city like a thief or an offender" and he even ascribed an ulterior motive to Escombe's advice as an attempt to show that Gandhi was a coward.

Laughton offered to accompany Gandhi if he chose to walk down the streets as if nothing had happened. Gandhi, touched by his arguments and responding to the challenge, decided to face the situation. Without informing police or anybody else, he landed in the afternoon at about 4.30 pm. Gandhi, while in the ferry boat, was spotted by his turban by some boys even before he landed on the shore. Gandhi could have gone back to the ship instead of landing but he refused and calmly walked down to face the menacing crowd.

Gandhi was jeered, pushed around, separated from Laughton and pelted with stones, fish, and rotten eggs. He was assaulted and showered with hard knocks and kicks and could barely support himself by holding on to the rails of a building nearby. He got quite a few cuts and blisters and would have been lynched in no time. But before any serious injury was inflicted "a beautiful and a brave thing happened". [Doke 49]

Mrs. Alexander, wife of the police superintendent happened to pass nearby. She knew Gandhi personally and rushed to his rescue saving him by her presence and with her umbrella. The police, hearing yells and cries arrived soon after and dispersed the crowd.

Gandhi declined the shelter of police station and was escorted by police to the spacious house of his friend Rustomji. He was united with his family and was treated for his wounds. He had extensive cuts on his neck, ears and around his eyes; he had been saved in nick of time.

But the danger still loomed large. In the gathering dusk, a huge, menacing crowd surrounded Rustomji's house and threatened to burn it down if Gandhi was not handed over to them. The police superintendent, Alexander, humoured and cheated the crowd while Gandhi was made to escape incognito. He was kept at the police station till tempers cooled down.

All rumours about Gandhi having conspired to flood Natal with Indian artisans and professionals were cleared out in no time and Gandhi was proved to be totally innocent of all charges levelled against him. Advocate Laughton paid him a splendid tribute [*Natal Mercury* 16-1-97] "To vindicate him [Gandhi] before the public, it was decided that he [Gandhi] should not give his enemies an opportunity of saying that he was flunking on board *Courland* where he could have stayed for a week if he had so chosen…he should not sneak in Durban like a thief at night but that he should face the music like a Man and like a political leader. And give me leave to say, right nobly did he do it.

"I accompanied him simply as a member of the bar to testify by so doing that Mr. Gandhi is an honorable member of an honorable profession, in order that I may raise my voice to protest against the way in which he was being treated and in the hope that my presence might save him from that insult". [Hutten 61] "Throughout the trying procession, his manliness and pluck could not have been surpassed and I assure Natal that he is a Man who should be treated as a Man. Intimidation is out of question". [Chandran 316]

The hatred of the mob this time was directed, not toward Indian community as such, not even towards Gandhi's family but only him in person and he was the only hate figure.

But the assault changed everything. The press, the administration and the entire White community were now ashamed of themselves. There was a sudden change in the tone of the press and a severe verdict was passed on the actions of Demonstration Committee. The press condemned "the ungentlemanly behavior and the brutalities towards an un-convicted freeman".

The lawlessness and the targeting a single individual by a crowd were severely castigated as "un-English". The administration which was clearly happy with the anti-Gandhi agitation also came in for caustic criticism for its failure to uphold law and order. The Natal press throughout the episode played a very fair and balanced role. "We had not the slightest objection to take a mean advantage of the provisions of quarantine law to prevent landing of Indian migrants in Natal on the ground that they came from a country infected with a very dangerous infectious disease". [Natal Mercury Hutten 83]

Gandhi reacted with a laconic comment. "The peaceful behavior and the quiet resignation [of the Indian community] during the most stirring period excited the admiration of those who were least likely to notice the good traits of our people". [CWMG III 123] Gandhi condemned the Demonstration Committee, which incited the mob and the government for countenancing the rioters for too long.

The Indian community thankfully acknowledged the part played by police and gave ten Pounds for the department. Alexander was presented with a gold watch "for saving the life of one whom we delight to love" and Mrs. Alexander was presented a gold watch, chain and a locket for defending Gandhi "at no small personal risk to yourself". [CWMG II 230]

The colonial secretary, Chamberlain, wired instructions to the Natal government to prosecute all those who had attacked Gandhi: but Gandhi had other ideas. He told Escombe: "You allowed Europeans to be excited against Indians, you took some steps as seemed advisable to you for safeguarding the interests of Europeans in Natal, [a clear reference to the Immigration bill of 1896] This is a political matter and it remains for me to fight you in the political field". [SSA 63]

Gandhi declined to register any complaint or in any way to co-operate in the prosecution of ringleaders. Gandhi's decision saved Natal political leaders from a very awkward situation. The mob attacks was a normal experience of the Indians and for the reasons explained by Gandhi in his Green Pamphlet nobody ever complained about such things. "In all cases of assault, our mode of action is not to take any notice of them...Sufferance is really and sincerely the badge of Indians in South Africa, especially in Natal…We follow this policy not from any philanthropic but from purely selfish motives. We have found by painful experience that to bring offenders to justice is a tedious and expensive process… The offender would either be discharged with a caution or fined five shillings or one day. The very man…puts the complainant in an awkward position and the publication of such acts incites others to similar ones". [CWMG I 6/7]

The Natal governor sent [16-1-97] a garbled and oversimplified version of the incident trying to shift the blame on shoulders of Gandhi. "Mr. Gandhi, a Parsee lawyer who had been prominent in the agitation that took place among Indians against recent franchise legislation and the author of a pamphlet… some statements in which were resented here, landed at regular landing place but within the borough of Durban and was recognized by some disorderly persons who mobbed and ill treated him. Ministers have formally expressed their regrets at the incident for which however they could not be held responsible. The arrangements within borough are not under their control. I am glad to say that Mr. Gandhi was not seriously hurt. I learn that Mr. Gandhi in coming ashore at so inopportune a moment when ill disposed persons were angry… and before the passions had had time to cool down, acted on the advice which he now admits to have been bad and accepts the responsibility of his action in the matter". Gandhi was "an individual who by his actions as an agitator has made himself socially odious". [Hutten 61]

Based on such a report, Chamberlain declared in Parliament "The landing took place without any opposition except in case of one person who was assaulted but not seriously hurt". [CWMG III 64]

Escombe requested and obtained a written disclaimer from Gandhi who wrote a note to Chamberlain. "I do not wish that any notice should be taken of the behavior of some people towards me last Wednesday which I have no doubt was due to misapprehension on their part of what

I did in India in reference to the Asiatic question". "It is due to the government that under instruction from you, the Superintendent of Water Police offered to take me to town quietly at night, I proceeded to the shore with Mr. Laughton on my own responsibility without informing the Water police of my departure". Gandhi thanked government for kind inquiries and the kindness shown by officials. [CWMG II P 127]

Gandhi had shrewdly mixed up his personal approach of Christian charity with the existing situation. In every evaluation of Gandhi we must continuously keep in mind the miraculous evolution of Gandhi's personality. There is a vast difference between Gandhi of 1897 and of Gandhi of 1908.One is the embodiment of sufferance and the other of forgiveness.

Gandhi rose tall in the eyes of Europeans for his forbearance and his Christian spirit of forgiveness made the Whites all the more ashamed of themselves. For the next two decades, Gandhi continued his strident campaigns against governments of Natal and Transvaal. He continued to excite controversies and he was intensely hated by the Whites for his activities: but never again was Gandhi subjected to the fury of the White mob in South Africa.

The opponents of Gandhi also reaped rich benefits from this incident. Escombe became immensely popular for the part he played in anti-Gandhi agitation and all the rowdies who led the mob got elected to either the Assembly or to the municipal council.

Chapter 12

THE LAWYER LEADER

Gandhi was by now, the most outstanding leader of Indian community in South Africa and his eminence continued undimmed through this decade of comparatively low level of political activities. His most famous performances as a political leader dates either before 1897 or after 1906.

This decade [1897-1906], a period of lull in public life of Gandhi is overcrowded with events, experiments and experiences in his personal life. These ten years, most of them spent in happy domesticity, constitute the most momentous and the most decisive era in the personal life of Gandhi on account of startling changes that shaped him into a very unusual personality so vastly different from what he was before 1897.

The leader and the lawyer slowly paled away as Gandhi passed through an amazing metamorphosis that made him a Mahatma. This ascent to Mahatmahood converted a constituionalist into a revolutionary, a law- abiding citizen into a determined satyagrahi and a man of compromises into a dogmatic master.

Such a Pilgrim's Progress is hard to describe and still harder to date. We have no way of knowing which incident or idea or experience led to what and when and why. There are no referents by which such spiritual vibrations can be recorded on the seismograph of history.

Those who presume that Gandhi was born a Mahatma have their task easy and mapped out: they have only to focus on a few flashing growth points. But Gandhi himself has repeatedly insisted that he made and continued to make strenuous and persistent efforts to raise himself to sainthood. Gandhi never was an ordinary mortal: but he was not born a mahatma, he *became* one.

The inquiry as to 'how' and more importantly for us 'when' the changes began to come over him is a journey in uncharted ocean with only a few buoys bobbing up here and there. We would therefore describe the process by resorting to what is known as Occam's Razor, going by hard facts and making as few assumptions as possible to account for the changes.

The process must have begun very early in Gandhi's life but it became clearly manifest more and more after 1897. By 1908, Gandhi had arrived at the apogee of this spiritual growth when he not only forgave his tormentors, but also strived unsuccessfully to save them from the legal consequences of their murderous assault on him.

Gandhi's firm refusal to prosecute the mob leaders of Durban [1897] was more an act of wisdom than an act of forgiveness. Every Indian in Natal had to do the same. He accepted his 'mistake' in sidestepping police protection and he escaped incognito from the fury of the mob. But in 1908, he declined to retreat from a clear danger and faced the assault without rancor or remorse.

These years [1897-1906] witnessed acute internal restlessness within Gandhi but there was hardly any visible change in his exteriors. He led a family life and had children: he carried on highly lucrative professional activities in Durban and then in Johannesburg: he lived in very comfortable and posh houses—Beech Grove Villa in Durban and an eight-bedroom bunglow with gardens on both the sides in

Johannesburg. He dressed in the most fashionable and costly Western clothes. He owned a thousand acre farm at Phoenix, a printing press and a newspaper as his personal properties. He loaned money to his friends. He helped to maintain the families of his brothers though for some time in 1898, Gandhi seems to have lost contacts with them. [CWMG III 57]

As he embarked upon his spiritual quest, he started changing from within. He was passing through awesome experiences and took more and more to a simple and even austere life style in midst of luxurious surroundings. He had been forced to shave himself because White barbers would not serve him. He now began to launder his clothes as a matter of economy and convenience. In Kathiawar every family, rich or poor, used to have a grinding wheel at home. Gandhi installed one in his home in Durban [1897] and himself ground grains for fresh flour. He now exercised regularly. In Johannesburg, he usually cycled to his office, a distance of six miles and often walked long distances. His dietary experiments date from London, but in South Africa, food became an adjunct to self-control. He developed a passion for serving the ailing and took to naturopathy as the best and most spiritual way of healing.

Educational experiments were forced on Gandhi. Gandhi was in charge of two young boys—his son Harilal and his sister's son Gokaldas and he was faced with the problem of their education. There were thousands of Indian children in Natal but there were no schools for them. Indian merchants were not much interested in educational activities.

"The Indian children are entirely shut out of the ordinary public schools as well as higher schools". [CWMG III 199] There were twenty-five missionary schools catering to the children of indentured and free labour, but Gandhi was too conscious about his status to send his wards there.

He undertook to teach his wards but he was too busy to do so and his wife was totally illiterate. So Gandhi hired a governess paying Pounds seven a month; but the arrangement does not seem to have worked well and was soon discontinued.

Too much has been made of his practice of cleaning the family toilet because Indians treat it as a very degrading activity to be undertaken only by the lower class. Cleaning toilets is not a big deal in western societies and Gandhi was a thoroughly westernised person living in a westernised society. Gandhi was always a very gracious and accommodative person but he was tyrannical enough to force his protesting and weeping wife to such a toilet service.

Gandhi always practiced what he believed and he never shied away from implementing novel and even weird concepts. He experimented with divers modes of self-discipline each being bolder and more bizarre than the earlier one. Such changes were incremental and with the passage of time began to be reflected in his opinions and his attitudes.

As his faith in divinity deepened, he felt it everywhere and he saw divine dispensation in every event and incident. "These untoward happenings [a disastrous accident in Paris] are not merely accidents but...divine visitations from which we may learn rich lessons...on this earth we are all mere sojourners...a grim tragedy behind the tinsel splendor of modern civilization". [CWMG III 500] "...the wonderful discoveries and marvelous inventions of science...is after all an empty boast". "This plague is a visitation of God's wrath on us for our accumulated sins". [CWMG IV 397] He described the earthquake of 1905 in Himachal region as 'divine wrath'.

Gandhi had revived his contacts with the London Vegetarian Society while in Pretoria [1893-4] and he often wrote to its weekly. Dr. Josiah Oldfield of the LVS had put Gandhi in touch with Edward Maitland and sent him the literature of the Esoteric Christian Union founded in 1891. Gandhi was very deeply impressed with Maitland's teachings and corresponded with him till latter's death in 1897. For many years while practicing as a lawyer in Durban, Gandhi's letterhead carried a logo of his being an agent of Esoteric Christian Union and of London Vegetarian Society.

Gandhi imported and sold the literature of both these organizations. It was Maitland who later on sent him Tolstoy's *The Kingdom of God Is Within You*, one of the three books that had had tremendous impact on the lifestyle and thinking of Gandhi.

He continued to read extensively on Christianity, maintained close contacts with missionaries of various denominations and almost regularly attended Welsian Church. He was greatly impressed by the teachings of Christian Esoteric Union and was struck by its closeness to Hinduism.

But all the while his faith in Hinduism was continuously deepening and widening. Max Muller's volume *India- What it can Teach Us* became, for Gandhi, almost a Bible and he profusely quoted from it very frequently between 1893 and 1900.

After returning to Natal [1897], Gandhi concentrated on building up his professional career. "His [Gandhi's] public career had helped him in building up his legal practice" [Nanda 74] and he soon emerged as an immensely successful lawyer with steady increase in his income. He was very highly reputed for his total honesty that precluded even minor misdemeanors so common in legal profession.

His professional career and his public activities were so closely intertwined that it would be difficult to say where one ended and the other began. As a lawyer, he had to fight for his clients who were the victims of the same laws against which he was waging political protests. He pleaded on behalf of his clients in the courts as well as in the administrative offices against enforcement of these laws by an arrogant and racist bureaucracy. He initiated and participated in several important test cases both in Natal and Transvaal.

Gandhi, on behalf of the Indian community, continued to keep a constant vigil in all the four political units of South Africa. He would be protesting immediately against every law and/or administrative measure jeopardising Indian interests. The memorandums and the petitions against any such happening were promptly submitted to the concerned authorities. He built up and maintained a relentless pressure on colonial governments by approaching the Colonial Office in England as also by vigorous crusades in local newspapers as well as in the press in England, and by keeping the Government of India and Indian public figures posted about the events and issues pertaining to Indian community in South Africa. All this involved enormous and continuous paper work and only a Gandhi could have coped with it.

Apart from professional and political activities, Gandhi was very busy in a variety of social service activities. He was the first political leader in Africa to add a new dimension to public life by organising non-political social services.

Immediately after his return to Africa in 1897, Gandhi raised Indian famine relief fund and sent more than 1500 Pounds to India. [4-2-97] During a far more severe famine in 1900, the viceroy of India had made an appeal for funds. The India Famine Relief Fund Committee was headed by the governor of Natal. Gandhi made an eloquent appeal for funds "Millions in India are engaged in a war in which there is no victory to be gained... the only reward is painful and lingering death". [CWMG III 181] The committee collected nearly Pounds 5000 from all the communities of the colony. The Europeans contributed 3000 Pounds while Indians and Africans donated 1700 and 300 respectively.

Gandhi's intense loyalty and faith in British Empire continued unabated. He had a great and genuine love for the Empire, sang its national anthem with gusto, and saluted Union Jack on all occasions.

"The Empire has been built on the foundation of justice and equity. It has earned a world wide reputation for its anxiety and its ability to protect the weak against the strong".

On the occasion of the diamond jubilee of the Queen Victoria's coronation, [22-6-1897], Gandhi prepared an impressive souvenir and drafted the Address "Most Gracious Sovereign and Empress, we are proud to think that we are your subjects... we can but reecho the sentiments of loyalty and devotion which are finding expression among all your subjects and in your vast dominions on which the sun never sets".

This address was inscribed in silver and was signed by twenty-one Indians including Gandhi. He organised a small Diamond Jubilee Library to be run by the Indian Natal Congress. But the library was more or less defunct and all the books and furniture of the library had to be handed over to the Durban Library. [10-1-1905]

When Queen Victoria died in January 1901, Gandhi organised a public meeting to mourn her death, led the procession to lay a floral wreath and spoke of India as 'a loyal and an important part of the British Empire'. He prepared a memorial souvenir and distributed it free.

When the Duke and Duchess of York visited Durban, [3-8-1901] Gandhi led the Indians to present a loyal address to them which spoke of the blessings of the munificent British rule. "It is because we are in the folds of Union Jack that we have a footing outside India".

South African experiences were responsible for the cracks beginning to appear in this solid loyalty. The scenario after 1902 forced a major shift in his opinions about the government and the society he was living with. "In Africa Gandhi had been struggling against racial prejudices that he firmly held to be both un-Christian and un-British and which he treated as a temporary and local aberration of British Justice". [Chandran 317]

In spite of repeated failures of Britain to protect its Indian subjects in South Africa, young Gandhi [he was only twenty-five] cherished a staunch loyalty to the British Empire and continued to do so for next twenty years. He has denounced Indian Anarchists as murderers in his *Hind Swaraj*. Gandhi's last act of loyalty was his exertions for recruitment to British army in 1915.

The erosion of such ingrained loyalty took a long time. All the while Gandhi was hoping against hope about the benevolence of British rule. The final disenchantment came in 1919. The Jallianwala tragedy finally shook him out of his fantasy and "Gandhi turned into one of the most determined opponent of the British Imperialism". [Chandran 319] He denounced British rule as strongly as he had supported it earlier. He even called it satanic and diabolical. "I do not believe that it [British Empire] protects the weak. It gives free scope to the strong to maintain their strength and to develop under it. The weak go to the wall".

By 1926, Gandhi's loyalty was completely shattered and he was aware of the distance he had travelled between 1897 and 1926. "If I had today the faith in British Empire that I had then entertained and if I now cherished the hope which I did at that time of achieving our freedom under its aegis, I would advance the same argument word for word in South Africa and under similar circumstances even in India". [SSA 110]

II

In the political arena, Gandhi had no respite from the bush fires that flared up all around to scorch and singe Indians in Natal. The Indian question became a volatile issue and now assumed criticality.

Gandhi converted the assault on his person into a public issue. The very first thing that Gandhi did after tempers had cooled down a bit, was to send [28-1-97] a detailed narration of the landing incident to political leaders like Dadabhai Naoroji, Manchersha Bhavnagree, W.W.Hunter and to the British Committee of Indian National Congress besides the colonial secretary in England "not to ventilate a personal grievance" but to highlight the sufferings and disabilities imposed on Indian community in Natal. "The assault was the work of irresponsible persons and by itself need not be noticed at all" [CWMG II 132] He thanked the government of England and the officials in Natal for their kind inquiries about the incident. "I was treated kindly and was given protection". Gandhi traced the incident to the seven-month old anti-Indian agitation naming names of persons and groups involved.

The copies of this memorandum were circulated widely to several other leaders of public opinion in England and India. [CWMG II 237] This detailed summary was written in very impressive language but produced no effect either on the Colonial Office or the government of Natal.

During the anti-Gandhi agitation, [December '96-January '97] the Natal government had conceded "the desirability of preventing the overrunning of the colony by Asiatics" [CWMG II 152] and Escombe had pacified the Demonstration Committee by promising to curb the influx of Indians and also to reduce and finally eliminate business rivalry of Indian merchants.

He was as good as his word and in the very next session of Natal Assembly [Mar-April 1897] Escombe introduced, in quick succession, four bills to achieve these objectives. While introducing them, the prime minister spoke of a systematic conspiracy to overrun the country with Indian migrants and hinted at still more stringent measures to counteract it.

The Quarantine Bill empowered the government to detain any ship coming from plague infected India or with Indian passengers for an indefinite period in quarantine, to debar such passengers from landing in the colony and to compel that ship to take them back to from where they came.

The Immigration Restrictions bill declared persons who were paupers, prostitutes, criminals, unsound in mental health, or suffering from loathsome diseases and those who failed the language test as Prohibited Migrants. These literacy or pauper tests would not apply to European migrants. [CWMG II 263] The bill did not name Indians and would not apply to those Indians who were already domiciled. The permitted migrants had to pay twenty-five Pounds and to fill in a form in any European language.

The third bill was for the Protection of the non-covenanted Indians and provided that vagrancy law would apply to only indentured Indians.

The last and worst of the quartet was the Dealers' License bill and it proved to be the most insidious instrument to root out the Indian elite from Natal. All trading activities were prohibited without licenses. The officers appointed by Town Councils were to issue, renew or deny annual licenses to all wholesalers and retailers. The accounts were to be maintained in English and shops maintained in proper sanitary conditions to the satisfaction of the officer concerned who can refuse to renew the existing license.

The licensing officer was to act 'at his own will'. The aggrieved party could appeal to municipal councils against the decisions of officers but the right to appeal to judicial courts was expressly denied. No other British colony had the laws so drastic in their potency and so wide in its application. But the Indians could do nothing much to stop the bills from being legislated.

These four ingenuous sidewinders effectively blocked the entrance of new migrants from India and the business activities by Indians who had settled in the colony without even mentioning Indians in the bill. But these bills left the doors open for importing as many Indian labourers as Natal needed or desired.

Between 1897 and 1911, 40,000 Indians were imported as indentured labour while free Indians could hardly enter. Gandhi was aghast. "Natal must have them [Indians] under indenture. She would not have them as free men. Would not the Home and Indian governments stop this unfair arrangement and stop indentured emigration to Natal"? [CWMG II 282]

There was a loud protest against these laws in India and the press in England took up the refrain. The *London Star* denounced the laws as "One of the most contemptible tricks which a government can be a party to". [CWMG II 267] *The Times of India* advocated stoppage of labour supply to the colony, which must either allow all Indians or have none of them.

Gandhi was the first to protest against the bills [CWMG II-152] calling them 'arbitrary and unjust measures' and "an un-British way to debar Indians from entering the colony". Gandhi was an embodiment of reasonableness in his critical appraisal of the bills mentioning the brighter side of each measure before criticising all of them.

He appreciated the concern of Natal in taking preventive measures like quarantine against the menace of plague. There was a genuine and a hysterical scare against plague spreading from India where there were frequent outbreaks of the disease.

Gandhi expressed his happiness that the license act would inculcate sanitary habits in trading community and force it "to keep their premises in good conditions and to provide proper accommodation for their clerks and servants...We will for the sake of arguments assume that there exists undue competition and there is a great deal of insanitation among Indians and these two evils ought to be removed by some legislation". [CWMG III 543] Gandhi conceded the right of Europeans to enforce immigration curbs against the flood of migrants and promised the help of Indians in restricting such flooding.

Having said whatever good there was to be said about these bills, Gandhi condemned them by pointing to the provisions and powers therein that could be misused to prevent Indians from landing and trading in the colony. Preventing Indian migration would be a deathblow to the Imperial unity.

There were very few 'free' Indians in the colony and their presence was in no way a threat to the colony or to Europeans because Indians were a floating group and were only temporary residents in the colony. He called for a census of the Indian population in order to prove his contention.

The treatment given to Indians as migrants and settlers was a grave violation of the 'gracious' proclamation of 1858. "It affects not only Her Majesty's subjects residing in the colony, but the whole population of India. May British Indians when they leave India have the same status before law as other British subjects"?

"It is preeminently an Imperial question in its implications—may or may not they [Indians] go freely from one British possession to another and claim the rights of British subjects in the allied states. The Europeans in Natal say they may not as far as they are concerned". [CWMG II 238]

Gandhi also pointed out that these laws were class legislation as they treated European migrants differently from coloured ones. He pleaded that these harsh laws "ought to be tempered with a large amount of discretion, reason and justice".

All such protests proved futile. Gandhi's appeals and efforts to block these laws failed. All the four bills were converted into laws and were forwarded to the colonial office for approval. Gandhi submitted a lengthy and detailed memorandum that was a strong and sober plea to Chamberlain [2 July 1897] with a request to veto them all. He pointed out that "all the four bills taken to-gather would pose a very serious threat to the very existence of Indian community in Natal".

Gandhi urged the Indian traders to get reformed. Sanitation and proper regulations were to be accepted and implemented "to show that...we are ever ready to rectify error and cooperate with Europeans". [CWMG IV 25]

The Colonial Office decided to set its seal of approval on these measures on the spacious ground that these measures satisfy the specifications prescribed by British authorities. Any discriminatory legislation was open to objection *only* if it persecuted any particular community by name. These bills did not name Indians as such and were applicable to all. This was a sheer casuistry because all these acts were meant to be and were used almost exclusively against Indians. They were sidewinders to be used with telling effects against Indian community.

The Natal government was quite frank about their objectives. The prime minister himself agreed that these acts were anti-Indian steps and were sidewinders. "Ships would not bring those people [Indians] if they knew that they can not be landed and people would not come here to trade if they knew that they would not get licenses". [CWMG II 269]

The prime minister defended the indirect approach because "We could not remove Indians from our midst, nor could we withdraw the privileges they possess as British subjects...When a man met difficulties, he fought against them, and if he could not knock them over, he went round them instead of breaking his head against the wall". [ibid 263]

Gandhi urged the Government of India and even the governments of the provinces to pressurise Africa, but nothing came out of it. He warned the community. "Unless there is a powerful public opinion in India against the disabilities that are being heaped upon Indians in Natal, our days are numbered". "The colony as an autonomous unit was powerful and Britain was aloof, so Indians will have to submit to whatever restrictions were placed upon them".

As Gandhi had foreseen, the enforcement of these laws was much worse than the wordings stipulated. The combined impact of these laws dried up the flow of Indian migration. In very few years, the number of free Indians migrating to Natal turned into a mere trickle. Between 1897 and 1903 only 158 new Indian migrants could enter Natal.

The Immigration Act was enforced very strictly and the rules and the procedure became more and more stringent with the passage of time. "The Act was administered in such a way that most of the Europeans were judged eligible to enter Natal, while virtually all Indians were not". [Hutten-64]

Even for Indian settlers returning to Natal, very costly and very cumbersome affidavits became necessary to prove previous domicile. Such affidavits were scrutinised minutely for every minor flaw and rejected if it was found.

The returnees were admitted only after tedious, costly and humiliating formalities and forms. Domicile documents were scrutinised minutely and were interpreted very strictly so that very often even genuine resident Indians were driven back. Indian migrants were often harassed and handled roughly by police and those without valid papers were not allowed to land but were confined to the steamers like prisoners.

The shipping companies bringing prohibited migrants had to pay heavy penalties and they had to take them back at their own risk and expenses. Very few ports were allowed as entry points for Indians. Indians coming as merchants or their employees knew no English and the language test proved an unsurpassable barrier for such new migrants: only twelve such Indians could enter Natal in the very next year. Even the temporary visitors had to pay heavy fees for a short stay or for passage through Natal.

Indian firms found it very difficult to find qualified and competent servants, while coolies continued to pour and settle into the colony in ever increasing numbers.

The frequent outbreaks of plague in India were used as excuses by Natal for strict enforcement of the Quarantine Act. "Indian ships were pushed back without even landing the cargo". [CWMG III 140]

The Natal authorities and the White press accused Indians of a conspiracy for attempting massive illegal infiltration. Gandhi not only strongly denied but he resented all such allegations. "What we object to is the circulation of false rumors and assumptions based thereon". A few Indians had indeed misused earlier leniency; but "Many innocents were made to suffer for the lapses of a few guilty persons". [CWMG III 197] "The cordon of restrictions in Natal has grown tighter with the lapse of time". Gandhi's anguished cry "Natal leads both [the Boer] republics in its studied persecution" of Indians was lost on British overlords. [CWMG II 263]

Gandhi repudiated the charge of conspiracy "Any evasion of law would be suicidal for the community. There has been no wholesale attempt to defy the law…The Indian ship-owners have been requested to co-operate in enforcing the Immigration Act and have agreed to do so". [CWMG II 294]

The laws of Natal were imitated by the Cape Colony and the screw was turned more and more tight over the years. "The door in South Africa that was formerly so wide open has been almost closed…" [SSA 51]

Most Indians now landed at Delgoa Bay and headed for Transvaal "as long as Transvaal continues to absorb Indians and the government is good enough to let them come". [CWMG II 292] "It is that country which has the capacity to absorb larger number of new-comers of various nationalities".

Gandhi bitterly noted that "Mr. Chamberlain has practically granted that an Indian as soon as he leaves India, ceases to be a British subject with the awful result that we have to witness a painful spectacle of British Indian subjects deported or debarred from Natal only to be driven to Transvaal or Delgoa Bay-both foreign territories". [CWMG II 288]

The Boer leaders too missed no opportunity to point out the inconsistency of Imperial government in coercing Transvaal to do justice to Uitlanders, while allowing the Natal government to do as it liked to with British Indian subjects.

In 1903, the Natal Immigration act was made still more severe. All Indians were considered newcomers till proved to be old residents by affidavits and evidence. The language test became more and more stiff and it was almost impossible to clear it to the 'pleasure of the local officer "when most of Indian merchants cannot even sign their names in English" [CWMG IV 220]: domicile was granted only after three years of residency and was lost by absence of three continuous years. The coolies would never be granted domicile rights.

In 1902, Natal renewed its request that indentures for coolies be terminated in India so that no coolie could ever settle in Natal as free labour thereafter. It was hinted that if such a provision is made, disabilities imposed on free Indians might be somewhat eased.

Lord Curzon curtly rejected the demand and Gandhi too opposed sacrificing rights of coolies for the comforts of merchants. "Such a stipulation should not be agreed upon even in the exchange for a grant of rights to free Indian settlers in Natal...To give away the liberties of indentured Indians... for the sake of better treatment of free Indians would be highly immoral". [CWMG III 526]

More than the Immigration Act, it was the Dealers' License Act that most adversely affected the trading interests of Indians most of them being Gandhi's clients. "The Dealers' License Act was the monstrous product of racial vindictiveness and was being deliberately used as an engine of oppression for driving away the Indian trade competition". [Hutten 235] The law succeeded in its objective and by 1903 all rich Indian merchants had been ruined. Only petty shopkeepers, coolies and free labour survived in Natal.

As noted by Gandhi, the sword of Damocles hung over the head of every Indian trader on account of very capricious enforcement of this law. Gandhi entered a bitter and strongly worded protest against "this terrible engine of oppression" with the colonial secretary citing concrete examples.

"All licensing officers are being chosen with one condition of they being anti-Indians". Gandhi listed [CWMG V 102] the towns and cities where for many years not a single trading license was either issued or renewed for Indian traders. In other places, Indians who had been trading for decades had their licenses revoked on the flimsiest ground. The term for the license in some towns was reduced to three months and the uncertainty ruined Indian trade. There was no judicial remedy because the courts had no jurisdiction in the matter.

Gandhi pointed out that denial of appeal to judiciary against the decisions of the persons and bodies "not unoften guided and carried away by popular feelings or prejudices would be deemed to be an arbitrary measure in any part of the civilized world: in British dominions it would be an insult to the British name and its constitution which is rightly deemed to be the purest in the world". [CWMG II 233] This proviso "violated one of the most vital principles of the British constitution and was without a precedent in any part of British Empire". [ibid]

A bitterly disappointed Gandhi wrote to Dadabhai: "We are powerless...We do not know where we are and where to go" [CWMG II 287] Gandhi called for a strenuous agitation till this disgraceful act is blotted out of the statute book" [CWMG V 72] but nothing happened.

Gandhi was never an escapist nor would he accept defeat even under most trying circumstances. Having failed to prevent the anti Indian legislation or to get it vetoed, he doggedly fought for several years against the Dealers' License Act both in the courts of law and in the press.

Gandhi fought numerous cases and lost all because the courts had no jurisdiction and no power to grant any relief. Even in the most celebrated of such cases, the Shambhunath Maharaj case, Gandhi could secure only paltry and temporary relief about the procedure to be adopted in denying a license.

The situation turned grave and continued to deteriorate. New licenses were never issued and existing licenses were most often not renewed. There were several towns where not a single license was issued for several years. The worst aspect of the act was that the uncertainty about renewal at the end of the year kept Indians in feverish anxiety about the continuity of business and about their stock and their credits. The Town Council of Durban was reported to have issued secret instructions not to issue fresh licenses to Asiatics.

Gandhi was driven to petition the colonial secretary about the woeful condition of Indians on account of the laws on immigration and license.

The license act with its blatant violation of established rights of Indian traders was "a real, present and tangible grievance". The act was a crude and violent expedient of depriving Indian merchants of their livelihood and was followed by very stringent measures to destroy Indian trade and to drive Indians out of the country.

Gandhi was intensely worried about the possibility of immense mischief under the license act and sent a pathetic SOS to the leaders in India about the need of 'immediate, urgent and continuous attention'. "All other grievances can wait for academic discussions; this brooks no delay", as it was the question of bread and survival for Indian merchants.

Gandhi appealed [27-1-99] to Lord Cruzon to pressurise the Natal government to get the law changed or to stop labour supply to the colony. Natal law was much worse than the Transvaal situation and the "active and effective intervention by the Government of India is necessary if the rights of British Indians outside India are to be rescued from extinction". [CWMG III 59]

In a series of articles that Gandhi wrote in *The Times of India* in 1899-1900, he described the conditions of Indians as 'the most wretched' and declared that "if the Home or Indian government do not give more attention than hitherto to the Indian question in South Africa, the effacement of the community in this country was a matter of time", [CWMG IV 136] and the term 'British subject' would become a meaningless phrase in Natal.

Gandhi very correctly interpreted these four acts as 'a notice to free Indians to quit the colony'. He was sharp enough and quick enough to understand that these acts sounded the death toll for Indian trade and Indian prosperity in Natal. This change would personally affect him too. After a few years there would be no Indian merchant left in Natal and coolies would hardly need his legal services. He was then earning quite well, but with the repeated failures in license cases, he would be banging his head against the wall and his practice would soon dwindle and dry up. This was therefore the end his professional career as far as Natal was concerned.

His decision to quit Natal by 1900 was in no small measure dictated by his professional interests which he saw going up in smoke before his very eyes. He must have made up his mind quite early but the work in hand and the Boer war delayed his departure for two more years.

When Barrister Talyarkhan offered to settle in Natal {1898}, Gandhi dissuaded him from coming because the prospects for Indian professionals had dimmed on account of these four acts.

These anti-Indian measures were copied by the Cape Colony though the Cape laws were far more mild and reasonable and were enforced with proper safeguards but restrictions on Indian immigration and trade in that colony also became more and more stringent. All the colonies vied with one another to drive Indians out by irritants and hardships.

The frustration among the Indian community was widespread and intense. When Gandhi failed to ameliorate the situation, Indian merchants turned their fury on him and accused him of misguiding them into trouble by political agitation against the franchise bill. The desperate merchants mounted their first open and bitter challenge to Gandhi's leadership. "It has been said that if we had not started that movement to obtain the redress, our position might not have been so bad as it now is". [CWMG III 124]

Gandhi defended himself by citing the example of Orange Free State "where Indians did nothing and lost all," and of Transvaal "where we awoke when half the ground was lost and we hope to get some redress".

This defense convinced nobody. Gandhi lost face with the merchants who up to now were his staunchest supporters. The conditions in the republics were entirely different from Natal and the strong arm of Britain protected Transvaal Indians and secured several facilities for them in practice if not in law.

In spite of all that was happening in Natal and despite his frustrations and disappointments, Gandhi's love and loyalty towards Britain did not diminish even a wee bit. This might explain his settling in Transvaal {1903}. He preferred to live in a British colony rather than in autonomous Natal. "If I had no faith in the strong sense of justice of British government... I would not be here. British love for justice and fair play are the sheet anchor of India's hope". [CWMGII 296] But even in Transvaal, his hopes were going to prove futile as British regime turned out to be much worse than Boer rule.

But even in Natal the situation was not entirely hopeless. The Government of India had lodged a strong protest against the Dealers' License Act and Lord Curzon was so upset that he threatened to discontinue the labour supply to Natal. The colonial office as also the entire press in England was breathing down the neck of Natal to ensure justice to the Indians.

The government of Natal was compelled to warn municipal councils that very blatant misuse of licensing powers might compel the government to restrict such powers and for next two years, the municipal authorities were more reasonable in issuing licenses.

Natal had to amend the license law and allow judicial appeal against improper refusal to renew the licenses. But this was not enough and an angry Curzon wrote to the India Office: "Our position has always been that appeals to the Supreme Court [be allowed] against all decisions of the licensing boards and we not prepared to accept as sufficient a proposal to allow appeals only against the withdrawals". [Hutten 261-62]

By 1898 Gandhi had become more active in Transvaal than in Natal because Transvaal was providing more opportunities for Indians. Britain had accepted the Bloemfontein award but resisted its implementation The British authorities actively helped Indians by preventing the enforcement of the law under various pretexts. The British high commissioner encouraged Indians to ignore the notices issued to them by the authorities and the Law no 3 of 1885 continued to be a dead letter.

"Prior to the outbreak of war [1899], the rights and position of Indians in Transvaal were far more aggressively protected than ever before or after as Chamberlain and Alfred Milner sought to increasingly assert British authority over Transvaal by interfering vigorously in opposing the infringement of the rights of the British subjects". [Swan 87] All this was done not out of any love or regard for the rights of the British subjects but to spite the Boers and to put them down.

The legal position of Indians in Transvaal was much worse than in Natal. They had no right to property and were expected to live and work in locations allotted to them. But Indians took full advantage of the non-implementation of anti-Indian laws. Indians were freely entering in Transvaal to set up business anywhere they liked. Many of Gandhi's clients in Natal had their branches and associates in Transvaal and had invested huge amounts in the Republic. By 1899, there were some 13,000 Indians in Transvaal. They were mostly merchants and hawkers with their total assets estimated at 800,000 pounds. They evaded the property law by either leasing European properties on very long-term basis or held them benami.

In Natal most of Indians were poor, ignorant and docile ex-indentured coolies who were either Hindus or Christians. In Transvaal, Indians were fewer in numbers but they were mostly rich and assertive Muslim merchants. Though largely uneducated, they were intelligent, successful and shrewd but often unscrupulous and shifty businessmen.

Chapter 13

BOER WAR AND INDIA

The entire landscape underwent a dramatic change and all issues and controversies in Natal were dwarfed by the outbreak of the third and last Boer war. [October 1899-May 1901] Transvaal and Orange Free state faced the mighty British Empire supported by Natal and Cape Colony. The Boers in a sudden and surprise attack on Natal occupied nearly half of it and Maritzberg as well as Durban were under a threat of being run over. This war gave an unexpected twist to a more or less placid life of Gandhi.

This "cruel war with no holds barred on either side" was "one of the most sordid of all Imperial wars." [Ash 73] The war was the outcome of several factors but one of the issues was the treatment given by Boers to Indians. War Secretary Lord Lansdowne went on record saying "of all the misdeeds of the Boers, none fills me with so much indignation as their treatment of British Indians in Transvaal". The Indian cause was used as one of the main casus belli raising thereby the hopes of the Indians.

Thousands of Uitlanders fearing detention and worse fled Transvaal; Indians followed suit and rushed out of the Republic to take refuge in Natal and India. Natal discriminated amongst the refugees. European refugees were welcomed, sheltered and helped. Indians were debarred even from entering Natal as per the Immigration Restrictions Act and were arrested for illegally entering the colony. Indians were given temporary permits on payment of pounds ten per person.

Gandhi's strong protest forced Natal government to suspend the act and Indian refugees were very reluctantly allowed free entry after some delay. Natal refused any relief or maintenance to Indians who were looked after by Natal Indian Congress and Indian community.

Gandhi in SSA and his Autobiography has discussed at great length the issue of Indian support to Britain during Boer war. But his presentations deviate very significantly from contemporary records. Gandhi asserts that the pros and cons of helping the British Empire were discussed thoroughly by the entire Indian community.

"Indians in Natal had always been denounced as money grabbers, deadweights and termites which are useless for war. We carefully considered this charge. All of us felt that this was the golden opportunity for us to prove that it was baseless...if we missed this opportunity ... we should stand self condemned and it would be no matter of surprise if the English treated us worse and sneered at us more than before". [SSA 97-98]

But "knowing as we do that a small nation like Boers is fighting for its existence, why should we be instrumental in their destruction? If they [Boers] win, they will wreck vengeance on us for siding with the British. [ibid]

But this never happened. "Some local English speaking Indians met together a few days ago and decided that because they were British subjects and as such demanded rights, they ought to forget domestic differences and irrespective of their opinion about the justice of war render some service…on the battlefield during the crisis". [CWMG III 133] "We had nothing to do with the issue whether war was right or wrong". [CWMG III 261]

The considerations of practical politics make a more interesting reading in view of the metamorphosis that Gandhi underwent between 1899 and 1929. The admiration and the sympathy for Boers expressed in SSA and his Autobiography are clearly afterthoughts and later day sentiments of a Gandhi greatly disillusioned by British regime.

Gandhi in 1899 had no love or respect lost for Boers and he had no reason to have any soft corner for them as can be seen from his contemptuous and often sarcastic references to Boers. In the contemporary records, not even once has Gandhi expressed any admiration or sympathy for Boers "The oppressive treatment of Indians by Boers together with his own experiences in Transvaal… did not give him sympathy for the Boers' case at that time". [Chandran 252]

He fully shared British dislike and hostility for Boers who were simple and brave but very racist and violent tempered. Seventeen out of the twenty-four members of their Volksraad [Parliament] had bullet wounds secured either in war or fights.

Gandhi's support to Britain during the Boer war was not an outcome of any rational analysis: it was an act of loyalty rooted in deep emotional attachment and also in several unarticulated expectations. Gandhi and the Indian community perceived a great stake in war and had very high hopes from British victory. Gandhi supported Britain for same reasons and with same hopes as Indian community as a whole did. It was universally and firmly believed that support to Britain would lead to a significant amelioration of all discriminations and disabilities suffered by Indians under Boers.

Gandhi had a blind faith that Britain can do no wrong. "It was to take several more years for Gandhi to become disenchanted with the British Empire and to lose his conviction that Indians in South Africa needed only to convincingly prove their loyalty to British Empire to be accepted by the White population". [Hutten 125]

The reasons advanced by Gandhi in SSA for supporting Britain are very important for understanding the inchoate and perplexing political philosophy of Gandhi even in 1929. "Our existence in South Africa is only in our capacity as British subjects. In every memorandum we have presented, we have asserted our rights as such. We have been proud of our British citizenship or have given our rulers and the world to understand that we are so proud. Our rulers profess to safeguard our rights because we are British subjects, and what little rights we still retain, we retain because we are British subjects ....To suggest that in case Boers won and the Boer victory was well within the range of possibility...our last state would be much worse than our first and Boers would exact a frightful revenge would be doing injustice to the chivalrous Boers as well as to ourselves". [SSA 98-99]

Then there follows a theoretical justification that is simply staggering. "It must largely be conceded that the justice was on the side of the Boers. *But every single subject of the state must not hope to enforce his private opinion in all cases.*[auto] *The authorities may not be always right but so long as subjects owe allegiance to State, it is their clear duty generally to accommodate themselves and to accord their support to the acts of State".* [SSA 98. Emphasis added]

This argument raises a very fundamental issue about satyagraha and renders it impossible. Gandhi here discusses the problem of political obligation of citizens-undoubtedly the most perplexing issue of political theory. Gandhi's acceptance of state as *the* final deciding factor for the behaviour of citizens would be a total rejection of liberalism and even of democracy. Such an emphasis on total obligation to the state would have immensely pleased political theorists from Plato to Neitschze who are the enemies of Open Society.

Such an emphasis on the total compliance with decisions of government, if extended from war to peace time, would entirely blast away the foundation of Satyagraha and would effectively shut out even a protest against the doings of the ruling junta. Such protests are 'an attempt and a hope to enforce private opinion of a subject' against the doings of state. The line of argument presented by Gandhi in 1929 would effectively rule out even the conscientious objectors and indeed the entire democratic process. Satyagraha is a protest of good Man against a bad State.

It was a very bad state that Gandhi supported and he was not unaware of it. The Boer war became infamous on account of British army burning down farms and villages. More than 1,50,000 Boer women and children were detained in concentration camps. More than 26,000 of them died of starvation and diseases after suffering at the hands of British soldiers all sorts of cruelties and indignities including rape. Gandhi himself has blamed Lord Kitchner for having deliberately inflicted such atrocities. [SSA] Gandhi's obsession with Satyagraha had become so intense by 1929 that he describes such involuntary sufferings as 'key to Satyagraha'. [SSA 22-23]

British Liberals behaved in much better way than Gandhi did. They denounced the war as 'cruel and unjust' and Sir Henry Campbell-Bannerman, the future prime minister of England organised open prayer meetings "for God to decree defeat to British forces".

"Boers and Britain were locked in a death struggle with the Golden Colony as prize" [Doke 64] and there was an atmosphere of war in Natal. Many English traders and lawyers from Natal, Cape Colony and Rhodesia left for the front.

"As soon as the war was declared, irrespective of their opinions as to the justness or otherwise of war, Indians to a man made up their minds" [CWMG III 174] and considered "the desirability of unreservedly and unconditionally offering their services to the government or the Imperial authorities in connection with the hostilities now impending". [ibid 134]

This is only partially true. Gandhi in fact played a very active role in persuading Indians for war efforts. "We were among those who assured the skeptical Indians that the bonds of British Indians in the two Republics would fall away with the close of war and we were able to silence any misgivings by pointing to the fact that as Indian disabilities were one of the causes of the war... a successful end of the later was bound to bring about the end of the former also". [CWMG III 533] "The war efforts became an integral part of Indians' attempts to validate their claim to the rights and privileges of citizenship". [Swan 15]

Gandhi was spoiling for armed service. "If Gurkhas or Sikhs were there, they [Indians] would have shown what they could do in way of fighting" and he regretted that "we do not know how to handle arms... it is perhaps our misfortune that we can not: but it may be, there are other duties, no less important to be performed on the battlefield... we would consider it a privilege to be called upon to perform them. ...If an unflinching devotion to duty and extreme eagerness to serve our Sovereign can make us of any use on the field of battle, we would not fail".

Indians volunteered for active military service but the offer was rejected because Indians had neither experience nor training for the use of arms and would become a liability rather than an asset.

The 8215 soldiers sent by India to fight Boers covered themselves with glory in many battles but more especially during the siege of Ladysmith. After the war many of them settled down in Transvaal.

Gandhi's offer that 'If in no other direction, we might render some service with the field hospitals or commissariat' was also turned down. Gandhi faced formidable obstacles in getting his offers even being considered but he persisted with his offer to serve in any capacity.

All such offers created very good impression amongst the Whites. Indian community came in for a good deal of praise by the White press. But the strong racial prejudice stood in the way of accepting Indian help. War has no respect for such prejudices and inhibitions and a severe crisis compelled British army to turn to Indian civilians for help. Britain suffered a series of reverses creating a severe crisis with ever mounting heaps of dead and wounded. "The government was in the need of as many men as it could get" [SSA 102] to reach the dead and the dying to the base hospitals.

The Protector of the Emigrants was asked to raise a corps of dhollie [stretcher] bearers out of coolies who were to be released by plantation owners. Gandhi's offer for even such menial work was accepted [15-12-99] with great reluctance and the enthusiastic Indian volunteers took lessons in hospital work under Dr. Booth.

It was a coolie job totally unsuited to educated Indians and was given to coolies. Gandhi led a small group of thirty-seven professionals who volunteered to act as leaders of coolies-stretcher bearers-who were paid fairly high wages of one pound a week.

The corps consisted of 1100-300 free and 800 indentured-coolies and theirs was hard menial labor involving long distance marches-often 25 miles at a stretch and at least 125 miles a week, with heavy loads of human bodies. But it was not a risky job except when they volunteered to work within the firing line. Not a single Indian was ever wounded.

The volunteers were not required to carry the stretchers but they had to march with them and act as their guides and leaders. Gandhi's insistence on sharing everything with coolies and the long distances he covered on foot completely shattered his health and it took him more than a year to recover. Gandhi's duty was to collect the wages and to distribute it among the coolies.

They did a wonderful job of carrying 700 wounded and 150 dead bodies. Though occasionally they were jeered at, they covered themselves with glory and were mentioned in dispatches.

"I think sufficient attention has not been paid to the devotion of Indian dhollie-bearers who do their work of mercy on the battle field. ...These Indian fellow subjects of ours are doing a work which requires more courage than even that of a soldier". [Gen. Sir Olphits]

But when Gandhi tried to publicise the good work being done by the corps, he was prevented form doing so. "Their part was merely to do without speaking". [CWMG III 159] The corps was disbanded after a week but was regrouped almost immediately and served for about six weeks. All the thirty-seven volunteer leaders including Gandhi were promised war medals but only eight were actually given. [CWMG IV 298]

The prime minister of Natal thanked Gandhi for his "timely, unselfish and most useful action in voluntarily organizing a corps of bearers... when [their] labor was most sorely needed. ...All engaged in that service deserve the grateful recognition of the community".

Such expressions of goodwill made Gandhi very optimistic. "The attitude of Natal during the crisis is a silver lining to the dark cloud that is hanging on our heads in Natal as also in other parts of South Africa". [CWMG III 133]

He saw the clear signs of Imperial unity. "If the present war brings about ... a better feeling on the part of European British subjects towards their Indian fellow subjects, it would have served one good purpose". [ibid 140]

Gandhi's enthusiasm for war and victories shines through all his actions and writings. He praised officers and soldiers of British army in spite of their sordid actions and there is hardly any trace of Ahimsa to be seen in these writings.

"Indians could not be too joyful in connection with British victories in South Africa". [CWMG III 162] He organised a thanks giving meeting where 1000 Indians and 60 Europeans were present to congratulate, felicitate and honour the victorious generals with proper addresses.

Gandhi praised volunteers of the ambulance corps for "a service both to your own self and to your mother land". Gandhi gave special gifts to all the thirty coolies who belonged to his group and promised them free legal services up to five pounds.

Gandhi was pained that Whites condemned Indians for keeping away from the armed service during war. The Indian elite had done nothing and Gandhi led only thirty-nine volunteers. Gandhi defended Indians by pointing out "Indians in Natal again and again petitioned government to be allowed to go to the front in any capacity", [CWMG IV 356] and that "It was with very great difficulty that they could get their services accepted even for ambulance work". [CWMG V 134] Gandhi rejoiced when, after 1904, Natal Indians were allowed armed service and he suggested regular Indian militia with military training.

Gandhi's attitude to war remained ambivalent till the very end of his life. He participated in Boer war and Zulu war. His efforts to raise an ambulance corps in 1914 was frustrated by protocol and in 1915 he strived to recruit soldiers for British army. He supported the use of the Indian army in Kashmir [1947].

In his speech at Calcutta [1902] Gandhi very highly praised war camps and talked a lot of rubbish. He found there 'the same holy stillness' as at the monastery of Trappists. "As a Hindu, I do not involve in war but if anything can even partially reconcile me to it, it was the rich experience we gained at the front",...[where] "proud, rude, savage spirits [were] converted into gentle creatures of God". [CWMG III 265]

However minor or insignificant be Gandhi's role in Boer war, it would be a grievous error to attribute it to an ulterior motive or to political ambition he has been accused of. "He was a political figure and all other work…would have to yield precedence to the politician whose motives were far more complex than perhaps he acknowledges. The iron or ambition had entered into him". [Payne 115]

Gandhi did not have any political ambitions in South Africa. In a strong rejoinder to the accusation by the Natal Mercury, he had clarified [25-4-97] "I have no political ambition whatever. Those who know me personally, know well in what direction my ambition lies". [CWMG II 246]

He was a hardheaded realist to understand that any political ambition would be unattainable in Natal. He never had any desire to settle permanently in Africa. Rich and educated Indians always returned to India after one or two decades having their fill of South Africa and Gandhi did the same.

By 1900, Gandhi had had enough of Africa. All the gates and windows were closing on Indians in South Africa that was fast becoming too uncongenial for Indians to stay and work.

Gandhi by now had developed wings and was quite confident of professional success in India. He had already decided to quit Africa for good and settle in India and was deliberately and methodically winding up his business and residential establishments.

His statements "eight months after my release from the war duty, I felt my work was no longer in Africa but in India" [Auto] and "I intended to do public work in India. I had learnt in Africa the lesson of service instead of self interest". [SSA 109] are rather tenuous. There was no dearth of political and public work in South Africa and he did no public work in India during the year that he stayed here.

In spite of uncertainties in Transvaal and Natal, Gandhi did not change his decision to quit Natal. His services to the community were warmly appreciated at several felicitation meetings held in his honor and he was presented with addresses some of them carved on gold and silver.

The most memorable of such meetings was held [15-10-01] at the Congress Hall—Durban. The hall was packed to capacity with his Indian and European admirers. Numerous gifts in cash and seven costly ornaments of gold and diamond were presented to him by his friends and colleagues. The address given to him by Indian leaders in Natal spoke about "The domestic duties which necessitates your going to India" and expressed the hope that "You would decide to cast your lot with us again". [CWMG III 567] The Indian community was sore to loose his services.

Gandhi gracefully accepted their love and promised to return if his services were needed within a year. "I was allowed to leave only on one condition that if within a year any unprecedented situation arose in South Africa requiring my presence, the community may recall me any day and I should go back". [SSA 109] He was to be recalled only for a period not exceeding six months and in that case the community would pay for his travels and stay for any such temporary and short visit.

Gandhi, however, decided not to accept costly gifts as that would be a sort of reimbursement for his public services. "What I value is the affection that has prompted the gifts but not the gifts as such". [CWMG III 246]

He persuaded or rather coerced his wife and children to return the gifts that amounted to about a thousand pounds. He handed over the cash and jewellery including those he had accepted and kept in 1896 to the African Banking Corp. and established a public trust to utilise the deposit as a sort of emergency fund, if Natal Indian Congress so needed.

Gandhi felt that the gifts were a sort of tribute to the Congress principles. He retained the right to withdraw part or all of jewellery but stipulated "neither I nor my family can make any personal use of the costly presents which are too sacred to be sold".

Gandhi together with his family sailed for India on 18th October 1901 and traveled very leisurely taking nearly two months on the way. He stayed for three weeks in Mauritius and was accorded several receptions by the Indians in that island and the governor Sir Charles Bruce hosted a party for Gandhi who by now was the most prominent leader of Indians settled in various colonies of the British Empire. Gandhi sailed from the island on 19th November 1901.

II

A dog-tired and a very sick Gandhi arrived at Rajkot by the middle of December 1901 and almost immediately left for Bombay on his way to Calcutta to attend a session of the Indian National Congress.

Gandhi yearned for a Congress resolution demanding rights for Indians in South Africa. He was somewhat put off by Pheroze Shah Mehta's dry comment "What rights do we have in our own country? So long as we have no power in our own country, you can't fare better in the colonies".

Gokhale helped him in getting such a resolution put on the agenda of the session and it was passed as a mere formality after Gandhi was allowed to speak on it for barely two minutes. Gandhi was shocked by the filth and chaos he witnessed at the venue of Congress session and tried to put things into order.

Gandhi tried hard through Turner, the president of the Bengal Chamber of Commerce, to set up an all-party delegation [CWMG III 251] to Viceroy Lord Curzon whom he rated very highly. "We have a vigilant and a masterful Viceroy in Lord Curzon and we hope His Excellency would not permit any serious injustice to be perpetrated". [ibid 309]

The delegation was to request some relief for Indians fighting against heavy odds in South Africa. Natal was fast becoming 'a sealed book' but there was still some hope. "Authorities here and in the Downing Street are not and cannot be unsympathetic. [ibid 250] But Gandhi did not succeed in getting anything beyond a very sympathetic letter from the Viceroy through Mr. Turner". [ibid 258]

Gandhi stayed back at Calcutta for a month and delivered two lectures—one about Boer war and the other about Trappists. He advocated a sustained agitation and "a unanimous, emphatic, temperate and continuous expression of public opinion on the subject of South Africa".

While at Calcutta, Gandhi stayed with Gokhale and through him met several public figures of Bengal. Gandhi made a short trip to Rangoon and advised his relatives about the good opportunity for business there.

A believing Hindu that he was, Gandhi visited various centers of pilgrimage in north India travelling in third class compartments of the railways. This was his first acquaintance with Indian society in its stark reality. His experience was very happy. "I feel all the richer and stronger in spirit for the experience". [CWMG III 273] Claiming that he had travelled third class compartment of railways in Europe, he declared that "I would far rather be in the third class compartment in India than in Europe", [ibid 282] where it was far more dirty and far much worse company.

For the first six months in India, Gandhi chose to relax and recuperate from a totally shattered health but he did not remain idle. He won all the three court cases that he conducted at Rajkot. But Gandhi did not take up too much of professional work. While at Rajkot, [February 1902] he became a secretary of the State Volunteer Plague Committee, carried on correspondence with Gokhale promising help in raising the Ranade Memorial fund.

Even after six months, he was still very weak and emaciated from the strain of the war services in Natal. "I am supposed to be taking rest, not that there would be much work for me in Kathiawar even if I opened a regular office" [CWMG III 305] "I shall try to take my weight, but [there is] a desirable change for the better". [ibid 310]

Poor health was not his only problem. He had to carry on a long and bitter correspondence with his clients in Natal to recover his dues from them. "I did not expect my pecuniary position to be so bad as it is.... You will understand how great must be my need for money... it will be possible for me to stay in Bombay if the amounts due start coming in from your end regularly... If I receive the funds expected from Natal, I would settle in Bombay and give it a try for a year". [CWMG III 306-7]

It was in July that he received a remittance of Rs. 3000 and immediately shifted to Bombay to build up his practice there and also to get launched into the political orbit by staying closer to Gokhale. He stayed in a bunglow at Santacruz and took a one-room office just opposite the Bombay High Court building. He felt free "to lounge about the High Court, letting the solicitors know of an addition to the ranks of the brief-less ones". [CWMG III 313]

But he was discouraged from all sides. "Phiroze Shah Mehta told me that I would be foolishly wasting my small savings from Natal... Solicitors...say that I would have to wait long before I get any work from them.... The work is uphill. But I do not despair. I rather appreciate the regular life and the struggle Bombay imposes on one. So long therefore as the latter does not become unbearable, I am not likely to wish to be away from Bombay". [CWMG III 313]

Gandhi was more fortunate and better connected than others. His friends in Rajkot kept him supplied with work and he started earning enough to cover his office expenses. "I have begun to feel my way about here". His practice grew up but at a rather sluggish rate and "a desultory, uncomplicated and not a very prominent career was opening up before him". [Payne]

Neither sickness nor financial worries held Gandhi back from public activities. He has no loco standi in the political arena of India but he strove to advocate the issue nearest to his heart and head—namely the condition of Indians in South Africa. While in India, he kept himself in close and continuous touch with the happenings in South Africa by securing newspapers and official documents from his friends and associates there.

He spoke very frequently and wrote extensively about his African experiences and about the difficulties and disabilities suffered by Indians there. He emphatically protested against the Natal bill to impose the poll tax on children of coolies as they reach the age of maturity [boys sixteen, girls thirteen].

He was amazed and pained that leaders of the Natal Congress who were rich did not care to protest against this 'children's bill' and also against the 'civil service bill' because they were not directly affected.

Gandhi never charged anything for public service but at this time he was so much in financial trouble that he proposed to charge twenty-five pounds to the Natal Indian Congress for his travels and office work.

He tried to sell his typewriter to the Congress and to employ his nephew Chhaganlal for office work with what then was a huge salary of rupees forty per month. "If it [the proposal] is accepted, it will enable me to carry on public work whenever expenses are necessary". [CWMG III 306]

He was upset with Indian leaders in Natal and chided them. "Indians are rent by dissentions and are suffering from disgraceful revelations and scandals… Our Congress and our associations are to no purpose if we are unable to carry out the very ordinary principles of morality…

I have to ask you to cleanse our homes of moral leprosy and...be prepared to suffer insults and to work for the sake of work and not for any name or distinction". [CWMG III 288]

Gandhi, a formidable fighter and a brilliant leader in Africa was rather quiet in India. The man who spoke so loudly in Durban was almost tongue-tied in Bombay as he had no occasion to speak and no theme to talk about. No one in India was much interested in the conditions of a handful of merchants or poor coolies who went to that distant land to enrich themselves.

Gandhi had written off Natal as a colony where Indians could have any prospects of an honourable existence and he wanted to concentrate on Transvaal and Orange River Colony. He still hoped that British authorities would sooner or later quash or at least considerably soften anti Indian legislation of Boers because Britain had denounced these laws in very strong terms.

In spite of his promise to return, he was very unwilling to go back to Natal and tried hard to get released from his commitment. "It would be gracious to free me unless it is to be enforced in the near future". [CWMG III 281]

In November 1902, when Gandhi was requested to go first to London and then to proceed to Transvaal, he declined to go "unless it was absolutely necessary... I do not yet feel strong enough for the mental strain, a visit to London and South Africa would require". [CWMG III 314] The request was repeated and his fees and his expense money were remitted. ["Barrister Gandhi, committee requests fulfill promise. Remitting".]

Gandhi still hesitated. "As I have not left in me sufficient energy to cope with the difficulties there, I have asked certain questions before deciding to leave, so that my way would be as smooth as possible... at any rate as the internal management is concerned". [CWMG III 315]

But he felt that he would have to go. ... "99 chances to 1, I will have to leave". Finally Gandhi decided to comply with the request for his presence and went South Africa for six months even though the issues and problems in Transvaal or Natal were nothing new.

He had been in Bombay only for four months and the work had already started coming in. Gandhi was eager to have more Indian lawyers in Africa and he requested several of them but could not get anyone eager to go.

"South Africa can accommodate 6 Indian barristers if not more and if some ... of the right stamp were to come with one eye on their living and the other on public work, much of the burden may be distributed". [CWMG III 315] Gandhi left in a hurry and did not wait even to meet his mentor Gokhale before leaving India. He was hoping to be back after a short break but once he went there, he stayed on for twelve years.

Chapter 14

TRANSVAAL

The South Africa to which Gandhi returned in 1903 was vastly different from the one he had left a year ago. The political configuration had changed beyond recognition. The republics were now Crown colonies controlled and directly administered by Britain. Gandhi had come only as a temporary visitor but the circumstances forced him to stay on. With full faith in British justice and their sense of fair play, Gandhi chose not Natal but Transvaal as the fulcrum of his professional and political activities during the ensuing decade.

The landscape he witnessed was a surprise and a shock to him. The power equations had so completely changed that Britain, an erstwhile protector of British Indians during Boer regime had now turned into their tormentor on behalf of the Boers and the Whites. British authorities were continuously on the horns of dilemma and were caught between the cross fire of their past promises and their postwar policy.

In Transvaal, history was moving very fast but in a retrogressive direction for Indians. After an embarrassingly difficult war, Britain had conquered [May 1901] the richest country in the world. The martial law regime [May-December 1901] under Lord Milner was converted into a civilian government and Milner functioned as the governor of Transvaal and Orange River Colony up to March 1905. Transvaal was granted responsible government in 1906 and became a self-governing colony in 1907.

In post-war Transvaal, a raucous debate raged around Indians – their numbers, their trade and their residences. The triangular debate between Britain, Transvaal and Indians got converted into a bilateral confrontation [1906] between autonomous Transvaal and Gandhi as the leader of Indian community.

Before the war, the British authorities had severely denounced the treatment given by Boers to Indians and "the British Agent at Pretoria had often told me that if Transvaal became a British colony, all the grievances under which Indians labor would be immediately redressed".

But after the conquest, Britain needed local support and co-operation in order to fully exploit the wealth of the region. Boers though defeated were un-subdued subjects to be placated and Europeans in Transvaal-Boers as well as British had nothing but contempt for all coloured people including Indians and they were determined to keep them away from sharing the prosperity of the land. So the thrust of the new British policy was that all earlier policy statements as well as the promises given to Indians were to be quickly and quietly replaced by evasions and equivocations.

Much of the confusion, animosity and heartburning caused by these controversies were the legacy of Boer republic. The Boers had enacted most severe anti-Indian laws in South Africa but then could not or did not implement them. The law required Indians to get registered before entering; they were to be confined to locations for residential and trade purposes; they could trade or hawk only with licenses; they had no property rights.

But the opposition of British overlords, inefficiency and corruption of the Boer administration and the clever evasion of laws by Indians had created a strange situation in which not a single provision of any such laws could ever be enforced.

The anti-Indian laws of Transvaal were much worse than in Natal but the actual situation was much better. Before the war, Indians could come and go freely, could stay anywhere they liked, start, close, restart, shift and transfer business anywhere and trade with or without license. Such illegalities were very common and were practiced on a massive scale—"an extraordinary state of things but nevertheless a fact".

In post war Transvaal, the local Whites and the British rulers insisted on enforcing all such laws that Boers had never enforced. The doors of Transvaal were now to be closed to newcomers from India and resident Indians must now stay and trade only in locations.

The Indian community had other dreams and expectations. They had entertained high hopes from the bonhomie during the stressful period of war. Indians had hoped that as a reward of war services, British assurances given frequently before the war would be implemented; all anti-Indian laws would he quashed or at least considerably softened to remove disabilities imposed upon them by Boer laws and the entire area would be opened to Indian traders and settlers. These hopes started vanishing by 1902. "We are all very nervous about it". [CWMG III 202] The Natal Indian Congress [December 1902] called upon British authorities for "a just, equitable and liberal treatment of Indian settlers in the colony" of Transvaal.

European and Indian refugees who had fled Transvaal [1899] and had taken shelter in Natal and elsewhere were very eager to return to their homes and shops. But the conditions in Transvaal immediately after war were greatly unsettled and there was an acute shortage of everything including food and clothing.

Taking advantage of post war confusion and unsettled administration, Europeans and Indians rushed into Transvaal. British military officers allowed free entry to all of them irrespective of whether they were newcomers or old residents. The genuine refugees took longer in returning. Many Indians who were new entrants secured licenses and began trading activities.

Indians were accused of infiltration on a massive scale. Lord Milner declared that 'a large number of people have come in…without proper authority' and Haji Omar Ali agreed that Indians have intruded "in far more numbers than the Whites". [CWMG III 370-71] Ali blamed the railways. "Any Indian who said that he was a refugee was brought in". [ibid]

The Europeans protested vehemently against such a rush and Peace Preservation Ordinance [1902] was issued prohibiting entry to all undesirable and dangerous characters as well as to political offenders. Only refugees who were old residents were to be allowed entry and that too only with permits.

A disconcerting shock was administered to the Indian community in issuing such re-entry permits. Entry permits were immediately and freely issued to European refugees on the basis of active war service while thousands of Indians had to wait anxiously and indefinitely to return to Transvaal.

A new department—Department of Asiatic Affairs was established on a temporary basis [1902] to handle the cases of Indian permit seekers.

Since three departments—Asiatic, Colonial and Registrar of Asiatics—in addition to the permit secretary were involved in the process, a long and circuitous procedure now took minimum of three to six months to get a permit after an Indian had proved his bona fide. Only seventy permits were issued per week and this would take three to four years to clear the applications of nearly ten thousand Indian refugees. Frequent changes of rules and procedure of the department was a torture for genuine refugees while the dishonest ones would sneak in by bribery. The officials were very anti- Indian. "Its [Department's] business is to invent new engines of terror". [CWMG III 392] Indians had to submit special applications with thumb impression and needed two European references. Gandhi's strong protest against such referees was effective and the rule was quashed.

The delays and uncertainties led to rampant corruption and there was "a gang of permit agents who simply fleeced innocent refugees" [CWMG IV 145] forcing each one of them to pay between 15 to 30 pounds. This was a very thriving and lucrative business. There was a wide spread permit racket and an assistant Consul of Greece was punished for getting involved in such illicit activity. Numerous Indians were also involved in such rackets.

Gandhi offered [1903-05] his legal services to those seeking permits and contacted the department on their behalf; but he never was a tout or an agent in that sense though he was accused to be such. In fact, Gandhi exposed the prevailing corruption and the Asiatic department had to sack two of its senior officers.

Things improved very soon. The Permit Regulation Act [October 1903] provided simple, free and quick issue of permits eliminating thereby the need for agents and touts. "Corruption has already disappeared and bona fide refugees are able to get permits without unreasonable delays". [CWMG IV 96] The Department of Asiatic Affairs became redundant and was closed down by the end of 1903.

The issue of permits was stopped by the end of 1904 and by then 8129 permits had been issued to Indians. There were nearly ten thousand Indians in Transvaal and nearly half of them lived in Johannesburg and Pretoria.

The Indian community experienced second and a more severe jolt when military authorities declared [24-11-1904] that they had no intention to alter the existing laws and regulations. The colonial secretary assured Transvaal and Orange River Colony that 'the existing laws...would be adopted by the new regime as far as possible.

The statement of policy issued by Britain also had an ominous ring. Before war, Britain had insisted upon "equal rights to all *civilized* races and fair treatment to natives". This was now changed to "equality of *all White* races and fair treatment to the natives".

Gandhi was sharp enough to notice the change and warned his people. "If the change to White is deliberate, it suggests a cause for grave anxiety...The question is most serious and our position most painful". [CWMG III 220]

The British administrators accepted all anti-Indian laws of the old regime "to the horror of every Indian in South Africa and they are now being enforced with a rigor unknown before". [ibid 218] The Indian protest against such a decision was brushed aside.

These laws were very old but they had never been enforced and 'they were more or less dead letters'. "Readiness of the last government to allow the evasion of its own laws when strict application became inconvenient or when influence was brought to bear in favor of the fortunate individual" was quite well known. But now "every anti-Indian ordinance of the old government is unearthed and with strict British regularity applied to the victims". [CWMG III 218]

Under the Boer rule, Indians had no right to own property. Many Indians believing that British rulers would now permit property rights had purchased properties on a massive scale and Europeans had sold properties to them under the same belief. But the registration office rejected all purchase documents under the old and hated law no 3 of 1885.

Indians were worried but felt that all was not lost yet. British rulers had condemned these laws and they had repeatedly promised to rescind them at the first opportunity.

Lord Milner had constituted a committee to scan the Boer statute book and to repeal "all laws repugnant to the spirit of British constitution and inconsistent with the rights and interests of Her Majesty's subjects". [Nanda 61] Boar laws affecting Europeans were forthwith quashed but anti-Indian laws were separated in a different schedule to be enforced till they were abolished.

Gandhi quoted old promises and assurances and asked an anguished question: "Is then the very evil to remove which ...the war had been entered upon, to be continued under the British flag"? [CWMG III 219] All that he met with was a stony silence that spoke eloquently.

The Indians who had stayed back and those who had returned to Transvaal were now to be driven to live in separate and distant locations "removing them like cattle or criminals at the sweet will of [municipal] corporations". [CWMG III 481] This would humiliate them and ruin their business.

Location laws were old but "prior to 1899, not a single British Indian was ever compulsorily removed to location or prevented from trading outside locations". [CWMG III 493] "The location laws were never enforced against respectable Indians and only a few, very few actually suffered from the indignity of the footpath and other laws". [CWMG III 218]

II

The occasion that motivated Indian leaders in Natal to urgently request Gandhi's presence was quite different. The colonial secretary, Chamberlain, was for the first time visiting Durban on his way to Pretoria to receive thirty-five million pounds from Transvaal [Auto. Part IV chap I] and the Indian leaders were keen to apprise him about the deteriorating situation for British Indian subjects in Natal as well as in Transvaal where locations had become a grave issue.

By the end of 1902, Indians were being pushed into locations in almost all the towns in Transvaal and now Natal proposed to enact a similar legislation. Moreover, the Dealers' License Act was likely to be copied in Transvaal.

Gandhi's proven abilities and long experience made him the ablest person to draft the necessary memorandums and to lead delegations of Indian community in both the colonies to the visiting celebrity. The services of Gandhi were therefore needed rather urgently but only for a temporary period.

Gandhi arrived on 25th December 1902 and not a day was to be lost. He drew up the necessary memorandum and led [27-12-02] deputations to Chamberlain in Durban and Maritzberg to protest against new disabilities being imposed on Indians by Natal. In a trite presentation without fire or fury, Gandhi concentrated on five issues— Dealers' License Act, the Immigration Act, Transvaal refugees who were stranded in Natal, education facilities for Indian children and a three Pounds tax on coolies that was now starting to be collected.

Chamberlain was polite but cold, distant and non-responding to Indian plea. He pleaded that these laws were old, "the Imperial government had little control over the internal affairs of a self governing colony".

He advised Indian leaders to placate local European community rather than appeal to Britain because Britain would be able to do but little. Gandhi commented wryly "He has brought home to us the rule of might being right or the law of sword". Chamberlain was not insensitive but he was confessing the self-imposed limits of Imperial authorities while dealing with autonomous colonies.

"This was not the only occasion when laboring under deep and natural disappointment at his [Gandhi's] failure to redress the humiliating disabilities, Gandhi failed to apprehend the inherent quality of constitutional relations between Britain and self governing colonies... to whose autonomous status India was already aspiring. Once the period of dependent minority was ended and that of majority attained, the autonomous unit had the freedom of choice of right and wrong action with all its consequences. This is what made the Imperial government, even though the protective powers have been reserved in the self governing constitutions regarding the minorities or unfranchised sections of the population, increasingly hesitant to interfere". [Polak 40]

Nothing much could be done in the Natal, which was a self-governing colony; but Indian hopes were pinned on Transvaal that was still a Crown colony under full British control. Indians hoped for the quashing of anti-Indian laws that were manifestly un-British and violated the proclaimed assurances given by British authorities. Transvaal Whites were jittery about such an eventuality.

Gandhi's arrival in Durban had made Transvaal officials nervous. Davidson, the colonial secretary in Pretoria wrote "A Mr. Gandhi...a lawyer from Natal should not be allowed to pose as a champion of Asiatics". [Hutten 148]

Gandhi now prepared to go to Pretoria but the time at his disposal was very short and attitude of the officials was very hostile. It was impossible for him to secure entry permit from Pretoria. Gandhi utilised his old friendship with police superintendent Alexander and got a permit issued to him by the Durban office as a returnee on the ground of his stay in Pretoria in 1893.

That stay had been very short, it was only a professional visit and it had ended long ago. But technically Gandhi *had* resided in Transvaal. The bureaucrats at the Asiatic office fretted and fumed to no end, but they could do but little as the permit was legally valid and binding.

There was an all round fear and dislike for Gandhi: he was a renowned lawyer and a clear-headed leader in whose presence Indians could neither be frightened nor cheated. The ignorant, corrupt and arrogant officers hated his very presence and very strenuous efforts were made to ignore him and even to insult him on every possible occasion.

"The government officials had resolved to remorselessly fight with Gandhi and if possible eliminate his influence from Asiatic politics in Transvaal". [Doke 71] The assistant colonial secretary remonstrated with Indians for calling in Gandhi and Davison avoided Gandhi with a gratuitous insult. "I do not want to see you or discuss matters with you". [Doke 71]

Gandhi arrived on 2nd January 1903 and drafted a memorandum to be presented to Chamberlain enlisting eight disabilities imposed on Indians in Transvaal. Indians were being forced to reside and trade in locations and could own property only in those areas. Indians could not use footpaths, or vehicles or higher classes for rail journey. They were subjected to registration and had to pay three pounds as the fees. They were confined to their houses during night and the gold laws denied them diggers' licenses or right of trading in raw gold.

Gandhi himself was excluded from the delegation as 'an outsider'. Chamberlain declined to see him on two grounds. He had already heard him in Durban and secondly "I might learn about the situation in Transvaal first hand from local residents". [SSA 114]

Gandhi and the Indian leaders were very upset at this, not very subtle, attempt to denigrate and sideline Gandhi who earlier had made several representations on behalf of Transvaal Indians. "I was fully conversant with Indian situation there... but then arguments based on reason do not always appeal to men in Authority". [SSA 115]

Gandhi swallowed the insult and persuaded other members of the delegation not to cancel the appointment. The merchants could not speak English. So the delegates were led by a supervisor of Asiatics. Nothing much could be expected from such a meeting.

Chamberlain advised Indian leaders to "try and conciliate public opinion and work with the authorities in Transvaal" [CWMG III 339] and "it was their duty to agree with the sentiments of European population so long as these sentiments do not interfere with your rights".

Gandhi had urged "It is the wretched anti-Indian legislation inherited from the Republic that we are struggling against". [CWMG III 340] Gandhi argued that 'if self governing colonies like Natal and Cape Colony had no locations for Indians, how can a crown colony push Indians into locations'?

Chamberlain explained the futility of quashing anti-Indian legislation or enacting pro-Indian laws "which would soon be repealed by the responsible government in two or three years". Chamberlain was equivocal to anti-Indian delegation of Whites. "Indians are our fellow subjects entitled to fair and honorable treatment" but he also sympathized with "your opposition to the unrestricted influx of millions from India who may easily swamp you". He advocated restrictions on immigration but those who have already settled here should not suffer any disabilities.

Gandhi insisted on a thorough overhaul. "Patchwork was useless and palliatives were dangerous. Uproot the tree, cutting branches is of no use". But Britain had neither the machinery, nor the time and nor again the Will for any such policy decision.

"Chamberlain was not unfriendly; but he was deeply impressed by the intense and universal hostility which existed among the whites against free Asiatic immigration and he was worried that if he exerted pressure beyond certain point, his action would be resented so as to set on foot a movement for succession from British Empire". [Hutten 140]

"It was impracticable to secure any important concession for British Indian subjects resident in Transvaal since the policy of Transvaal appears to be approved by a great majority of the Europeans both English and Dutch in various colonies". [ibid]

Gandhi was now very eager to return to India. He had not allowed his law office in Bombay to be vacated. "I may leave in March 1903...If it does not involve the breach of duty, I shall make every effort to return home. ... It is no bed of roses here". [CWMG III 336]

"I have been in the thick of a fight... The struggle is far more intense than I had expected... It probably means my having to stay here longer than March '03". [CWMG III 341]

Frequent and kaleidoscopic changes in the attitude of British rulers in Transvaal created a pendulum of hopes and frustrations that kept Indians on tenterhooks and delayed Gandhi's departure. By June 1903, he was in despair. "It will be almost impossible for me to get away for several years—at least 3/4 years". [CWMG III 425]

Gandhi has never explained reasons for his staying on in Africa. But the reason choosing Transvaal over Natal is very convincing and very obvious. The Indian community in Transvaal faced very severe and stressful problems that were novel and there was some hope of securing justice from the British Crown. Almost all the rich merchants of Natal had their business branches located in Transvaal and needed Gandhi to be there to look after their commercial interests. There was not much to be done in Natal. The community needed his services more in Transvaal than in Natal.

From a personal point of view, the prospects for earning and for a good life were much brighter in Transvaal, which was a still a British colony than in self-governing Natal where Indian business was being systematically smothered and eliminated. Gandhi decided to stay and work in Transvaal "if need be all my life". [SSA]

He had promised his wife to call her to Africa if he had to stay for more than six months. As soon as he realised that it would be much longer, he tried to dissuade hir from joining him. He wrote to inform her that he intended to return to India in three or four years; but if she chose to come, it would be ten years because living was very expensive in Transvaal. She had not got enough company in Natal and felt lonely: but it could be much worse in Transvaal.

"It will be best for her to remain in India but... I wish to be guided entirely by her sentiments and I place myself absolutely in her hands". [CWMG III 425/6] This is a rare view of Gandhi as a doting husband who had to communicate indirectly to his wife. Kastur was illiterate and the letters had to be read to her. She chose to come and Gandhi left Transvaal after ten years as he had said he would. [CWMG IV 426]

Gandhi got himself enrolled as an advocate with the Supreme Court of Transvaal [April 1903] and settled down in Johannesburg. Almost immediately he became the most reputed and highly paid lawyer in the city, employing about thirty junior lawyers and clerks. His clientele grew so vast and the inflow of work was so enormous that even such a large staff could barely cope with work. Gandhi's practice thrived as never before. There was a steady rise in his income that climaxed to 5000/6000 Pounds per annum by 1907 which would be equivalent to more than two crores of rupees a year in our days.

Johannesburg was a flourishing city with a large population of Indians many of whom had sneaked into the colony with the connivance of notoriously corrupt Asiatic department. Johannesburg was the richest city in Transvaal, "a city without a soul" where "everyone is engrossed in thinking how to amass maximum wealth in minimum time". [SSA 4-5]

"Johannesburg, a polyglot city was a Monte Carlo superimposed upon Sodom and Gemmorah, a central sin spot of civilization" [Hamilton Fye quoted by Hutten] It had a large population of Jews who were a persecuted minority in Transvaal.

Rev. Doke mentions Gandhi's contacts with the Dutch Reformed Church and Gandhi himself has mentioned his prolonged discussions with several Christian mystics and missionaries. For a number of years in Africa, Gandhi was very close to Christianity. As he told Millie Polak, [p.30] "I did once seriously think of embracing Christian faith". But he was not ready to accept Christ as the only saviour and rated Buddha a bit superior to Christ offending thereby his Christian friends.

In Transvaal, Gandhi was also in very close touch with Theosophists and often spoke at their meetings. Nearly all his European friends in Transvaal were the ones he met in Theosophical circles or at vegetarian restaurants and most of them—Ritch, Polak, Schelslin, Keelenbach— were Jews.

The four lectures on Hinduism that he delivered at society meetings created for him endless troubles and misunderstandings with Muslims in South Africa. Gandhi now turned more and more to Hinduism, read Hindu scriptures including *Upanishads* and *Yoga Sutras* of Patanjali. Tolstoy's *The Kingdom of God is Within You* and the *Gita* became a sheet anchor of his faith. The one book that influenced him greatly was *Dharmavichar* of a Gujarati poet Narmad who had passed through similar phases. "Christian Evangelists ultimately converted Gandhi into an evangelical Hindu"—a person with a missionary zeal to convert all others to his own beliefs. [Chandran 258]

By 1904, Gandhi had imbibed the principles of voluntary poverty and began to spend most of his earnings for public causes and activities, supporting causes and ventures that were close to his heart.

Gandhi activated and utilised British Indian Association of which Sheth Haji Habib was the president and the moving spirit. Gandhi worked as its secretary during almost his entire stay in Transvaal. This Association was 'a party not on the Western lines but on lines well recognized in India' [Swan]. Like the Indian National Congress before 1919, it had no constitution, or a formal structure or formal membership. It had no permanent funds.

The association had a more or less informal structure in Johannesburg and in Pretoria and convened meetings of the delegates of other bodies and associations in Transvaal as and when needed.

The low level of political activities undertaken by Gandhi during his first three years in Johannesburg is indicated by the fact that "during these years, there were only three mass meetings, only 6 deputations and a few petitions and letters all of them "uninspired and un-inspiring". [Swan 110] But then there was hardly any occasion for such presentations.

The oppressive and discriminatory anti Indian laws were very old laws and were established since long. There was no specific legal or political ground to protest against such laws. Gandhi through British Indian Association repeatedly pointed to the misuse of such laws but Britain would not and India could not give any effective help. Gandhi in Transvaal was not idle or quiet but he was helpless. He could do but little to secure any concrete relief.

By the time the offensive in the form of new anti-Indian legislation began in 1906, Gandhi had lost faith in such representations and he handled the situation not with petitions but with confrontation.

During these [1903-06] years of dormant leadership and political hibernation, an alert, industrious and indefatigable Gandhi fought ever-mounting upsurge of anti-Indian hatreds. Gandhi's efforts to get anti-Indian laws rescinded on the basis of promises given by Britain, elicited only flowery verbiage from London and Pretoria-both promising to look into the matter at proper time but nothing happened. It was a "great words, little sympathy and no action" syndrome.

Unlike Natal, Indians in Transvaal were too few [hardly 10000] and were scattered in various cities and towns in midst of an overwhelming number of the Europeans [128000] who bitterly complained about the increasing number of Indians sneaking in by bribery and through an open land frontier. Early in 1904, 579 Indians were expelled for such illegal entry. Gandhi denied the allegation of large-scale infiltration but Governor Lord Milner supported the allegation. "Had we to deal with Asiatic population as it existed before war, it might have been possible to remain passive... but with so many new comers pouring in and applying for licenses to trade and with the European population protesting with increasing vehemence against them... it becomes impossible to persist in the policy of complete inaction". [Huten 132]

The crux of controversy was the number of Indians residing in Transvaal before war. No census was taken between 1891 and 1911 and so there was no objective data nor was any reliable information was available on this crucial issue. Whatever scanty record was there had been destroyed during the war.

There were some 5000 Indians in Transvaal in 1890. "Transvaal was absolutely open to free migrations of British Indians". [CWMG III 455] A large number of Indians had entered and had settled in the republic between 1895 and 1899. The Registrar of the Asiatics had no precise figures because two-thirds of such Indian migrants never cared to get registered so as to save three pounds.

The figures about the pre-war resident Indians that were bandied about varied from 9000 to 19,000—Boers pushing the figure down and Indians claiming higher figure. "It is an undisputed fact that there were over 15,000 British Indians adult males in Transvaal". [CWMG V 69-72] But Gandhi could cite no source of definite information and his statement was treated as a mere guesstimate.

Indians were also charged with cheating the administration and there was a long list of allegations and accusations against them. The domicile permits issued by the Republic were shoddy and bore no names of the holders. It was alleged that such certificates were never returned to government after retirement or death of the persons concerned but were sold and bought by the new comers in Bombay and Durban. It was known that 144 permit holders had died but only 4 permits had been returned. A few Indians using such certificates purchased in Bombay for Rupees ninety, were found and expelled.

Indians were also accused of bringing adult children to the colony as underage dependents and employ them in shops; children of relatives were often passed off as their own. Quite often the related females were brought in as wives. Gandhi angrily repudiated all such charges and allegations as attempts to malign Indians and the last one he called "an infamous lie and a libel on Indian women". [CWMG V 435] But Gandhi had to admit about isolated cases of such misdemeanours.

The permit rules became more and more stringent and insulting. Indians were treated as dirt and were required to prove their previous residency. The wives and children would be admitted only after the evidence of their being genuine and children after being proved to be under the age of twelve. At that time neither marriages nor births were registered in India and therefore it was extremely difficult to submit any legal proof. The permit had to bear fingerprint of the holder for identification. By 1904, strict police search and other measures were afoot to hunt out Indians who had no permits. [CWMG V 28/29] Indians led by Gandhi submitted several petitions and memorandums against such harassment to the genuine returnees.

Indian refugees had taken shelter in Natal where a few, isolated cases of plague were reported. Using this as a pretext, Indians were prevented from entering Transvaal though Europeans from the same area were freely admitted. Gandhi half in jest and half in fury demanded to know "Is there anything special in Indians so that they will bring the plague more quickly in this country than other races"? "All this savors more of persecution than precaution". [CWMG III 459]

The returning Indians faced most urgent and most distressing problems about residence and business. The Europeans insisted that Transvaal should not become another Natal and the law No.3 of 1885 must be implemented to force all Indians to reside and trade only in locations. During the Boer regime, only poorer Indians with unsanitary habits had to live in locations on the outskirts of cities and towns.

After 1901, fifty-four locations were set aside for returning Indians. These locations were unfit for human habitation being largely devoid of sanitation, water supply and electricity. Most of them were very far away without any transport facility. The location at Johannesburg was thirteen miles away from the city.

Most of locations were just wilderness, being mere vacant plots of land. Indians were being forced to move to such locations by arbitrary arrests and continuous harassments. They were given only residency right: they could neither buy nor sell nor transfer the area where they lived. It was difficult to trade and dangerous to live in these dirty and unhealthy Locations. Moreover, locations kept on changing and Indians were subjected to frequent shifting.

In April 1903, notice no 356—the Bazaar Notice—empowered municipalities to establish and manage such bazaars and Indians were required to reside and trade only in such specified areas.

The deputation led by Gandhi [22-5-03] was told by Governor Lord Milner that "Whites not unreasonably object to the scattered settling of Indians in their midst and that they would resist any large and indiscriminate influx of Asiatics". [CWMG III 368]

Gandhi fought several cases on the ground that law no. 3 had never been implemented so far and that Indians had lived and traded anywhere convenient to them. He argued that disregarding usage and established rights would be a miscarriage of justice. But his pleas were rejected by courts because defiance or non enforcement of law is not a valid ground for protest.

Gandhi argued that shifting to locations would ruin Indian trade; this was the policy to hound Indians out of Transvaal by 'starvation cure'. He felt that it would be more merciful to throw Indians out rather than subject them to such vivisection 'to kill them by inches'. "Indians

want nothing except liberty to trade and reside where they like".
[CWMG IV 78]

Gandhi, while dealing with location and trade, always emphasised usage. Whites insisted that Indians have defied and disobeyed laws for very long and they should no longer get away with it. Thus Transvaal became a classic case of conflict between Law and Usage.

The horizons were dark and Indians lived in midst of an ocean of uncertainties. Gandhi was fighting single handedly against an avalanche of anti-Indian pamphlets, press reports, letters, petitions, violent and inflammatory speeches and writings in the press.

The deliverance came from a totally unexpected quarter. In a test case [Habib Motan Vs. Government of Transvaal] regarding Bazaar Notice, the Supreme Court ruled [22-5-1904] that law no. 3 enjoined locations only for residency. Trade or commercial activity is not residency and therefore that act provides no valid ground to prevent Indians from trading outside locations. The orders restricting Indian trade to Bazaars were quashed.

The court declared that locations were enjoined only due to the unsanitary mode of Indian life in midst of European population and not to avoid inconvenient competition with European traders. The act therefore would not apply to better placed and cleaner Indians. The officials and the municipalities were severely criticised by the court for taking heartless measures to force Indians into locations.

Indians were jubilant. The verdict would save Indian trade from extinction. After a prolonged struggle of fifteen years [1891-04] the Indian position had been fully vindicated by the highest judiciary.

Gandhi was intensely happy. The verdict reconfirmed his faith in Britain. "How much there is to love in British constitution and British rule in spite of temporary aberrations on the part of local authorities who whether out of selfishness, weakness or prejudice are unable to take a just view". [CWMG IV 190]

Gandhi was wise and cautious to foresee the trouble ahead that the verdict would create. 'A new and stricter law may come'. He advised moderation and restraint. "The representatives of the community should refrain from the ardor of its members and make a moderate use of the right of trading... If people go mad and begin to apply for licenses here, there and everywhere, a great deal of harm can be done". [CWMG IV 191]

Gandhi explained to his countrymen that even though Supreme Court has granted the right to trade anywhere, "life is made up of compromises and policy of conciliation is preferable to any other".[CWMG IV 258]

As Gandhi had foreseen, there was a furious protest against the verdict and Europeans were determined to get it reversed by another law. There erupted "a violent, aggressive and uninformed agitation against British Indians". [CWMG IV 324] The Europeans were determined to maintain their monopoly on trade by law if possible, by force if necessary. There was widespread defiance and disobedience to the order of the Supreme Court. Municipalities clamored for a new law but Britain refused to enact any such law.

The press incited violence to push Indians into locations and furious anti-Indian agitation continued through out 1904-05. A virtual terror reigned in several towns and cities of Transvaal: Indians were boycotted and their stores were shunned. Gandhi called these tactics "unworthy of people who call themselves British" and he lamented that "We are weak, less intelligent and unable to unite". [CWMG IV 365]

The British colonial secretary insisted on total obedience to Court and a skeptical Gandhi commented. "Let us hope his deeds will be as good as his words". The British administrators in Transvaal now insisted on proper licenses from Indian traders. Indians in the colony were mostly petty traders and hawkers. They were not allowed to trade if they could not prove to have held old licenses. New licenses were not being issued and even existing licenses were cancelled on flimsy grounds.

In an exhaustive memorandum submitted to the British colonial secretary, Gandhi summarised and reviewed the entire issue. There were five categories of Indian traders whose claims were to be considered by the authorities. A few, very few Indians possessed license documents issued by Boer regime and they faced no problem in getting them authenticated. Many Indian merchants had paid necessary license fees, but no regular documents had been issued to them due to the laxity of Boer administration and the license fee receipt had been treated as regular license. Lord Milner accepted their claim after some hesitation.

During the period of confusion in post war Transvaal, civil and military administration had issued licenses to many new comers who had already started trading activities. Milner agreed to validate their licenses.

During the Boer regime, a large number of Indians had traded without getting any license issued to them and British authorities had encouraged them in such evasion of law. The fifth category consisted of Indians who had traded in the name of their English friends.

In spite of their cases being so strongly argued by Gandhi with facts and figures, no licenses were issued to the last two categories of traders because evasion of law or non-implementation of law does not establish any legal right.

The new license rules caused a lot of conflict and much litigation. The licenses could not be transferred to another person and were not valid with change of address. When partners in business separated, no fresh license would be issued to those who left the firm. Many returnees who had shifted to new cities or towns lost their licenses.

The issue was the most serious one for the community. "A right to reside outside locations was [for Indians] a matter of sentiments but right to trade was a matter of bread and butter". [CWMG IV 45]

In his memorandum, Gandhi made very reasonable and moderate suggestions. Only pre-war traders be allowed in general areas: all new-comers were to be confined to locations; but they should have right to property in locations: fresh licenses should be issued only if Europeans in the area do not object. 'These proposals', said Gandhi 'were as moderate as moderate can be but then they are the irreducible minimum'.

The only response which Gandhi got from British authorities was that Britain was bound to protect Indians but "there is no justification in dealing with Asiatic question in a manner opposed to the voice of the vast majority of Europeans".

The Indian question got further complicated on account of a terrible shortage of labor in Transvaal. The Colony needed 1,29000 labourers [1903] for railway construction and mines and the projected shortage would be 3,65000 by 1908. Lord Milner turned to India with an urgent request to immediately supply 10,000 indentured coolies promising them good wages and good treatment on condition of compulsory return to India on expiry of indenture. Gandhi criticised this condition as 'unjust, un-Christian and un-British'.

Lord Curzon whom Gandhi praised as "a strong and sympathetic Viceroy" vigorously championed the cause of Indians and emerged as a defender of their rights. He firmly refused labour supply till certain conditions were accepted.

Curzon insisted on good treatment not only to the coolies but to all Indians. Locations were to be only for the poor and the dirty: rich and better Indians were to have a right to use footpaths, public facilities and first class travel. Indians had to be given all reasonable facilities for trade. He was more forthright in his dispatch to the Home government. "The name of South Africa stinks in the nostrils of India. The most bitter feelings exist over the treatment meted out to Indians in Transvaal and Natal...No arrangements which did not provide good treatment…would be tolerated by public opinion here". [CWMG III 476] Curzon expressed his anger in a language more blistering and more assertive than ever used by Gandhi.

Gandhi was immensely happy. "It is refreshing to find Indian government sticking out on behalf of Indians". [CWMG III 476] He always wanted government of India to support the rights of Indians in South Africa and was quite happy with Curzon's budget speech in the Indian Assembly.

But Gandhi was opposed to Curzon's policy. "Rights for Indians are not to be extorted but to be secured as British subjects…not to be exchanged against labor…We would not exchange freedoms of free Indians for the virtual slavery of indentured Indians".[CWMG IV 103]

Gandhi rather advocated a stoppage of labour supply. "Why should (the) Indian government go out of its way to accommodate a government which is callous to all ideas of justice in treating resident Indians with fairness".

Lord Milner hard pressed with labour shortages agreed to grant some facilities to better placed Indians but he refused any further concessions to Indian trade. Lord Curzon was adamant. Milner withdrew his request and rued "We …are in an absurd position of being flooded with Indian traders and hawkers who are of no benefit to the community and are not allowed Indian laborers whom we need". [CWMG III 467]

Transvaal imported 45,000 Chinese laborers. This would add to the racial complexity in South Africa and would adversely affect Indian interests because with such an alternative source for labour, India would lose a lever to pressurise South Africa.

Gandhi conceded that Transvaal had a right to import labor from anywhere, but his initial reaction to the import of Chinese labor was quite hysterical. "Chinese would not be allowed to use their brains, pen or brush". A rumour that the Chinese would not be coming made him immensely happy. By the beginning of 1904, Chinese labourers started arriving but Europeans always wanted Indian coolies. The Chinese were as hard working as the Indians but the former were more violent while the Indians were more docile.

While struggling strenuously to secure safety and dignity for his compatriots under very trying circumstances, Gandhi never lost his balance. His wisdom and moderation shines through his acceptance of ground realities.

He repeatedly emphasised that Indians demand no political rights but only civil securities; they want no power but only peace, dignity and trade. Gandhi only asked for freedom and dignity for those who are already settled. "We wish to live side by side with other British subjects in peace and amity and with dignity and self respect". [CWMG V 150]

"The country being suited for European settlement, it should be kept for them so far as it is consistent with the well-being of the Empire". [CWMG III 407] He pleaded that supremacy of Whites had been accepted by Indians and appealed "do not use it to do us injustice, to degrade us and to insult us". [CWMG III 439]

British administrators advocated a policy of restricting the immigration of Indians so that "it would be possible to gradually settle the status of those who are now residing in the country on a fairly satisfactory lines". This would entail a virtual stoppage of Indian migration to a British colony but then "this was the only practical solution for this difficult [Indian] question". Gandhi too never asked for free and open immigration of Indians and was always agreeable to restrictions that were general and non racial.

"Restrictions on immigration would be perfectly justified within reasonable limits. We believe in the purity of race as we think they do…[but] purity of all races not of one alone…Whites in South Africa are and should be a dominant race". [CWMG III 548]

Gandhi supported the Immigration Restriction Bill [Jan 1904] that was more or less on the same lines as in Natal. In a memorandum to Governor Selborne, [CWMG V 145] Gandhi accepted language test for migrants but suggested that Indian languages should be permitted for the test. He advocated free entry to all refugees with their wives and children and pressed for free entry for Indians of education and attainment.

He informed the governor that established business houses find it impossible to secure competent and confidential staff from local population and therefore they should be allowed to import them from India. This last was not a very reasonable demand.

The bill had to be abandoned for other reasons but it was decided "no non-refugee Indian would be allowed to enter the colony till a representative assembly has considered the question". [CWMG V 144] The authorities in London mooted [1905] the grant of self-government to bring Boers closer to Britain. Gandhi resented that Indians were totally excluded from discussions. "British Indian is only a step child and has been left out in the cold...[and] insulted by deliberate exclusion". [CWMG IV 422]

Gandhi was enraged by the spacious arguement of British High Commissioner Sir Arthur Lawley who sought to evade the earlier commitments made by Britain to the Indian community. The Indian problem was complicated because of strong local prejudices against Indians who had rendered great services to the Empire. Britain had to hold the scale even between rights of Indians and local prejudices. But "the earlier promises made to British Indians having been made in ignorance, it would be a greater duty to break them than to keep them". [CWMG IV 427]

Gandhi was furious and forthright in denouncing both Sir Arthur and Lord Milner too. "They are no friends of Indians". Gandhi conceded that reasons of state can be a valid ground for violating promises but in a masterly analysis of facts he demonstrated that no such reason existed in the situation obtaining in South Africa.

When it was decided to grant partial autonomy to Transvaal and Orange River Colony [February 1906]. Gandhi called for "special and specific protection for British Indians" to be included in the new constitution as "there was no hope of justice from the colonies about the very painful conditions of Indians".

Chapter 15

THE ASCENT

During the latter half of this decade [1897-1906] that Gandhi spent at Johannesburg, there are four major incidents and activities that had far-reaching consequences in sculpting his personality and approach.

Gandhi in Transvaal was in close and daily contacts with all sections of Indians—rich as well as poor and he was acutely aware of the deplorable conditions in which more than 1600 coolies, petty traders and hawkers were living in a dirty and overcrowded Indian location in Johannesburg. It was a dumping ground for the city refuse.

A large number of Kafirs were also living in this location. A few of them had been taken as lodgers by Indians but many more pushed into the area by local authorities. A mass meeting of Indians had protested against this dirty, distant, overcrowded and mixed location because Indians hated to live with Kafirs.

Gandhi also was very angry and upset with such mixing of races. "The Town Council must withdraw Kaffirs from the location: about such mixing of Kaffirs with Indians, I must confess I feel most strongly. It is very unfair to Indian population and an undue tax on the proverbial patience of my countrymen". [CWMG IV 131]

Gandhi, fully aware of the conditions prevailing in this slum, was greatly worried because "the outbreak of some epidemic disease is merely a question of time". From February 1904, he repeatedly warned municipal authorities about the shocking state of sanitation and increased mortality in the area. But all such warnings and pleading fell on deaf ears and the health officer pleaded shortage of staff for inaction.

Johannesburg had incessant rains for seventeen days from 18 March 1904 and the sanitary conditions in the location deteriorated sharply. Such unsanitary conditions together with weather led to the outbreak of deadly pneumonic plague with great fatalities. [March 1904] Fifteen Indian mine workers were the first to be affected and Gandhi, together with Dr. Godfrey, Dr. Pareira and some volunteers rushed to the spot. The patients were taken to "a house which Indian community had vacated and isolated": funds were collected and necessary materials as well as medicines were procured. This was an improvised hospital and Gandhi inspired the volunteers to rendering yeomen's service to the sick of the community.

The municipality offered a better and a larger Customs warehouse for temporary hospital with twenty-five beds and supplied medicines as well as the nursing staff. Its doctors and staff did very good work after the initial lethargy was shaken off. There is no reference to any breaking open of any godown in the contemporary reports.

In spite of all efforts, the epidemic spread amongst all communities and by the end of month of April, 72 out of 107 affected patients could not survive. Indians were the first to be affected and Gandhi was the first to be very active in fighting against the scourge. Indians suffered most [51 out of 54 died] and the total death toll rose to 86 out of 125 affected.

Gandhi had to very strongly chide Indians for concealing plague cases for the fear of further harassment. "The Indian community can not be held free from blame. The nemesis that has overtaken it more than any other community is, we fear, more or less deserved". [CWMG IV 156]

This ghastly tragedy had political repercussions and was used by Europeans as an excuse and an occasion to harass Indians. The outbreak of plague was blamed on 'dirty' Indians and that bugbear was used for a 'Banish dirty Indians' crusade and for more severe restrictions on their shops and homes. Hawkers were prohibited from entering market places. "There is some ulterior motive in imposing extra-ordinary restrictions especially when they are applied only to Indians".

As a precaution against further spread of plague, the Town Council decided to vacate the location and the entire location was burnt down together with the belongings of Indians—a step that Gandhi described as pure "theatrical display" [CWMG IV 169] Gandhi, however, was fair enough to praise the municipality for providing good care and good food for the Indians shifted to the camp.

When the Town Council tried to shift the entire blame onto the dirty life style of Indian community, Gandhi was furious. "The danger to the public health arising out of the conditions in Indian location was brought to the notice of Town Council...and in fact was one of the reasons which led Town Council to press for the power to expropriate the whole area". [CWMG IV] Gandhi pointed out that the conditions deteriorated *after* the area was taken over by municipal authorities and it was the Town Council that was to be blamed for the plague. "It and it alone must be held responsible for the awful death march". [CWMG IV 287]

The compensation given for loss of shelter and belongings was meager and for the time being no alternative accommodation was provided for the residents. Gandhi filed and fought seventy-five cases on behalf of the poor Indians for compensation and won seventy-four.

Gandhi's share in the legal fees paid by the municipality came to about pounds 3000 and was set aside by Gandhi as hospital funds: but nothing came out of it except a very ugly controversy in 1913 about the so-called hospital funds that Gandhi was accused of misappropriating.

The occasion served to demonstrate the unquestioning faith that poorer Indians had developed in Gandhi's integrity. During the plague and when the location was being shifted, Indians handed over their entire savings and valuables to Gandhi for safe custody. The total amount so deposited came to the staggering figure of 60,000 pounds or Rs. 2,70,000,000 at current price level. No receipts or any other documents were either demanded or even expected from Gandhi.

Gandhi's great service during the plague and in securing adequate compensation for the victims of plague went practically unrecognised and unappreciated by authorities and even by leaders of the Indian community. But the memories thereof made coolies follow the call of Gandhi in 1913.

II

From the very beginning of his public life [1896], Gandhi had felt the need for a newspaper to voice the grievances and aspirations of Indians as a counterpoise to the White press. He was expected to bring Indian types and press artisans with him while returning to Natal. [December 1896] But he did not succeed in his assignment and his efforts to establish a printing press [1897] did not succeed.

He renewed his efforts and sounded the correspondent of *The Times of India* for starting an Indian paper: but the correspondent was returning to India and declined the offer. Gandhi inspired and encouraged Madanjit Vyavaharik to start [1898] 'International Printing Press' for job work in Durban. But the newspaper could not be started. There was no competent Indian who could edit a paper and Gandhi himself was too busy in professional and public activities to undertake the responsibility.

Mansukhlal Nazar came forward [1903] to work as an editor. The *Indian Opinion*—a weekly—was launched in Durban. [1903] Gandhi was then staying in Johannesburg but from the very beginning, he was deeply involved in the enterprise by contributing the editorial and financial inputs. Gandhi wrote so many editorials in the paper that he could be called its virtual editor.

When Nazar and Vyavaharik were leaving for India [October 1904], Gandhi paid 3500 pounds to purchase the printing press and as well as the weekly and became its owner proprietor. But he never became its editor. Gandhi's European, theosophist friends—Albert West, Herbert Kristchen and Henry Polak worked as the editors of *Indian Opinion*. West and Polak gave up their lucrative careers to edit the paper and both settled at Phoenix. The management of *Indian Opinion* was always a great headache for Gandhi as he struggled to manage the ego problems of his staff. West and Chhaganlal Joshi often clashed and there was endless trouble with Kitchen. "Money is paid to him not because of his efficiency but because of my [Gandhi's] folly". [CWMG V 125]

Gandhi's career as a journalist dates from London when he started contributing articles to *The Vegetarian*. While in South Africa, Gandhi wrote hundreds of letters to various newspapers. He spent a fortune in getting his Open Letters and pamphlets printed and circulated free of charge. He wrote a series of articles in *The Times of India*. [1899] He had great faith in the efficacy of press publicity and always maintained a list of papers and journalists friendly to his cause. His rise to fame and leadership is partly based upon his superb handling of publicity and he firmly believed "publicity to be our best and only weapon". [Green Book]

The lawyer leader now [1904] turned into a part time journalist guided by the lofty ideals as he sought to mould *Indian Opinion* into a sober, balanced and critical journal on the lines of the *London Times*.

The first issue of the journal under Gandhi specified its basic objectives—to ventilate the grievances of the Indians, to eliminate the communal and linguistic divisions and factions among Indians, to educate public opinion, to remove causes of misunderstandings between Indians and Whites and "to put before Indians their own mistakes and to show them the path of their duty while insisting on their rights... because mere flattery would be an act of enmity". [CWMG IV 320]

"While championing their rights, if we happen to observe any of their short comings, we must bring these to their notice...It is our duty to administer the bitter pill". [CWMG V 114] The *Indian Opinion* was to become a friend and an advocate who will not flinch "believing firmly ...in the ultimate triumph of Truth and Justice having full faith in the good sense of British People." 'Its aim is Imperial and... it does and must lay stress upon the grievances of British Indians in Africa..." [ibid 340]

We will "strive to highlight the grievances and the defects of Indian community, to spread knowledge about glory of India and to promote harmony and goodwill between different sections of one mighty empire." "We are far from assuming that Indians here are free from all the faults that are ascribed to them" one of its functions would be to point out the faults of Indians and suggest remedies. [CWMG III 377] "Our basic objective is... to serve humanity but our first duty is to serve India and to earn our bread through public service". [CWMG VIII 276]

Gandhi was as good as his word and the *Indian Opinion* was often very highly critical of the community it served. This often made it very unpopular with its readers. Even though Gandhi had a paper of his own, he continued to write in other English papers but with diminishing frequency. This was greatly disadvantageous to his cause because his communication links with European community became more and more tenuous and he lost many opportunities of directly appealing to

Europeans and of conveying his views and opinions to them. Gandhi thereby crippled himself. During the registration controversy, Gandhi resumed writing to the English press.

There was a copious flow of articles, editorials and comments on contemporary events and issues from Gandhi's pen. Gandhi's interest in human affairs widened and he wrote on a wide variety of subjects— from Indian affairs to karate training in British army; the evil of juvenile smoking to the rise of Japan as world power—touching contemporary affairs in India and world at large as he commented on the week that passed.

He wrote about Tolstoy, Elizabeth Fry, Abraham Lincoln, Florence Nightingale, Ishwarchandra Vidyasagar and several others. He translated eight chapters of Saltter's *Ethical Religion*. He wrote thirty-four articles on naturopathy and a series on 'the duty of civil disobedience' based on Thoreau, a very long article on Brahmacharya. He translated books of Tolstoy. He intended to translate Amir Ali's *Spirit of Islam*. He translated Irving's *Life of Prophet Mahomed* but could publish only a chapter or two. The furious protests from Muslims forced him to discontinue the series as Gandhi submitted to Muslim obscurantism.

Gandhi was deeply impressed by Plato's *Dialogues* and translated a few of them. He adopted dialogue form to defend the compromise with Smuts [January 1908] and also for his *Hind Swaraj*. [1909] Ruskin's *Unto This Last* was translated but it was presented in context with Indian ethos foreshadowing almost verbatim the entire *Hind Swaraj*. The cultural anarchy of western countries was denounced. 'British rule in India is an evil but no advantage would accrue to Indians if it is ended "because of our disunity, our immorality and our ignorance"'. Expressing great respect for Tilak, Gandhi rejected his views. "Uprooting British rule by violence will exchange one slavery with another". Gandhi read and wrote so much that he felt "a Triton among Minnones". [Auto]

But Gandhi studiously restricted *Indian Opinion* to Indian question "We are, as a rule very reluctant about expressing opinions on matters not coming specially within the preview of this journal". [CWMG IV 347] "We must recognize our limitation and not enter into questions of high policy that do not directly affect Indians in this country". [CWMG VII 1] The *Indian Opinion*, with its pugnacious presentations and its vitriolic language, was a leadership tool for Gandhi. It was always a very unprofessional enterprise—more a mission than a business. This journal shaped Gandhi more than Gandhi shaped it. It was a superb training school for Gandhi as a writer, as a conscientious journalist and as a maker of public opinion.

The *Indian Opinion* was never much read. It had a mere 687 subscribers when Gandhi took it over [CWMG V 289] and many of them never bothered to pay their dues. Its circulation fluctuated between 800 and 1500 copies and it touched 3500 at its climax, the average being 800-900. More than 500 copies were sent as complementary to prominent leaders in South Africa, England and India. Most of Indians were too poor to buy it and those who could afford to pay were not much literate even in Gujarati. The *Indian Opinion* was a loss-making concern. In the initial stage, the loss was shared by Natal Indian Congress, British Indian Association and Gandhi. After the Congress withdrew its support, [April 1906] Gandhi poured his hard earned money into this bottomless pit.

The weekly therefore had very limited resources, very few correspondents and even fewer contributors. Gandhi tried very hard and searched for honorary as well as paid correspondents from England and India; he even requested Gokhale to occasionally write for the paper but all this never came to much.

The weekly had to be mostly filled up by numerous and lengthy quotations from other English papers making Indians aware of feelings and opinions of the Europeans. But this was a one-way traffic because

Indian Opinion was never read by many Whites. It was read only by Indians and that too by very few of them. But even then the *Indian Opinion* was a major force and a strong link to hold Indians together. After 1908, *Indian Opinion* became "the most authentic voice of the Indian Community in South Africa-a sort of weekly newsletter for all those...interested and concerned with Indian affairs. It proved to be the most useful and the most potent weapon in our struggle...a faithful mirror of the current history of Indian community". [SSA 194 and 198] During Satyagraha movements it became a compulsory reading for officials as well as the leaders of European community.

The *Indian Opinion* had four sections—English, Gujarati, Hindi and Tamil, catering to major linguistic groups of Indian community. But severe financial crisis, paucity of competent manpower and total absence of subscribers forced Gandhi to discontinue [3 February 1906] the Tamil and Hindi sections. Such discontinuance also indicated "a failure to reach either the indentured labor or their descendents" [Hunt 53] and also a gap between Indian elite and Indian labour.

Both the sections were resumed in December 1913, as a tribute to "the great sacrifices of the Hindi and Tamil speaking coolies" whom Gandhi had enlisted for 1913 satyagraha. This resumption emphasises a major shift in Gandhi's leadership. Gandhi up to 1912 was a leader mostly of upper and middle class Indians. He now [1913] had a following mostly of the down trodden and the depressed.

Gandhi struggled hard to secure advertisements for the *Indian Opinion* up to the end of 1913. The struggle to collect the bills was even harder. He was keen to bring in more revenue by publishing puzzles and riddles "if somebody pays for it". [CWMG VI 320] The advertisements from rich Muslim merchants got more and more diverted to *Al Islam* after 1910.

The *Indian Opinion* never printed any news that might create discord among Indians. Gandhi specifically banned a review of a book written by his old and notorious tormentor Sheikh Mehtab [CWMG V 80] and blacked out the news about Habib Motan. "We are not to publish anything relating to Hindu Conference" [not even its advertisement]...The whole thing is a humbug". [CWMG XI 303]

Gandhi always treated *Indian Opinion* as belonging to the community but legally it was his property and he had to suffer a lot of censure from the community on that account. The *Indian Opinion* together with *Phoenix* became a Trust property in the middle of 1913.

III

Phoenix grew out of a seed planted in Gandhi's mind when he visited his cousin's shop and garden at Tongart that set him thinking about having a farm. Ruskin's *Unto This Last*, that he read [October 1904] during a professional trip to Durban proved to be a catalytic agent. "[I] decided to change my life according to its principles" [Auto] and thus began one of the most daring experiment in Gandhi's life.

He paid a thousand pounds to purchase a thousand acre farm situated only two miles from Phoenix and fourteen miles from Durban. He purchased property in Natal because Indians had no property right in Transvaal.

Gandhi, in a brilliant move, merged two of his ventures—*Indian Opinion* and *Phoenix* into one by shifting the press and the paper to the farm. It was a very wise mixture of Ruskin's ideals and shrewd business economy. The decision to run the paper from Phoenix by manual and voluntary labour helped Gandhi to cut down financial loss and to experiment with the life style advocated by Ruskin.

For seven years, Gandhi spent all weekends at Phoenix swinging between his Johannesburg office and his farm. A shed was constructed to house the machinery of the press and the office of the *Indian Opinion*: a small colony of six families—some Indians and some Europeans—quickly grew up around it.

Gandhi sought to implement the teachings of Tolstoy and Ruskin about simple life of labour, purity and poverty in close proximity of nature not only for himself as an individual but also as a patriarch of a band of faithful followers.

Phoenix was a non-religious organisation seeking to live a life of unselfish objectives. Apart from the workers who were paid usual wages, there were Schemers who as farmers lived on a plot of land sufficiently large to maintain them. The profits if any were to be divided among these Schemers. The workers could buy a plot of land at Phoenix.

Phoenix had several very attractive features—immediate prospect of owning land on the most advantageous terms, with direct and tangible participation in working for an ideal; an opportunity to live under very healthy, sanitary, natural surroundings far away from the town without too heavy expenses; a close, brotherly union between Indian and European families. Gandhi persuaded three of his European friends to join the scheme that was fully operational by December 1904.

Gandhi was aware of the far-reaching consequences of his experiment. "If it is successful, [the scheme] will mark revolution in business methods". [CWMG IV 340]

Gandhi had many dreams: he planned a residential school at Phoenix to fill up the vacuum because there were no educational facilities for Indian children in South Africa. Gandhi experimented with a novel educational system where elders would be educating their children during the normal routine of life.

Polak secured several scholarships, stipends and even books for the students. When Dr. Mehta offered [1909] to sponsor one son of Gandhi for getting educated in England, Gandhi altered the offer to apply it to the best boy from Phoenix and chose Chhaganlal Gandhi. [CWMG

IX 382] Gandhi had planned a sanitarium for naturopathy but that project never came up.

Till 1908, Gandhi "strongly believed that Indians must come to England to acquire the qualities of leadership". [Hunt 97] and to get themselves trained as lawyers and doctors. He was always very eager to send all capable Indians to England for education. He had great regards for English Character. "They deserve all that they have and for the most part it is necessary to behave as they do".

After Gandhi discontinued his legal practice and vowed voluntary poverty, [September 1908] Phoenix faced a severe financial crisis that worsened more and more. The Durban office of the *Indian Opinion* had to be closed; the residential school was sold off to Anjuman-I-Islam in Durban. Gandhi sold family jewellery, he sold his law books and law reports, office furniture, and even the volumes of encyclopedia. While in London, Gandhi surrendered [20-8-09] the life insurance policy for 660 Pounds [a lakh of rupees] that he had taken out a few years back. "I would like to receive back the large portion of the premium I paid". [CWMG IX 363] It was financial stringency rather than any question about faith in God [cf.Auto] that made him do so.

Gandhi later on designated Phoenix as an ashram and this was the first of his several experiments in organising group living to implement the ideal way of life. Phoenix remained a personal property in his name and under his sole control up to 1913 and gave rise to the allegations against Gandhi for misusing public funds to save this property from insolvency. Gandhi explained that both the *Phoenix* and the *Indian Opinion* were public institutions and were devoted to public service. But legally and technically they were in his name. Gandhi handed over the entire Phoenix property worth 5130 Pounds to a public trust in 1913. [CWMG XI 326]

Not very far from Gandhi farm, there was another such altruistic colony run for a different purpose and on different lines. John Dube, a U.S. educated Zulu had established a 3000 acre educational farm— a center for educating Zulus and other natives in various trades and crafts to prepare them for the battle of life. [CWMG V 55]

Dube was editing a weekly *Ilanga Lase* and often spoke to European groups. Gandhi knew his activities and wrote about him in *Indian Opinion* but he does not seem to have ever visited him. The British Indian Association, of which Gandhi was general secretary contributed a smithy at Dube's farm. Phoenix was a precursor of Tolstoy farm and a pioneer amongst many ashrams of Gandhi in India. It was the nodal point for conducting the last and the most famous satyagraha of 1913. Gandhi had shifted his residence to Phoenix in 1911.

The name ashram dates from hoary traditions of ancient India. Gandhi's ashrams have nothing similar to the Indian prototypes. His ashrams were more a blend of communes of Utopian Socialists in Europe and America and the monastery of Trappists that Gandhi greatly admired ever since he visited it in 1894.

IV

The Zulu war is the last major event that added important dimension to the personality of Gandhi. Gandhi was dragged in the whirlpool called Zulu war which does him no credit and which must have intensified the turmoil within him.

The so-called Zulu war was an uprising led by Bombata [April 1906] the leader of Ama-Zulu (People of Heaven), against heavy taxation imposed upon his people. Bombata was killed in June 1906 and twelve Zulu leaders were hanged. The uprising was crushed [July] with great and unnecessary cruelties. It was not a war but a sheer massacre of scantily armed innocents. The Natal army raided Zulu territory, set fire to Kraals, killing and wounding people just for the fun of it. "This was no war; it was a man-hunt". [Auto] Within a period of mere five months, nearly 3500 Zulus were butchered and the doings of Natal army greatly shocked General Smuts. There were strong protests from London against such ghastly cruelties.

The army tortured even totally innocent Zulus. The Whites refused to touch black bodies. "The British would not even treat wounded Zulus who were left unattended for days together". [SSA]

But Gandhi fully supported Natal and even defended its atrocities by citing the doings of British army in Egypt and he appealed for war funds. [CWMG V 346] "If Indians claim rights of citizenship, they were bound to take their natural share of responsibilities". [ibid 291]

Unlike 1899, Natal government permitted Indians to join armed forces and Gandhi was intensely happy about it. [ibid 353] He extolled the virtues of military training. [ibid 366] "If we car. prove our willingness and ability to fight, our disabilities may probably disappear". [ibid 303] He advocated a permanent voluntary corps of Indians hoping that anti-Indian prejudices might disappear thereby. [ibid 373-74]

Gandhi offered ambulance services as he had done during the Boer war and served on the side of Natal government. 'Major' Gandhi led a small group of nineteen Indians and served for only three weeks. [22-6-06/10-7-06] It was a very strenuous and frustrating piece of work. "Gandhi just to prove that he was not anti-British, ... volunteered the ambulance service... and was given the care of the Zulu bodies lacerated by whippings under the martial law". [Payne]

Gandhi's mission of mercy proved to be of great help and solace to Zulus but Gandhi had sided with cruelty; he never protested against what was being done and what he witnessed every day. His silence spoke very loudly. Gandhi, not only held his tongue about all such happenings —that is unpardonable for a seeker of Truth—but he even defended his decision with an excuse that is totally untenable and extremely naïve.

"But then I believed that the British Empire existed for the welfare of the world. A genuine sense of loyalty prevented me from even wishing ill of the Empire". [SSA and Auto]

"Gandhi speaks with great reserve of this experience. What he saw, he would never divulge... it was not always very creditable to British humanity". [Doke 70] "Mr. Gandhi does not like to speak his mind about what he saw and learnt on this occasion. But many times he must have had the searching of his conscience as to the propriety of his allying himself even in that merciful capacity with those capable of such acts of revolting and inexcusable brutality". [Polak—*Speeches and Writings of Gandhi* xii]

Helping Britain or even standing on its side during the Zulu war is indefensible even as an act of loyalty or a mission of mercy because he went much beyond what was expected from him. In the long reports that Gandhi wrote, there is not a single word of sympathy for Zulus probably because of his loyalty to the colony or his contempt for blacks. Gandhi is often inexplicable and incredible.

The Gaelic American from New York denounced Gandhi's action as "an act contemptible beyond expression" and Shyamji Krishnaverma from London called it "disgusting and despicable". [Indian Sociologist July 1906] The Zulu war is an important landmark in the personal life of Gandhi. It was during this fortnight that he met all those who had organised and led the Durban mob against him in January 1897 and who by now had turned his admirers. The governor as well as the prime minister of Natal thanked him profusely and praised him very highly.

It was during hard and haunting experiences of Zulu war that Gandhi was set on the high road to sainthood. He came to realise that totally selfless and continuous public service would require him to limit the growth of his family and his property and would necessitate the vows of Brahmacharya and Aparigraha—the same as Jesuit vows of voluntary poverty and celibacy.

He decided to use thereafter all his income for the public and not for self or for his family, [letter to Laxmidas] and soon after returning home, he broke up his family life and sent away his wife and children to Phoenix.

The years that follow mark Gandhi's growing identification with humanity and his willingness to undergo great sufferings for their sake. Gandhi who led Indians in 1894 and Gandhi who led them in 1908 are two different persons. By 1908, Gandhi was a transformed person feeling no difference between self and others. He was by now a total devotee of God, a servant of humanity and a crusader for Truth. "Gandhi, by now, saw the face of God in the most humble and the most hostile and the most ignoble of his fellowmen". [Polak]

By 1907, the pragmatic, compromising political leader had changed into a dogmatic and unbending saint. It was the failure of satyagraha and his hopes that mellowed the saint to a very large extent.

In this first decade of the twentieth century when Gandhi was growing into a Mahatma, the Indian community that he led suffered a great splitting on the communal lines. The partition of Bengal with its resultant communal dissentions in India and the foundation of Muslim League and Hindu Mahasabha had very disastrous repercussions in South Africa. Gandhi could never digest the support given by the Muslims to the partition of Bengal and that was the beginning of his drift away from the rich Muslim community in Natal.

By the first decade of the twentieth century, several political and social organisations of Hindus, Muslims and colonial born coolies cropped up though most of them were ephemeral products of egocentric leadership. The Tamil leaders in Durban established the Hindu Young Men's Association and insisted on using only Tamil language for its work excluding thereby not only Christians and Muslims but also the Hindi speaking Hindus from its activities.

Gandhi's leadership was hardly ever challenged and he remained a quiet center of many hurricanes. Gandhi has lamented "many bitter experiences have been my portion of life". [Auto] The communal disunity was the most bitter of them.

The establishment of the Hamidia Islamic Society and the visits of Bhai Parmanand and Swami Shankaranand created new stresses for Indian community that was more or less united in South Africa.

Gandhi had welcomed both of them for their efforts to spread education and also as educated Indians coming to Natal but he had never supported their ideology. "His [Shankaranand's] very ways and doings seem crooked". [CWMG X 355] In a letter from London [1909] Gandhi severely criticised Swami's views on Islam and his anti-Islamic education to the Hindu youths.

Prof. Parmanand [Bhai Parmanand] of the Anglo-Vedic college of Lahore was a visiting missionary trying to promote educational activities and bringing communal passions with him in South Africa. Professor Parmanand organised Ved Dharma Sabhas. Shankaranand's Arya Mandal at Durban was largely an anti-Congress and anti-Gandhi organization of Arya Samajists.

Swami Shankaranand arrived in Natal in October 1908 and stayed on for nearly three years. He was very active. The communal twist that he gave to the Indian community had a very disruptive impact.

The tension between the communities flared up on the issue of sharing of the income of Durgah Mosque Market that resulted in a communal riot. [20-5-09] The area was owned by mosque authorities and used by Hindu farmers for marketing their goods. The farmers used to pay a handsome rent. Hindus now demanded a share thereof to be spent for Hindu festivals. Muslims argued that the income was religious property and refused to share it. Swami led a boycott of the market and anti-Muslim crusade.

Shankaranand encouraged separate organisation of Hindu festivals: Hindu participation in Muslim festivals was now discouraged. The Natal Patriotic Union [1909] was responsible for Hindu revivalism and was an anti-Muslim, anti-Congress and anti-Gandhi organisation.

Chapter 16

A PYRRHIC VICTORY

All the disabilities and discriminations against which Gandhi had been fighting all these long years in Transvaal were dwarfed by registration ordinance of August 1906. The clamour of Europeans against being flooded by Indian migrants had compelled British administrators to prevent the entry of Indians in the colony except with permits.

Such permits were to be granted only to Indians who were old residents and their wives and underage children. Permits were issued after prolonged and detailed inquiries involving procedural delays. This long and tedious process was over by December 1906. By then, 12,899 permits had been issued.

All old records had been lost during war and it was not possible to say who were old residents and who were not. Therefore Lord Milner decided to get all Indians registered so that the newcomers could be identified and expelled. The existing permits were cancelled and Indians were asked to get registered for getting new certificates.

The new permits would contain full personal details—name, family, caste, community, height, age, occupation, and would bear the signature or thumb impression in order to prevent impersonation. The permits were to be dated, numbered and signed by the concerned officials.

"Although Indians were not bound by any law, they voluntarily agreed to get themselves re-registered in the hope that no new restrictions would be imposed upon them and it might be clear to all concerned that Indians as a community did not wish to bring in fresh immigrants by any unfair means. ... This was the proof of their veracity, tact, large-mindedness, common sense and humility. It also showed that the community had no desire to violate any law in force in Transvaal. The Indians believed that if they behaved towards the government with such courtesy, it would treat them well and show regard for them and confer fresh rights upon them". [SSA 94-95]

It was a voluntary action but "this self effacing courtesy has been misinterpreted as a docility of nature that would stand any strain or indignity". [CWMG V 436]

The Europeans were not satisfied even with such re-registration and alleged that a rigorous and exact registration would reveal that the actual number of Indians was at least double the figure registered.

The European community kept on complaining about surreptitious intrusions by Indians on a massive scale. They were bent upon finding out the exact number of Indians and then rigorously ban the further entry. The fist step was an accurate registration of all Indians.

A new and very strict law was proposed for compulsory registration with identification drastic enough to detect every case of misuse of a certificate. The Asiatic Law [1885] Amendment Ordinance was published [11-8-06]. The ordinance presumed every Indian to be an illegal entrant. The existing permits were cancelled. Every Indian- male and female above the age of eight must get registered on the penalty of imprisonment or fine. Women and children had never been registered before and had no documents of any earlier residence.

The registration certificate besides usual personal details would carry a description of body mark and an imprint of ten digits for identification as if he or she were a potential criminal. The certificate was to be produced whenever and wherever demanded by any official and was needed for all official dealings with the government - be it a job or a license for a shop or a vehicle or for anything else. The police could enter residential or business premises to check or verify certificates and could accost any one including women and youngsters for the same purpose. Non-registration or refusal to show the certificate was a crime punishable with a fine of hundred pounds or imprisonment of three months or deportation.

The blow was sought to be softened by making such registration free and there was a promise that existing rights of registered Indians would be guaranteed. Indians would be granted permission to drink hard liquor and religious bodies of Indians would get the right of property. The properties purchased before 1885 would be legitimized.

The Indians reacted with fury. Gandhi denounced 'the horrible ordinance' that was much worse than the law of 1885 and 'a serious and wanton injustice'. Registration of women and children was "a shock to Indian sentiments and a violation of female modesty".

"This wicked and unjust law is designed to strike at the root of our existence in South Africa", and it "seeks to humiliate not only us but also our mother land". [CWMG V 417-18] The ordinance "dripping with hatred for Indians and spelling absolute ruin for the community" was abominable. Even "the adjective abominable is not enough, the act is criminal—a crime against humanity". [CWMG V 409]

The government and the White press defended the ordinance as an effective and foolproof barrier against all illegal entry in future and Indians did get a few more rights. Gandhi tore such defense to pieces.

The right to property was illusory except for very, very few individuals. Freedom to drink was an insult to Indians and an anathema to Muslims.

There would be a long and insulting inquiry and strict examination prior to the issue of certificates and all this harassment of innocents was for a few who had entered the colony without proper authority and the inefficient and corrupt officials had failed to prevent them. "In Russia, subjects are killed. In Transvaal, Indians are killed by inches". [CWMG V 412] They were now to be inflicted with an indignity that would rank them lower than Kafirs.

Gandhi had correctly gauzed the intentions underlying the ordinance- worst of all anti-Asisatic measures so far. He called it a 'Black Act' because "it was aimed at hounding us out of the colony" [SSA 138] and eventually out of South Africa. Gandhi explained the implications of the ordinance to the leaders of Indian community and advocated a total defiance of law. "No submission, no registration, no payment of fines; go to gaols". [CWMG V 414]

Up to 1906, Gandhi had resisted racism with "feeble weapons of petitions and publicity". [Hunt 47] But now he was bent upon total defiance. "It is impossible to pinpoint exactly when and why Gandhi himself experienced the moment of metaphysical rebellion out of which the passive resistance grew…The politics of polite protests had been tried and found wanting…The politics of confrontation can be seen as an attractive alternative in the face of… the kind of threat posed by the registration ordinance". [Swan 116]

Before taking the final plunge, Gandhi was keen to exhaust all legal and constitutional avenues. He therefore submitted a memorandum and led a deputation to Duncan, the colonial secretary of Transvaal. In a prolonged and very heated discussion, Gandhi rejected the ordinance as totally unacceptable under any circumstances and he assured Duncan "I will be the first to go to gaol rather than be registered or pay the fine". [CWMG V 414]

Cables were sent to colonial secretary in London and to viceroy of India requesting immediate intervention: it was decided to send a delegation to London to stall the Imperial sanction to "a wicked and unjust law".

After several meetings to make Indians aware of the situation, British Indian Association called a conference of delegates from all over Transvaal who met at Empire Theatre in Johannesburg on 11 September 1906. This was a day of complete *hartal* for the Indian merchants all over the colony. More than 3000 delegates crammed the theatre and a huge crowd waited outside. The significance of this packed and peaceful meeting was not lost on European observers and the Rand Daily Mail called it 'unprecedented'.

"The united protest of the British Indian community against the draft Asiatic Ordinance constitutes one of the most remarkable gatherings Johannesburg has seen. The size of the meeting, the enthusiasm of the audience—practically the entire Indian population ceased work for the day—and the depth of feelings expressed form a striking testimony to the indignation which the proposed legislation has aroused". [*Rand Daily Mail*, Hutten, 168] Chimney and four other Europeans together with reporters from three major newspapers attended the meeting.

Gandhi has described this crucial meeting at some length in his autobiography and in SSA but he seems to have forgotten details of what happened because his recapitulation is at great variance with the report that was published in *Indian Opinion*.

Sheth Haji Habib spoke with great passion and threatened violence if women were required to go to government offices for registration. He proposed a solemn oath to oppose the ordinance. He mentioned Tilak. "There is no disgrace in going to the jail. It is an honor... are you prepared to take the oath? ...We tried this method in the days of Boer government... the time has come for us to go to jails and go we will.... We will not take up the rifles as they [Uitlanders] did but like them we will go to gaols. ... We will not wait for the police to come and arrest us, we ourselves will go there". [CWMG V 442-443]

The meeting passed four resolutions with acclaim and the most important of them—Resolution No.4 was moved by Haji Omar Ally the founder of the Hamidia Islamic Society.

"This meeting of the British Indians here assembled solemnly and regretfully resolves that rather than submit to the galling, tyrannous and un-British requirements laid down in the Ordinance, every British Indian in Transvaal shall submit himself to imprisonment and shall continue to do so until it shall please His Most Gracious Majesty the King Emperor to grant relief".

Gandhi, speaking on the resolution in a more quiet tone, vowed to die rather than submit to the law. "We will be unworthy sons of India if we submit to the contemplated degradation...We are conscious of the mark of slavery that the act will put upon us. We will meet it and refuse to submit to it. The brave rulers... can only respond to bravery and practical action". The responsibility of advising them to go to jail was his. The step is very grave but it is unavoidable; it is not a threat but only a readiness and a plan for action. When people pass a resolution it is their duty to adhere to it. [ibid]

Gandhi pointed out that simple passive resistance will face the brute force but this is the time not for arguements but for action and Indian character would be judged by this trial. Resistance will enhance their prestige all over South Africa. If the resolution is not acted upon, "we will lose face, bring disgrace to the community and all our petitions would be worthless...Indians would become a laughing stock to be spurned and spitted upon.... The resolution will be a touch stone by which the national and self respecting spirit of Indians in Transvaal is to be tested". [CWMG V 449]

The elaborate distinction between pledge and oath involving perjury and divine contract etc. that Gandhi emphasised in his later narration is not mentioned at all. In fact this distinction was drawn in an article that Gandhi wrote in *Indian Opinion* of a much later date.

If the birth of satyagraha is to be dated and located, it would be this date [11-9-06] and this place [Johannesburg]. Gandhi had advised [January 1904] Indian merchants not to cooperate with government on the license issue and to refuse to pay and go to jail for doing business without license. But that was for private interest; now it was a question of public honour.

The Johannesburg meeting was followed by several such meetings in other parts of Transvaal to explain the implications of the ordinance and of the decision to resist it. The government retreated a step and exempted women and children from personal participation in the process of registration. On the other side, Indians began to waver even before the fight had begun and the signs of weakness emerged when the written pledges were being collected about the defiance of law. "Many signed the pledge...but even among those who had originally pledged, there were some who hesitated to sign it". [SSA 160]

Transvaal was still a Crown colony and every measure would require prior approval of the Crown. The meeting therefore decided to send a delegation to plead Indian case before Colonial Secretary Lord Elgin and also before India Secretary Morley so as to stall the Imperial sanction to 'a wicked and unjust law' that reduced Indians to the status worse than pariah.

Gandhi was greatly disappointed that after very brave speeches at the Empire Theatre meeting, very few came forward to pay the money needed for the delegation and there were acute factional bickering. [CWMG V 453]

It had been decided to send Haji Omar Ally as one-man delegation because Gandhi's presence was necessary to keep people firm and steady on the path. Later it was decided to send Gandhi also. Gandhi insisted on written pledges being taken from the leaders to stick to the jail going resolution. Gandhi had been repeatedly urging Indians for going to jail, but he doubted whether many people would do so because of the great fear of jails. [CWMG VI 336]

Indian leaders had high hopes for very sympathetic hearing by British authorities after the victory of Liberal Party in 1905. Lord Elgin, an ex-Indian viceroy was in charge of Colonial office with Winston Churchill as his assistant.

The European press in Africa strongly condemned passive resistance as a defiance of Law and criticised "the bad leadership for the Indian community." Indians who were 'expensive nuisance' were threatened with wholesale expulsion. [CWMG V 429]

The dissentions about the composition and number of delegation degenerated into long, complicated and at times bitter discussions. "We had a full experience of all the bad habits which are generally prevalent in Associations". [SSA] There were several factions among Indian community. A lot of Gandhi's time and energy were wasted in holding them together and he was not always very successful. There was a strong insistence on sectional representation and dissentions opened along communal lines. It was with great difficulty that Gandhi finally pacified the opposition of Dr. Godfrey, Mr. Pillay and others. But this discord was going to plague Gandhi in London.

"There was for all practical purposes no Hindu-Muslim problem in South Africa. But it can not be claimed that there were no differences between the two sections and if these differences never assumed an acute form that may have been to some extent due to the peculiar conditions in South Africa". [SSA 161]

Lord Elgin had already approved the principle of full and strict registration and he tried to stop the visit of the delegation. He felt that Indians have misunderstood the ordinance. Registration was only a verification of old documents to make the new register a more complete and more authentic document.

Governor Selborne informed the British Indian Association "Lord Elgin has already approved the ordinance and His Excellency does not consider that any useful purpose is likely to be served by sending the proposed delegation to England". [CWMG V 449] But Elgin also promised that the delegation, if sent, would be properly heard. [ibid 456]

The choice finally fell on Gandhi, Abdul Gani and Haji Omar Ali but Gani withdrew and the two-member delegation left for England on 20 September 1906. Gandhi at the age of thirty-seven was a widely discussed personality, famous both in England and South Africa. Ali was the founder president of Hamidia Islamic society—an Islamic missionary group and Gandhi mentions a controversy of its being a rival of British Indian Association. [CWMG V 392] Ali was a well-known leader of the Indian community before Gandhi. But compared to Gandhi, he was a mere non-entity and he resented the eminence of a novice like Gandhi. Ali had publicly expressed grave misgivings about the resolution No 4 and he was opposed to any form of satyagraha. After returning from London, Ali left Transvaal. He was a very strong critic of Gandhi-Smuts understanding of 1908 and established the British Indian Reconciliation Committee. [June 1909] He was to denounce Gandhi-Smuts settlement of 1914 in very strong terms.

The delegation travelled in first class comforts of a train as well as by ship and arrived in London on 3 October 1906. Gandhi was visiting London after more than fifteen years. Gandhi's dress, manners and activities were those of an English lobbyist. The delegation stayed for five weeks in Cecil Hotel, one of the finest and costliest hotels, a proper and prestigious location in London and employed an expert shorthand typist as a secretary.

Ali suffered from acute rheumatism and stayed at Lady Margaret Hospital most of the time. It was therefore virtually a one-man delegation though Gandhi always used 'WE' to give the necessary credit to Ali. Gandhi also was suffering from shaking teeth and ailing nose. He could not eat any solid food on account of a painful molar. But he refused to be treated and plunged into work. He had no time to go to a dentist and got his molar extracted by his friend Dr. Joshiah without using anesthesia. [Shukla]

Gandhi single handedly bore the enormous burden and strove hard to build up pressure on the Colonial as well as India Office by seeking support for his cause from all parties except Conservatives. He was actively supported and helped by leaders like Dadabhai Naoroji, Manchersha Bhavnagree, Amir Ali, Sir Henry Cotton, William Wedderburn and by many others.

Gandhi whipped up a wide publicity campaign, hosted lunches almost every day, made speeches, saw all important persons who could help the cause, gave six interviews to the press. In addition to all this work, he wrote 257 letters, issued more than 2000 notices for the members of parliament, drafted five memorandums, wrote 8 articles and led three delegations—all this in forty-one days [20-10-6/1-12-06] He used 5000 penny post stamps during his stay in London. There was not a moment for Gandhi to rest. He hardly ever slept before 1.00 am and was always up and ready for work by 8 in the morning. Besides all this work in London, he attended to his weekly contributions to *Indian Opinion.*

Gandhi was able to handle this unbelievably enormous burden of work by enlisting the clerical services of five Indian students from South Africa who were studying in London. Gandhi was always able to charm young people by his sincerity and his sweet nature and he was always very eager to train younger people for public work.

Gandhi got British exporters in London to petition Lord Elgin about their opinion of Indian merchants in Transvaal being "an honest and honorable body of men...[whose] presence was a distinct gain to the European community in general". [CWMG VI 106] He persuaded the

Chinese ambassador to protest against the ordinance on behalf of the Chinese Community in Transvaal. Five ex-coolie students from Natal studying medicine and law in London were persuaded to petition that the new law would prevent them from practicing in Transvaal.

More than 100 members of the parliament belonging to labor, liberal and nationalist parties met to hear Gandhi and Ally [7-11-06] and resolved that the Indian question was an Imperial issue and should be put above party politics. In his interviews with the British press, Gandhi was forthright. He described locations as "Jewish Ghettoes" and accepted reasonable restrictions on Indian immigration. "British Indians in their wildest dreams have never claimed the right to free migration into Transvaal". [CWMG VI 5] Racial prejudices were known and accepted; "the colonies were British in name and very un-British in conduct".

Gandhi succeeded in hammering out an all-party deputation of twelve carefully chosen members of Parliament. There was no Irish member, no one from Labor Party and none of the pro-Indian radicals. The total exclusion of Conservative party members proved to be a costly mistake later on.

Sir Lepel Griffin, a strong critique of nationalist movement and leaders of India, was initially very hesitant to lead an Indian deputation to Lord Elgin but he finally consented to do so. Gandhi prepared a very highly factual, sober and balanced memorandum to be submitted to the Colonial Office. The deputation waited on Lord Elgin. [8-11-06] Sir Lepel Griffin submitted "such registration is meant only for criminals and is unheard of in any other British colony or in Europe with the only exception of Russian legislation for Jews.... Indians are the most orderly, honorable, temperate and industrious race. Transvaal is a colony by conquest and this legislation and anti-Indian prejudices are fomented by aliens, by Russian Jews, by Syrians, by German Jews, by every class of aliens-the very offspring of the infernal sewers of Europe". [CWMG VI 111-112]

Gandhi argued that "Indians were struggling for removable of degradation and the only method short of violence and disorder which is open to those who have neither votes nor representation is that of passive resistance...a movement which for Indians means suffering and ruin and for the colony, a scandal and a disgrace".

"Our task is made difficult because you have already approved the principle of the ordinance, which is fit only for thieves and robbers. Since anti-Indian laws were often copied by colonies from one another, this ordinance may be copied by other colonies in South Africa". [ibid] Gandhi then pleaded for a Commission of Inquiry about Indian question.

Lord Elgin replied that Indians had accepted finger printing in earlier registration; so why is it debasing this time and if one impression is acceptable, why do ten digits make it more objectionable?

But then he played his trump card. Gandhi and Ally might be representing the large meeting, but he has with him "a petition...that has been largely signed in opposition to the views which has been placed before me today. I therefore cannot entirely subscribe to the opposition... in this matter". [CWMG V 125]

Gandhi demanded to know the names of Indians sending the cable and he was told about the petition signed by 437 persons and forwarded by Dr. Godfrey and there was a letter from Mr. Pillai that was signed by 107 Indians.

Dr. Godfrey had challenged the right of Gandhi to speak in the name of all Indians as he had no mandate from the community. Pillai, the leader of the colonial born Indians expressed his anger against Gandhi. His second letter was much worse than his first. Gandhi was charged having minted money as a permit lawyer. "Mr. Gandhi, a well known professional political agitator whose mischievous views upon Indian question in South Africa has been productive of greatest possible harm to the Indian community and anti-Asiatic laws in various colonies here have been the direct outcome of such views from which Mr. Gandhi derived considerable financial advantage while Indians in South Africa gained nothing". [Quoted by Hunt]

Sir Lepel Griffin dismissed Dr. Godfrey's petition as "a somewhat silly petition—a work of some mischievous school boy". The Godfrey-Pillai documents were shocking and were finally proved to be of no importance but a great deal of damage was done. "The delegation was a good deal discredited being apparently mainly representative of the interests of permit agents whose occupation would be threatened by registration". [Hunt] Gandhi was maligned and misunderstood because he was the ablest and most successful lawyer advising his clients and acting as a Permit Agent to secure entry permits for them.

Gandhi did not lose his cool and quietly faced the vicious and embarrassing challenge to his person and to the cause he espoused. There is no rose without thorns and Godfrey-Pillai were just that. He pointed out that Dr. Godfrey was present at the Empire Theatre meeting and had supported Resolution no. 4. Godfrey had offered to be a delegate but was not so chosen. He is "a little insane...he looses his mental balance when any problem is presented to him; [CWMG VI 151] he is a child and lacks understanding. He is more to be pitied than scorned. He is madly doing all he can to injure the cause while his brothers here are assisting it". Gandhi was rather harsh about Pillai who "has been found to be worse for liquor and may be described as a loafer". [CWMG VI 196]

Gandhi denied any financial gain from public work. "Thirteen years of service rendered by me to my countrymen has been a labor of love and a matter of keenest pleasure to me." The only reason for giving such an explanation was that "The sacred mission...may not be prejudiced in the eyes of public". [CWMG VI 166]

Lord Elgin was greatly impressed by Gandhi's strong arguments as also by his cogent and factual presentation. "Mr. Gandhi's marshalling of facts and his submissions on them betrays a skilled as well as a determined hand". [*Rand Daily Mail* Hunt 80] Elgin was polite and evasive to the delegation but he wrote to Selborne. "They have protested against the ordinance... on the ground that it actually aggravates the disabilities from which they at present suffer and they have urged that retention of the un-amended law of 1885 would be preferable to the allowance of the new ordinance". [Hutten]

The deputation then met Morley on 22 November 1906] Gandhi urged that the ordinance was a matter of life and death to Indians. "We have a right to come to India Office to protect our interest and the ordinance imposes a color bar which Britain has always opposed".

Morley fully supported the Indian claims but he had no power to handle colonial matters. He however expressed his doubts. The Crown would not be able to dictate the colony about its internal matters. The commissions never solve any problem and we cannot control a self-governing colony that Transvaal was going become within a few months.

Gandhi sought and secured an interview with Churchill and met him 27 November 1906] Churchill felt it was desirable to keep whites and coloured people separate. Gandhi argued "this would lead to locations and would be ruinous to Indians".

Gandhi's plea received strong and vocal support in Parliament and from almost entire English press. Anti-Boer prejudices in England were very strong. Gandhi was intensely happy and even euphoric. The all round sympathy made him optimistic and confident about the success of the mission. The support that he had secured was "beyond expectation. Everybody considers that a stronger deputation on Indian affairs has never waited upon the government". [CWMG VI 134]

But Gandhi was not blind to the undercurrents. "The rulers here think in the heart of their hearts that we are an inferior race and there is no harm in piling up endless burdens on us". [CWMG VI 222] "If the weak are not protected, Sun of the Empire is about to set because God would deprive it of its power". [CWMG VII 210]

While in London, Gandhi organised [15-11-06] a permanent body to be known as "South African British Indian Association Committee". Lord Ampthill was its president and Gandhi's old colleague and a devoted follower Louis Walter Ritch became its secretary.

It was to be an active pressure group financed by Gandhi who provided it with pounds 300/500 every year. Gandhi remitted 10 pounds for expenses with almost every letter he sent to the committee. This committee was the most concrete result of Gandhi's activities in London. But it soon became defunct. Once Transvaal became a self-governing colony, British control over the colony was reduced to the minimum. Britain had hardly any role to play in Transvaal after 1907. Thereafter this Committee lost all its utility though Gandhi struggled hard and long to keep the committee going and on many occasions praised the work done by it.

In midst of such hectic activities, Gandhi found the time and energy to meet several of his old associates of London Vegetarian Society and Theosophical society whom he had befriended during his student days in London. He also met Syamji Krishnaverma for long discussions. Gandhi was "always ready to confront his opponents directly attempting to win them over through his candor and his reasoned convictions". [Hunt 94] But Gandhi's approach and methods were so abhorrent to Krishnaverma that discussions were entirely fruitless. Krishnavarma insisted that Britain must be driven out of India. "Indians should refuse them all help so that they become unable to carry on administration and are forced to leave". [CWMG VI 84]

Gandhi in 1906 was a strong supporter of British rule in India. "It would be a calamity to break the connection between British people and the people of India...The connection cannot be only beneficial but is calculated to of enormous advantage to the world religiously and therefore socially and politically". Gandhi was compelled to adopt the Kishnavarma line of action in 1921-22 and thereafter.

It was during this visit that Gandhi was very strongly impressed by suffragette movement and he met Mrs. Emuline Pankhurst. He witnessed their demonstration where eleven arrested women declined bail, refused to pay the fine and went to jail for a month.

Gandhi wrote rapturous articles in *Indian Opinion* about this movement and exhorted his followers to emulate them. "If even women display such courage, will Transvaal Indians fail in their duty and be afraid of gaol"? He never approved of their methods but had genuine admiration for their bravery and sacrifices. The strategy of his satyagraha movement carried a deep impression of this movement in terms of concepts and tactics- demanding equality not as a concession but as a right.

Satyagraha, like the suffragette movement, started with moderate steps—petitions, press campaigns, demonstrations and then a deliberate defiance of law.

Gandhi spoke to the Union of the Ethical societies and warned that England would find it difficult to hold India 'if her people...are insulted and degraded as if they belonged to a barbarous race'. He repeated his plea at the meeting of the East India Association and asked a rhetorical question 'whether India is to be lost or retained simply because of the colonial sentiments'. He pointed out that since the laws are in the name of King, every Englishman is responsible for the acts of colonies. "The term British Indian becomes an empty platitude" and the empire "ceases to have any meaning for British Indians in Africa". [CWMG VI 252]

In his farewell speech, Gandhi mentioned encouraging support from all sides. "Ours has been a policy of strictest moderation...we have been able to enter into the feelings of our opponents... in South Africa and we have examined the whole question from their standpoint." [CWMG VI 245] Just before leaving England, Gandhi arranged an early breakfast meeting for sympathisers and associates as a token of his gratitude and wrote a farewell letter to the press thanking it for the cooperation.

The Polak family was the only relief for an overworked Gandhi and while Polak senior helped Gandhi to establish contacts with several persons, young Polak sisters were his toys whom he teased and joked with. "Were I young and unmarried and believed in the mixed marriages, I would have married them or accepted them as my daughters". [CWMG VI 17]

Lord Elgin was deeply impressed by the force of Gandhi's arguements and presentation and he realised that the ordinance did violate British policy that status quo should to be maintained and nothing should be done to worsen the conditions for Indians. The ordinance was not a mere re-registration but a further deterioration of the situation as far as Indians were concerned.

A cryptic note from his assistant Churchill was also effective. "What can we say to the deputation after what we said to Kruger"? This was a clear reference to the British protest to Boer government about discrimination against Indians. Churchill argued that new legislature of Transvaal should shoulder the burden. Churchill was for inaction. "Why should we say anything? Either dawdle or disallow, preferably the former. ...Why should Britain take the odium for the racist ordinance"? [Hutten]

The colonial office was caught in a dilemma. Elgin had approved the ordinance but there was a strong current of anti-Boer and pro-India feelings that supported Indian cause. It was also impossible for Elgin to overlook the intense anti-Indian prejudices of Europeans and the need to placate the politically dominant community of Boers.

Transvaal was soon going to become an autonomous colony and could not be neglected: many British statesmen were already envisioning a union of all the four colonies of South Africa to be led by Transvaal. But the Empire and India weighed the scale. Britain would not sanction the legislation based upon racial discrimination which would be a departure form the fundamental principle of British Empire and which would produce untoward reactions in India. Britain would not accept any restrictions on Indians that were more severe than those imposed in pre-war Transvaal. Lord Elgin therefore disallowed the ordinance. [3-12-06]

Gandhi had triumphed. As in Natal [1894] so also in Transvaal [1906] Gandhi's presentation and his efforts had checkmated the dominant community and the government of the concerned colony and had saved the dignity and rights of the Indian community. The delegates returned to South Africa and participated in a bout of immense jubilation. This was the most important event of the year for the community and Gandhi humbly accepted the praise showered upon him. "God be praised".

There was a shower of congratulatory messages [more than 30] on him and the event reaffirmed Gandhi's faith in Britain. "British rule is essentially just and we can find redress of our grievances". He expressed "a confident conviction that any reasonable and just grievance when laid in moderation before English rulers at Home would not go un-redressed". [CWMG VI 264:266]

At a reception in Durban, Gandhi was as wise as he was moderate. "Europeans must be honored as a dominant race". He harped upon the communal unity so as to secure civil rights and got a resolution passed that "Indians desire to work in cooperation with European colonists and to yield to their wishes in all reasonable ways". [CWMG VI 261]

But something else had also happened in London. If Gandhi was busy pursuing his mission, the government of Transvaal was not idle either.

Sir Richard Solomon, lt. governor of Transvaal had left by the same boat that Gandhi and Ally sailed in. Gandhi was unaware of the currents flowing behind his back. The date for granting autonomy and for transferring all administrative powers to Transvaal had been fixed for January 1907. Lord Elgin assured Sir Richard that if the new regime passed the same or similar measure about registration, the Colonial office would have to accept and approve it. The logic of self-government would then prevent any interference from Home government.

Lord Elgin's disapproval of the ordinance would thus be a temporary postponement of the registration for Indians only by a few months at the most. The Europeans need not worry as the question was to be left to the government they would elect and control.

This was the British double-dealing to keep Indians happy and at the same time allow Transvaal to do what it wanted to do. "That this was a secret decision and a clear collusion between White Hall and Transvaal racists has been proved by the documents at the colonial office". [Hunt 84]

The odium for anti-racist measure was to be transferred to Boers. Gandhi was greeted with good phrases but "in the moment of his triumph, he would discover that he was put into his place". [Hunt 60]

"It could be interpreted as an empty gesture, one of the type that in the absence of any real risk [because the transfer of power was imminent] the colonial office was from time to time fond of making". [Hutten 170] Britain would not accept injustice being done to Indians and would not overlook the sentiments of the whites in the colony.

The colonial office showed "a greater concern with the form than with the substance—an apprehension lest the crisis in Transvaal shred the veil of decency surrounding the Imperial scene. When all rhetoric is put aside, what the colonial office was desperate to achieve was not the welfare of the Indian population but the avoidance of embarrassment". [Hutten 174]

Gandhi says [SSA 170-71] that he came to know about Elgin's betrayal as soon as he reached South Africa. "Our disappointment in Transvaal was as deep as had been our joy in Madeira"…"The sole topic of conversation was the trick played upon us by Lord Elgin and by the British government and our disappointment in South Africa was deep"…" I have characterized it as a crooked policy but I believe that it can be given a still harsher name with perfect justice". But the contemporary documents do not support Gandhi's statements. He continued to praise Lord Elgin up to the end of 1907 and even beyond. "Lord Elgin has dared to do justice in the teeth of official opposition". [CWMG VI 365]

Gandhi was to understand his total defeat very slowly. It was after many, many years that Gandhi came to know about his being double-crossed in London. He was to learn very late that his heady and short-lived victory was not a triumph but that he was a victim of a very dirty joke.

Gandhi's work in London turned into a shallow hoax and a total waste of time, effort and money. The delegation had wasted 900 pounds and six precious weeks. Lord Elgin continued to make proper sounds and he even requested Transvaal government about "the desirability of relaxing the restrictions to which Asiatics are at present subject". [Hutten 179] "The Indian government feels strongly in the matter and insists that Indian community should be granted relief". [CWMG VI 338]

Gandhi was naturally very livid at such double-crossing by Elgin when he knew about it, but for the moment it was the White community that denounced Elgin furiously and even threatened violence for disapproving the ordinance.

Chapter 17

SATYAGRAHA

Transvaal was granted autonomy in February 1907 and the campaign for Assembly elections revealed "clear evidence of virulent racial hatreds displayed by all political parties and all candidates". [Hunt 83]

General Botha promised to drive away all 'coolies' within a period of four years. General Smuts was more specific. "The Asiatic cancer which has already eaten so deeply into the vitals of South Africa ought to be resolutely eradicated". [Polak 56]

After the elections, General Botha became prime minister and General Smuts was in charge of Asiatic department as colonial minister. The Dutch were thrilled by the formation of Botha ministry. They had won back in politics what they had lost in war. Gandhi noted that "There is nothing for Indian community to rejoice or regret". But he was as generous as he was wise. "No matter what Dutch have done us, we ought to congratulate them". [CWMG VI 357-8] "Why do Dutch and British both hate us-our skin, our cowardice, our unmanliness and our pusillanimity". [ibid] Gandhi was worried about apathy of Indians. "People seem to have gone to sleep elated by the rejection of the ordinance. We should be wide awake". [CWMG VI 298]

Gandhi and Smuts - the titans to clash very soon were both the products of very similar social and religious orthodoxy. Both were very sincere, very honest and very inflexible. Both were generous and kind in personal life. Both were lawyers and they fought so cleanly that when the struggle was over, they developed great mutual respect for each other. But at the outset there was no love lost between them and each suspected the bona fides of the other. "The arrogance of this man can be equaled only by his ignorance...a man mad with rage", wrote Gandhi. [CWMG VII 279] Smuts hated and despised Gandhi as the chief-the only-agitator with whom co-operation was impossible.

The confrontation between the two was an experience for both. Later on there was a profound turn around in the lives of both of them. Smuts, a rebel, turned a loyalist to the British Empire: Gandhi an ardent and a confirmed loyalist turned into a determined rebel against the British Empire.

The pervading atmosphere of anti-Indian hatred was a clear indication that the ordinance would be revived in no time. The elected Assembly of 58 members met and on the very first working day [23-3-07], an exact replica of the old ordinance now renamed as Asiatic Registration Act was adopted unanimously with very great haste, its three readings being finished in two hours. Within twenty-four hours, it was forwarded to England.

Indians had not expected the law so soon. Gandhi wondered "Is self-government a license to deprive Asiatic of all his liberty?" [CWMG VII 70] "We welcome the draft bill as a challenge...[Indians] have to show of what stuff they are made...the bill will test the power of Imperial government to protect British Indians and the ability of Indian community to enforce the famous resolution regarding passive resistance". [CWMG VI 370]

"We can not say whether Imperial government will cancel the ordinance or not." [ibid 378] "This [act] proves that there is no equality between whites and blacks and all British subjects are not equal... It has fallen to our lot to be treated as Bhangis here in Transvaal". [CWMG VI 470]

Elgin hesitated for a long time to approve the new law and Whites were worried about its disapproval: but Sir Richard Solomon assured them that law will have to be approved and will be approved. Elgin had little option left because Boers threatened bloodshed and Botha offered to resign and create a constitutional crisis. The act was approved after three months, [8 June 1907] Elgin requested Botha to make the regulations under the act so generous that it would not hurt the feelings of Indians.

Gandhi deplored the approval as "a calamity as great as plague" and that "Lord Elgin's fear proved to be a stronger motive than his inclination to do justice. Out of the fear of whites, he had done injustice to Indians". [CWMG VI 469]

The Act that applied to all Asiatics was to come into operation from the first of July and Indians were required to get registered within a month as and when the registration office was opened in their areas.

Gandhi was depressed. "I saw nothing in the black act except hatred for Indians". [SSA 99] He decided to pick up the challenge and offer passive resistance to the brute force of law and government.

As was his wont, Gandhi dispatched numerous letters and memorandums to the authorities concerned and to the leaders in England and India as he quietly prepared for the struggle, which was to be a new experience for Gandhi himself.

By 1908, Gandhi had emerged as a very mature leader of the community with a very dignified and impressive behaviour. "Mr. Gandhi with his intellectual face, his low, intense voice, and unusual powers of concentrating all his thoughts carried all before him in a personal sense". [Cartwright quoted by Hunt 104]

By now, Gandhi had been transformed in to a crusader who was more assertive and more self-righteous and to whom principles and values were far more important than success or popularity. "God is always near me: he is never away from me". [CWMG VI 265] There was a marked change in his demeanour, in his style and even in his language.

Gandhi was not unaware of the change. "There was a change in the style of language used, in methods of work and in other things besides". [SSA 273] "His felicity with words at times led him along dangerous paths and sometimes he believed in his own rhetoric". [Payne 189] He went to the extent of calling Smuts a 'murderer' when Mrs. Naidoo had a miscarriage during the agitation.

Prior to 1907, Gandhi had conducted his campaigns by legal and constitutional devices. But Gandhi was sharp enough to understand that constitutional agitations would yield no results when laws themselves were unjust and oppressive and when people have no effective voice to change or repeal them. After repeated failures and frustrations spread over a period of more than a decade, Gandhi was convinced about the inefficacy of such methods.

After 1908, he increasingly relied upon his new methods of disobedience and confrontation in a peaceful manner and experimented with these new techniques in a variety of ways and with superb flexibility. There was much advancing and retreating. But to call him a strategist would be to misread him and to doubt his spontaneity. He hardly ever planned his moves and very often acted on the spur of the moment.

There were several forces dragging Gandhi in diverse directions. Therefore satyagraha as it took its shape and form in Africa had had a chequered history. The final outcome of satyagraha was so ambiguous that each side chose to depict it as a victory and both the sides were right in their own way.

The battle lines were being drawn up. There were several small meetings to rouse and prepare Indians for the struggle ahead.

Gandhi had been advocating now for some time the defiance to law involving jail going as the only effective way to oppose the registration act.

At the mass meeting called by British Indian Association at Johannesburg, there was a consensus that the new registration rules with ten-digit finger printing would not be submitted to. A resolution sought British protection. British Indian Association was "willing to cooperate in the program of voluntary registration as in 1904" in order to satisfy the government and the popular prejudices. The government was requested to trust Indians.

Gandhi reminded people of resolution No. 4 and harped upon jail going otherwise Indians would be ridiculed and crushed. Registration was worse than jail. Gandhi condemned the White Press for denouncing passive resistance. Passive Resistance was a recognised method for the redress of grievances and was an extreme step justified in exceptional circumstances. Gandhi felt confident. "Government would be unnerved by the list of jail goers". [CWMG VI 393]

No fresh oath was taken at this meeting. "Whether or not we should take an oath or whether or not September [1906] oath still binds us is no longer a question to be decided". [CWMG VI 420] "Let us show to Britain that we are fed up and would take no more any longer and Britain will help us. ... If many go to gaol, all would be released and the law would be amended. The battle is already won". [ibid 442]

Gandhi promised that the jail goers' families would be looked after by British Indian Association and that jail going is not that dangerous. 'Enjoy life in jail.' "Anybody anxious about the result has little faith in Truth and God".

Gandhi warned that if the pledge is not implemented, more stringent and humiliating laws will follow and Indian community will face contempt and ridicule in the colony, in England and even in India.

Gandhi led a deputation to Smuts offering voluntary registration and cooperation, [4-4-07] Smuts was non-committal about the act but rejected voluntary registration as useless. He justified body marks for speedy and exact identification and warned that there will no further concessions for those who defy law.

Gandhi replied that passive resistance is not defiance of law but a readiness to accept the ultimate penalty of law. He charged the government "You are creating animosity between two communities living under the same flag". [CWMG VI 450] Gandhi repeated his pledge. "If I am the only one left who has not taken a permit, my pledge still stands".

The events were rushing fast to a climax of confrontation. The Chinese community threw in their lot with the Indians under the leadership of Quinn.

Gandhi, by now, had completely lost faith in applications and petitions and repeatedly exhorted his compatriots to undertake passive defiance of law involving intense suffering: imprisonment was the only way to resist registration. 'The new ordinance was as much a mark of pure and simple slavery as the earlier had been and was a challenge to Indian manhood... The act was meant...to humiliate Indians'. He told them to give up all thoughts of family and of business in fighting against the ordinance and to look to suffragettes. "While English women do manly deeds, shall we though men act like women"? [CWMG VI 336]

Gandhi felt that government was nervous and shaken because of Indian decision of passive resistance. "If many people go to jail, all will be released and the law would be amended." "If Indian community remains firm in the resolution about gaol going, we may as well take that the new law has not been passed at all. [ibid 421] If Indians stand united...no Indian will be ruined...The brave Boers will recognize our courage and the law will go". Gandhi was aware that the struggle would involve enormous funds and all through the ensuing struggle, Gandhi repeatedly and desperately appealed for funds. He suffered intense disappointment as nothing much came out of these appeals.

Gandhi was very eager to be the first one to be arrested and jailed: he was worried about others. "Through years of disuse, such a mode of showing resentment is new to my countrymen... The results of passive resistance were unpredictable as we have been unused to it especially on such a large scale. Respectful non-submission is no disloyalty...[it is] communal suffering...not a mere matter of sentiments". [CWMG VII 61] "Gentle Jesus, the greatest passive resister that the world has seen is our patron." [ibid] Gandhi relied on God. "Even if the whole Transvaal is against us, God is with us". [ibid 89]

He clarified that ostracism and excommunication were the most powerful instruments often resorted to in India for trivial social and caste matters and these weapons would now be used for common good and for higher purpose in South Africa.

In midst of steadily mounting tension, there came a jolt for Gandhi. Some of Indian leaders were rather uneasy. Haji Omar Ally raised a communal issue. Ally telegraphed Ameer Ali in London "Gandhi's campaign would ruin thousands of my co-religionists who are all traders while the Hindus are mostly hawkers...Gandhi has totally ruined the Muslims and has been doing it for the last fifteen years". [CWMG VIII 100] Amir Ali persuaded the S. A. British Indian Committee to advise Gandhi to desist from confrontation and defiance of law. [CWMG VII 59] Gandhi of course rejected that advice, but he was furious with Ally. "It is a disgrace to the Indian community that Ally penned such words". [CWMG VII 124] But the rift that was opened thus, was going to deepen as the movement progressed further.

Gandhi hoped for British intervention and confidently expected help from that direction. "Indians are waiting to see whether the Imperial arm is to protect the weak Indians from the strong whites or whether it is used to strengthen the arms of the tyrant and to crush the weak and the helpless".

The registration office opened at Pretoria [1 July 1907]. In order to implement the decision taken at the public meeting, the first step required that no Indian should go to or deal with that office. Gandhi chose young persons for peaceful and courteous picketing with their badges and with posters to effectively dissuade Indians from getting registered. They were instructed not to obstruct traffic and keep moving and to be peaceful and polite and to submit to police violence and arrests.

The picketing was denounced by the White press as an imposition of the crowd will on individuals: Gandhi refuted the criticism by comparing the pickets with the Salvation Army girls who only persuade the misguided to their duty and exert no compulsion on anyone to fall in line.

The police never interfered with such peaceful picketing. The White press accused pickets with violence and intimidation and Gandhi himself mentions a group of rowdies among the pickets who threatened and harassed those who wanted to get themselves registered. [SSA: CWMG IX 125]

Barring a few stray and very rare incidents, picketing was so peaceful that none of the picketers was ever arrested and it was so effective that almost none of the Indians got registered. There was no violence but ostracism and social disapprobation were very potent determents.

The government, municipalities and railways threatened to dismiss Indians who did not get registered. Proclaiming that Indians were afraid of boycott and physical assaults by pickets, the government stooped very low and the officials started visiting homes and stores to receive registration applications at night. Gandhi protested against such a practice that was both illegal and undignified for the government.

But such a move did have some results. Twenty Indians got themselves registered. They "blackened their faces and hands and brought the slur on the good name of the community...this ghastly betrayal was a treachery of the community and our success becomes doubtful". [CWMG IX 134]

Gandhi warned his followers that threats and violence against renegades would harm the movement and that anger, malice arrogance, selfishness and violence are worse than useless in this movement.

Of the countless meetings and discussions that were going on all around, there is one that ought to be noticed at some length. Gandhi has given it a place of crucial importance in his later narration of events. It was on 31 of August when a mass meeting was organised at Pretoria to take stock of the emerging situation.

Mr. Hokson—a prominent Member of Parliament and a staunch supporter of Indian cause—was deputed by the government to inform the meeting that the law will not be altered, voluntary registration is not acceptable and cooperation is impossible in view of the defiance of law. Hokson advised Indian leaders to submit to the inevitable because it was like 'smashing your head against a wall'. Resistance to law would be fruitless and ruinous for Indians. He ended by advising the submission to law and loyalty to the king.

Gandhi translated his speech to the audience and then in a spirited reply full of cold, repressed fury explained that such submission would be slavery and might bring in more cruel, more humiliating laws and finally the expulsion. The loyalty to king also involves loyalty to the king of kings. For a people who had "no vote, no voice and no support" such resistance is the only available alternative left to them after their petitions have been rejected.

Gandhi again offered voluntary registration if the black act was withdrawn. Indians have suffered many insults and indignities but now the cup is full and the community could or would take no more.

Passive resistance is a legitimate method to secure redress of a felt grievance. [CWMGVII 140] "The struggle may be bitter and long before they make a breech in the impregnable wall of prejudice...but then there is no remission of Sin without shedding blood". [ibid 152]

In SSA and the Autobiography, Gandhi describes the event that took place after Hokson had withdrawn Ahmed Cachalia, pledging his support, invoked God as his witness to his pledge to resist the law 'even if I am hanged". Gandhi "felt as if the scales have fallen away from my eyes... a pledge to initiate Satyagraha must be taken in the form of a solemn oath". Very solemnly and in great detail he explained to the meeting the distinction between a pledge and an oath.

The pledge is to resolutions that are majority decisions and they can be altered, evaded and even disobeyed. The oath is an act of faith and is a stipulation between an individual and his God. It cannot be altered and its violation is both a legal crime-a perjury and a moral crime-a sin. Death is to be preferred to violation of an oath.

Kachalia who occasioned such a discourse was a very sincere person and got himself ruined to keep his word. "I have never in Africa or in India come across a man who can surpass Mr. Kachalia in courage or steadfastness". [SSA 181] Gandhi then drew an elaborate picture of the worst that can happen to those who chose the path of defiance and he was quite candid about the disastrous results of the passive resistance. But he promised the final victory to those few or even one satyagrahi who persisted to the last.

The speech that Gandhi delivered at this meeting could be one of the best that he ever delivered in his life. This was the most crucial moment in his life and before the very eyes of a crowd that could hardly comprehend what was happening, a political leader was being transformed into a saint—a Mahatma. The entire meeting very enthusiastically took the oath not to ever get registered and to face all the consequences that this may entail.

It is sad to note that this account is somewhat incongruent to the contemporary reports in *Indian Opinion*. Kachalia, then a very minor leader is not mentioned as a speaker at this meeting and the distinction between pledge and oath is nowhere referred to. Gandhi did mention jail but he drew a rather rosy picture of jail life.

Gandhi had had mentioned oath, perjury etc for the first time in a letter he wrote to *Rand Daily Mail* [6-7-07]. "Indians have sworn before God that they will not submit to this law...Perjury before a court of law can be expatiated by suffering the punishment that may be awarded by the judge. What expatiation is possible before the Judge of judges who never errs! If we perjured before Him, we would be unfit associates of any civilized society of men and the Ghettoes of old would be our proper and deserved lot". [CWMG VII 87] There is no mention of any distinction between pledge and oath and in fact Gandhi continued to use both these words as synonyms for a long time thereafter.

Registration process was a long drawn war of attrition and went on at a leisurely pace. After a month at Pretoria, the registration office shifted from district to district waiting for a month in each of the district H.Q. for Indians to get registered. Its last stop was at Johannesburg and the process was over by 31 October.

During these four months, the administrators had tried very hard to persuade Indians even by going from house to house. But after the final date, no further applications were accepted. The month of November was spent in scrutiny and in preparations for action.

In spite of the government's threat that no licenses would be issued to unregistered Indians, the community had displayed a rare solidarity and out of some 7000 Indians, only 551 got themselves registered or "played upon the piano"—a phrase that was coined by Gandhi as the process involved imprinting ten digits. Gandhi's efforts had met with a roaring success and the pickets had done a wonderful job. Pretoria proved to be the only weak spot but even there, out of 1500 Indians only 100 got themselves registered.

This boycott and the agitation were strongly supported by Mr. Bhavnagree in London and by Agakhan in Bombay. Anjuman-e-Islam sent Jinnah to London to pressurise India office to involve itself in the issue. The press in India as well in England came out very strongly in support of Gandhi. He wrote to *Johannesburg Star* [30-12-07] that his love and loyalty to Britain urged him "to resist the Act in the most peaceful and shall I say Christian manner".

But the vitriolic language used by *Indian Opinion* throughout this campaign was certainly not very Christian. Gandhi's fiery journalism was at its pugnacious best. Permit office was "Plague office" and the officers were the 'tauts' while the Registration act was 'a demon devouring victims and was fond of Indian blood'. Registration certificates were warrants of slavery and death.

Indians who fell out of line were furiously denounced. A list of such persons with their religion, caste and even region of origin was regularly published. They were 'black legs,' 'black faced,' 'traitors', 'cowards', 'mentally deranged' 'enemy of self and of the country' and "curs who deserved to be kicked and despised".

Gandhi's vehemence did lose him many followers. Some prominent Muslims had got themselves registered and such denunciations and ugly names alienated them from Gandhi. Many prominent Indian leaders like Haji Omar Ally, Sheth Haji Habib deserted the movement by quitting the colony to settle elsewhere and a large number of Indians left Transvaal. "It will be better if every worthy son of India were to leave

the colony or to commit suicide rather than to submit to this law".
[CWMG VI 489] Nearly 6000 Indians, finding it difficult to withstand
the government pressure and community ostracism, left Transvaal
during the last three months of 1907.

Adverse publicity and name-calling must have exerted tremendous
peer pressure on those who were wavering. Swan [150] mentions that
"Social and even economic boycott against such black legs was
practiced". The shame and the fear of being marked out by the
community must have been the most effective factors to maintain the
solidarity of the community. Gandhi's rhetoric often did become
unbalanced but then it should be remembered that the cry of the
anguished is never very musical to the ear. Gandhi was fighting against
very heavy odds with his back to the wall in midst of increasing
disaffection and desertions. Gandhi had great fears about the collapse
of the movement as "the public agitation of this magnitude [was]
undertaken for the first time.

Smuts declared that most of the Indians had offered to get registered
after Gandhi was arrested; many Indians had alleged undue pressure from
pickets to prevent them from registration. The White press spoke about
the terror of the pickets. Gandhi issued a strong denial. "We have no
desire to resort to questionable methods in order to compel obedience
to the wish of majority...by minority". [CWMG VII 303]

During these months of suspense when the process of registration was
going on, Gandhi oscillated between the hope of British intervention
and the fear of intransient Transvaal. Gandhi's faith in British
government and his illusion about the weakness of Transvaal proved to
be very costly mistakes. Britain did nothing.

The Transvaal government had held its hand back during this period
and Gandhi grew more and more contemptuous of Gen. Smuts. "The

aggressive spirit that Gen. Smuts showed four months ago has now disappeared"...."A speech like this is the raving of a mad man."... "Not being in his right mind, he says whatever comes in his head". [CWMG VIII 20, 21, 24] 'The threats of Gen. Smuts need not frighten anyone'. Smuts was often depicted as a combination of cowardice and idiocy and Gandhi often mocked his "bravery".

Gandhi mistook the warnings in the White Press about impending action as showing "a nervousness of rulers". "There is no limit to the weakness of government which is afraid of its own tyranny". "Government was climbing down step by step". "Government is demoralized and it does not know what to do". "Government is losing its grip and courage and would soon surrender". [CWMG VII 421, 427, 438]

"The government is afraid that if Indian community does not submit to law, no action can be taken against it". The government will have to come to a settlement with Indians because there are not enough jails for all Indians and in case of massive deportation "Imperial government can not keep aloof". "Imperial government must have impressed upon him [Smuts] that he would not be able to touch any Indian". "The signs that we see on every side indicate that if we fight till the last, we shall win. Even today we have as good as won". [CWMG VII 341,339] Gandhi believing that Government would not dare to take action against such a large number of determined Indians kept on mocking Smuts with contemptuous references.

Smuts on his part was equally contemptuous of the 'Coolies' who are 'detrimental to our prosperity'. All Boer laws thwarted earlier by British intervention were now to be enforced strictly to plug further influx of Indians. "We have made up our mind to make this a white men's country and however difficult the task before us, in this matter we have put our foot down and shall keep it there". [CWMG VII 287] Strict registration was necessary because old certificates and registration has failed. Since one Indian cannot be distinguished from another, fingerprints were needed and "Indians have to and do give finger prints before they leave India". [CWMG VII 286] Ten digit fingerprints were only for identification and there was nothing dishonorable or criminal about it. The provisions of the Registration Act would be fully enforced. "If the resistance of Indians...leads to results which they do not seriously face to day, they will have only themselves or their leaders to blame". [CWMG VII 162]

For Gandhi, the Asiatic law was so degrading to the manhood of Indians and so offensive to their religion that the struggle against it was as much a moral and religious fight as it was a political one. He continuously referred to faith and God. Such references were hardly ever mentioned during his earlier agitations. "In resisting the wretched act, Indians would be seeking the Kingdom of God". "Even if every white is against Indians, God is with them and that is enough". [CWMG VII 151, 194] "Indian cause is God's own while Government's is that of devil". [Ibid VIII 4]

Gandhi was quite aware of the transcendental nature and the universal applicability of his crusade. "Indians in Transvaal will stagger humanity without shedding a drop of blood...Gentle Jesus, the greatest passive resister the world has known is their patron". [VII 118]

Gandhi was simultaneously fighting against Asiatic Registration and against the new immigration law. The Immigration Restriction Bill [9-7-07] introduced severe language test on the lines of Natal and this was made applicable to all entrants including the refuges. Many of these refugees did not know English and would lose their right of entry. Educated Indians could enter but registration was compulsory of them all. By this immigration law the government acquired the power of deportation that was absent in the Asiatic act.

Gandhi's petitions against immigration bill to the Assembly and to the colonial secretary went unheeded and Lord Elgin approved the law in December 1907. Gandhi called it a savage, barbarous act and accused Britain of neglecting Indians.

The government had delayed taking action against Indians refusing registration because Smuts waited for the approval of Immigration Act. Gandhi had treated this delay as a sign of weakness and vacillation and therefore he was almost stunned when the whiplash fell so heavily against Indians.

The action began on low key. The government, municipalities and railways dismissed those Indian servants who had not got registered. The licenses to traders and hawkers were denied. Gandhi was unfazed. He advised the persons concerned to trade and hawk without licenses, not to pay the imposed fines but allow their merchandise to be auctioned for recovery of such fines.

Satyagraha and its theoretical formulations by Gandhi were about to be put to the acid test. Satyagraha proved to be an ordeal by fire that burnt away all dross and shaped Gandhi's leadership and tactics making his wooly concepts more precise and firm. Gandhi grew though and because of this struggle as he perfected his techniques of mobilisation and management of masses. He was quite confident about the potentiality of satyagraha. "Our example on a small scale in this colony, whether successful or unsuccessful may well be adopted by every oppressed people and every oppressed individual as more reliable and more honorable instrument for securing redress of wrong than any which hitherto been adopted". [CWMG VII 334]

Count Leo Tolstoy, the most famous intellectual of the day endorsed Gandhi's faith. "Your activity in Transvaal...is the most essential work, the most important of all the work that is being done in the whole world where in not only the Christians but the whole world will unavoidably take part". [CWMG VII 118]

The struggle was now joined and prominent Indians were issued individual notices for deportation for non-registration. Twenty-five pickets were arrested on 8 December. Pandit Ram Sunder Das who had very actively participated in the campaign and picketing was the first [8-12-07] to be arrested. He was sentenced to a month in prison and instantly became a hero praised to the sky by Gandhi. But he proved to be an imposter and entrained for Natal as soon as he was freed from prison. Gandhi denounced him as a rascal, a traitor and a demon, "as far as the Indian community is concerned, Ram Sunder is dead from today". [14-1-08], 'a hypocrite has been unmasked' [CWMG VII 473].

The situation was not at all rosy and Gandhi had many reasons to worry about the developing scenario. A large number of Indians had drafted a humiliating note of total surrender [CWMG VII 199] "Many stalwarts have fallen: more may fall". [ibid 473] Rattled by such large number of defections, Gandhi made frantic appeals. "Please in the name of God…if you will show a little courage, the fight is easy enough".

He appealed to the Muslims "not to allow the ship to go down just as we are about to sight the land". [CWMG VIII 26] Hamidia leaders also appealed to Muslims all over the world in the name of pan-Islamism and appealed to Muslim League: but all to no purpose.

Gandhi was depressed by the rumours of large-scale desertions and increasing rift between Hindus and Muslims. His appeal to the British high commissioner came to nothing. "We had hoped for support from (the) Imperial government". He had to face the bitter truth that people did not have the courage and the capacity to sacrifice that he possessed. He was worried and was unsure about Indians standing the acid test. He sought to remind the merchants that the community was suffering because of trade rivalry and poorer Indians also risked their jobs by non-registration.

The Whites alleged that the opposition to registration was to shield illegal migrants who had infiltrated and who were still coming. Botha denounced Indians for opposing the law on flimsy grounds of ten digit-finger-printing that was compulsory even for European immigrants. But he was confusing the issue. Finger-prints were never the central issue. The act was resented by Gandhi not for finger-printing but because it ascribed criminality to the entire community, insulted their traditions and challenged their manliness by the sting of compulsion.

Times without number, Gandhi had emphatically clarified that finger-prints was not the core issue though it was an important point because of implied degradation. Though Gandhi had always underplayed this issue, the lesser leaders had made finger-prints a focal point of anti-registration campaign. *Indian Opinion* too had often emphasized fingerprints as a core issue.

The Indian resistance began to crumble down the moment government struck the first blow. The panic button was pushed and several merchants "informed the government that they were prepared to conform to the law if the pickets and other mischief makers were removed from their path".

The crucial moment arrived on 28 December when Gandhi was arrested and was given a week to quit Transvaal. He spent the interval between arrest and trial in hectic activity consolidating the morale of his followers. He spoke at numerous meetings and wrote extensively in *Indian Opinion* and in English press.

In his last speech, Gandhi clarified several issues. "I do not want the public to leave this place under the impression that the whole of this fight is in connection with the thumb or finger impressions". [CWMG VIII 3] It was not so much as finger-printing or naming wife or mother as the underlying spirit of the Act. "It is not possible to describe in words the underlying spirit...the condemnation of the whole community". [ibid 34]

A huge and disciplined crowd of Indians attended the trial of Gandhi. A cool and collected Gandhi walked in, offered no defense and asked for the maximum punishment as a leader of the movement. The magistrate acknowledged that Gandhi was a thorough gentleman but law had to be enforced. He gave Gandhi two months of simple imprisonment. His last message to Indians was to remain firm and faithful. Gandhi was led away to jail by a side door to avoid the waiting crowd.

When alone in custody, Gandhi was in deep thought and was assailed by doubts and misgivings. "I may have misled myself". [CWMG VIII 38] "The home, the courts were I practiced, the public meetings—all this passed away like a dream and now I was a prisoner". [SSA Chap XX] If people fail to fill up the prisons, "the two months would be as tedious as an age." He soon regained his posture, "the second train of thought acted...like a bracing tonic". [ibid]

Gandhi had no reason to worry and his followers did not leave him in the lurch. Seventy-six more satyagrahis joined him within a fortnight. In all there were some 220 satyagrahis in jails. All satyagrahis including Gandhi were non-Whites and hence were put into Negro wards and given Negro food and dresses. The famous Gandhi cap that became the badge of Indian nationalists is a replica of the cap of Negro prisoners in Africa.

Gandhi felt degraded by being classed with the natives. He was troubled by "the horrible din and yelling of the native prisoners ...[who are] only one degree removed from animals and [were] fighting among themselves". [CWMG VIII 120] "To be placed on the level with the natives seemed too much to put up with" [ibid 130] "Kafirs as a rule are uncivilized... they are all troublesome, very dirty and live almost like animals". [ibid 135] "Kafirs are intellectually backward, they are unlettered and have no arts". [ibid 191]

There was no privacy in jail while urinating or defecating or bathing. Prisoners were stripped in groups for medical examinations and then often left naked for hours till the doctor arrived. After his experiences in African jails, Gandhi lost his sense of shame: nudity became natural to him in later life.

Gandhi started pressing jail authorities for proper diet for Indian prisoners and spent most of his time in reading Bible, Koran, Bacon's essays, lectures of Huxley besides *Gita* and Socrates. He started to learn Urdu. This was his first experience of jail and he was greatly worried about the impact of his absence on the movement that now was almost leaderless. [SSA 204] Gandhi so far had never bothered about preparing a second line of leadership to act on his behalf in his absence.

The government was also in great predicament. Smuts confessed it in a public speech [2 May 1908] while explaining why he agreed to the compromise of January 1908. Only 500/600 Indians out of a population of 10,000 had got registered. They could not be exiled because neighboring colonies refused to receive them. They could not be imprisoned because there were not enough jails and it would be a great loss of prestige. Registration was a drastic law for the colored and "British Empire is largely a black Empire-an important fact never to be forgotten".

The failure of registration had created a very awkward and in a sense a very dangerous situation. "There is no more awkward position for government than a movement of passive resistance. It is a movement that is really tantamount to war...a state of anarchy as far as the government is concerned. In primitive society, this is suppressed with cruelty, but civilized government could not do it". This was Smut's reason for agreeing to the compromise. [January 1908]

Chapter 18

COMPROMISE

The Transvaal happenings reverberated all over the civilised world and were a great embarrassment to Botha ministry. There were hardly 200 Indians in the jails but they were able to discredit the government as a bully. "The conscious breaking of the law by an entire community and a demand by the transgressors that they be given the maximum penalty was so novel and so foreign to the bureaucratic mind that it tended to create a panic. There were after all only 12,000 Indians in the whole of Transvaal and yet they were able to essentially immobilize the colonial government and to hold the attention of the whole Empire". [Hutten 20]

The Transvaal government was worried about the impact of Indian agitation on the huge mass of very poor natives who suffered far more severe restrictions. Government therefore could not afford to yield even an inch for the fear of an upsurge among the natives.

Smuts was in deep trouble. Britain egged on by Indian government and public opinion in England was breathing down his neck and he felt stung by the calumny tarnishing the image of the first responsible government of the colony.

India was in agony and expressed great resentment at the events in Transvaal; a mass meeting of 10,000 in Madras resolved to boycott Transvaal; British press and public figures extended strong support to Indian cause; questions about Gandhi and Indians were asked almost every day in British Parliament; Britain was making efforts to ease the situation and the British prime minister agreed that the law was bad. Britain could not directly interfere as Transvaal was a self-governing colony; but the Prime Minister did promise to use 'pressure and persuasion'.

Gandhi was in no less a quandary. Even before he was arrested, the movement was flagging down. Indian merchants were being squeezed by White wholesalers who shut off credits and supplies. Indians were worried about the financial ruin as well as about the expulsion from the colony: they were keen to stay in Transvaal at any cost.

Reports about defections poured in from many areas and Gandhi realised that he was standing not on a rock but on a quicksand. He was ready, even eager for a compromise at the earliest opportunity.

Gandhi was not left alone in prison for long. Albert Cartwright, the editor of *Transvaal Leader* and a personal friend of Gandhi was a great supporter of Indian cause. He sought and secured special permission to see Gandhi and met him on 21st of January. He and Gandhi agreed that if Indians got themselves voluntarily registered, the 1907 act would become redundant and could and would be repealed.

Cartwright returned with a letter "the draft [of which] he and other prominent persons had prepared". [CWMG VIII 161] "Cartwright drafted the letter". [CWMG VIII 66] This would contradict Gandhi's statement [SSA Chap. XXI] "the compromise letter was either drafted or approved by Smuts." An enthusiastic Cartwright might have given the impression that he was speaking on behalf of Smuts. He accepted two major alterations made by Gandhi in the draft. Gandhi, Naidoo and Quinn signed a compromise proposal of voluntary registration, with finger printing being optional. Such registration was to be legitimised. All persons who left Transvaal and all refugees outside Transvaal would be allowed to get registered. Fingerprints will not be insisted upon for the educated, rich and well known Indians as well as for the conscious objectors. There would be no prosecutions during the grace period of three months allowed for voluntary registration. [CWMG VIII 76]

Smuts consulted several senior leaders of his party and then called Gandhi for a meeting. Gandhi was taken in great secrecy to Pretoria to meet Smuts at night [30-1-08]. Smuts was very conciliatory. But Gandhi's demand for reinstatement of dismissed Indians in government service was rejected.

Gandhi was taken again next day to Smuts and was informed in very clear and precise terms. "The demands that you have made in your letter are rather excessive but government has decided to accept them. If fingerprints are found necessary you will have to give them".

The new form for registration would be prepared in consultation with Gandhi. Smuts requested that the 'black legs' may not be harassed and Gandhi promised it. "Other things were discussed besides but these need not be reported here". [CWMG VIII 67] Gandhi waited till the cabinet in another room accepted the settlement.

Gandhi was released after spending twenty days in prison, satyagraha was postponed and 220 satyagrahis were released next day. "Gandhi in no way is inclined to consider his release from jail as a victory". [*Rand Daily Mail* 31-1-07] He did not allow any demonstrations of victory. Gandhi thanked all those who had sent numerous telegrams and declared the he is "ready to suffer any hardship for Truth, honor and self respect".

Gandhi's release came as a perfect surprise to Indian leaders. He explained that the agreement was honourable to both the sides with neither climbing down. In Gandhi's opinion, acceptance of voluntary registration by government implied that the black act would be repealed.

But all hell broke loose. Gandhi was strongly denounced for agreeing to registration without specific and written commitment to the act being repealed. Gandhi argued "It would have been of no use having anything in writing since the final authority is that of Parliament." [CWMG VIII 46] "As soon as Parliament meets, the Act would be repealed and Immigration law amended". [CWMG VIII 4]

Gandhi-Smuts settlement enjoining registration and fingerprinting on voluntary basis was a sudden reversal of gears and had a very disconcerting effect on the community, which was suddenly thrown off the balance. Gandhi was severely criticised for hasty action and for unilateral decision without consulting other leaders while Smuts consulted his party and his cabinet colleagues.

The compromise was opposed both in Transvaal and Natal. Even those who respected Gandhi very highly as a person rejected the settlement that was too vague, entirely one sided and oral in its most important aspect. Smuts too was denounced by the whites for compromising with the evil. "The whites are dumbfounded and wonder how all this came about". [CWMG VIII 61]

The community was shocked that Gandhi who had so strenuously opposed both the registration and fingerprinting was now advocating both in the vain hope of the act being repealed. "If we are required to give fingerprints against the repeal of the act, it is worth it". Gandhi defended the oral assurances; "there are some things which can be put down on paper; for others one has to rely on oral understandings".

Gandhi accounts for the intense opposition by a vague and oblique reference to Indians who had illegally sneaked into Transvaal and who were opposed to registration as such for the fear of being exposed. "This clique could have instigated Pathans. The reader will now see how Pathans got excited all of a sudden". [SSA 224]

Gandhi had time and again clarified very emphatically that fingerprinting was not the main or even a major issue for opposing the act. "This struggle is not for giving or not giving fingerprints; but it is a struggle for the honor and the dignity of the Indian community". [CWMG VII 346] "There are many Indians who have mistakenly assumed that our campaign is against giving fingerprints". [CWMG VIII 62] "Finger print has never been as essential objection but of course an issue, it has a ring of criminality about it and is used for criminals trying to hide their identity". But Gandhi *had* roused bitter feelings against fingerprinting by pointing out that such prints were taken only from convicted criminals. "Those who give ten digit fingerprints confess to have lost their virility".

The intensive propaganda against such prints by the lesser leaders had been countenanced by Gandhi; Maulavis and Pandits had added a tinge of fanaticism to the movement thus negating any compromise on any issue. Gandhi strenuously defended the settlement in *Indian Opinion* but he could not convince anybody. "Gandhi always described the settlement as a victory, but almost the entire community considered it a defeat and defeat it was". [Walpart] Gandhi stuck to his guns and refused to accept opinion of the community as valid.

The settlement is an interesting exhibit to understand the developing pattern of Gandhi's leadership. What were the factors that prompted or pushed Gandhi into such a precipitate settlement and why did he not consult other leaders of the community?

The movement had started fizzling out by the beginning of January and as a strategist, Gandhi might have his own reasons to retreat. "The offer came from the government... Elderly and the respectable businessmen were to go to jail... it was my duty to prevent this from happening if I could". Discouraging reports about people losing courage were a galore. "Those who went to gaol, lost their nerve in few days and some of them hinted that they would not go to gaol again... all these things could not be just ignored by a person who had been deeply involved in the struggle for sixteen months". [CWMG VIII 114] "The settlement, while securing government aims would enable Asians to retreat from a position which had become untenable". [Hutten 185] The nagging question whether Gandhi could have avoided such an abject surrender admits of no objective answer. The evolving scenario may have forced Gandhi to climb down.

But there is no surprise in the fact that Gandhi took such a momentous decision all by himself without caring to consult any one else. In Africa, Gandhi was not primus inter pares, he was the only primus; he had no companions, he had only supporters and opponents. He had developed a habit of acting on his own and taking unilateral decisions; he never felt the need or the usefulness of consulting others.

On account of his long innings in South African public life, Gandhi came to look upon political leadership as some sort of legal profession. He was the best barrister, the most erudite and the best leader of the community. The community can choose or change the leader, but then it should leave him free to decide and act in the best interests of the community. "I will strive to obtain the best [terms] that I can for the community". [CWMG VIII 46]

This style of Gandhi continued in India even though in India he was working with the stalwarts almost as tall as he and they felt frustrated with his style of functioning as in Chouri-choura or Quit India decisions that he imposed upon them without prior consultations.

Now that the settlement was a settled fact, Gandhi hoped that wounds would be healed but it did not happen. "With the passage of time ...implications of the settlement became clear; the misunderstanding on the other hand began to thicken. The letter we had written to Smuts was open to misinterpretation". [SSA 225]

For all the struggle and sufferings by the community, Gandhi had merely earned three months grace period during which the registration, in no way materially different from the compulsory one, was permitted with only a fig leaf of its being a voluntary act. He had to face the ire of Indian community on account of all-pervading mistrust of government and the fear of law being not repealed. He was widely accused of betrayal and of some sort of personal deal; the figure of 15,000 pounds began to make the rounds.

At a meeting of British Indian Association [2 February 1908] a threat of violence was held out for those who go for registration. Gandhi spoke out. "If violence is to be used against any one, let it be first used against me... I shall thank the person who assaults me, grateful for the blows from one of my brethren and feel honored by it. I alone am responsible". [CWMG VIII 55-56]

Pathans had a longstanding grudge against Gandhi. "We will finish him" for his rumoured 'derogatory remarks against our religion and our Prophet'. A Pathan, Mir Alam Khan, vowed to kill Gandhi if he ever got himself registered, but Gandhi stood firm against all calumnies and threats.

His response to such threats was as noble as Gandhi alone can be. "To die at the hand of a brother or in some such other way can not be for me a matter of sorrow...if in such a case I am free from the thoughts of anger or hatred against my assailants...I am willing to die or do anything for the cause". [Polak 64-65] Pathans were mere stooges. "I am sure that there is the hand of a well known Indian behind it". [CWMG IX 152]

The forms for voluntary registration, prepared in consultation with Gandhi, were ready by first week February and new registrations were to begin from the 10th of the month. Gandhi decided to be the first one to be registered and to give his ten digit prints. A mass meeting [9 February 1908] expressed strong opposition to giving fingerprints but Gandhi was adamant. Gandhi chided as 'childish' the demand for giving only thumb impression and not ten digits. Government has given great concessions but it is to be used in a limited way.

Gandhi, accompanied by Thambi Naidoo and Esop Mian started a campaign for registration: he was accosted and murderously attacked by Mir Alam Khan and his gang. "As the blows started, I uttered the word He Ram...as I came to, I got up with a smile, [there was] no anger or hatred". [CWMG VIII 93-94] Gandhi thereby created a myth that was potent later on. Like Christ's last anguished cry, there was nobody to hear what he then said.

Gandhi was very seriously injured and was left with a life long disability for deep breathing. He was taken to the nearby residence of Rev. Doke. "He was not exactly a friend...I have hardly met him three or four times...It was thus a stranger that he took to his home". [ibid]

Gandhi insisted on getting registered before he was treated and brought tears to the eyes of registration officials. He was nursed for a week by the Doke family with love and devotion much to the chagrin of the white community. Doke was threatened with expulsion from his parish for sheltering a black rebel but he stood his ground.

Gandhi appealed for peace. "Let the blood spilled to day cement the two communities indissolubly". [CWMG VIII 76] Gandhi's appeal not to prosecute the assailants was disregarded and the gang was sentenced to three months. "Whatever view Mr. Gandhi might hold as regards punishment to the criminals, they can not be given effect to in South Africa". [SSA 230]

Gandhi's forgiveness was limited only to himself. When Naidoo and Esop Mian were attacked, Gandhi was vehement. "The instigator... [Maulavi Mukhtiar Ahmed] of...the attack ...has been traced...If it is possible, the man must be deported. He is more or less a maniac and many dissatisfied Indians simply hang around him". [ibid 253-4] His views on nonviolence are developing. "Non violence needs to be cultivated; till then we have to defend ourselves with sticks or weapons and strike back in self-defense". [CWMG VIII 251]

As soon as Gandhi was a little better, he insisted on facing the Indian community in Natal and he was surprised at the reception. "The discontent in Durban…I did not expect it in such vehemence. … Many people have turned against me". At a mass meeting, Gandhi was closely questioned, even hackled by a hostile crowd of about a thousand Indians and not a single person was ready to believe him.

A second attempt on his life was made at this meeting and he was saved by defensive firing by his friend and the timely arrival of police. He was escorted out "amidst much booing and hissing" [Swan 167] and was taken to Phoenix under police protection, which continued for some time with bodyguards. "I was week enough to feel safe in their presence and I wonder if I could have slept with the same ease if the guards had not been there". [SSA 254]

Gandhi discussed the compromise in *Indian Opinion* in a dialogue form that foreshadowed *Hind Swaraj*. The questions are inane and the answers are smug and evasive. "Only malicious persons will pick holes…Our real victory is treated by the ignorant people as defeat".

Gandhi presumed much, imagined a lot and hoped for unbelievable. He failed to convince anyone. He mellowed down after some months and confessed to his mistake. At the mass meeting at Johannesburg [24-6-08] "to consider the breech of the spirit of the compromise", Gandhi made a great speech in a tense atmosphere. He referred to great discontent "over what…I myself have done and that the community has been sold for selfish purpose... I approached Gen. Smuts on the strength of a letter that was placed before me...I acted according to my conscience. But time has shown that they [his critics] were right ...I need not have gone to Gen. Smuts as I did". [CWMG VIII 318-9]

The political blunder of not consulting other leaders widened the Hindu-Muslim rift. "It is not Hindus who have blamed me. The condemnatory letters that I have received are all from Muslims." [CWMG VIII 99] Muslims denounced the compromise and approached Jinnah for his advice on the future course of action.

For Gandhi there was nothing new in all this. "When the passive resistance movement was at its height, Mr. Ally could not trust me because I was a Hindu". [ibid]

Haji Omar Aly, Haji Habib and Godfrey formed a group of moderates who would fight for rights of Indians but who were not ready for confrontation and jail going program. They denounced Gandhi for his haste and his unilateral decision. Gandhi was in great agony at this growing rift between Hindus and Muslims whom he considered to be one and the same community. Gandhi warned against the enemies who seek to divide the community. "I have only one duty to bring Hindus and Muslims together and to serve them as one community". [ibid 101]

Now that the resistance movement had been suspended, Indians had no option but to get registered and by the end of grace period [9 May 1908] 9178 had applied for registration out of which 7793 were accepted and certificates were issued while 1214 applications were rejected. There was hardly any opposition to fingerprints—7010 gave ten digits while 1960 gave thumb impressions and only 70 declined fingerprints. The facility for voluntary registration was withdrawn and such registration was legitimised by an act of 1908.

Gandhi was accused of charging two pounds only from Muslims for securing such certificates. This was a vicious misrepresentation. Gandhi had charged all his clients two guineas for the legal work and had forwarded 235 such applications.

Then came the most cruel blow to the prestige and political leadership of Gandhi. The repeatedly expressed hope and confidence of Gandhi over the 'black' act of 1907 being repealed proved to be a mirage. The law was not repealed. On the contrary, permit holding Indians who were out of country and could not get registered by 9th May were brought under the old act.

Gandhi had repeatedly assured the Indians that total registration by the community would render the law deadwood and it would be naturally repealed. "Government has placed the key to repeal the law in our hands...The law will then automatically stand cancelled". "When Parliament meets, we shall be delivered from this law i.e. the act will be repealed. [CWMG VIII 46] "The compromise implies the ultimate repeal of the act. Registration outside the framework of law, if carried out would mean the end of law".

The intense and unseemly controversy about the repeal of the act is a clash of the titans and is an area of total darkness where it is almost impossible to unearth the truth. Gandhi had already attained an impressive stature in public life and would never tell a lie; Smuts was the ablest and the most conscientious leader of the day and was destined to rise to great heights in future. "Both have been adjudged honorable men by History. Yet they told diametrically opposite stories and only one can be right as to what actually happened". [Hutten 191] There is no hard evidence to prove or disprove either side. Smuts agreed that the repeal was discussed with Gandhi inconclusively but he clearly and emphatically denied that he ever gave any such promise. "I could not promise that a certain class of population in the state should be outside the law. All I could say was that...there should be this interim state of affairs and...as soon as parliament met, it should deal with the situation. It was impossible for me to promise that at a future date, Asiatics coming to this country should be left free to register as they wished. That was the request with which I could not comply and which the law of the land would not sanction". [CWMG VIII 508]

Gandhi insisted that a definite promise about repealing of the act had been orally given to him and squarely accused Smuts of going back on the promise given but he was not always clear or specific. Gandhi's statements are contraries and create confusion rather than clarity. "The promise was given there and then that if all the Asiatics applied for voluntary registration, the act would be repealed". [CWMG VIII 260] "We have been assured that the law will be annulled". "This is double crossing pure and simple". [ibid 272] "Gen. Smuts now wants to gull us by putting a wrong construction on the promise he gave in writing". [ibid 268]

But Gandhi also said that "While it is true that there was nothing written in so many words as to the repeal of the Asiatic act, reading between the lines one can read the repeal of the act in the written terms of the compromise". [CWMG IX 125] Since the number of voluntary registration is very large, "the act ceases to have any meaning. It will be noted that repeal of the act was implied, not explicit in our letter." [CWMG VIII 284] "The unconditional acceptance of our letter "therefore implied... that if all or majority of Indians took out voluntary registration, the law would have to be repealed".

Gandhi did concede some confusion. "The draft did not make very clear the condition that required the repeal of the black act". [SSA 211]. The letter that Gandhi mentions is more specific. "We have noticed your repeated public declarations that there is no likelihood of the Act being repealed". [CWMG VIII 42] In three letters written by Gandhi to Smuts between February and May, Gandhi never mentions any such promise. But then the letters deal with immigration and secondly the oral understanding precludes any such reference.

Gandhi often quoted the Richmond speech of Smuts where he said that the law could not be repealed 'till every single Indian in this country has been registered'. Gandhi interpreted this to mean that full registration would lead to repeal.

"Asiatics have fulfilled their obligation in both spirit and letter of law. It now remains for the government to complete the performance of its duty- to repeal the Asiatic law and to legalize voluntary registration'. [CWMG VIII 222] "Full and speedy registration would fulfill the law...law will then automatically stand cancelled". "Registration outside the framework of Law which is fully carried out would mean the end of law". [CWMG VIII 64]

In view of such expressions, there can be no certainty whether a definite promise was given or whether Gandhi hoped and believed that the law would be repealed. Gandhi does mention "We have been assured that the law would be annulled". But then he immediately adds "victory does not lie so much in the expectation that the law will be annulled ...even if the repeal of the law does not come about..." [ibid 130]

Gandhi seems to have expected a quid pro quo from the government. "The essence of the compromise is that the undertaking of Indian community being fulfilled ... the act should be repealed". ..."I have risked my life and if the registration act is not repealed, I will prove guilty of selling away Indian interests...Were I ever to consent the act to be applied to the newcomers, I would be unworthy as a leader and their suspicions would be justified...In order to make good my word and to assist the government...I very nearly lost my life". [Ibid 232]

When the voluntary registration facility was withdrawn, Gandhi wrote to the authorities and to Cartwright about such facilities being extended to Indian refugees who were absent and had been left out. But the former residents of Transvaal holding Dutch permits who arrived after the expiry of the grace period were compelled to get registered under the old act and Gandhi's protest letter was brushed aside by Smuts with a clear assertion that 1907 Act was never going to be repealed.

Gandhi was besides himself with anger. "The abnoxious law has to be repealed now...If government plays foul, what sort of settlement is this". [ibid 248] "Indians have fulfilled their part of the compromise...the act is considered a dead letter and the British Indian community would consider it a breach of compromise if the act is enforced".... Men do repudiate the written word...that is what has happened on this occasion...Gen. Smuts should rectify his error and repeal the act. [CWMG VIII 259]

Though Gandhi called Smuts names, we are not sure whether Smuts was lying or whether there was some misunderstanding on the part of Gandhi. It is one man's word against another. Smuts had no authority to withdraw or repeal any law. But the matter of repeal was discussed at the highest level and there was some move to replace the act by more stringent provisions in the Immigration Act. Smuts might have referred to it so as to give an impression that law was about to be repealed.

The government's refusal to repeal the act put Gandhi into an impossible situation. He was being taunted, hackled and ridiculed even by his supporters for his credulity and his leadership nosedived. Gandhi was forced to publicly acknowledge his folly in rushing through a hasty compromise and he was never again allowed such freedom of action. He candidly apologised to the community. "You must take me as you find me, with my defects no less with my quality". [SSA 261]

"The nailed fist was too apparent behind the velvet glove and the thin veil of self respect by the voluntary registration was also forfeited". [Hutten 192] Now that it was clear that the act is not going to be repealed, Gandhi advocated the resumption of resistance. "I will have to sacrifice myself".

Cartwright arranged a meeting and Gandhi met Smuts and three other officials: [6-6-08] but the meeting proved to be futile. They met again on the 13th and Smuts offered to repeal the act on condition that all categories of Indians—educated Indians, refugees and even the old permit holders-lose their right of entry. The talks finally broke down on 22 June 1908.

Gandhi was fighting also against Immigration Act and decided to test the government about the entry of educated Indians. He chose Sorabjee Shapurji Adajania—a highly educated Parsi from Natal to enter Transvaal without permit. Adjania was not prevented from entering: [24 June 1908] but on 20 July was prosecuted for his refusal to get himself registered and was sentenced to one month of hard labor. After serving his term, he was deported; but he returned again and again and went to jail till his right to enter and settle was granted by Transvaal.

At a mass meeting at Johannesburg, Gandhi reemerged as a leader by his candid confession and by his readiness for sacrifice. He mentioned widespread discontent against his leadership. After a detailed narration of his discussions ending in compromise, Gandhi agreed that "the assault on me is justified. How can people trust me? Why should they? ...[But] I state most emphatically and definitely that Gen. Smuts did promise that he was going to repeal the act". [CWMG VIII 321]

Gandhi explained that satyagraha was a war without weapons and would involve many battles and many ups and downs. He reminded the audience of the triumph of the delegation of 1906 when an ordinance was disapproved. Indians in 1908 had "earned...a name as a brave community [that] compelled Boers to yield by sheer dint of courage and Truth. Now was the opportunity to complete what was prematurely abandoned". ...This last battle of war must be won". [CWMG VIII 323]

Gandhi still hoped for a negotiated settlement and a compromise but "the people of the East will never again submit to the insults from the insolent whites". [ibid 328] Gandhi was allowed by British Indian Association to negotiate with Smuts but was warned not to commit to anything and to regularly report back to the committee.

Gandhi hammered out [17 August 1908] a formula in consultation with Smuts and Botha in the form of a Validation bill. This was a vast improvement on the Asiatic bill that was to continue to be on the statute book but only as a dead letter. "I can freely advise [my countrymen] to accept the validation act as a compromise. This was much further than I should ever care to go under present circumstances". "Majority of Asiatics [would] choose to accept the benefits that the government have so generously given". [CWMG VIII 474] "I was unwilling to impose on my countrymen further suffering and was therefore prepared to waive a substantial repeal of the act". [ibid 464]

But extremists in British Indian Association rejected Gandhi's advice and insisted on a formal repeal of 1907 Act. Gandhi agreed to honour 'the deliberate promise to lead them in passive resistance if the promised repeal was not granted'. Gandhi was thus dragged into a fresh struggle much against his better judgment and he was forced to lead them into headlong struggle that promised to be a bitter and strenuous fight. His mistakes of unilateral decision and compromise in 1908 had robbed him of assertive leadership and he was now tied down to lesser leaders.

This second phase of satyagraha was for the two remaining issues-namely the repeal of the 1907 law and the right of educated Indians to enter Transvaal. Neither of them were any very crucial questions. But "My fight has always been for principles and it shall be for principles".

To launch satyagraha again, it was necessary to revert to the position that existed before the compromise. [January 1908] For getting deregistered, Indian applications must be retrieved and certificates returned to the government. But the government refused to return applications or to receive back certificates issued. Gandhi went to the court to withdraw the application forms submitted to the government. The court blocked the way. The applications were declared to be government property that cannot be parted with.

Gandhi came up with a brilliant and dramatic alternative. The certificates were to be burnt in public and passive resisters should then trade and hawk without licenses. "We have undertaken to break certain statutes that are miscalled laws, but which can be more properly described as the engines of tyranny". [CWMG VIII 365]

Gandhi started collecting certificates for burning but by middle of July could hardly collect 300 out of some 9000 certificates. Gandhi was always a realist and was aware of the lukewarm response to his call. He calculated that there would not be more than a thousand Indians who would join the movement and half of them would be Tamil speaking ex-coolies.

He tried hard to whip up the enthusiasm of Indians by meetings and discussions. The attendance at such meetings was often as low as 500. Swan has alleged that for these meetings people were brought to swell the crowds. The elite support to Gandhi was falling off and he was now being supported mostly by poor Indian settlers. He had very serious misgivings about the ensuing struggle and he wrote to Gokhale: "whether I can carry them [Indians] with me or not, I am not in a position yet to tell you definitely". Events were to justify his misgivings.

Gandhi denounced Smuts in unmeasured terms. "The vessel of his sins is about to burst". He "does not keep any promise written or oral. He says one thing and does another". [CWMG VIII 373] The English press denounced Gandhi for such intemperate and unjustified denunciations. There was an open split in the Indian community and there was a rush for trade licenses before the certificates were burnt. Smuts had no desire to provoke 7000 Indians who had got registered and he was confident that 'except for Gandhi and a few of his mischief makers', most of Indians would comply with law.

Gandhi petitioned the Assembly to repeal the act by 10 August 1908, failing which, "the certificates would be collected and burnt and Indians would humbly but firmly take the consequences". [SSA 271]

Smuts misused this personal letter that Gandhi had written to an official and in a deliberate twist treated the date as an ultimatum.

The Assembly as well as the government were stunned by 'the audacity as well as the insolence' of Indian community for throwing such a challenge'. Smuts thundered in the Assembly. "People who have offered such a threat to the government have no idea of its power...Some agitators are trying to inflame poor Indians who would be ruined". The petition was unanimously rejected and the defiance of law 'by the barbaric and savage Indians' was condemned.

Unmoved by such outbursts and undaunted by the possible lack of community support, Gandhi stuck to his decision and he dramatized the burning of certificates at a public bonfire. The date was 16th August and the ground chosen for the bonfire was the vast compound of Hamidia Mosque.

A mass meeting attended by 3000 Indians was organised and the huge iron cauldrons used by natives to cook food were used to burn the certificates collected from Indians during past two months. Before setting them on fire, Gandhi offered to return the documents to those who wanted them. But that was not needed. Those who wanted to keep and use them can always get duplicates for a mere five shillings.

Gandhi delivered a long and passionate speech and promised to fight to the finish even if he was the only person left fighting. Mir Alam Khan apologised for misunderstanding Gandhi and was assured that Gandhi bore no ill will against him.

The *London Daily Mail* compared the incident with Boston Tea Party and the Storming of Bastille. The event, however, marks the beginning not of a victorious revolution but of the decline of satyagraha as a movement. Gandhi himself has noted that the response from the community was rather mute and there was a noticeable lack of enthusiasm.

Out of more than 9000 registration certificates, Gandhi had expected to collect 1500, but only 1300 were offered for burning and 500 trading licenses had to be burnt. [CWMG VIII 456] Five hundred more certificates were burnt a week later. [23-8-08] "I do not know if all these are true men who would fight to the last and suffer every form of hardship". [ibid 451]

The government reacted with masterly inactivity. Nobody was prevented from burning the documents and nobody was punished for the act. Government took the stand that certificates were the property of holders and they were free to do whatever they wanted to do with it. Burning certificates was not a crime: not showing them on demand was a crime making Indians liable to fines, imprisonment and deportation.

Other Indian leaders were pressing Gandhi to widen the scope of the movement to include all anti-Indian laws. But Gandhi added only the recently passed Immigration Act. Satyagrahis would enter Transvaal without permit, would neither get nor show any certificates and would trade and hawk without licenses after giving due notice to the authorities concerned.

Gandhi did teach a few un-Gandhian tricks to his followers. In order to avoid loss of property, they should nominally transfer property to their wives or European sympathisers and trade in their names. He even named some Europeans who would help for such transactions.

"Those who hold the licenses in their names should prepare a servant or a relative to go to gaol". Those who are unwilling to risk jail should donate generously to the movement. "Our objective is to tire the government". [CWMG IX 2/3]

Gandhi persuaded Indian war veterans who had settled in Transvaal after the Boer war to renew [14 September 1908] the application they had earlier submitted to British colonial secretary. "Should His Majesty's government be unable to obtain just treatment to King-Emperor's soldiers...[they] be spared the degradation of imprisonment or deportation...and [they] further wish that King-Emperor will command that they be shot by Gen. Botha or Gen. Smuts on one of the battle fields of South Africa where they had been under fire while serving".

Gandhi was aware that the British government was uneasy at the turn of events and had requested Transvaal to give consideration to Indian demands. Gandhi was quite confident that in spite the tenuous support from his compatriots, satyagraha "WILL succeed some day no matter when" [CWMG VIII 295]

Chapter 19

AT THE CROSSROADS

The second phase of satyagraha that opened with the burning of certificates was for Gandhi an era of financial difficulties, intense physical torture and great mental anguish. Gandhi was now a prophet in wilderness—highly respected but neither obeyed nor followed. He had suspended his legal practice [September 1908] and had no personal income. Gandhi had foreseen a long and bitter struggle but the actual experiences far surpassed his expectations. After the Validation Act of 1908, most Indian leaders lost interest in satyagraha that was now a struggle not for any gains but for principle of legal status of Indians in South Africa.

The exasperated government had decided to crush the movement by sheer brutalities and it uncovered all its ferocious fangs with which Gandhi's followers were to be dealt with by all organs of government. The White community with all its might and means supported government efforts to teach Indians an unforgettable lesson and all the niceties of civilised encounter were pushed aside in what Gandhi described as "a wicked misuse of power".

Gandhi personally, and the Indian community in general, faced the full blast of all the satanic devices like unbelievable and savage punishments and tortures. The courts were now very harsh. All imprisonments were for longer periods and were always with hard labor. Some satyagrahis were sent to Diepknoof prison meant for hardened criminals and where the jailor was notorious for his cruelty. Satyagrahis were often put on starvation diet and no visitors were allowed.

Gandhi was not touched for two months but seventy-five satyagrahis were arrested. [September 1908] All of them were given long sentences with hard labor and were treated very cruelly in jails. Gandhi considered such cruelties as signs of weakness. "The government is at the end of its tether....its resources are getting exhausted and it is using up all its ammunition". [CWMG IX 99] So the struggle is ending in our success because "suffering is our only remedy. Victory is certain". [ibid 104]

Gandhi was arrested in October 1908.He was given two months of hard labour and was released only after serving full term. [12-12-08] Gandhi denied that he was maltreated but his statement—"I was every well treated in jail"—borders on un-truth.

There was no distinction between political and criminal prisoners in South African jails and Gandhi cheerfully suffered all the indignities. All Indians, including Gandhi were put in Negro wards and would get cells, food and clothing meant for Negroes. This led to untold troubles because Negro diet also did not agree with Indians and they would get animal fat for cooking which was taboo for them.

Gandhi underwent the most harrowing and shattering experience of physical torture and tormenting insults. He passed through an ordeal that would have broken the spirit of any one except Gandhi. "The experience impelled me to agitate against the government more tenaciously". [CWMG IX 149]

The one night that he passed in a cell with hardened criminals—both Kafirs and Chinese—was hellfire and brimstone and he barely escaped being sodomised. "I spent the night in great misery and fear...I became very nervous...extremely uneasy. The Kaffir and Chinese prisoners appeared to be wild, murderous and given to immoral ways". [CWMG IX 148]

Gandhi was jeered and questioned by them. "A Chinese came near the bed and looked closely at me. I kept still...Then he went to the Kafir lying on the bed. The two exchanged obscene jokes, uncovering each other's genitals. Both had been charged with murder and larceny. Knowing this, how could I possibly sleep? ... Other Indians too would feel the fear that I did. [ibid]

Next day Gandhi was put with other Indians. "I worked for a day breaking stones". He was made to dig pits for trees on municipal grounds very near the road. Then for two days, he was put to digging a tank and clearing the earth. His hands got bruised, his back pained and he was roundly abused by the warden for not completing the assigned work. Then he was made to clean the latrines.

When taken to Johannesburg [27 October 1908] as a witness in another case, he was made to walk in the streets in prison uniform with handcuffs on and carrying his luggage on his head in full public view.

The treatment given to him raised furious controversy in British press. There were angry outbursts in British Parliament and government slurred over the facts in defending such a treatment to a distinguished person that Gandhi was. Botha was brazen enough to say that "It is a universal rule and applies equally to European convicts and there was no reason to exempt an Indian from its operation. Mr. Gandhi was however allowed to conceal his handcuffs and was allowed to carry a book".

Such a callous attitude met with universal condemnation in British press and in India. But Gandhi justified the treatment. "They are... entitled to compel submission to their laws". [CWMG IX 155]

One incident in Johannesburg was nightmarish. A Kafir prisoner lifted Gandhi up from his toilet seat and flung him away. Gandhi could barely avoid the fall by holding the bar of the doorframe. He says he just smiled and walked away. Actually he was so frightened and nervous that he had no bowl movement for four days.

The news of such treatment created a furor and after his return to Volkrust he was given light work of mending torn clothes and caps on the sewing machine. He was released on 12 December 1908. He was free only for two months.

He was rearrested and sentenced to three months with hard labour on 25th February. A week in Volkrust was comparatively comfortable but the torture started when he was transferred [2 March 1909] to Pretoria. "I… was obliged to undergo hardships not warranted by the sentence passed upon me…avoidable misery was inflicted on me. I was not likely to succumb … If I fared ill, majority of other passive resisters fared no better. [CWMG IX 223]

After a few days in solitary confinement, he was put into a small cell [10'x7'] too small even for pacing. There was only a small window at the top and the room was dimly lighted. He was made to stitch blankets and torn clothes on a sewing machine seven hours a day. His health broke down. He suffered from severe neuralgia with intense back pain, headaches and chest pain. The prison food did not agree with him and he refused to accept special food offered only to him. He ate only once a day and was reduced to a skeleton. "I am being subjected to brutal treatment but I will not bend". [CWMG IX 239]

Polak created a stir by publishing the details. "He is being subjected to every humiliation to break his spirit…Mr. Gandhi is being half starved and the lack of exercise is telling upon his constitution. Mr. Gandhi will make no complaints so long as he is in jail—you know the spirit of the man—but it is heartbreaking to me as an Englishman and a friend to feel that this high-minded gentleman who has all along conducted the campaign with clean hands and a lofty spirit is being tortured in this way". [quoted Huten 203]

After one and a half months he was put in the European ward and was supplied with books. The labour now taken from him was also very light like sweeping the gardens. In midst of all such torture and humiliations, he read Ruskin, Carlyle, Thoreau, Emerson and Tolstoy besides the Upanishads and books by Rajchandra and thirty other small pamphlets on Hindu rituals.

To the physical torture was added an emotional one. His wife Kasturbai was almost on her deathbed. Gandhi yearned to be by her side but he refused to accept parole or he would not pay the fine to get out of jail. When released, [25 May 1909] Gandhi rushed to Durban and nursed her back to health. He gave up the use of salt and pulses to encourage Kastur to accept proper diet.

The government as well as the entire White community was determined to crush this movement of the small Indian community. The merchants began to exert tremendous and constant pressure on Indian merchants who had links with European wholesalers and denied them normal credit facility. By foreclosing their debts they drove a few of Indian merchants to bankruptcy.

Most of the merchants buckled under pressure and started to keep away from the movement. The Muslim merchants started deserting Gandhi and he was realistic enough to acknowledge it. "Many have given up the fight... others it appears are about to do so". [CWMG IX 152] Only two merchants stayed with Gandhi till the very end.

Several small traders and poor labourers were suffering from great financial hardships on account of their participation in the movement. But Gandhi could give but little financial assistance to them. He had no such funds at his disposal and large payments would bring all sorts of wrong recruits to the cause.

The satyagraha movement was being crushed by a pincer of government repression and faction fights within the Indian community.

With the exception of a very few brave souls, most of the satyagrahis lost heart and began to withdraw from the movement. Only fifty-nine satyagrahis crossed the border into Transvaal between January and June of 1909 and the movement was virtually dead as a dido.

"Satyagraha has for the most part collapsed and ...the remaining Indians would also give in". [CWMG IX 245] Gandhi conceded that satyagrahis are too few and too weak to face the government repression. But his faith was unshaken. "Since Truth is on the side of Indian community, it must win". [CWMG IX 259] Much worse was the move made by Haji Omar Ally who established a "British Indian Conciliation Committee' [June 1909] with Haji Habib as the chairman and George Godfrey as secretary to bring about the end of the struggle against the government by goodwill and surrender. Gandhi's political opinions, his tactics of confrontation and even his language were severely denounced and his leadership was repudiated.

II

The second phase of Satyagraha coincided with the process for transforming the political map of South Africa and establishing a union of four colonies. The colonies were engrossed in prolonged and complicated negotiations and London authorities were also involved in these discussions. It had been decided to bring about such a Union by the end of 1909.

The impending union made Indians nervous because this would be 'a Union of hostile forces' "desirous of suppressing Indians...it would go hard with the community when they [colonies] came together". [SSA 310] The Union would make virulent anti-Indian laws and apply them in all colonies.

"The proposed Union has dangerous implications for Indians and other colored races who have no votes and no rights". [CWMG IX 186]

"How could Britain approve a scheme of unification which would mean reduction of Asiatics and natives to a state of practical slavery ... It would mean greater restrictions of their liberty unless [Union] meant unification not only of white races but of all British subjects colored or white". [CWMG IX 78]

Leaders of Indian community in Natal and Transvaal decided to send a delegation to London to oppose such a union, to hold a watching brief for Indian interests and to preclude the racial bias from being incorporated in the constitution that was being framed in England.

Those leaders of the Indian community who had totally forsaken Gandhi and his movement turned to him in their hour of need for advice and guidance. His abilities were undoubted and his eminence unchallenged. He was still the most outstanding leader of Indians.

"Gandhi neither wanted nor approved of any such delegation". [Swan 175] There was hardly any hope of success. He had lost faith in constitutional methods and was convinced that "Delegations and petitions are vain if there is no real sanction behind them". [CWMG IX 272]

He cherished a firm faith in satyagraha as the one and the only method to redress all ills. "A delegation is inconsistent with Satyagraha which is only sufferings and God...[they] will not be needed when the force of Truth grows stronger than the falsehoods of the government of Transvaal". [ibid 256] "I do not at all like going to England in these circumstances". [ibid 259]

But Gandhi was also a man of practical wisdom. "All Indians are not satyagrahis and all satyagrahis do not have complete faith", and "delegation was needed as a crutch for the disabled limb of the community". [SSA] The Indian community had developed deep fissures along the communal lines and the choice of delegates involved long and bitter debate.

"Having yielded to others on sending a delegation, Gandhi was able to control its composition". [Hunt108] Moreover Gandhi insisted on a delegation being simultaneously sent to India to rouse the country to its duty and to collect funds for the movement because the local sources had dried up. Gandhi had felt all along that Satyagraha movement was not properly understood in India and in England and his own visit to England and Polak going to India might help correcting many misconceptions.

After long discussions, four names were selected for each delegation. But four of these eight leaders were arrested as Satyagrahis and Gandhi and Haji Habib were left to proceed to London. The duo had been at loggerheads for a long time. "[Habib] has not been able to see eye to eye with us up to now" [CWMG IX 252] and "his [Habib's] withdrawal had led many persons to withdraw from the movement".

An extremely reluctant Gandhi left [23-6-09] for England together with Habib. "I would advise everyone to expect nothing from the deputation" [Ibid 271] and "Our efforts against Union are bound to fail. ... There can be nothing but empty bubbles where we are going. ... The deputation is proceeding unconcerned. For we are, to a great extent, indifferent to what will happen in England". [ibid 269] "The deputation shows only Indian weakness—mere children dependent upon the baby pushcart".

The end result proved that Gandhi was absolutely correct but these statements raise an uncomfortable question as to why he consented to waste his time and community funds. The delegation could not have expected to have any impact on the unification issue: but then Gandhi might have hoped to secure some sort of Imperial guarantee for safety and rights of Indians that were likely to be jeopardised by the dominant position of Transvaal in Union affairs.

"The whites are strong and favored sons of Empire, we are weak and neglected ones", but "The discussions will impel the Imperial government to seek an understanding from the colonial governments". [CWMG IX 273] Some such hopes might have been the only reason for Gandhi agreeing to go to London. It would be useful to take a stand rather than allow to case to go by default.

In spite of his firm belief that luxuries of first class travels are obstacles to spiritual progress, Gandhi insisted on travelling first class and poured scorn on African delegation for travelling cheap. "I do not consider traveling by first class to be wrong always and under all circumstances. Indians must travel first or second class to refute the charge of miserliness and to maintain status". [CWMG IX 272].

The delegation arrived in London [10 July 1909] and put up at the expensive Westminster Palace Hotel. Gandhi was in proper conventional dress—a silk hat, a well-cut morning coat, smart shoes and socks. [Polak 175]

Misfortune plagued the delegates from the very first day. They arrived to face a hostile atmosphere for no fault of theirs. Sir William Curzon Wyllie and Dr. Lalkaka had been shot dead [1 July 1909] by Madanlal Dhingra creating thereby an intense anti-Indian fury. Gandhi denounced Dhingra as a coward and mentally sick but this was not enough to clear the atmosphere. English politicians shied away from anything Indian and the delegation suffered thereby.

Gandhi, unsure of his purpose and objectives, could take no definite stand or evolve any strategy. The delegation decided to depend entirely on Lord Ampthill and the Colonial Secretary Lord Crewe. Ampthill was to cultivate personal relations with the White leaders of South Africa and carry on negotiations on behalf of Indian community.

Ampthill and Crewe insisted on a policy of 'reticence and expectation' "avoiding all public discussion of Indian issues so as to facilitate a private settlement". [CWMG IX 304] "If private moves bear no fruit, there is precious little possibility of gaining anything through public representations".

Gandhi and Habib were forced into total inactivity and were not allowed so much as to open their mouth in public. Both of them were kept absolutely in the dark about the negotiations rendering them to mere shadows. A vocal Gandhi consented to such agonising silence because the atmosphere in England had turned hostile to everything Indian.

Gandhi himself had no faith in such negotiations. He was merely going through the motions but his heart was not in it and it showed in his behaviour. "We are endeavoring, by private negotiations to arrive at a settlement; but I know Mr. Smuts too well to put much faith in such negotiations". [Ibid 308] 'All these efforts are no better than pounding the chaff'.

He had no faith in leaders of the South African White community and no hope of getting anything out of such discussions. But he still defended his decision to join such a futile delegation. "Delegation is a confession of community's weakness. It becomes something of a duty to come here on behalf of the weak". [CWMG IX 386]

Gandhi took some time to realise that he has become a persona non grata for the Imperial government. No minister and no official would like to meet a person who had defied law and had been punished as a criminal. In spite of his wide and long-standing contacts in the corridors of power, Gandhi was being avoided by English leaders so as not to displease Smuts and Botha.

"[Gandhi] became somewhat embittered that he could obtain no hearing from any of the politicians in England". [Shukla 189] Even Morley declined to see Gandhi who was a rebel and a failure because 'a vast majority of Indians in Transvaal had already submitted to Law'.

The first two months were spent without anything happening and Gandhi's repeated requests for an audience with Lord Crewe came to nothing. 'Why do you want to meet me?' asked the colonial secretary.

During these eight weeks of total inactivity, Gandhi was practically gagged and his plans for a public campaign to justify Satyagraha came to nothing. Gandhi felt miserable at the total inactivity during this long and absolutely useless stay. He got more and more disgusted.

Gandhi wasted time meeting a few celebrities and journalists. Nobody talked to him and he to none. "We are where we were", wrote Gandhi on 11 September 1909.

Lord Ampthill continuously assured Gandhi about the progress in talks but revealed no details. Smuts refused to even discuss Indian question with anybody because "Indians are not on my agenda". He declined to see Bhavnagree and left without answering the last letter from Ampthill.

Both Smuts and Botha insisted [8-9-09] that whatever concessions are granted to Indian community can be a matter of grace and not of any right. The Transvaal government was willing to admit six educated Indians every year for permanent residency as a grace without any legal equality or legal status. Lord Crewe was willing. "If India Office accepts the compromise, it would not be impolite to press Transvaal…" [CWMG IX 390]

After long delays and several requests, Lord Crewe agreed to meet Gandhi [10 August 1909] as an individual for an unofficial visit. Crewe advised acceptance of the substance but Gandhi argued that legal equality, even if fictitious, is necessary to remove the racist taint. The admission of six Indians must be a matter of right as was the case in all other British colonies. The discriminatory bar existed only in South Africa. Gandhi insisted on legal equality of treatment between Europeans and Indians to remove the racist taint and was willing to allow administrative discrimination as was done in Australia, Canada and other British colonies.

Gandhi assured Crewe of his earnest desire to promote compromise but "We fight for ideals" and legal equality would 'keep up Indian

Honor'. Crewe was blunt. "I do not hold out much hope". When Gandhi complained about avoidable hardships suffered by political prisoners in Transvaal, Crewe declined to use any compulsion on self-governing colony. 'Britain could only give advice'. [CWMG IX 359]

Lord Crewe wrote to Lord Hardinge describing Gandhi as "a quite astonishingly hopeless and impractical person for any kind of a deal but with a sort of ardent though restrained honesty which becomes most high handed obstinacy at critical moment". [Hunt 122]

The conversation about Habib accepting the proposed concessions and Gandhi rejecting them [SSA page 316] is not reported anywhere in the otherwise copiously detailed documents of the day. Habib in fact had also rejected the compromise [CWMG IX 531] and supported Gandhi's demand.

All hopes were dashed when Union Constitution bill was passed in Parliament with racist bias intact. Europeans in the Colonies insisted and secured a clause in the constitution that "Every member of the Union Parliament must be a British subject of European descent".

A bitterly disappointed Gandhi whined about the Whites "being convinced about us being inferior people". [CWMG IX 365]

The mission accomplished, Smuts prepared to depart without any definite move on the part of the colonial office for settlement of Indian quesion. Smuts told Reuters before leaving England that "It [Indian question] is in a fair way to disappear from the horizon of Transvaal politics. The vast majority of Transvaal Indians are sick to death of the agitation being carried on by some of their extremist representatives and have quietly submitted to law". [CWMG IX 376]

Gandhi had been totally neglected and bypassed by all public figures in England in all discussions about South African issues and he was bored with nothingness. "I am tired of reporting every time that I have no news to give about a settlement". [CWMG IX 383] 'I am now fed up" [ibid 494]

Lord Ampthill and Lord Crewe had rendered the delegation totally innocuous by imposing a total silence. This was a rather strange way of conducting negotiations. This approach barred even a presentation of Indian case and benefited none. Unlike 1906, Gandhi this time had no support or encouragement from the leaders of opinion in England. Crewe did not respond for a long time to Gandhi's persistent inquiries about the talks with Smuts. In England, there were no negotiations as such. Crewe merely accepted Smut's stand and informed [3-11-09] Gandhi that legal, theoretical equality demanded by Gandhi was impossible. Gandhi was intensely disappointed. 'Sun of justice has set.' "It does not seem likely that Western Civilization will survive much longer".

The press in England had charged that Satyagraha was being financed from India and was being fomented by Indian extremists. Gandhi vehemently denied the charge and explained that he had received neither money nor support from India. Gandhi had been cautious enough to totally keep away from extremists. He had given specific instructions to Polak then in India "not to come in touch with Extremist leaders but to be guided by the editor of Times of India, Prof. Gokhle and Agakhan". [CWMG IX 330]

Gandhi was left wondering whether to stay on in London or return to Transvaal. He was also toying with an idea of visiting India to rouse public opinion with the help of Bombay Presidency Association and Anjuman-I-Islam and then to return to England to pressurise Imperial authorities to intervene in Transvaal. "Many educated men in India do not realize the significance of the struggle...knowledge of soul force is lost in darkness". [CWMG IX 392]

But Polak reported about Sir Pherozeshah's hostility to Satyagraha as a defiance of law. A meeting to support the movement was prevented by the governor of Bombay.

Smuts returned to Transvaal [16-9-09] but Gandhi lingered on for two more months considering various alternatives. Haji Habib had already been recalled by his supporters. The Transvaal British Indian Association finally requested the delegates to return and they finally left England on 13th November.

Gandhi's London visit was a political disaster but it was fruitful in several other directions. He was invited by Ms. Winterbottom to speak at the Union of Ethical Societies at Emerson Club and spoke [8-10-09] on the Ethics of Passive Resistance where he repudiated the concept that such resistance is the cry of the weak. Gandhi declared passive resistance to be a weapon of the strong.

His speech on 'East and West' at Hampstead Peace and Arbitration Society was the precursor to what he was later going to write in *Hind Swaraj*. He drew a sharp contrast between East and West and condemned the society, the ethics and the approach of the West. His speech roused tempers and he was heckled both for such opinions and for his disloyal sentiments.

He presided over the Dussehra meeting [30-10-09] of the Indian Union Society in London that was organised by Indian extremists in England. Gandhi praised Rama as a national hero to be revered by all Indians. V D Savarkar was the next speaker after Gandhi. Gandhi also addressed Indian students at Cambridge [7-11-09] He addressed a meeting of Indians [3-10-09] and asked for volunteers to carry on propaganda for Transvaal agitation.

While at London, Gandhi cultivated many Indians of all shades of opinion. Though staunchly opposed to violence, he had long discussions with some Indian Anarchists at the India House of Shyamji Krishnaverma and discussed the implications of terrorist activities with them 'to show them the error of their ways'. But he had to concede "I have met practically no one who believes that India can be free without resort to violence". [CWMG IX 509]

Gandhi had met suffragettes on his earlier visit [1906] and he interacted with them again in 1909.He met their leaders and attended their meeting at Albert Hall. [7-10-09] He admired them very highly and was deeply impressed by their bravery, their sacrifices, their skill and their organisation, their resources and pluck but he disagreed with their tactics of violence against property.

"There is much to be learnt from them but some of their faults ought to be avoided". "These women are no satyagrahis and are resorting to physical force". [CWMG IX 433] He disliked their militancy and violence. "Being women, they escape the punishment of their misconduct". [ibid 402] They are agitators. His earlier enthusiastic admiration for them had by now cooled down considerably.

While in London, Gandhi actively promoted his own biography written by Rev. Doke. "I am very anxious to see it published as early as possible". He collected pre-publication subscriptions for the volume. He bought out the entire edition of the book and sent most of the copies free to the press. Polak, as requested by Gandhi, sold 250 copies to Natesan publishers in India. The book was hardly noticed in England, only *Times* acknowledged it in four lines. [CWMG IX 415]

Gandhi wrote [1-10-09] to Count Leo Tolstoy seeking his permission to translate and publish Tolstoy's letter to a Hindu in *Indian Opinion*. Tolstoy had originally written it for *Free Hindustan* published from Canada.

Gandhi wrote to Gokhale inviting him to visit Transvaal and participate in Satyagraha because such an event would draw the attention of the whole world and may help to bring the movement to a successful termination.

What Gandhi wrote in *Indian Opinion* from London will sadden the hearts of many of his admirers. "What good will it do mankind if planes fly in air...life would grow intolerable if there are too many planes flying in air...I, at any rate have grown disillusioned with Western civilization...If Dr. Cook goes to the north pole, what does mankind get? ...Unless its [west's] entire machinery is thrown overboard, people would destroy themselves in so many months". [CWMG IX 389] "It is beyond my understanding what good the discovery of North Pole has done the world...I, for one regard all these things as symptoms of mental degeneration". [ibid 401-402]

The most important and the most astonishing outcome of all the experiences and discussions and churnings in London was *Hind Swaraj* that he wrote on board during his return voyage. Gandhi was returning empty handed after spending four fruitless months. "All the disgust and disappointments of recent weeks in London, fortified by the thoughts of Carpenter and Chesterton and above all of Tolstoy and brought to a fine edge by his encounters with the radical anarchists took shape in this work". [Hunt 155]

Hind Swaraj was an immediate response to what he saw, felt, read in England during the months of enforced idleness—a workaholic smarting and fuming within. "I have written because I could not restrain myself. I have read much, pondered much during the four months in London". [CWMG X 6]

His disillusionments and frustrations made him spell out his basic faith and principles in *Hind Swaraj*, the first book he wrote in Gujarati. It was the most shocking and controversial book that he ever penned. It was "a real blast from the Triton's horn" announcing the emergence of a strange man from the sea of history. It was serialised in *Indian Opinion* and was banned in Bombay Presidency: Gandhi had already translated it into English to seek a wider audience. The English version, not an exact translation of the original, escaped the ban.

Hind Swaraj was written straight from his heart and his opinions— rash as well as mature—simply gushed out and present Gandhi at his worst. "It is so crude and so hastily conceived that Gandhi himself will destroy it after spending a year in India," said Gokhale. [Chandran 374] Gokhale went on to describe it as "a product of a sick and insane mind". "It was full of several crudities and much of it is unwarranted, half baked nonsense". [Chandran]

The concepts that are at the root of this volume are outdated medievalism and in a way they go back to Kathiawar of his childhood remembered through romantic hues. The volume is probably rooted in intense Puritanism and it is a negative evaluation and a total repudiation of modern civilisation ["a loathsome disease"] with *all* its institutions denounced as immoral and materialist.

Such a total condemnation is both unreal and undeserved. Gandhi's picture of modern civilisation is a caricature that is unfair to the West: his projection of ancient Indian culture is unwarranted and illusionary. Such a depressing clash of stereotypes could be only a product of cultural mythologies.

Gandhi, for a number of years, had been an ardent admirer of Western lifestyle and etiquette and he had made strenuous efforts to train Indians into educational and behavioural patterns of the Europeans. He himself still donned western attire and maintained a western lifestyle.

Even while denouncing the West, Gandhi was a westerner. The criticisms he voiced and the views he expressed are largely if not entirely shaped by European thinkers. Gandhi quotes Tolstoy, Ruskin, Thoreau, Max Muller, Edward Carpenter and many others. "I claim no originality", he said and he has listed twenty titles including six by Tolstoy, two by Thoreau, two by Ruskin and one by Carpenter in this small book. "The views are mine and not mine. They are mine because I hope to act according to them. They are almost a part of my being". "They [the concepts] are not new but now they have assumed such a concrete form and have taken a violent possession of me". [CWMG X 481] "My present mind set is such that even if the whole world were against what I have written, I would not be depressed". [CWMG X 139]

Gandhi was deeply influenced by all that he read since 1893, and he was ardently devoted to several thinkers but Gandhi was no blind follower of any one. Gandhi always was an original genius and "though inspired by many, it [Hind Swaraj] was nevertheless his own creative response to the unique situation facing Indians in South Africa". [Hunt 153]

Hind Swaraj is written in the form of a dialogue in which Gandhi responds to the cult of violence for securing political freedom for India—a dialogue that "actually took place between several friends-mostly readers of Indian Opinion and myself".

Though an expanded and extended version of his speech at Hampden, Hind Swaraj is focused on India and the struggle of Independence as it was being waged there. But Gandhi's analysis of that struggle is neither very deep nor very comprehensive. The basic and largely unarticulated axiom underlying Hind Swaraj is that ancient civilization of India "in my opinion represents the best the world has ever seen". Modern civilisation, a mere worship of body and not of soul "is based upon violence of the blackest type and is largely a negation of Divine Spirit in Man...it is rushing headlong to its own ruin".

Gandhi is not so much anti-West as he is anti-Modern.

He argued that India was crushed, not under British rule but under the modern civilisation from which Europe also is suffering. "If India copies England, she will be ruined...India's salvation lies in unlearning modern culture and in discarding it in its entirety because material comforts are incongruent with moral fiber". We must return to the simple, rustic and religious life of the peasants. Gandhi insisted on cultural rather than political emancipation. Real Home Rule-Swaraj is the rule over self or self control

Pax Britannica has emasculated Indians and made them cowardly but replacing British rule by Indian rule through violence would do India no good except stopping financial drain because Indian leaders would be mere imitators and would try to make India a second or fifth copy of England or America. Gandhi's discussions about the communal unity in India is the most lucid and the most rational portion in *Hind Swaraj*.

He described the parliament of England as a sterile woman ['it has not yet of its own accord done a single good thing] and a prostitute. [It is under the control of changing executives.] Hospitals and railways are maddening conveniences. Modern medical science is the concentrated essence of black magic…hospitals…are the instruments of devil…it is sinful to get medical training. Railways promote famines and plague. Indian cities have become the plague spots. By speedy travels, "man is disregarding the natural and biological limitations to travel". [CWMG X 28] What he calls it the mad rush of modernisation has unhinged us. Hind swaraj thus marks the final step crossing over the divide between barrister M.K. Gandhi and Mahatma Gandhi.

In spite of its political overtones, *Hind Swaraj* is not a political manifesto because Gandhi's nationalism is not geographical but ethical and cultural. *Hind Swaraj* is a step towards universalisation of Gandhi. He now does not belong to South Africa or to even India but to the humanity at large.

This small volume is "the most imaginative, the most intense and the most idiosyncratic of all his writings". But it also reveals a total ignorance about the evolution of human civilisation and the way societies grow by learning from one another.

"*Hind Swaraj* was a profound challenge and an extreme one at that. His closest followers were baffled by it and were embarrassed. But Gandhi has never repudiated it". [Hunt 56] "The convictions that I state in this book have grown stronger...I see no reason at all to revise them...The results of its teachings has been to create a hatred for British and to suggest that they should be expelled through armed fighting or use of violence...I bear no ill will against British...I am an uncompromising enemy of the present day civilization of Europe...

The key to the understanding of *Hind Swaraj* lies in the idea that worldly pursuit should give way to Ethical living. This way of life has no room for violence in any form against any human being black or white". [Preface to II edition 1914. CWMG XII 411-12]

But he did warn his readers in 1921 against thinking that "I am today aiming at Swaraj described therein. I know that India is not ripe for it... I am individually working for self rule pictured therein but to day my corporate activity is wholly devoted to the attainment of parliamentary swaraj in accordance with the wish of people of India". This would be enough of a confession of the impracticability of ideas expressed therein.

It was very un-Gandhi-like that he himself never acted upon the beliefs and opinions presented in that book: he continued to use all the modern gadgets and facilities in transport, communications, medicine and printing. Gandhi denounces western dress and wears it, denounces postal services and uses them, denounces newspapers but edits one and writes for several others. He denounced modern medicine and yet continuously used it. He was traveling comfortably in a ship while he wrote this book.

Gandhi's increasing fetish with puritanism, his total disillusionment with western civilisation he once admired so ardently, and depression due to a complete failure of his mission might be the genesis of *Hind Swaraj*. His intense adherence to spiritual quest blinded his vision and clouded his understanding of the world he lived in.

The four months that Gandhi spent in London were the most frustrating period of his public life. The British leaders had to concede the racist approach of the Union leaders. Britain was very eager for the earliest formation of the Union and she needed South Africa more than the other way around.

While in London, Gandhi kept a tight vigil on the satyagraha movement in Transvaal, though his followers were dwindling very rapidly. Since there was not enough accommodation for all the satyagrahis they were often deported across the borders. They almost immediately re-entered Transvaal making such deportation a farce and a nuisance.

A batch of satyagrahis had been deported to India leaving their families and their properties behind them. They were virtually starved during the voyage and on reaching India they were just abandoned without any support whatsoever. These coolies had settled in South Africa for many years and had neither contacts nor resources in India. Gandhi wrote to Natesan who organised some relief for them. Fortunately for these deportees, the Supreme Court of Transvaal held such deportations illegal and they had to be brought back South Africa at government expenses.

Chapter 20

IN WILDERNESS

An empty handed, crestfallen and a very depressed Gandhi arrived at Cape Town, [30-11-09]. Gandhi had to plough his lonely furrow and he strove in wilderness for one more year. He crossed Transvaal border arriving at Johannesburg on 2nd December. A small, motley crowd of Indians, Chinese and a few Europeans greeted him. He had expected to be arrested for violation of Immigration Act but nothing happened. Though Gandhi crossed and re-crossed Transvaal-Natal border several times, he was not arrested again till 1913.

At a meeting at Johannesburg [4 December 1909] Gandhi summed up the benefits of delegation. The Union government has shown readiness to repeal 1907 act and the issue had now narrowed down only to the entry of educated Indians. The government was ready to permit the entry and residency for six educated Indians as a matter of grace: Gandhi had insisted on such facilities being granted as a matter of right. The deputation had evoked worldwide sympathy and colonial office now had a much better understanding of the issues involved in Indian question.

Gandhi had to face the stark reality that satyagraha as a mass movement had died on his hands by March of 1909. "By February of that year, 97% of Transvaal Asians had taken out the registration certificates" [Swan 174] and the government was intensely happy that "the passive resistance movement is breaking down in all directions as the great bulk of the Indian population in Transvaal is submitting to law". [Hutten] Gandhi lamented "It has become my sole occupation to seek out people wiling to go to jail". [CWMG XI 273]

The harsh sentences meted out by courts, the intensely cruel treatment in jails, the fear of being exiled and loss of domicile and the strain of Satyagraha disrupting normal family life were some of the factors that forced lesser spirits among his followers to fall away and withdraw from the movement. "It is no wonder then if many lose heart now and decline to give even pecuniary help". [CWMG X 97]

Only about 100 satyagrahis were active; "others were found only in meetings, petitions and protests". [ibid] This was inevitable "considering the material one has to work with and work upon". [CWMG X 381] "The community was torn by internal dissentions and the principal workers left one after another". [SSA 388]

By the end of 1908, 2124 persons had served jail sentence—1373 for crossing borders and 751 for non-registration—and 450 had been deported to various colonies in South Africa. But by the end of 1909, the movement was virtually dead and only 150 satyagrahis were in various jails.

Gandhi was fully aware of what was happening around him. "Indians on their part were not in a position to put up a strong fight. There was not sufficient number of Satyagrahis for the purpose…[Indians] looked upon staunch satuyagrahies as so many fools…Stray satyagrahis now and then went to jails". [SSA 309 and 353] In spite of all the coaxing that Gandhi tried, the movement could not be revived. Nanda mentions the boredom and the fatigue felt by Gandhi 'for a mission so thankless and so fruitless". The Indian community had become so apathetic that nobody cared to even greet the satyagrahis on their release from jail.

"The community has failed in its duty of courtesy and does not show sufficient interest in satyagraha campaign". [CWMG X 144] Gandhi was totally neglected by the government and Indians avoided him.

But just as the satyagrahis were tired and listless, so was the government. Severity in jails continued, but the satyagrahis were now very rarely arrested. By 1910 the satyagrahis were objects of ridicule rather than hatred and were often mocked by police and even by magistrates. "Transvaal agitation is petering out. Indians have lost heart and there is no need for stronger legislation against them". [*Sunday Times of Johannesburg*]

But Satyagraha, or what was left of it, continued. Gandhi was left without any funds or followers. Satyagraha was a costly movement. The enormous paper-work, the cost of publicity and travels consumed a lot of money. Gandhi was faced with a very taxing problem of maintaining the families of the satyagrahis who were in jails and this was a crushing burden.

By the middle of 1908, Gandhi's legal practice had dried up due to his public engagements and he closed it down in 1909. He was financially ruined. He had borne the entire expenses of movement for two years [1907-09] and had by now nothing left with him. Gandhi was maintained by Kallenbach and lived in severe simplicity. Gandhi started selling everything. He sold family jewellery, his office furniture, his law books and even the volumes of his Encyclopedia.

Gandhi, hard pressed for money decided to surrender his insurance policy of 660 pounds, [nearly a lac of rupees] a huge fortune in those days. "I have no longer any use of it and I would like to... receive back a large portion of the premiums paid". [CWMG IX 363] Insurance being a lack of faith in god as mentioned by Gandhi in his autobiography is clearly an afterthought. He never believed in insurance but he had to take out the policy because of family feud—"because of your bitter letters...in order to escape from your imprecations in case of responsibility for supporting my wife and children fell upon you as I was at that time engaged in helping the plague victims". [CWMG VI 431]

Gandhi continuously appealed for funds and more funds but there was hardly any response from local sources as rich merchants had turned away from the movement. He was facing a severe cash crunch but he was enormously relieved when due to the efforts of Gokhale, funds began to flow from India just at that moment [November 1909] beginning with Tatas donating Rs. 75,000 in three installments: Petit was generous and princes of Mysore, Bikaner, Baroda and Nizam of Hyderabad sent in their contributions. The list is fairly long and representative.

Gandhi received in all about pounds 8000 from India and he acted as the sole dispenser of this fund refusing to account for it to any one in Africa. Gandhi spent a part of these funds to pay back the debts incurred for running *Indian Opinion* and *Phoenix* both of these he claimed belonged to the community and were part of the Satyagraha movement. But legally speaking both were his personal properties. In 1914, a very ugly controversy about such spending was raked up by Muslim leaders when he was leaving South Africa

Gandhi was facing a haunting problem of providing shelter and work for destitute satyagrahis and their families. He conceived of a farm for satyagrahis to stay and work so as to maintain themselves by physical labor. Kallenbach invested in a farm and spent 600 pounds to construct buildings to house passive resisters there. Kellenbach named it Tolstoy farm and handed it over [30-5-10] to Gandhi to be used without any charge or dues for the duration of struggle. [CVWMG X 263]

This 1100- acre farm, two miles long and one mile broad had two wells and about 1000 fruit trees with very fertile soil. It was a rich and self-sufficient farm and it was to become "a center for self purification as a prelude to the final campaign". Situated at distance of twenty-one miles from Johannesburg, it was a sort of war camp sheltering sixty males, ten women and about twenty-thirty children of all ages. The inmates belonged to different religious and language groups. They subsisted on physical labour like farming, fruit gardening and sandal making etc. It was here that the simple, hard, corporate ashram life—with its common kitchen, separate wards for males and females, evening prayers followed by religious discourses and Bhajans—began to shape itself. Celibacy was compulsory and everybody slept on the floor.

The continuation of Satyagraha would not have been possible without this farm because from this base, Gandhi could carry on his fight indefinitely. Gandhi adopted a life of voluntary poverty often walking to and from Johannesburg—a distance of forty miles. The Tolstoy farm was closed after three years and all the satyagrahi families including Gandhi moved on to Phoenix farm that became the base camp for the last and the most famous phase of Gandhi's Satyagraha.

Satyagraha as a movement had failed but as a concept it proved be a roaring success. If the purpose of Satyagraha was to focus public attention on the plight of Indians, it had succeeded beyond all imagination. Gandhi's movement astonished the entire civilised world by the novelty of its techniques and the maturity of principles that were now being admired all over the world.

Public opinion both in India and England was profoundly agitated by what was happening in Transvaal and there was a good deal of disquiet and unease even in official circles. "No question stirred the people of India as the sufferings of Indians in South Africa". [London Times] A meeting of the most prominent Indian leaders in London added to the pressure that was being built up on Botha and Smuts to settle

Indian question. The Colonial Office was greatly worried about the turn of events; several questions were being asked in British Parliament about the treatment given to British subjects and about the sullen reaction it was producing in India.

The *Bengal Weekly* commented: "Indians are powerless to help Indians in South Africa…Europeans do not care for oppression and injustice meted out to Asiatics…Have Europeans lost their human attributes by losing all virtues of kindness, justice and spiritual truthfulness"? [Hutten 204]

The Colonial Office informed Transvaal "His Majesty's government cannot remain unaffected by the continued movement of passive resistance in Transvaal arousing as it does considerable interest in this country and the agitation in India which shows little sign of abating… The controversy has led to the imprisonment of many Asiatics who are normally respectable and law abiding British subjects and to deportation of considerable number. It has been and is a source of very grave embarrassment to His Majesty's government in their relations with Indian Empire". [Hutten 200]

The struggle was rousing the tempers through out British Empire and protests were pouring in from all parts of India against the treatment that Indians were subjected to. The viceroy was forced to confess that Indian public opinion was very excited. "We regard it as a very serious matter… the political effects in this country of the measures taken to enforce the law". [Hutten]

Gandhi was so frustrated by the failure that he often broke down at public meetings but he refused to either surrender or accept defeat. When Gokhale wanted to know the number of satyagrahis, Gandhi cheerfully replied that the number was sixty-six maximum and sixteen at the minimum. But Gandhi was firmly set in his faith in God and Satyagraha and refused to relent this futile and hopeless war of attrition that continued for one more year.

The Satyagraha was by now a desultory movement with "a few satyagrahies occasionally going to jail". Gandhi continued to roam in wilderness but he never withdrew the movement. Between 1909 and 1911, Satyagraha was more or less a token fight - a mere shadowboxing.

The Transvaal government was confused and inert. The government did not enforce the black act though it was never repealed or withdrawn. The prosecutions were stopped after July 1910. The European press and leaders scoffed at the movement by offering to keep all satyagrahis in jails on a permanent basis and provide all comforts to them, because they were so few.

Meanwhile, the root cause of the Indian question was being hotly debated in Natal and in India. The presence of indentured coolies and free Indian labour had created a lot of bad blood on all sides. Gandhi considered system of indentured labor an evil per se leading to moral degradation of individuals and a loss of prestige to nation. The Indian National Congress called for a total stoppage of such labour supply and Gokhale's resolution [25-2-10] for putting an end to the system was passed by Indian Council requesting to end the system from 1st. July 1911.

The 1908 Satyagraha was centered round the repeal of the Asiatic Registration [Black] Act 1907 and the Immigration Act of 1908 imposing restrictions on the entry of Indians into Transvaal. With voluntary registration by almost entire Indian community and total prevention of new entrants, the act of 1907 had lost its centrality. But the Immigration Act and the right of educated Indians to enter the colony on the same footing as whites remained the core issue.

Gandhi had never supported the demand for free and unfettered immigration to Africa and he was wise enough to always concede the dominance of white community in this region. "If equality of rights in law is conceded under the Immigration Act Indians would not object to the prohibition of further Indian immigration". [CWMG XI 425]

Gandhi only demanded that domiciled Indians should enjoy civil rights of security and trading. Indians would feel insulted if they are treated as inferior race and prevented from coming on racial grounds. The influx of migrants ought to be regulated only by educational test and Gandhi was ready to accept more severe and even discriminatory test for Indians. He insisted on equality of legal status with administrative discrimination.

The Asiatics and the coloured citizens advised by Gandhi kept away from all festivities to inaugurate the Union of South Africa in 1910 and refrained from welcoming the Duke of Cannought. "There was no other way to express the community's deep grief caused by the protracted struggle in Transvaal and its future being endangered by the Union". [CWMG X 363] Indians treated this Union as "a combination of hostile forces arrayed against us".

After the Union was formed, all matters pertaining to Indians were put in charge of Union government. Gandhi's worst fears came true and anti-Indian laws were more rigorously enforced all over South Africa.

During the campaign for elections to Parliament of Union, General Botha promised: "fair and sympathetic treatment to the colored races in a broad and liberal spirit". The Union would not admit any more Asiatics but all those who are already settled in the land were to be treated well.

Europeans living in midst of a vast mass of the natives felt that to open the door to one more non-White race would endanger their existence. The Prevention of Asiatic influx was the basic urge for Union and therefore a new and comprehensive Immigration Law was being formulated to replace various immigration laws of the colonies.

The Asiatic Immigration Act of Transvaal, which Gandhi had described as Asiatic expulsion act, was also to be replaced by this Union Immigration Act.

The drafting of such a law acceptable to all parties concerned was a Herculean task. The Union was very eager to encourage Europeans to come to South Africa in large numbers and wanted to totally exclude Asiatics. "The act must have the same terms and conditions for all migrants, but certain types of people should be able to come in and other types were to be kept out without naming either of them. This looked very much like a Chinese puzzle. The bill that emerged was a labyrinth without either an entry or an exit". [Hutten 291] The South African press described the bill as "a new born baby that was very sickly and had plenty of enemies".

It is a tribute to Gandhi's leadership, his eminence and his maturity that in spite of his disastrous failures and nearly total loss of following, Smuts chose to rely on Gandhi as the one and the only spokesman of Indian community. Smuts initiated the contact and frankly discussed with him the contours of his new immigration policy.

A very stiff language test was prescribed for migrants. A migrant could choose any European language but he must be able to speak and write fifty words of that language, words being selected by the officer on duty. The entry would be free and there would be no registration. The act provided theoretical and legal equality for all migrants and the Act of 1907 was to be repealed. Domicile would be granted after three years residence and would be lost by three years of continuous absence. Wives and children of the residents would be exempt from any test. Persons who failed language test or were found to be unsuited to the requirements of Union or of any particular province on economic ground or on the grounds of standard of living or habits were declared prohibited migrants.

The bill, with prior approval of Colonial Office was introduced [February 1911] in the very first session of the new Parliament. The

Union Immigration Bill was more liberal than the old Transvaal law but it was more restrictive than the similar laws of Natal and Cape Colony.

The bill conceded both demands of Gandhi—repeal of 1907 law and legal equality—and Gandhi publicly [10-3-11] promised to withdraw Satyagraha if the bill became a law. Indians in Natal were opposed to the bill and warned Gandhi "not to ruin the whole community and run after shadows...[and] not to blunder at the concluding stage". [CWMG X 433] Gandhi of course disregarded such warnings. He still did not trust Smuts and was wary "to see to it that Gen. Smuts does not surreptitiously create a color bar"..."Gen Smuts—absolutely disloyal or intensely stupid" 'a schemer', 'a liar' [CWMG X 467, 473, 480 492].

Gandhi suggested a few changes. He wanted Sanskrit and Arabic to be allowed for language test, he demanded trading rights for Educated Indians admitted in South Africa and wanted free inter-colonial migrations for Indians settled in the Union.

Smuts was generous and kind and made many conciliatory gestures [CWMG XI 227-8] but he could not and would not accept any new demand. He assured Gandhi that domiciled Indians would be allowed to stay anywhere they liked, all racial bars against the Indians would be removed and visitors would be issued temporary permits. Gandhi had burnt his fingers too often and he pointed out that there were no such provisions in the Immigration Act.

Smuts found himself squeezed between adamant Gandhi and racist Europeans. The Europeans opposed the bill because at some future date, the language test could be used by Indians to gain entry into South Africa and it could be used against the Europeans too.

This first Immigration bill was rejected by the Assembly and a new Immigration bill was introduced in the assembly after a long delay. The new bill was much worse for Indians and Gandhi entered a strong protest. "The new bill consolidates the worst features of the provincial laws…conditions in Natal is leveled down to Cape in stead of leveling up Cape practice to Natal". [CWMG XII 56]

Gandhi took the initiative by writing a very friendly letter to Smuts [19-4-11] and Smuts opened up to him. Smuts was very hard pressed for time and was harassed by extremists of his community. "You, the Imperial government and I want to avoid…ferment". [CWMG XI 30] Gandhi needed and asked for assurances from Smuts to enable him to suspend Satyagraha and they were given to him. Gandhi thanked: "the Union government for conciliatory and generous attitude, His Majesty's government for their friendly and effective intervention to bring to a happy ending the unfortunate situation".

Indian leaders were not happy. The huge and stormy meeting at Hamidia Hall [2 May 1911] declined to trust Smuts; but Gandhi was not ready to be guided by them. "Those who kept aloof from jails, now claim to shape the policy".

Gandhi by now relied entirely on Polak and Ritch to deal with the passage and changes in this bill and hardly ever gave any importance to Indian leaders who had not stood with him during the struggle.

Gandhi and Smuts met and talked on the post-peace situation and Smuts showed readiness to concede every demand of Gandhi who made only minor and very reasonable demands.

Smuts convinced Gandhi about his sincerity and after a very long and very frank discussion between the two, Gandhi agreed to suspend Satyagraha for an indefinite period.

The bill took a long time to assume its final shape. A very nervous and anxious Gandhi stayed in Cape Town to watch over the passage of the bill. "It was intensely sad for Gandhi to see the prospects of final settlement so tantalizingly near and yet so difficult to achieve". [Hutten 280]

Gandhi was very eager to quit South Africa by this time but till the Immigration bill was passed, Satyagraha could not be withdrawn and Gandhi was tied up in South Africa. The bill met with strenuous opposition from Orange Free Colony and it had to be withdrawn, [10-4-11]. Gandhi who was planning a short retirement and was very eager to quit South Africa was intensely disappointed.

Smuts was keen to avoid a fresh struggle. Since the Union Immigration bill could not be passed, it was decided to amend Transvaal Immigration Law of 1908 so as to repeal the black law of 1907 and to grant equality of status to educated Indians as far as Transvaal was concerned, thus satisfying Gandhi's original demands.

Gandhi was generous and he acknowledged: "the settlement has gone beyond our expectations". [CWMG XI 95] After discussions and some correspondence, all issues were settled to the satisfaction of Gandhi. But the Transvaal Immigration Amendment bill could not be passed for a long time and till it was passed, Satygraha could not be withdrawn.

The Indian community participated enthusiastically in the festivities on the occasion of the coronation [22 June 1911] of Emperor George V and Gandhi's great persuasive powers justified such enthusiasm.

"It may seem anomalous to a stranger why and how British Indians in South Africa should tender their loyalty to the Throne and rejoice over the crowning of a sovereign in whose domain they do not enjoy even ordinary civil rights of orderly men... The British sovereign represents, in theory, the purity and equity of justice... the British statesmen make an honest attempt to realize that ideal. That they fail miserably in doing so, is too true but irrelevant to the issue before us... In tendering our loyalty, we but show our devotion to the ideals just referred to; our loyalty is an earnest of our desire to realize them".[CWMG XI 112]

Such sentimental outburst goes to prove that in spite of all his bitter experiences and repeated rebuffs, Gandhi still believed in and trusted the British sense of justice and fair play.

II

There was a strange and an inexplicable incident when Gandhi was contacted with a proposal that he should preside over the Indian National Congress session to be held in December 1911. Gandhi did not know who proposed his name, on whose behalf and by what authority.

After some hesitation Gandhi accepted the offer on condition that he should be allowed to return to South Africa after the session was over and that he should be allowed complete freedom to speak his mind. But nothing came of it and Gandhi never heard about it from anybody afterwards.

Gandhi had been requesting Indian leaders to visit South Africa but there was no response from any quarters. "No Indian had been to South Africa or... to any other place outside India where Indians had emigrated to examine their conditions". [SSA 355]

Gopal Krishna Gokhale, a member of the Central Legislative Assembly in India, had always taken a deep interest in the Indian question in South Africa. He had been in close touch with Gandhi through correspondence and personal contacts. Gokhale decided to visit South Africa on his way back from England and spent nearly four weeks [22 October 1912 to 14 November 1912] in South Africa.

Gokhale, "the coolie King" was on a private visit but was treated as a state guest and was received with great pomp and ceremony by Whites and Indians alike. Gandhi planned a royal welcome for him at an estimated cost of 1000 pounds.

Gandhi repeatedly warned his compatriots against "false hopes and expectations out of the visit of Gokhale". He expected only a better understanding and goodwill. "They [problems] are too large to be settled in a single visit of one distinguished legislator."... "Gokhale would not be giving rights they [Indians] were eager for; Indians would have to fight for it". [CWMG XI 335]

Gandhi was very eager to avoid any exhibition of communal disunity during this visit. "We should not shut our eyes to the disunity amongst us and say that there is none". [CWMG XI 274] "Even if there is disunity and public bodies refuse to come together on the same platform...unity should prevail on this occasion". [Ibid 301] But this did not happen and Gokhale was presented separate addresses by Hindus, Muslims and Parsis.

Gokhale had a bitter experience of colour prejudice while travelling to South Africa. No White was ready to share a cabin with him and he was made to pay for the entire cabin. He landed at Cape Town, travelled to various cities, addressed two largely attended meetings, charmed mixed audiences of Europeans and Indians by his oratory and vision. Gandhi accompanied him throughout his travels and acted as his secretary and his valet and "as my guide, philosopher and friend".

Gokhale paid him a splendid tribute. "a marvelous personality of the stuff of which heroes and martyrs are made... He has in him a marvelous spiritual power to turn ordinary men around him into heroes and martyrs". [CWMG XI 579]

Gandhi, in his enthusiasm, tortured Gokhale by taking him to Phoenix Ashram. Gokhale had to walk a long distance and share the austere and uncomfortable ashram life. Gandhi insisted that Gokhale should speak to the ashramites in Marathi though neither the audience nor the speaker were comfortable with that language.

Gokhale was fully briefed by Gandhi before he talked for over two hours with Prime Minister General Botha and his ministers [14th November] and met the governor next day. Gokhale assured Gandhi that all problems faced by the Indian community had been settled and would be solved in no time. The Black Act of 1907 would be repealed, poll tax of three pounds would be abolished, and racial bias in Immigration Act would be corrected.

Gandhi's report on Gokhale's speech [SSA] is rather inaccurate because Gokhale spoke in Bombay what Gandhi says he spoke on his departure day [CWMG XI 586] and told the cheering crowd that "the actual working of Immigration Act would become milder and more considerate; the outrageous 3 pounds tax will, I fully expect would go in course of this year... the ministers have authorized me to say that they would do their best to remove all the grievances as early as possible. In the matter of education also the position would materially improve and the actual administration of laws such as the Gold Law and the Townships Act will tend to be less and less burdensome". [Hutten 301-02]

The speech shows Gokhale to be rather naïve and a daydreamer. He was so carried away by his own enthusiasm that he advised Gandhi to immediately sail for India as there was nothing left for him to do in South Africa. But Gandhi had suffered greater and more frequent disappointments and he knew better. He was naturally more skeptical than Gokhale and told him so in very clear terms. "I am not as hopeful in the matter as you are". [SSA 366]

Gandhi accompanied Gokhale to Dar-es-salam to see him off [18-12-12 and was dressed for the first time in Indian style probably in imitation of Gokhale who always dressed Indian. Gandhi apologized to Gokhale for the last minute confusion resulting in non-reimbursement of his ticket and many other inconveniences caused to Gokhale. "I know I made a bad secretary in South Africa". It was an emotional parting. "I want to be a worthy pupil of yours ... We have many differences of opinion but you shall still be my pattern in political life. ... I want to learn at your feet...I will scrupulously observe the compact of silence for one year after my arrival in India except on South African question".

The hopes raised by Gokhale proved to be a mirage. "Nothing happened and nothing was expected to happen". [Ash 122] Gokhale's optimism was utterly baseless as he was only promised by the ministers "to give consideration to all the points raised by him during the talks and more especially in regard to 3 pounds poll tax paid by Indians". [Hutten 302]

Gandhi while returning from Zanzibar had great trouble in disembarking at Delgoa Bay as he had no registration certificate for Transvaal. Gandhi was detained and he felt angry at the harsh treatment he received by the officer on duty. [CWMG XI 358-60]

Gandhi and Gokhale were severely denounced by Phirozeshah Mehta and other Indian leaders for agreeing to barter away the immigration rights of Indians against good treatment to local elites in South Africa and Gokhale was forced to defend his position in three major speeches.

From the middle of 1911, Gandhi had been preparing to quit Africa at the earliest convenient date. "My work can be only in India and rather in Kathiawar". "I shall go the moment I become free here". [CWMG XI 166] He expected to go latest by June 1913. [CWMG XI 440, 460] The Tolstoy farm was closed down [1 January 1913] and all the inmates were shifted to Phoenix.

Chapter 21

EMERGENCE OF MAHATMA

Satyagraha had been suspended in May 1911 and its embers were smoldering to extinction. The comatose Satyagraha got a shot in the arm from a totally unexpected quarter and it blazed forth in its third, final and the most memorable phase in South Africa. In this phase, Satyagraha turned into a mass agitation involving for the first time the poorest class of Indians. Gandhi skillfully dovetailed the social grievance of the elite with economic hardship of the poor. A nervous government resorted to extremely cruel and repressive measures forcing the government of India to decisively intervene. The Indian question was dragged to a settlement that ended Gandhi's career in Africa.

The bolt from the blue that ignited this conflagration was a verdict of the Supreme Court of Cape Colony that declared all marriages by Hindu and Muslim rites null and void. The issue of marriages among the Indian community had been simmering for a long time in South Africa but the boil over point was reached with this verdict.

The European society and law of South Africa recognised only monogamous marriages. Therefore polygamy amongst Hindus and Muslims was creating problems for Indians in South Africa. Such polygamous marriages were not recognized in law but were tolerated in the colonies for a very long time.

In several cases prior to 1913, courts had ruled that an Indian with more than one wife could bring only one wife and her children to the Colonies. This had become an established practice. The rich Muslim merchants claimed that polygamy was a religious right for them and were sore because they wanted to bring all their wives and children with them. Gandhi had been consistently supporting Muslim demand as it involved religious faith.

When the Transvaal court had held [1911] that when a man sought admission for a woman on the ground that she was his wife, he must prove that she is his only wife. Gandhi protested: "Will the office bearers of the Hamidia Islamic Society realize that Islam is being insulted"? [CWMG XI 244] But there was hardly any reaction among the Indian community.

But J. Malcolm Searle of the Supreme Court of Cape Colony delivered [14 March 1913] a judgment that implied most explosive and disruptive consequences for Indian community. The case was very simple. One Marriam had married Esop according to Muslim rites and she was his only wife. But she was denied entrance into South Africa by Cape Colony because Justice Searle chose to strike at the system of polygamy itself.

He argued: "all polygamous systems by themselves were invalid in law. When a person marries only one wife under a system that permits polygamy, such a marriage is still a polygamous marriage and hence invalid in law". Marriam was therefore not a legally married wife and hence not entitled to stay in the country.

This sweeping verdict invalidated all marriages performed according to Hindu, Muslim and Zoroastrian rites and with a single stroke of pen reduced the wives of most of Indians in Africa to the status of concubines. Their children would become bastards.

The verdict was an unbearable affront to Indian community. It would put them to untold hardships and shame and would result in enormous psychological and material disturbances in several aspects of their family life. Their families would be disrupted and their children would lose right to inheritance. "The judgment shakes the existence of the Indian community to its foundations". [CWMG XII 9] Indians in South Africa would be forced into a terrible dilemma of either staying single or of renouncing their religion in order to get married by Christian rites.

Gandhi considered this verdict to be an insult to Islam as also to the honour of Indians. The Imperial intervention would be necessitated because personal laws of Indians were protected by 1858 declaration.

But Gandhi took his stand on the prevailing practice. "What is of greater importance is that... Indians may not bring more than one wife here. Hitherto those who had more than one wives have been allowed to bring them without let or hindrance. If the Judge's dictum is sound in law, the law will have to be altered. In British dominions where all religions are respected, it is not possible to have the laws insulting to any recognized religion flourishing under it". [CWMG XII 120]

The Union government took the stand that there was nothing new in the judgment. "The law of the land has recognized as valid union, only the marriage... of one man to one woman to the exclusion, while it lasts, of any other". [ibid 2] "The judgment in this case is merely a repetition of what we have always understood to be the law in South Africa. It is preposterous that a small community of say 150000 all told can expect to enforce a different and frankly an inferior, alien view of marriage in South Africa".

The Government of India and the India Office pressurised South Africa to maintain status quo. The Union government assured the leaders of Indian community that they would not be troubled on the basis of Searle judgement and that the government had no intention to debar the introduction of wives and children of British Indians who have been lawfully residing in South Africa.

But such declarations would have no force in law and government was bound to enforce the judicial verdict unless the law was reversed by another law. "With all the good will in the world, the government can grant no relief". [CWMG XII 15] The government may admit Indian wives as a matter of administrative grace but the Searle verdict will be a sword hanging on their heads.

Moreover despite government assurances, the Searle verdict was being acted upon and marital status and inheritance rights were being denied to polygamous families. A test case to reassert the old position had failed [June 1913] rendering wife and child of every Indian illegitimate who were permitted to live in the country as a matter of grace and could be expelled any time.

If viewed in the light of a deliberate policy of riding South Africa of Indians, this was the last straw that would break the camel's back and would lead to the extinction of Indian community within a decade or so.

Gandhi was worried and baffled and he warned: "There is a possibility of Satyagraha being revived on the issue affecting wives and minors…If the objectives are not met, a revival of the awful struggle is a certainty". [CWMG XI 513/XII 10] but his warnings were treated as so many threats that the government was determined not to yield to.

Gandhi insisted on a specific law to recognise non-Christian marriages as valid but the Union government was helpless. A law "permitting polygamous marriages is entirely opposed to the principles of European civilization". [ibid 27] However, he pointed out that special marriage officers had been appointed in Natal to solemnise marriages according to Muslim rites and that by a 1907 law, Natal had permitted polygamy for indentured Indian labour. "It was inconvenient to the then government not to recognize polygamy because indentured Indians were wanted by an influential class. It is now inconvenient to recognize it for the free Indian settlers because they are intruders". [CWMG XII 34]

The Natal Immigration office—Gandhi called them the 'tin Tzars of the department'—issued 'a high handed' circular demanding clear evidence that the woman is really a wife [with marriage certificate] and that she was the only wife and her children belonged to the migrant, [by authenticated affidavits]. They also insisted on the birth certificates of the children to prove that they are minors.

In India at this time neither births nor marriages were registered anywhere and there was no legal proof about the marriage and the names of the parties concerned and the dates of birth of children were just unavailable. The Indian migrants had to submit several affidavits and official testimonials to prove the marriage and the parenthood as well as the age of children.

Gandhi suggested that the situation could be corrected by the impending Immigration bill that was under discussion. The Act could validate marriages under all religious rites. [CWMG XI 496] Gandhi was being consulted by Smuts about the immigration bill and he hoped for some such protection. But the immigration bill presented to the Assembly on 12 April 1913 contained no such provision and there were several other provisions that Gandhi considered to be violating the spirit of settlement of 1911.

The invalidation of marriages on such a massive scale was, most certainly, a very serious issue and any protest against it was fully justified but Gandhi was surprised and pained that Indian community was inert in the face of such a serious danger. "Our lethargy would be our ruin". [CWMG XII 20] Gandhi deplored that there was no reaction and no stir in Natal and the Indian community seemed to have accepted government assurances at its face value.

Gandhi had to come out of his retirement and return to active leadership. He very reluctantly decided to revive Satyagraha. "I am not itching for passive resistance". The British Indian Association called a protest meeting [30 April 1913] and condemned the 'terrible judgment' that was much worse than the black act of 1907. "This is an insufferable situation for women, no less than men". [SSA]

There was an all round condemnation of the verdict and it deserves such condemnation. It would condemn Indians to live permanently without leading a family life. Gandhi and others condemned the verdict as anti-woman and an affront to womanhood.

The verdict certainly was a very arrogant and impulsive measure that negated the entire system of polygamy so widely prevalent in Asia and Africa. But there is nothing anti-woman in it, nor is any insult to womanhood involved in it. In fact, the judgement denounced polygamy, which is very anti-woman and feminists all over the world are unanimous in demanding the abrogation of this obsolete and unjust marriage system; it is polygamy that is an insult to womanhood.

The issue was clearly and closely connected with the family life of Indians and Gandhi, for the first time decided to involve women in the fray. The Transvaal Indian Women's Association consisting of the wives of satyagrahis decided to join Satyagraha and forty women came forward to join the campaign.

Kasturba Gandhi's decision to join the struggle has been reported by Gandhi in very confused and mutually contradictory statements in Auto and SSA. Gandhi tried very hard to keep his wife out of the melee. But she protested very vehemently "What defect is there in me that disqualifies me for jail"? [SSA]

This presentation is squarely contradicted by a reconstructed conversation in Gandhi's Autobiography. The contemporary report in *Indian Opinion* [1 October 1913.] shows that report in SSA is not true and Autobiography is more accurate. Kastur's decision to join the struggle was conveyed to Gokhale by Gandhi.

However marriage was not a major issue of any practical importance for the vast mass of poorer Indians. The sex ratio among indentured labor and ex-indentured labor was very low- hardly 350 or 400 women per 1000 males. On the estates, hundreds of coolies lived with very few women and often shared them amongst themselves. "Those who know the conditions of life on the estates wonder that there is any purity of life left among the inmates and that violent crimes are so rare as they are". [CWMG XI 319]

Gandhi's focus had changed after his experiences during the second phase of Satyagraha [1909-11] and he got more and more concerned with the sufferings of indentured labour. "Indian traders and businessmen are sometimes accused of being so busy with matters directly concerning themselves that they have no time for looking into their poorer brethren's misfortunes". [CWMG XI 205] Gandhi himself had neglected them up to 1908. Gandhi had learnt his lesson from the betrayal by the rich merchants and from the support given by poor hawkers and coolies.

He had already taken up the issue of the three Pounds tax collected from ex-indentured coolies. "The inhuman annual tax exacted from the freed indentured Indians, their wives and little children...is a burden that cannot but oppress the conscience of every Indian". [CWMG XI 81] P.S.Aiyer, the editor of the *African Chronicle* had launched a campaign for the abolition of the three pounds tax and had established an anti-tax league.

Only very few coolies, hardly one in twenty could afford to pay the tax and Gandhi denounced it as 'criminal and cruel...driving men to crime and women to prostitution'. Very often the coolies would re-indenture themselves to escape the tax. Gokhale had discussed this question with ministers of Union government and he had expressed confidence that the tax would be abolished by the end of 1912.

General Botha was willing to quash the tax but the bill abolishing it was postponed. [April 1913] This was "a shock and a bitter disappointment not only to ex-indentured but to the entire Indian community because it is a tax upon its honor and social integrity."...[Natal had no objection to its abolition and there was no valid excuse except] "a cowardly fear to rouse further antagonism from Free State reactionaries ...[and] their notorious obsession with anti-color mania". [CWMG XII 42-43]

Gandhi informed the Union government [21-6-13] about the resumption of Satyagraha from 13th July 1913 and formulated an elaborate agenda for the same. The Satyagraha was launched for 'not one but many important issues unrelated to one another'. Three major issues were selected—[a] validity of non-Christian marriages, [b] poll tax and [c] the black act of 1907.

There was a ray of hope. The Immigration Bill of 1913 provided partial relief and poll tax on women and children was to be withdrawn. Non-Christian marriages were to be registered and the polygamous marriages would be accepted but only one wife would be allowed in South Africa. Plural wives currently staying in South Africa would be allowed to stay. But there was no hope that the bill would pass the muster of Assembly.

Gandhi was extremely doubtful about the support he would be able to get for Satyagraha. "I could not count upon hundreds going to jails...but what satyagrahis lack in numbers would be made up by the earnestness and the unconquerable Will of the few. ... Whether we have five hundred or fifty or five...with even one true passive resister, the victory is ours". [CWMG XII 53] Gandhi had assured his followers. "If the struggle is revived, the impending third campaign will be the purest, the last and the most brilliant of all". [ibid 58]

Gandhi was worried because of his past experience. "During the previous campaign, those who did not go to jail sought to thwart the community's efforts and joined hands with the enemy... our cause thus received a set back". He therefore advised them to support the movement with funds and constitutional agitations.

Gandhi submitted a list of Indian grievances and had a long discussion with Home Minister Fisher. The government was willing to repeal the act of 1907 but firmly refused to give legal recognition to polygamous marriages. Gandhi too was adamant. "We warn...even *if this {marriage} question is the only one left unsolved, revival of passive resistance is a certainty.* [emphasized by Gandhi. CWMG XII 79] He also made it clear that 'not a single existing right can be surrendered'. [ibid 94]

The negotiations with the government failed [11-9-13] and Gandhi launched the campaign with a declaration that "a settlement without the spirit of the settlement is not a settlement.... It is much better to have an open fight than a patched up truce. The fight this time must be for altering the spirit of government and of European population of South Africa and that result can be attained by prolonged and bitter suffering that must melt the hearts alike of government and of the predominant partner". [Nanda 113]

This was a struggle of "a microscopic minority against the might of government and the dominant community". "This Satyagraha is not merely against the government and Europeans of South Africa but it is equally against Imperial government... for criminally neglecting their trust". [CWMG XII 193] It was to be a movement "for the honor, self-respect and the financial relief for the dumb, helpless coolies".

In spite of severe shortage of men and money, [only 13 women and about 100 males] Gandhi was confident of success. "Satyagraha needs no money, no public support, no meetings or demonstrations. All these are impurities". There was also no definite program. "In the present Satyagraha campaign, we can take new issues whenever we think it right.... This time it has no program and no plan of action except defiance of laws". [CWMG XII 231/188]

Gandhi had so completely lost the support of the mercantile community that he could raise no funds and satyagrahis were asked to travel on foot and beg for their food and clothes. The Satyagraha was to be confined only to Natal and Transvaal. The government was in no less trouble than Gandhi. Mrs. Fritzerald led 40000 whites to strike work; the agitation turned violent and riotous and the chaos spread all over the Union.

The 1913 Satyagraha was a two-layered movement. The satyagrahis were to cross the border of Transvaal and hawk without license, while the coolies, who were not satyagrahis, were to strike work against the imposition of the three pounds tax. "The men were to withdraw from the collieries and to court arrest and imprisonment in Natal and failing that they were to cross the border into Transvaal and get arrested there". [CWMG XII 253] Gandhi and Thambi Naidoo visited coalmines to persuade coolies to strike work.

The Satyagraha began on a low key without any fanfare and on 15th September 1913, eleven men and four women led by Kastur Gandhi crossed the border into Transvaal to court arrest. The government sought to kill the movement by policy of non-action; no arrests were made. Gandhi's passive resistance was to be countered by passivity on the part of government. "There were not many men willing to go to jails... and those who were ready, could not easily have their wish". [SSA 380]

These women were arrested after a week [21-9-13] and sentenced to three months imprisonment. The arrest of women created a furor all over India and excitement rapidly mounted to a crescendo. Some Tamil women from Tolstoy Farm led by Kallenbach crossed over to Orange Free Colony. The police declined to take any action against them. These women then marched back to Natal and exhorted coolies in the coalmines of New Castle to go on strike. They were successful. "They defied authorities to arrest them and then went from door to door, barrack to barrack at New Castle to incite strike". [CWMG XII 492] "If women had been arrested...the strike might not have taken place". [ibid 511]

The strike spread like wild fire. Two thousand coolies in six collieries struck work [15th October] and the strike soon spread to sugar farms and railways involving some five thousand coolies by the end of the month. Gandhi had been very strongly opposed to the strike on the plantations and he wanted it limited only to the collieries. But the strike kept on spreading and soon engulfed entire sugar belt. The strike in the sugar farms and collieries stopped all mills, markets were dead and the economy became sluggish.

There were a few scuffles at the mines and the collieries were put under the protection of armed and mounted police. "With the long delayed entry of women and labor, Satyagraha scored high". [Ash 123]

The mine owners invited Gandhi for talks at Durban and he met them in Durban Chamber of Commerce Hall, [25-10-13] Gandhi agreed that Satyagraha was not for any labour issue that would justify the strike. The mine owners criticised Gandhi for using labour as fodder for his satyagraha that was a political fight and he was taunted whether he would compensate the misguided coolies for the damage that the strike would cause them.

But the mine owners had to concede that abolition of three pounds tax was a legitimate demand of the coolies and they promised to pressurise the government for its abolition if the strike was withdrawn. After the talks failed, mine owners drove striking coolies out of their residential quarters by cutting off electricity and water supply and by withholding their rations.

Thousands of coolies faced the problem of starvation and loss of shelter. "The strikers could not hold out in these circumstances" and "the Indian merchants were mortally afraid and not at all ready to help me publicly because they had trading relations with the coal miners and other European merchants". [SSA 391] Some of them did help privately by supplying food grains and other necessities. But very few rich merchants would risk to even host Gandhi.

This Satyagraha was fought with the support and sacrifices of poor and faithful coolies, who suffered more than any other class of Indians while all the beneficiaries from earlier agitations deserted Gandhi.

But even at this crucial hour, Gandhi had nothing but contempt and misgivings about the qualities of coolies. He describes their filthy habits and their proneness to crimes. "Some of them were murderers, thieves and adulterers" [SSA 404] Gandhi considered them to be totally unfit for agitating for any public issue and yet he decided to use them for his satyagraha with a very strangely argued out escape route. "I did not consider myself fit to sit in judgment over the morality of strikers. It would have been silly on my part to attempt to distinguish between the goats and the sheep". [SSA 394]

Nearly 5000 coolies were on strike and it could have lead to violence. Europeans were afraid of Africans joining hands with them. But the strikers behaved in the most exemplary manner and remained peaceful even under very severe stress. There were only a few minor acts of violence but not a single theft.

Gandhi realised that he would not be able to feed and shelter strikers for any prolonged period. They were fed only dal, rice and vegetables often with millie pep and bread. But even then the monthly expense to feed them would come to nearly 7000 pounds a month and Gandhi had no money. "To house and feed thousands... was a stupendous problem". [CWMG XII 513]

The idle crowd could indulge in violence and crime. There was a fear of epidemic. This terrible crisis might have temporarily blinded Gandhi to the purity of means and simple honesty of purpose when he decided to get the coolies arrested and thereby use the prisons of Transvaal for shelter and food for strikers. To achieve this purpose, it was necessary to make them cross the borders and get arrested as satyagrahis. Such a fudged relationship between methods and goals can, in more simple language be described as duplicity and can be excused in Gandhi only because of the dire necessity to safeguard the interests of Indian community in South Africa.

Aware of torturous conditions in South African jails, coolies were hesitant to court imprisonment and Gandhi offered them the alternative of going back to their cruel and vindictive masters. This was a very brutal alternative and Gandhi was fully aware of its implications. "I had no alternative but to harden my heart and declared that those who wished, were free to return to the mines". [SSA 396]

These poor, ignorant, faithful coolies were very loyal and courageous followers but they were very reluctant satyagrahis.

Gandhi decided to lead them and march thirty-six miles from Charlestown to Tolstoy farm. "I am marching out presently with the strikers in order to court arrest for ourselves". [CWMG XII 255] He put himself at the head of 2023 men, 130 women and 40 children.

Gandhi underwent an impressive sartorial revolution by giving up fashionable Western dress. He donned the dress of a simple, poor coolie. A little later he would shave off his head and go without shoes to mourn the death of coolies who had been shot dead by Natal police.

The news of this march that began on 16th November created panic in Transvaal as if it were an invasion by Indians. It was nothing of that sort. The marchers were under strict instructions not to touch anything that was not theirs and not to react to any type of abuse or violence.

They marched in a mile long procession and Gandhi with Kallenbach brought up the rear.

The women and children got tired on the very first day and most of them were left behind. The rest of the marchers proceeded peacefully and with great discipline in spite of starvation diet of a loaf of bread and some sugar.

There were many acts of kindness from the European community and Gandhi recounts many cases where Whites helped and comforted strikers supplying medicines and even food to them. [CWMG XII 480] The marchers arrived at and crossed the border of Transvaal without any incident.

Such courage and sufferings were an astounding demonstration of faith and trust that Gandhi had won from poor, illiterate coolies. Gandhi described it as "my most wonderful experience in South Africa. A wonderful thing for 2000 men to have marched so long and so far without violating law and without stealing and rioting". [ibid]

The London press had denounced harsh measures that were being taken against the striking coolies and now showered praise on this march. "The march of the Indian laborers must live in memory as one of the most remarkable manifestations in the history of the passive resistance", wrote the *London Times*. [Polak 88]

The *Sunday Post* was more descriptive. "The pilgrims, Gandhi is leading are an exceedingly picturesque crew. To the eye they appear most meager: indeed so emaciated that their legs are mere sticks but the way in which they are marching on starvation ration show them to be particularly hardy". [Hutten 371]

The destination of the marchers was Tolstoy farm where arrangements were made to receive them. Gandhi, time and again, made it very clear that the march was not for the settlement of any labour dispute but was in the nature of a public protest.

Gandhi's repeated efforts to open talks failed. The government had closed its eyes and ears and heart. Gandhi's letters and telegrams were left unanswered. General Smuts refused even to hear him. "General will have nothing to do with you and you may do just as you please", was the curt reply from his secretary.

When the marchers arrived at the border of Transvaal, they found police ready in full force but nothing was done to stop them. Gandhi had led the marchers to get them arrested but Smuts refused to oblige.

By refusing to arrest the trespassers, Smuts foiled Gandhi's plan by inaction and Gandhi was greatly stressed. The cost of feeding the marchers was pounds 250 per day and though he had received 1000 pounds from India, there was a huge deficit left on Gandhi's hands. Gandhi made many appeals to the government to arrest the strikers because he had no means to feed and house them.

"Arrest me but arrange for rations and transport for the marchers to Tolstoy farm. Otherwise government would be responsible for the sufferings of the strikers and the deaths of babies. ... It is the duty of the government to arrest strikers and provide board and lodging".

"Mr. Gandhi is disconcerted by the inaction of government and has made representations that it was their duty to arrest the demonstrators. Mr. Gandhi appears to be in a position of much difficulty. Like Frankenstein, he found his monster an uncomfortable creation and he would be glad to be relieved of further responsibility for its support. If Gandhi is arrested, he can disclaim the responsibility of maintaining the strikers. But a 'free' Gandhi is a 'burdened' Gandhi." [CWMG XII 591]

"Government has no desire to make our work easy by arresting all of us or to provoke agitation in India on that account". [CWMG XII 518] But some [150] marchers were arrested and Gandhi offered to lead them to prison: but there were no jails ready to receive them. They were put in Gandhi's custody till some arrangements were made and police paid for their food for four days. The government was very anxious that the rank and file 'at present peaceful' be left undisturbed because failure of provisions will force them back to work. Mounted constables accompanied the marchers but there was neither crime nor violence.

The march could be stopped only if strikers turn violent and then they can be crushed. But for this, Gandhi will have to be removed from their midst. He was arrested late at night at Palmford on 6th November: but prosecution was not ready with the case. Gandhi was released on bail. Gandhi was arrested again at Standerston [8-11-13] together with five others. Gandhi requested bail and was released on bail of fifty pounds. He was again arrested [9 November] at Teakworth. Thus he was arrested thrice in five days. Polak who had come to see Gandhi before leaving for India was also arrested and sentenced.

Gandhi was charged with inciting indentured coolies to leave their employers and jobs. "The defendant, by his threatening conduct [was] bringing ruination on men...Indians were alienating the sympathies of Europeans who were one with Indians in requesting the government for the repeal of the tax". [CWMG XII 264] Gandhi was aware of the seriousness of the violation of laws and the great sufferings but that was "the only way to rouse the consciousness of the whites and the government".

Gandhi was sentenced sixty pounds in fine or nine months with hard labour. He was separated from all other Indians and was sent to Bloomfontain where he was treated extremely well. "He [Gandhi] would like to publicly record the manner in which prison officials had considered his comforts". [CWMG XII 272]

The marchers were arrested at Balfour and were deported to Natal by four special trains. The coolies refused to entrain as they would obey only Gandhi's orders, but Polak who was leading them after Gandhi was arrested, persuaded them to go. The coolies were sent back to New Castle [Natal] where compounds of coalmines were declared to be prisons. The owners and the European staff members were appointed as temporary jailors and wardens and work in the mines was to be the hard labour of jail sentence.

The coolies refused to be taken in by such a stratagem and declined to work. They were mercilessly flogged, beaten and kicked by European staff. There was a wave of indignation and colliery labour and plantation labour went of a sympathetic strike. [12 November]

This strike [unplanned and opposed by Gandhi and Polak] spread very rapidly and by 16th November, entire Indian labour force [nearly 6000] in railways, docks and plantations was on strike.

There were several clashes between police and strikers. The strikers were treated very brutally, mounted military police was used to mercilessly crush the strike; there were shootings—killing nine and injuring more than twenty-five strikers. "Those bullets hit me". Labourers were forced back to work with incredible and inhuman brutalities.

India watched these happenings with baited breath and mounting fury. South Africa was a burning topic of discussion all over British Empire and government of South Africa was denounced for such brutalities by the entire civilised world.

Chapter 22

FINALE

There was intense unrest and discontent in India about the happenings in South Africa and Gokhale started raising funds and tempers. There was no upsurge as such, but the sullen unease and increasing anger among the Nationalist Opinion were quite clearly visible.

The Indian authorities were apprehensive of an outbreak of anger and revolt. Lord Wellingdon, the governor of Bombay expressed great anguish about the events.

At this critical and dangerous moment, Viceroy Lord Hardinge intervened and in a speech in Madras violating the time honoured protocol, he denounced South Africa in very strong terms for barbaric brutalities against Indians.

"It is not very easy to find the means whereby India can make its indignation felt for those holding the reins of government in South Africa... Your compatriots in South Africa have taken the matters in their own hands and organized passive resistance to the laws, which they consider invidious and unjust—an opinion, which those who are watching the struggle from afar cannot but share. They violated the laws with full knowledge of penalties involved. In all this, they have the deep and burning sympathy of India and even of those like myself who without being Indians, sympathize with the people of this country".

Lord Hardinge then referred to measures allegedly being used in South Africa to crush passive resistance. He went on to say that "the most recent developments have taken a very serious turn… this movement of passive resistance has been dealt with by measures which would not, for one moment, be tolerated in any country which calls itself civilized".

The government of South Africa, the viceroy agreed, had categorically denied the charges leveled against it "but in the process, [it] has admitted those which at best were neither wise nor discreet". In concluding his address, the viceroy urged the appointment of an impartial committee to investigate and report on Indian problem in all its ramifications.

"Lord Hardinge has, in fact, spoken as would an Indian patriot… the speech will ever remain enshrined in the hearts of Indians". [*Sind Journal* Hutten 321] "He has transformed an indignant and resenting India into a hopeful and trusting country. People at a distance cannot imagine what danger has been averted and what confidence has been restored. He has saved India from a rising or a deluge of objectionable statements. He has rescued it from the clutches of scheming Extremists. He has brought a hesitating India closest to English throne today and by a well thought out and earnest expression of Imperial truth, has crowned the King-Emperor in every Indian heart. Let the critics look at the Indian hearts and judge". [*London Times* Hutten 320] The *Kaiser-e-Hind* commented "Lord Hardinge spoke at that psychological moment when India's feelings were at its boiling point. His words fell like oil on the angry waves". [Hutten 321]

But Smuts and Botha fretted and fumed. The government of South Africa severely criticised Lord Hardinge and pressed very strongly for his recall. The British Cabinet did consider such a recall but abandoned it as any such move would set entire India afire. Hardinge had become immensely popular. No other viceroy had identified himself so closely with Indian labour.

Hardinge was cool and confident. He was aware that emotional strain in India was quite serious before he spoke at Madras. "Many people claimed that there had been nothing like this since the mutiny… My speech was very unusual in character but it had an almost magical effect… people had a confidence in me and my government… they [Indians] are not clamoring at all for free immigration but what they demand is fair and proper treatment of the Indians domiciled in South Africa". [Huttn 321]

General Smuts was in great travail. He was opposed to brutalities but he could neither stop nor denounce them. Taking a cue from Hardinge, the Union government appointed [1-12-13] 'Indian Grievances Commission' of three headed by Justice Solomon to deal with Indian question in its entirety. Gandhi was released on 18th December to present the Indian case before the Commission.

But Gandhi objected to the commission on two grounds. The Commission was appointed without consulting Indian community and secondly two of its members - Edward Esleen and J.S. Wylie were well known India baiters. "The Commission is being appointed to give fair play [to the Indians] but it is a packed body, intended to hoodwink the public in England and in India". [Gandhi to Gokhale] Such a packed and weighed body would militate against Indian interests and would outrage Indian sentiments. Gandhi therefore vowed to boycott it.

Gokhle was angry and upset. "Gandhi had no business to take such a vow and tie himself up in knots. This is politics and the compromise is the essence of it". He wired to Gandhi. "Boycott a grave mistake…Protest but appear under protest". [CWMG XII 283]

Gandhi refused to relent. "[the]...struggle [is] beyond Viceroy, Imperial Minister-in fact beyond all temporal powers. It is in God's name. Anybody advising acceptance of Commission would be rejected and justifiably killed". [CWMG XII 293] The vow made it impossible for him to withdraw his boycott of the Commission.

Gandhi threatened to revive Satyagraha if the Commission was not reconstituted and made more balanced. Gandhi's offensive language and harsh tone created problems for his supporters and friends. Lord Ampthill pointed out that "[His] present attitude will alienate sympathies ... will place friends here and in India in false position and will wrack the cause. The peremptory tone is not in accordance with the spirit of passive resistance". [CWMG XII 293]

Solomon threatened to resign and the governor general wrote to the colonial office "Gandhi would not be allowed to get the lever to break up or block the commission's work". [CWMG XII 600]

Gandhi was compelled to climb down. He had to retreat and make conciliatory noises. He wrote to Gokhale requesting him to assure the viceroy that he would do nothing to embarrass Lord Hardinge and made very adulatory references to his speech. There was more pressure from Gokhale and Gandhi's tone and attitude changed completely under that pressure. Gandhi retreated all the way and now confined his demand to appoint one more member on the commission. The request too was curtly rejected. Gokhale insisted upon and secured from Gandhi conciliatory statement appreciating the viceroy's efforts and support and then formulating seven demands of the Indian community.

Gandhi wrote a very conciliatory letter to Smuts asking for an interview to "remove the deadlock without loss of dignity to the government and loss of honor to Indian community...Our letter was mis-described as ultimatum... Please grant interview". [CWMG XII 295] Smuts' reply was hesitant. He noted the conciliatory attitude but in view of the past misunderstandings, insisted "on a formal and written representation to be carefully considered". [ibid]

Gokhale wired to Gandhi that Hardinge would send Robertson "only if you promise him one week's time before you renew struggle...Do you promise? Cable explicitly". [ibid 300] Gandhi had no go but to surrender and he assured Gokhale that the date for starting Satyagraha was never fixed and he was ready for 'all reasonable postponements.'[26-12-13] Gandhi requested Gokhale to "please...exert pressure on Smuts to grant my requests before the arrival of Robertson". But that could not be done.

Robertson was arriving on 11th January 1914 and he made it very clear that he would assist Indians but "would disassociate himself if Satyagraha or violence is revived". Gandhi postponed Satyagraha to 15th January and offered to co-operate with the Soloman Commission.

Gokhale resented Gandhi fixing any date for Satyagraha and forced Gandhi to agree to "wait as long as needed by Robertson".

Gandhi again requested Smuts for an interview and suggested that shorthand notes be taken to avoid future misunderstandings. Gandhi was wise enough to disassociate himself from Natal Congress demand for "free and unrestricted immigration...and political franchise". He would rather concentrate on "gaining or regaining every lost civil right or every such right withheld from the community". [CWMG XII 310]

Charles F. Andrews and Pearson, sent by Gokhle for liaison between Gandhi and the Commission arrived on 2nd January 1914 and were accorded a public reception: Robertson declined any such welcome.

The Union government was facing very serious trouble. The European railway workers went on strike [9 January] and the strike became so violent that martial law had to be declared over entire South Africa.

Gandhi in a press interview declared "I have nothing to do with the Railway strike. I have no attitude to it. What attitude can we a voteless and neglected people have in such a crisis"? When asked by the press whether he would take advantage of the crisis and launch his agitation, "Gandhi paused and replied "that has never been our policy…I will be no party to embarrassing the government at a time like this… I mean to take no unfair advantage of government…We shall not resume operations till the railway matter is settled". [CWMG XII 323]

This statement earned for Gandhi the gratitude of harassed officials. "I do not like your people and do not care to assist them at all. But what can I do? You help us in the day of our need. How can we lay hands on you? I often wish you take to violence like the English strikers and then we would know how to dispose of with you at once. But you would not injure even an enemy. You desire victory by self suffering alone and never transgress your self imposed limits of courtesy and chivalry and that is what reduces us to sheer helplessness". [Polak 90]

Benjamin Robertson was deputed by the Government of India to present its views to the Commission; but he proved to be more anti-Indian than even Smuts. Robertson and Gandhi soon fell foul of each other. Gandhi praised him in public but Gandhi's real opinion of him was different. He "…has disappointed us. He has done hardly any good and he may do a good deal of harm….He undoubtedly consciously or unconsciously fosters divisions amongst us". [ibid 360] "His presence proved to be of negative value… he began to create factions among Indians and bully Satyagrahis". [SSA 450]

Robertson found Gandhi a very uncomfortable colleague. "He [Gandhi] is an altogether extraordinary person, very subtle minded and always ready to change his grounds… He has a terrible amount of conscience and is very hard to manage". [Hutten 326]

Faced with several problems and troubles on all the sides, Smuts softened: an interview was arranged between Gandhi and Smuts [16th January] in a very cordial atmosphere. Smuts accepted Gandhi as the only spokesman of Indian community and he was quite frank. "Our troubles are manifold and we have not a moment to spare. We therefore wish to put Indian question at rest". Smuts assured Gandhi: "We have decided to grant all your demands but we need the commission's report to act upon".

After prolonged and very frank discussions between the two titans, a compromise was worked out. The Gandhi-Smuts agreement was concluded with a final exchange of letters. All issues were settled at this single sitting and Gandhi returned to Phoenix on 21st January 1914. They met again in February 1914.

Gandhi withdrew Satyagraha [21st. January] and the Commission could work in an atmosphere of conciliation and goodwill. The Natal Indian Congress had refused to support Gandhi and had co-operated with the Commission: Gandhi, on his part, denounced the Congress as a group of less than hundred disgruntled leaders like Angalia and Dada Osman. Gandhi ridiculed Indian leaders who cooperated with the Commission with "flimsy and foolish submissions".

The Commission's report and its recommendations were based upon the understanding between Gandhi and Smuts. The Commission condemned boycott of its working by 'some' Indians but recommended the acceptance of all demands submitted by Gandhi on behalf of the Indian community. The Solomon Commission's report was presented to the Assembly and was accepted in its entirety by the government. It was embedded in Act 22 of 1914–the Indian Relief Act that had been previously shown to Gandhi and approved by him.

The Commission had found that the three pounds tax "was paid by very few and was evaded by most of Indians". It was a source of great and unnecessary irritation to Indians" and it was to be abolished. Educated Indians would be allowed to move more freely within the Union except in Orange Free State and domicile certificates would be treated as valid permits for all intents and purposes. Six educated Indians would be permitted every year to visit South Africa.

All existing polygamous marriages were to be recognised and registered separately so as to facilitate for members of those families their comings and goings out of South Africa. The future polygamous marriages would not be recognised and for all new entrants who had more than one wife elsewhere, only one wife and her children would be recognised and admitted in the Union.

Indian maulavis and priests would be appointed as marriage officers to maintain records of Indian marriages that took place in South Africa. Divorces would be permitted only on the grounds of adultery or desertion. [CWMG XII 340] The fact of married wives in India was to be verified by the officers in India and certificates issued by Indian officials would be accepted as valid.

Gandhi was not very happy with the report but "less than this we can not accept; more than this it is almost impossible to get. In any case...Satyagraha will not be justified to secure more". [CWMG XII 346] At Gandhi's insistence, the Indians Relief Act was promulgated with an assurance that "It has always been and would in future continue to be a desire of the government that all laws are administered in a just manner and with due regard to the vested rights". [CWMG XII 329]

The 1907 Act was gone and the poll tax was abolished. But there was not much yielding on the marriage issue. The Indian community secured no political right and its civil disabilities were not removed. All racial laws and discriminations—trade licenses, locations, gold laws, were to continue as before. There was to be no more migration of Indians either free or indentured to South Africa.

The Indians Relief bill was a climax and a termination point of Gandhi's career in Africa. This was the final end of the eight-year old Satyagraha that had been actively pursued for less than three years.

Gandhi had won a victory but it was more limited than either his followers expected or his opponents anticipated.

Satyagraha had hardly any spiritual impact. There was no sign that the hearts of either government or European community had softened as Gandhi had expected. The racial hatreds and the harassment of Indians continued unabated. Gandhi himself felt distressed and frustrated. His main purpose—to win the hearts of Whites and thereby to ensure the safety and dignity for Indian community in South Africa—went down to a permanent defeat.

There was no end to the hardships and discriminations faced by Indians and after more than a decade Gandhi himself was forced to comment on "the painful contrast between the happy ending of the Satyagraha struggle and the present conditions of Indians in South Africa". [SSA]

The Relief Act was a temporary and elusive victory. The Indian problem remained what it always was. A more ruthless and a more shameless racial tyranny that prevailed in the Union after Gandhi had left, shows that the settlement was a mere cosmetic achievement.

All the sufferings and struggles were in vain and conditions for the Indian community deteriorated very sharply thereafter.

Indians lost property rights; they were forced to live and trade only in locations in 1919 and lost municipal franchise in 1924. There was a re-registration with even more stringent requirements. South Africa did not change. Indians were undesirable in the country and must be driven away, not by use of physical force but by a steady pressure to make life miserable for them.

Gandhi's victory was mundane and political rather than spiritual and it was only a partial victory. The final outcome can, by no means, be attributed to any soul force or any victory of principles over politics.

The Indian Relief Act was more due to the pressure exerted by the labour strike. There was hue and cry in India as well as throughout the world against the senseless brutalities resorted to by the racist and cruel Whites in South Africa. The severe denunciation by the Viceroy and a possibility of violent reaction in India were as much if not more powerful factors as Satyagraha forcing Smuts to relent.

Europeans considered the settlement as a defeat for Gandhi. "Gandhi's outwitting by my father was complete and it was with a sense of defeat that he set out dejectedly to brood and scheme in India". [Smuts jr. Nanda 119]

Gandhi felt severely dejected but for quite other reasons. The 1914 settlement was not acceptable to the most influential sections of Indian community and Gandhi faced intense hostility from Muslim merchants who rejected him and repudiated his leadership. "It was rather difficult to get Indians to endorse the agreement". [SSA 450] "Some are opposed to the settlement and have moved heaven and earth that settlement should not become final".

Rich and polygamous Muslim merchants insisted on continuing their marriage system and denounced Gandhi for his failure to secure the privilege for them. Gandhi himself criticised the decision of the Commission of not permitting a second wife till the first was alive as "anti-religious". But then this was an impossible expectation. No Christian country would ever permit polygamy to flourish.

Gandhi faced a huge and a hostile crowd of Muslim merchants at Hamidia Islamic Society [15 July 1914] and was asked to answer specific questions as to by whose authority, the settlement had been finalized; where is the plague hospital fund started in 1904; where are the accounts of the funds received from India. "Did you not use 1200 pounds for Phoenix and the newspaper owned by you"? asked Habib Motan.

Gandhi replied to the points raised. The settlement was negotiated under the authority of British Indian Association of which Gandhi was the secretary: frequent references to the parent body would not be possible for any public person. The Indian community had gained several points without giving up any. The settlement was only about Satyagraha which was fought for strictly limited objectives and its doors are not closed; any one can use Satyagraha in future for any issue.

Gandhi had set aside the Plague hospital fund [about pounds 3000] in 1904, entirely from his own earnings. No further collection was made because Gandhi intended to go to England for medical education. [CWMG XII 490] He had used the fund in passive resistance struggle.

Funds from India were sent to him and he was "unable to hold himself responsible to the public in Africa in connection with those funds". The accounts had been presented to British Indian Association from time to time and were published in *Indian Opinion*. The books were with Polak and anybody could check them. *Phoenix* and *Indian Opinion* were used entirely for public purposes and belonged to the community and were only nominally registered in his name.

Gandhi's critics were unrelenting in their hostility. "We as a community are entirely dissatisfied with the Relief bill. There are questions like marriage question for the colonial born and others that were completely ignored by Transvaal government and by Mr. Gandhi who being a Hindu and not an authorized representative of our community and our co-religionists did not try to get the necessary redress for us".

"We wish to strongly protest against the credit which might be given to Mr. Gandhi for any alleged settlement of Indian grievances in South Africa and…as far as the Mohameddans are concerned, …the Relief Act is a complete farce and we want to disassociate ourselves from Mr. Gandhi and his few followers whose methods of passive resistance, strikes and violence do not appeal to us". [Letter from Hamidia Islamic Society to the Colonial secretary [30-7-14]

The secretary of Muslim League of India wrote even more bitterly. [16-11-14] "The largest sections of Indians in South Africa are dissatisfied with him [Gandhi]. He has posed, while there, as the representative of Indians while all the time he was only an authorized representative of his own few followers".

"Gandhi is a Hindu and it is ridiculous to suppose even for a moment that Mohmeddan community would trust him...What Gandhi has done, is by no means done with the approval of the vast majority of leading Indians. He is mistrusted by us in all matters".

"He has failed to render the accounts of large sums of money, which he was supposed to have used in the interest of all the Indians and for the purpose of getting redress for them. He has been repeatedly asked by different societies to postpone his departure and call a public meeting for the purpose of clearing himself of all suspicions and charges, which are directed against him but he has refused".

"The government imagines that by entering into an agreement with Gandhi and afterwards giving him dinners and fine speeches, they have settled Indian question. But the government has yet to learn that our grievances are far too real and serious to be settled in such an offhand manner: Gandhi will find that he is not such a great hero that the government and his followers wish to make the world believe he is... The marriage disabilities and one or two more points will have to receive serious consideration of the government before they make up their minds that there is going to be a final settlement". [quoted in Chattopadhyaya. 175-76]

Gandhi mentions a conspiracy 'in Johannesburg to take my life' and it was quite a serious threat but he avoids giving any details.[CWMG XII 386-388] Gandhi himself was not very happy at the turn of the events on the eve of his departure and he entertained doubts about the efficacy of Satyagraha when he considered its long-term effects. "When one considers... the present conditions of Indians in South Africa, one feels for a moment as if all the sufferings had gone for nothing and is inclined to question the efficacy of Satyagraha as a solvent of the problems of mankind". [SSA 458]

The settlement of 1914 wilted and withered away in no time and the environment for Indian community deteriorated sharply and steadily thereafter. But Gandhi's failure was not his fault. He was fighting for securing justice for a tiny and weak minority of Indians against not only the government or unjust laws but also against an entire community that was politically and economically in a commanding position. He was bound to fail by the very logic of his situation and circumstances.

But it would be a grievous mistake to overlook the fact that but for Gandhi's struggle, Indians would have been hounded out of Africa or forced to live under conditions much worse. Gandhi made the whole world aware of the Indian question by his novel and noble techniques, exposed the hollowness of British professions and provided a role model for the vast majority of Africans to overthrow the domination of the white minority at a later date. In spite of a ceaseless struggle against the Whites, "his mind was absolutely free from any bitterness against them…[and he too] was universally esteemed and loved by the Europeans as a person".

What Gandhi did in South Africa is far less important than what South Africa did to him. Most of his achievements in South Africa are personal than public. His personality got transformed in every which way. England had made him an activist; South Africa made him a Mahatma as he zealously strove to practice the ideals that he had garnered from a variety of masters and teachers both Indians and Europeans. The changes that came over him were too imperceptible to be dated and even to be accounted for, but at the end of the process he emerged as a rare piece of humanity. As a political activist South Africa transformed him in many significant aspects. Gandhi proved his mettle as a great and extremely capable leader employing many angled strategies to safeguard the interests of his community.

He had done all that he could do for his community in Africa and now he felt that his mission in Africa was over. Gandhi had decided to quit South Africa way back in 1911 but the uncertainties of the situation and his commitments had held him back. He now announced his firm decision to go to India. "I am going to India for good...and if I have to return to South Africa or leave India, it will be owing to circumstances beyond my control and at present beyond my conception". [CWMG XII 479]

There were personal reasons also that made Gandhi eager to leave Africa for good. The health of his wife was causing anxiety. She was bedridden. She could hardly sit up in bed and was hanging between life and death. "I doubt whether Mrs. Gandhi will survive the settlement". [CWMG XII 401] His children and dependents caused him a lot of anxiety. "You two started to point out at my faults ...Manilal took to evil ways to pleasure". [CWMG XII 368]

Gandhi was in great agony. "My heart seems to have gone dry. The agony I am undergoing is unbearable. I have often wanted to take out a knife from my pocket and put it through my stomach. Sometimes I have felt like striking my head against the wall opposite, other times I have thought of running away...I have committed terrible sins...I do not know what evil is in me. I have a strain of cruelty in me...such that people force themselves to do the things—even to attempt impossible things in order to please me. Lacking the necessary strength they put on a false show and deceive me. Even Gokhale used to tell me that I was so harsh that people felt terrified of me and allowed themselves to be dragged against their will our of sheer fear or in an attempt to please me and that those who found themselves too weak assumed an artificial pose in the end....I put, he said far too heavy burden on people. He too [he added] strained himself to do things beyond his capacity when he was asked by me". [CWMG XII 410-411]

His elder brother Laxmidas had died in March 1913. Gandhi was the only male member left "to look after the five widows of my father's family and of course their children". [CWMG XII 385] He did shoulder the family responsibilities till the very end of his life in spite of the crushing burden of his public activities.

There were several parties and farewells and meetings averaging twenty a day so that Gandhi often had no time even to eat. Most of such functions were organised by the coolies and very few by the richer sections of Indians. All the old friends and supporters of Gandhi now kept away from him. He expressed great admiration for the loyalty and devotion of the Tamil speaking coolies. "Of all the different sections of the Indian community, Tamils have bore the brunt of the struggle....so much pluck, so much faith, so much devotion to duty and such noble simplicity and yet so self effacing...A glorious and rich experience that I would treasure to the end of my life". [CWMG XII 494] "Gujaratis have failed in their duty...They care more for money, drinks, smuggling gold and for ill-gotten money".

By 1913, Gandhi had totally turned away from the rich, influential and sophisticated sections of the society. He now championed the causes of the poor and depended entirely on them. Gandhi was presented with very rich gifts in cash and he decided to keep them for public service in India. He was now an ascetic with no income and no personal property and all that he had or would get was for public service.

The last of such a farewell meeting was in Durban and Gandhi was deeply touched. "The honor that I have received today is the highest ever in my life" because it was by the labourers who loved him and have led him to success. He advised the colonial born. "South Africa is your motherland...do not waste on drinks and trinkets what you would be saving in tax. Gandhi indulged in a long narration of his experiences in South Africa. "I have gone through much in my life and a great deal of depression and sorrow has been my lot".

Gandhi worked for amiable relations between Whites and Indians till the very end and in his last speech in South Africa expressed such a hope. He appealed "to our European friends...to take a humanitarian view of the question, the Imperial view... rightly or wrongly, for good or evil, Englishmen and Indians have been knit together and it behooves both the races so to mold themselves as to leave a splendid legacy to the generations yet to be born and to show that though the Empires have gone and fallen, this empire is perhaps may be an exception: this is an empire founded not on material but on spiritual foundations". "I have always believed that there is something subtle, something fine in the ideals of the British Constitution. Tear away those ideals and you tear away my loyalty to that constitution. Keep those ideals and I am for ever a bondsman". [Hutten 331]

Gandhi left Africa never to return and Smuts heaved a sigh of relief. "A saint has left our shores, I sincerely hope for ever". [Smuts to Robertson.] But he was nostalgic. "It was a strenuous but clean fight. It was my fate to be the antagonist of a man for whom even then I had the highest respect... I must frankly admit that his activities at that time were very trying for me. Together with other South African leaders, I was busily engaged in the task of welding the old colonies into a united State...It was a colossal work which took up ever moment of my time. Suddenly in midst of all those engrossing preoccupations, Gandhi raised a tremendous issue. We had a skeleton in our cupboard. Since there was no personal hatred or ill feeling and the spirit of humanity was never absent, when the fight was over, there was an atmosphere in which a decent peace could be concluded". [Radha 282]

Gandhi left Africa on 18th July 1914] not for India but for England. He was quite eager to avoid a trip to London, but Gokhale who was sick there insisted that Gandhi must see him before going to India. "I will come if Mrs. Gandhi either dies or gets well". But she recovered very fast and Gandhi decided to go to India via England.

Eminent Indians in London organised a reception at Cecil Hotel in his honour and Gandhi chose to ridicule himself. "We come amongst you almost as barbarians isolated in a little farm cut off from the cities". [CWMG XII 523]

The outbreak of war left Gandhi stranded in London for six months and created several problems for him. His colleague Kallenbach was detained on account of his German nationality and even though he had lived for eighteen years in South Africa his application for naturalisation was rejected.

A far more baffling problem was the issue of war service and non-violence. "A Satyagrahi can not support war directly or indirectly. There are no two opinions about that but I am not such a perfect Satygrahi, I am trying to be one." He conceded that nursing the wounded is also an indirect participation in war. [CWMG XII 554] But such a total view was impracticable and no alternative exists. A satygrahi in a civil society would always be protected by 'force' of government and he lives by indirect violence. He therefore will have to support his society at war.

A meeting of Indians in London [13-8-14] unconditionally offered their services to the Empire. The Colonial Secretary Lord Crewe responded with a qualified acceptance of the offer. Gandhi's offer to enlist Indians for armed services was politely brushed aside by India office. He was told that the only service that is needed is for nursing the sick and the wounded.

A committee recruited Indian students for ambulance service and they underwent two months training. Indians insisted on presenting their demands and ventilating their grievances through Gandhi but Col. Baker resented it as a breech of protocol. The matter came to a head about the appointment of corporals. Gandhi in a short, curt letter insisted on being consulted on matters pertaining to Indian volunteers who had protested against the appointments. [13-10-14] The letter from Gandhi and the protest of students was treated by Col. Baker as a serious breach of discipline. The India Office sided with Col. Baker and Gandhi was forced to a total retreat.

Four hundred and seventy Indian soldiers were lying wounded at Netlley hospital but Gandhi was not allowed to visit them. "Unheard of difficulties are put in my way and I am prevented from going to Netley or any of the hospitals...because official...fear that I might make mischief". [CWMG XII 556]

Gandhi refers to his Satyagraha against the India Office but gives no specific details; he suffered serious illness during the last fortnight of October 1914. "My health was completely shattered...during the fast". He suffered severely from piles and had blood in his cough together with extreme weakness because of fasting. He was forced to stay mostly indoors, mostly in bed. Mrs. Gandhi had a relapse and was confined to bed.

Gandhi intensely longed for India but it was only on 18th December that he left England "with work uncompleted and health broken". He was severely depressed and a bit nervous about unknown and somewhat dark future. "I have been so often prevented from reaching India that it seems hardly real that I am sitting in a ship bound for India and having reached there, what shall I do? However 'Lead Kindly Light amid encircling gloom, lead thou me on...' that thought is my solace".

Gandhi was a celebrity in Africa and in England and he was quite well known to the political elite in India. But he was almost unheard of by the Indian masses whom he was soon going to lead for the next three decades. Gandhi sailed into the Indian tempest to end a remarkable era of his life and his arrival was the beginning of a still more remarkable and glorious one.

Bibliography

Alexander, Horace, *Gandhi through Western Eyes*, Bombay, Asia Publishing House, 1969

Ali Shanti Sadiq, *Gandhi and South Africa*, Delhi, Hind Pocket Books, 1994

Ash Geoffrey, *Gandhi New York*, Stein and Day, 1968

Athalye D V, *The Life of Mahatma Gandhi*, Poona, Swadeshi Publishing Company, 1923

Azad Maulana Abul Kalam, *India Wins Freedom*, Hyderabad, India, Orient Longman, 1988

Bolton J R Glorney, *Tragedy of Gandhi*, London, George Allen and Unwin, 1934

Bose Subhas Chandra, *Crossroads*, Calcutta, Asia Publishing House, 1962

Britton Burnett, *Gandhi Arrives in South Africa,* Canton Me, Greenleaf Books, 1999

Brown Judith Margaret, *Gandhi Prisoner of Hope*, London, Yale University Press, 1989

Chattopadhyaya Harprasad, *Indians in Africa*, A Socio-economic study, Calcutta, Bookland, 1974

Chopra Pran, *The Sage in Revolt*, New Delhi, Gandhi Peace Foundation, 1972

Doctor Adi, *Anarchist Thought in India,* Bombay, Asia Publishing House, 1964

Devanesen Chandran D S, *The Making of Mahatma, Madras*, Orient Longman, 1969

Doke Joseph John, M.K. Gandhi, *An Indian Patriot in South Africa*, London, London Indian Chronicle, 1909.

Durga Das, *India from Curzon to Nehru and After,* New York, John Day, 1970

Fisher Louis, *The Life of Mahatma Gandhi,* New York, Harper and Row Publishers, 1950

Gandhi M K, *An Autobiography or the Story of my Experiments with Truth,* Ahmedabad, Navjivan Publishing House, 2003

Gandhi M K *Collected Works, New Delhi*, Publications Division, Ministry of Information and Broadcasting, Govt. of India, 1956.

Gandhi M K *Satyagraha in South Africa,* Madras, S. Natesan, 1928

Gandhi Prabhudas, *My Childhood with Gandhi*, Ahmedabad, Navjivan Publishing House, 1957

Gandhi Rajmohan, *Gandhi, A Good Boat*, New Delhi, Viking, 1995

Gill S S, *Gandhi, A Sublime Failure*, New Delhi, Rupa & Com., 2001

Government of India, Census report of Bombay presidency, Kathiawar, 1891

Gregory R G *India and East Africa*, Oxford, Clarendon Press, 1971

Hancock W K Smuts, *Sanguine Years, Cambridge*, University Press, 1962

Hardiman David, *Gandhi in His Times and Ours*, New York, Columbia University Press, 2003

Hay Stephen, *M K Gandhi in London*, Victorian Studies, August 1989

Holmes J H, *Gandhi and Non Violence*, Delhi, Akashdeep Publishing House 1988

Hunt James D, *Gandhi in London*, New Delhi, Promila and Co., 1978 *Gandhi and Non-conformists,* New Delhi, Promila and Co., 1982

Hutenback R A, *Gandhi in South Africa, British Imperialism and Indian Question*, 1860-1914, Ithaca, Cornell University Press, 1971

Jai Narayan, *Gandhi's View of Political Power*, New Delhi, Deep & Deep Publications, 1987.

Joshi P C, *Unrest in South Africa,* Bombay, Kitab Mahal, 1958

Joshi P S, *Mahatma Gandhi in South Africa*, Rajkot, 1980

Karaka D F, *Out of Dust,* Bombay, Thacker, 1968

Karaka Dhanjisha Hormusji, *Kathiawar Directory, Part I and II* 1888

Kriplani J B, *Gandhi, Bombay*, Orient Longman, 1970
  Gandhi-A Political Study, Kashi, Sarva Seva Sangh, 1956

Law D A [Ed], Congress and Raj, London, Heinemann, 1977

Lester Muriel, *It Occurred to Me*, New York, Harper and Brothers Publishers, 1937

Mahadevan T K, *The Year of the Phoenix*, Not a novel, Chicago, World Without Wars Publishers, 1982

Marquard Leopold, *Story of South Africa,* London, Faber and Faber, 1955

Mathur D B, *Gokhale: A Political Biography,* Bombay, Manaktalas, 1966

Meer Fatima, *Apprenticeship of a Mahatma,* Phoenix, South Africa, The Phoenix Settlement Trust, 1979

Meer Fatima, *Gandhi in South Africa*, 1893-1914

Morton Eleanor, *Women in Gandhi's Life,* New York, Dodd Mead and Co., 1953

Mukherjee Hirendranath, *Gandhi-A Study, New Delhi*, People's Publishing House, 1958

Mehta Ved Prakash, *Mahatma Gandhi and his Apostles*, New York, The Viking Press, 1977

Namboodripad E M S, *Mahatma and his Ism,* Calcutta, National Book Agency, 1981

Nanda Bal Ram, *Mahatma Gandhi*: *A Biography, London*, George Allen Unwin, 1958

Nehru Jawahar Lal, *An Autobiography*, London, Bodley Head, 1989
  Nehru on Gandhi, New York John Day Company, 1948

Polak H S, *Mahatma Gandhi: the Man and his Mission*, Madras, Nateson and Company, 1943

Polak Millie, *Gandhi—the Man, London,* George Allen and Unwin, 1931

Pyarelal, *Mahatma Gandhi, the Early Phase*, Ahmedabad, Navjivan Publishing House, 1965

Rai Kauleshwar, *Indians and British Colonialism in South Africa*, Allahabad, Kitab Mahal, 1984

Ray Sibnarayan [Ed] *Gandhi: India and the World,* Philadelphia, Temple University Press, 1970

Rolland Romain, *Mahatma Gandhi*: *A Study in Indian Nationalism,* Madras, S Ganeshan, 1931

S. Radhakrishnan, *Mahatma Gandhi: Essays and Reflections on his Life and Works*, Bombay, Jaico Publishing House, 1977

Mahatma Gandhi 100 Years, New Delhi, Gandhi Peace Foundation, 1968

Shridharani Krishnalal J, *Mahatma and the World*, New York, Duell Sloan and Pearce, 1946

Sitaramayya Pattabhi, *History of Indian National Congress*, Delhi, S Chand, 1969

Swami Shraddhanand, *Inside Congress,* Bombay Phoenix Publication, 1946

Tarachand, *History of Freedom Movement in India*, New Delhi, Ministry of Information and Broadcasting, Govt. of India, 1961

Swan Maureen, *Gandhi—the South African Experiences*, Johannesburg, Ravan Press, 1985

Tendulkar D G, *Gandhi—His Life and Work*, Bombay, Karnatak Publishing House, 1944

Upadhyaya J M, *Gandhi—Early Contemporaries and Companions*, Ahmedabad, Navjivan Publishing House, 1971

Mahatma Gandhi as a Student, Delhi, Ministry of Information and Broadcasting, 1965

Shukla Chandrashekher, [ED] *Reminiscences of Mahatma Gandhi*, Bombay, Vora and Company, 1951

Walker Eric, *A History of South Africa, London,* Longmans Green and Com., 1941

Wolpert Sydney, *Gandhi's Passion*, New York, Oxford University Press, 2001

Gujarati Books

Desai Shumbhuprasad H., *Kanera no ker*, Junagadh, Prabhat Prakashan, 1984

Harilal Savailal, *Shamaldas Permanand*, Bombay, B H Shinde, 1912

Sedani Hasuta Shashikant, *Mahamati Sant Prannath*, Rajkot, Self, 1992

Index